D0754588

BIOLOGY OF *HYDRA*

CONTRIBUTORS

Allison L. Burnett
Marshall N. Cyrlin
Sondra Corff
Lowell E. Davis
Fred A. Diehl
Le Ming Hang
Robert E. Hausman
Julian F. Haynes
Philip G. Lambruschi
Georgia E. Lesh-Laurie
Ralph Lowell
J. J. Reisa
Norman B. Rushforth

BIOLOGY OF *HYDRA*

Edited by ALLISON L. BURNETT

Department of Biological Sciences
Northwestern University
Evanston, Illinois

ACADEMIC PRESS   New York and London   1973
A SUBSIDIARY OF HARCOURT BRACE JOVANOVICH, PUBLISHERS

LIBRARY

SEP 20 1973

UNIVERSITY OF THE PACIFIC

270776

COPYRIGHT © 1973, BY ACADEMIC PRESS, INC.
ALL RIGHTS RESERVED.
NO PART OF THIS PUBLICATION MAY BE REPRODUCED OR
TRANSMITTED IN ANY FORM OR BY ANY MEANS, ELECTRONIC
OR MECHANICAL, INCLUDING PHOTOCOPY, RECORDING, OR ANY
INFORMATION STORAGE AND RETRIEVAL SYSTEM, WITHOUT
PERMISSION IN WRITING FROM THE PUBLISHER.

ACADEMIC PRESS, INC.
111 Fifth Avenue, New York, New York 10003

United Kingdom Edition published by
ACADEMIC PRESS, INC. (LONDON) LTD.
24/28 Oval Road, London NW1

LIBRARY OF CONGRESS CATALOG CARD NUMBER: 72-77331

PRINTED IN THE UNITED STATES OF AMERICA

CONTENTS

Part III POLARITY IN *HYDRA*

Chapter 4. **The Developmental Significance of**
Interstitial Cells during Regeneration
and Budding

Fred A. Diehl

Chapter 5. **Expression and Maintenance of**
Organismic Polarity

Georgia E. Lesh-Laurie

Part IV GASTRODERMAL REGENERATION IN *HYDRA*

Chapter 6. **Ultrastructural Changes during Dedifferentiation**
and Redifferentiation in the Regenerating,
Isolated Gastrodermis

Lowell E. Davis

Part V   EPIDERMAL REGENERATION IN *HYDRA*

Chapter 7.   Regeneration from Isolated Epidermal Explants
Ralph Lowell and Allison L. Burnett

Chapter 8.   Epithelial-Muscle Cells
Julian F. Haynes

Chapter 9.   Regeneration of a *Hydra* Containing No Interstitial Cells from an Isolated Basal Disc
Allison L. Burnett and Philip G. Lambruschi

Chapter 10.   Interspecific Grafting of Cell Layers
Allison L. Burnett, Ralph Lowell, and Le Ming Hang

Chapter 11.   **Regeneration of a Complete *Hydra* from a Single, Differentiated Somatic Cell Type**

Allison L. Burnett, Ralph Lowell, and Marshall N. Cyrlin

Part VI   **DIFFERENTIATION OF NERVOUS ELEMENTS IN *HYDRA***

Chapter 12.   **Ultrastructure of Neurosensory Cell Development**

Lowell E. Davis

Chapter 13.   **Ultrastructure of Ganglionic Cell Development**

Lowell E. Davis

Chapter 14.   **Structure of Neurosecretory Cells with Special Reference to the Nature of the Secretory Product**

Lowell E. Davis

LIST OF CONTRIBUTORS

Numbers in parentheses indicate the pages on which the authors' contributions begin.

ALLISON L. BURNETT, Department of Biological Sciences, Northwestern University, Evanston, Illinois (223, 239, 249, 255)

MARSHALL N. CYRLIN, Department of Biological Sciences, Northwestern University, Evanston, Illinois (255)

SONDRA CORFF, Department of Anatomy, University of Pennsylvania School of Medicine, Philadelphia, Pennsylvania (345)

LOWELL E. DAVIS, Department of Zoology, Syracuse University, Syracuse, New York (171, 271, 299, 319)

FRED A. DIEHL, Department of Biology, University of Virginia, Charlottesville, Virginia (109)

LE MING HANG, Department of Biology, Case Western Reserve University, Cleveland, Ohio (249)

ROBERT E. HAUSMAN, Department of Biology, University of Chicago, Chicago, Illinois (393)

JULIAN F. HAYNES, Department of Biology, University of Maine, Orono, Maine (43, 233)

PHILIP G. LAMBRUSCHI, Department of Biological Sciences, Northwestern University, Evanston, Illinois (239)

GEORGIA E. LESH-LAURIE, Department of Biology, Case Western Reserve University, Cleveland, Ohio (143)

RALPH LOWELL, Department of Biology, North Park College, Chicago, Illinois (223, 249, 255)

J. J. REISA,* Department of Biological Sciences, Northwestern University, Evanston, Illinois and Department of Biology, Mundelein College, Chicago, Illinois (59)

NORMAN B. RUSHFORTH, Department of Biology, Case Western Reserve University, Cleveland, Ohio (3)

*Present address: Argon National Laboratory, Argon, Illinois.

PREFACE

For over 218 years the simple freshwater polyp *Hydra* has been used as an experimental animal by biologists throughout the world. Several books that deal with selected aspects of *Hydra* biology have been published, but until the appearance of this treatise no compendium has dealt with this polyp in such depth.

The editor has selected eight areas of *Hydra* biology that he feels will be of great interest, both in content and scope, to the modern investigator. While some of these fields are still in their infancy, others, such as the origin of nerve cells, have been previously discussed, but never with the authority presented in this work.

Over 2000 papers have been published on *Hydra,* but because of space limitations the authors have judiciously chosen to cite only those most pertinent to their contributions. References pertaining to higher animals have been presented to show that *Hydra* may be the metazoan of choice for experiments in ecology, neurophysiology, development, behavior, and differentiation.

The editor would like to express thanks to the contributors. Special thanks go to Dr. Robert Hausman, who not only proofread material but revised bibliographies and served as a most favorable and congenial "right-hand comrade" to the editor.

Dr. Paul Gerard Rose

IN MEMORIAM

Dr. Paul Rose, who was preparing a contribution to this volume, succumbed to cystic fibrosis on August 14, 1970. He was about to enter his thirtieth year. Thus, he was one of the "oldest" patients to have lived with this congenital disease.

During his graduate studies at Western Reserve University, Dr. Rose not only withheld the nature of his affliction from his fellow graduate students, but never asked for excuse or special treatment from the faculty. None of us knew that he was living from day to day. The same was true during the years he studied at Harvard for his A.B. degree. Paul was a selfless, brilliant, highly cultured individual who contributed generously to the training of countless undergraduate students.

Before his death, Paul published four papers in the Wilhelm Roux developmental biology archives. Listed below are the references to two of these papers that helped solve one of the most knotty problems encountered in our studies of differentiation in *Hydra,* the origin of the mucous and gland cells.

The contributors to this volume, many of whom were Dr. Rose's close friends, wish to dedicate their contributions to his memory.

Rose, P. G., and Burnett, A. L. (1970). The origin of mucous cells in *Hydra viridis*. II. Midgastric regeneration and budding. *Wilhelm Roux Arch. Entwicklungsmech.* **165,** 177–191.

Rose, P. G., and Burnett, A. L. (1970). The origin of secretory cells in *Cordylophora caspia* during regeneration. *Wilhelm Roux Arch. Entwicklungsmech.* **165,** 192–216.

PART I

BEHAVIOR OF *HYDRA*

If an observer looks into a *Hydra* culture bowl for an hour or two, an investigator would be hard-pressed to convince him that the animal possessed any "behavior" at all except for short contractions. However, continued observations, especially during feeding, or if the culture dish is shaken so that the animals are swirled to the middle of the dish in a mass tangle of tentacles and bodies, would convince the observer that the animals are far from inactive. Many different types of locomotion and feeding behavior are observed. In the following section various aspects of *Hydra's* behavior, not obvious in casual observation, will be elucidated. Our "floral" grazing animal will be seen as Trembley saw it over two hundred years ago — as a voracious carnivore whose limbs carry the most complex and deadly organelles in the animal or plant kingdom, the nematocysts. In this section we also include a small chapter on feeding and digestion, to follow an animal's fate after it has been ingested by a *Hydra*.

CHAPTER 1

Behavior*

NORMAN B. RUSHFORTH

I. Introduction

When Trembley first observed *Hydra viridis,* it was the shape of these polyps, their green color, and apparent immobility that led him to believe that they were plants. On further careful study, however, he noted the spontaneous movements of the column and tentacles, and the contraction of these body parts when the surrounding water was agitated. "This contraction of the polyps, and all the movements that I saw them make when they extended themselves again, awakened sharply in my mind the idea

*Supported in part by grants MH-10734 and GM-12303 from the National Institutes of Health.

3

of an animal" (Trembley, 1744). Their shape and color still made an impression on Trembley, and he began to consider them to be very sensitive plants. The seed of doubt had been planted in his mind, however, and led to the famous experiments in which he cut the polyps and observed the regeneration of the various parts. Having previously observed the locomotory activity of the *Hydra,* he was much more disposed at this time to think that they were animals, and fully expected to see the cut polyps die. Trembley, well aware of the regenerative properties of plants, believed that only if both halves lived, and each became a perfect polyp, would it show that the organisms were plants. He recounts in his memoirs the excitement of observing the regeneration of both halves, so that when seen under his magnifying glass ". . . each of the two appeared to be a complete polyp . . . ."

If Trembley had pursued the rationale originally leading him to cut the polyp, he would have concluded now that they were small plants. However, the spontaneous movements, extensions, and contractions, together with their "walking" behavior prevented him from fully believing it, and still puzzled he wrote to the famous biologist Reaumur, sending him some specimens. The mysterious organisms were exhibited at the Académie royale des Sciences, and Trembley's letter was read to a rapt assembly. Reaumur wrote to Trembley on March 25, 1741, to tell him of the proceedings at the academy, remarking in his letter: "They are certainly animals. I have indeed already given them a name, subject to your approval: that of polyps." As recounted in Baker's biography of Trembley: "This letter marks the origin of the word polyp, as the word is used in modern zoology."

In addition to providing a key to the organism's taxonomy, the behavior of *Hydra* was the subject of a controversy at the turn of the present century. The central issues in science at that time were the relationship of the external environment to behavior and the question of spontaneous activity. At this time the American psychologists William James and Edward Thorndike and the Russian physiologist I. P. Pavlov were vigorously questioning the usefulness of methods of introspection in the study of behavior. Pavlov's discovery of the conditioned reflex emphasized the important role of external factors in the control of behavior. His ideas were readily seized upon in America. Loeb, the zoologist, began to emphasize the role of the external environment in the control of animal behavior, and the psychologist James B. Watson founded the school of behaviorism which substituted more direct observational techniques for methods of introspection in describing behavior.

These developments did not go unquestioned, however, and such approaches were labeled by some as far too mechanistic in concept. They were criticized by the psychologist McDougall and the zoologist Jennings, who considered that such ideas neglected the importance of endogenous influences in controlling behavior. These men stressed the participation of internal changes, the role of spontaneity, and the "goal-directedness" of behavior. Jennings (1906) in his studies of the behavior of the lower metazoa placed emphasis on the constantly changing relationships between organisms and their external environment. Describing the behavior of *Hydra* he noted that ". . . contractions take place without any present outward stimulus; the movements are due to internal changes . . . ." He pointed out that the feeding behavior of *Hydra* depended on the physiological state of the animal, which in turn was determined by the time since previous feeding. "Hydra that are not hungry will not eat at all; moderately hungry specimens will take the solid food (chemical and mechanical stimuli); very hungry ones take liquid food (chemical stimulus alone)." Referring to the earlier studies of Wilson (1891), Jennings noted that starved hydras undergo complete cycles of behavior which are not exhibited when they have been recently fed. *Hydra* normally remains in the upper layers of the water, where the oxygen supply is abundent. "But when the crustacea on which the animals feed have become very scarce, so that little food is obtained, *Hydra* detaches itself, and with tentacles outspread sinks slowly to the bottom. Here it feeds upon the debris composed of dead organic matter which collects at the bottom, often gorging itself with this material." It then moves upward to the surface, remaining for a time, before repeating the cycle. Even in describing the response of *Hydra* to external stimuli, Jennings emphasized the internal control of the response. In discussing the movement of the polyp to heat stimulation, first described by Mast (1903), or under stimulation by chemicals, he stressed that "in all cases it was found that the direction towards which the animal moves bears no definite relation to the direction from which the stimulus comes."

Such descriptions of behavior are in stark contrast to those of Loeb, who in his tropism theory of animal conduct (1918) maintained that behavior consisted primarily of movements forced by environmental stimuli acting on bilaterally symmetrical structures of the animal. The conflict between the mechanistic viewpoint of behavior which stress reflex theory and the so-called vitalists who emphasized endogenous factors lasted in various forms for some time. However, the prevailing belief today is that both internal and external factors are important in all patterns of behavior. Marler and Hamilton (1968) in a recent text "Mechanisms of Animal Behavior" succinctly express the modern viewpoint. "No animal is a passive respondent to environmental commands. Rather, there is a process of interaction between the organism in which both have an active role."

Certainly our current views of the behavior of *Hydra* encompass both environmental and endogenous factors. Feeding behavior appears to consist of reflexly linked sequences, together with modifications of spontaneous activity patterns. At the present time there is a search for electrical correlates of such responses, in an effort to understand their underlying physiological bases. From the time of Trembley, *Hydra* and other coelenterates have intrigued investigators studying mechanisms underlying behavioral control. The apparent simplicity of both the structure and behavior of such animals led workers to believe that a "complete" description of behavioral mechanisms would soon be attainable. In *Hydra*, for example, the nervous system is relatively simple, consisting of a nerve net. The classic histological observations of Hadzi (1909) and McConnell (1932) have been confirmed by more recent ultrastructural studies (Lentz and Barnett, 1965; Davis *et al.,* 1968; and in Chapters 12 and 13 of this volume) showing that this system consists of small sensory cells which connect through bipolar and multipolar neurons, forming a network throughout the epidermis of the animal. While the behavior of *Hydra* has been often thought to consist mainly of stereotyped activities, the simplicity is more apparent than real. A careful perusal of Trembley's classic descriptions of the animal's locomotory activities alone should convince one of this fact. In the present chapter the wide range of *Hydra*'s behavior is discussed: its feeding behavior, locomotory activity, and responses to external stimuli. From a consideration of such activities, factors concerning the physiology of the animal required for behavioral control will be elicited.

II. Locomotory Activity

A. MODES OF LOCOMOTION

The locomotory movements of *Hydra,* first described by Trembley (1744), constitute a series of complex behavioral sequences. The most astonishing feature, however, is that locomotion may take any one of seven different forms. Trembley first observed that *Hydra* moves by looping like a caterpillar or inchworm, as shown in Fig. 1. By this method the animal places its free end against the substratum, releases its foot, and after contraction and elongation of the column, draws the foot forward reattaching it. The process is repeated so that the *Hydra* literally loops along the substratum. In other cases it attaches itself by its tentacles, releases its foot, and uses the tentacles like legs (Jennings, 1906). Trembley also noted that *Hydra* can locomote by means of a slow somersaulting movement, in which the polyp stands upright alternately on its anterior and posterior extremities. This form of locomotion is much less frequent than the inchworm movements, however, and is considered to constitute somewhat abnormal movements (Ewer, 1947b).

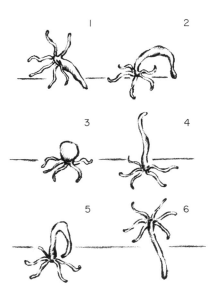

Fig. 1. Successive positions in the loco-motory sequence of "inchworm walking be-havior" in *Hydra*. (After Wagner, 1904.)

Several investigators have indicated that *Hydra* can move through the aqueous medium unaided by attachment to the substratum. For example, animals which have loosened themselves from a substratum close to the water's surface glide slowly downward with straightened tentacles, some-times being passively borne by water currents (Schaffer, 1754). On the other hand, *Hydra* has been seen to move upward to the surface of the water by producing a gas bubble attached by mucus to the base. Both Wagner (1904) and Kepner and Miller (1928) report this method of loco-motion, but Beutler (1933) seriously questioned the existence of this phenomenon. In reviewing this controversy, Kanaev (1952) points out that such a means of travel is probably the only one available for a *Hydra* at a depth of many meters to use in returning to the upper water layers.

The formation of a gas bubble at the base of the *Hydra* and the subse-quent floating of the animal have been investigated more recently by Lomnicki and Slobodkin (1966). They find that only starved or poorly fed *Hydra* will produce a bubble and float to the surface of the medium. Richly fed *Hydra* will not. Floating may be elicited by the water which has been "conditioned" by the presence in it of other hydras. This sug-gests that the behavior may be initiated by chemical factors released from the *Hydra* into the medium. However, the phenomenon is not at all clear-cut, since crowded animals are less effective in eliciting floating than are less crowded animals. Lomnicki and Slobodkin, nevertheless, believe that the floating behavior is useful in nature, providing mobility for hydras within a lake.

Hydra has still other modes of locomotion. Marshall (1882) observed *H. viridis* to glide slowly along a solid substratum with the aid of movements of the body and tentacles. Wagner (1904) also observed such creeping by the base along the substratum, but with no participation of tentacular activity. The method is an extremely slow form of transportation but, nevertheless, the hydra can travel by this means over considerable distances. The mechanism of this means of locomotion is totally unknown.

A final mode of *Hydra's* locomotion is "walking" along the water's surface film. This has been compared to the way flies walk along a ceiling, but the techniques used are of course quite different. Trembley (1744) studied this behavior in considerable detail; although the phenomenon has been observed by other workers, they have added little to the earlier descriptions. The base of the *Hydra* is located outside the water at the bottom of a small depression on the water surface. The polyp is supported by surface tension and if the dry base is moistened the animal immediately falls to the bottom. Trembley likened the suspension of the *Hydra* at the water surface to the way an unwetted pin may be supported on the surface.

The seven modes of locomotion are summarized in Table I, together

TABLE I

MODES OF LOCOMOTION IN *Hydra*

Mode	Reference
Inchworm or caterpillar movements	Trembley (1744)
Walking on substratum using tentacles	Jennings (1906)
Somersaulting	Trembley (1744)
Passive gliding downward from water surface	Schaffer (1754)
Floating by means of gas bubble	Wagner (1904)
Active gliding along substratum on base	
With aid of tentacle and body movements	Marshall (1882)
Without aid of tentacle and body movements	Wagner (1904)
Walking along water's surface film	Trembley (1744)

with documentation of sources of their description. In reviewing these forms of locomotion one cannot but be impressed both at the amazingly wide range of behavior exhibited and the complexity of some of these activities. While much has been learned about the pacemaker systems associated with simple contraction behavior in *Hydra,* virtually nothing is known of the mechanisms involved in locomotion. The obvious complexities of many of these locomotory sequences indicate that it will be many years before we fully understand their underlying mechanisms.

B. THE ROLE OF THE NEMATOCYSTS IN LOCOMOTION

In some forms of locomotion, such as inchworm movements, walking by means of the tentacles, and somersaulting, the nematocysts play a key role. Toppe (1909) was the first to observe that the tentacles attach by means of the isorhizas to the substratum. However, the most complete account of the role of the various nematocyst types in both feeding and locomotion was given much later by Ewer (1947b). An earlier observation by a Russian zoologist Zykov (1898), quoted in Kanaev (1952), was that pseudopods emerge on the ectodermal cells of the tentacles and are used during locomotion. Wagner (1904) questioned the existence of such structures, and believed that Zykov mistook strips of plasma, stretched by the adhesive cnidae, to be pseudopods. Although Beutler (1927) confirmed Zykov's observation, the concept appears to find no support in current views of tentacle attachment.

There are four nematocyst types in *Hydra*. The modern terminology is attributed to Weill (1934), although older names were given previously by Schulze (1917). The equivalent terms are stenotele (Weill) = penetrant (Schulze), desmoneme − volvent, holotrichous isorhiza = large glutinant, and atrichous isorhiza = small glutinant. The four nematocyst types are depicted diagrammatically in Fig. 2, in both the discharged and undischarged state. The stenoteles and desmonemes are the nematocysts used in prey capture. The stenoteles pierce the prey, even when a tough cuticle is present, and inject poison from the nematocyst capsule into the organism. The poison is released through the open distal end of the discharged thread. In contrast, the desmoneme contains no poison and the distal end of the nematocyst thread is closed. On discharge, the thread coils around the prey, and holds it tightly against the outer surface of the tentacle. This nematocyst acts somewhat like a lasso in wrapping around the bristles and projections of the prey organism.

The primary stimulus for discharge of both types of nematocyst is mechanical, since they may be released by prodding the tentacles with a clean glass rod. The threshold for such activation is considerably lowered, however, by the presence of food extracts. This has been shown by Pantin (1942) for the sea anemone *Anemonia,* and for *Hydra* by Ewer (1947b). Thus, in the normal feeding response of coelenterates both chemical and mechanical factors are involved. Extracts of food alone cause no discharge, but have the effect of reducing the threshold to mechanical stimulation.

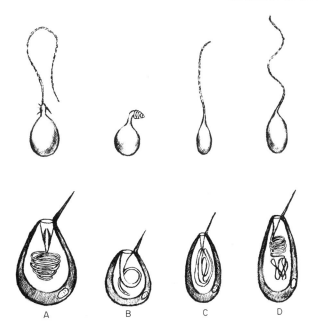

Fig. 2. Semidiagrammatic representation of the four types of nematocysts of *Hydra vulgaris attenuata*. Bottom row, undischarged; top row, discharged. (A) stenotele; (B) desmoneme; (C) atrichrous isorhiza; (D) holotrichous isorhiza. (After Ewer, 1947b.)

Ewer (1947b) investigated the mode of action of the atrichous isorhizas in the walking movements of *Hydra,* confirming Toppe's (1909) earlier observations that they were used in tentacle attachment. Ewer studied the vertical locomotion of buds of *Hydra vulgaris* on a clean glass cover-slip and described the attachment of the nematocyst thread in detail:

> . . . the thread adheres to the glass and the capsule remains embedded in the battery cell so firmly that the cytoplasm is often pulled out into a conical projection two or three times as long as the thread. This cytoplasmic projection can be seen to extend and contract according as the animal pulls or releases the strain on the particular nematocyst under observation . . . . When the tentacle is pulled free the capsule is torn out of the cnidoblast and remains adhering to the glass by the thread.

Ewer observed that a relatively small number of nematocysts is used in anchoring the tentacle at each step, usually fewer than ten per tentacle. She estimated that the number of nematocyst batteries would suffice for at least sixty locomotory steps, and that the rapid production of nematocysts described by Jones (1941) would normally replenish the supply. Thus, the animal is not reduced to inactivity by shortage of nematocysts.

Using buds of three different species, making measurements of the dimensions of the nematocysts, and employing differential staining of the nematocyst footprints left on the glass by the locomoting hydra, Ewer established that the atrichous and not the holotrichous isorhizas were used in the tentacular attachments of walking. The holotrichous isorhizas were not discharged in locomotion and their thresholds were not affected by food extracts. They were found to be discharged only when stimulated by animals such as *Paramecium,* which are not normally eaten by *Hydra* and evoke no feeding reaction. Their function was thought to be primarily defensive in nature.

Ewer (1947b) attempted to answer the key question concerning the differential use of the various nematocyst types. "How does it come about that in catching prey stenoteles and desmonemes are discharged, whereas in walking only atrichous isorhizas are used?" The first possibility that was considered was the secretion of some substance by the animal during walking which inhibits the stenoteles, desmonemes, and holotrichous isorhizas from firing, and sensitizes the atrichous isorhizas to mechanical stimulation. This hypothesis was eliminated since food animals placed on the tentacles of a *Hydra* in locomotion are readily captured. If the prey is removed from the tentacles only stenoteles and desmonemes are found to be attached to it. While chemical factors from the food might neutralize the inhibition of stenotele and desmoneme discharge, the absence of isorhizas on the prey remains unexplained. It was also found that when a *Hydra* was removed from the tank while walking and examined under a coverslip, the manipulation caused the usual discharge of some stenoteles, a very few desmonemes, but very seldom any isorhizas. If the latter had been sensitized by a walking hormone they, too, should have been discharged.

Ewer (1947b) then tested the effect of food extracts on the discharge of atrichous isorhizas. Coating the tips of small capillary glass rods with copepod extract she compared the numbers of nematocysts adhering to the rods after contacting the tentacles for a 30-second period with those attached to control rods coated with silica gel and administered to the hydra in a similar manner. Other series of experiments were run in which the rods were first coated in silica gel and then coated in copepod extract before touching the tentacles for shorter time periods. The results indicated that (1) food extracts inhibit the discharge of atrichous isorhizas; and (2) the duration of mechanical stimulation necessary to bring about discharge is greater for atrichous isorhizas than for stenoteles. "This is functionally significant, for in prey catching, discharge must be rapid, whereas in walking there is no such necessity; in fact it is undesirable that a brief accidental encounter with an inert object should at once cause the tentacle to adhere." Ewer also noted that the small numbers of nematocysts discharged meant that not all contacts of an atrichous isorhiza's cnidocil with the substratum resulted in discharge.

The findings of this excellent study may best be summarized and related in terms of their importance to *Hydra's* natural activities, in Ewer's own words (1947b):

> In the absence of the chemical stimulus of food the atrichous isorhizas have the lowest threshold to mechanical stimulation, but they are not discharged instantaneously. This means that a small particle of mud falling on a tentacle will not cause discharge, but if the tentacle is laid gently against the substratum the atrichous isorhizas alone will be discharged. This is what happens during the attachment of the tentacles in locomotion. When the chemical stimulus of food is present the thresholds of the stenoteles and desmonemes are lowered, while the atrichous isorhizas are inhibited. The former, therefore, discharge while the latter very rarely do so. Since the threshold of the desmonemes is higher than that of the stenoteles, they are discharged in large numbers only if that stimulus is violent. This is normally the case when the prey is bristly and offers them not only violent stimulation but also a suitable surface to grip.
>
> The case of the holotrichous isorhizas is less clear. They are not discharged in locomotion, therefore, their threshold must be higher than that of the atrichous isorhizas. They appear to be unaffected by food extracts. Nevertheless, they can be discharged by the very slight simulation of an encounter with *Paramecium*. To reconcile this with the fact that they are not discharged during locomotion it is necessary to assume that something in the *Paramecium* lowers their threshold. This has not been demonstrated, and needs further investigation; but if it is true presumably hydra's commensal ciliates, although of the same dimensions as *Paramecium*, do not discharge because they lack the threshold-lowering substance.

C. FACTORS LEADING TO LOCOMOTORY ACTIVITY

There are several reports in the literature that locomotion in *Hydra* is induced by external factors such as light, increased temperature, and mechanical stimulation. In addition, the upward movements of buds newly detached from parent hydras have been characterized as a response to gravity. Spontaneous locomotory activity occurs frequently in starved animals, and such behavior has been thought to be exploratory and food seeking in nature. The most detailed study of factors affecting locomotion in *Hydra* was undertaken by Ewer (1947a), who investigated the interactions of the influences of light and gravity on the locomotion of recently detached buds.

Trembley (1744) noted that *Hydra* migrates toward a light source, and performed experiments to verify this observation. He noticed one day that a large number of polyps had collected on the side of the glass turned toward the sunlight coming from a window. Curious to know whether this was merely an accident or a result of the light sensitivity of the animal, he turned the glass halfway round so that the majority of the polyps were on the least illuminated side of the glass. Returning next day he found this side to be almost depopulated, and that the polyps "were dispersed through the glass in the process of going to the better illuminated side." A few days later most of the hydras were on the illuminated side, after repeating the experiment several times with the same result, he "was convinced that the polyps had a special inclination for the best-lit place in the glass."

In further experiments he inserted the jar containing a large number of polyps into a pasteboard cover, in which he had cut a chevron-shaped aperture. When the aperture was turned to the light, the animals migrated to it and grouped themselves in the characteristic shape of the chevron. Placement of the aperture upside down induced a reversal of the pattern produced by the migrating polyps. Trembley found that the animals would continue to migrate some distance even after the light had been cut off. In addition, polyps at the bottom of the glass moved to the lighted aperture by a circuitous route, first moving up the side of the glass opposite to the aperture, then along the surface film to the light side. He observed these types of behavior with three different species of *Hydra,* finding the green species much faster in their locomotory activities.

More than a century passed before anything new was added to Trembley's original discoveries of *Hydra's* light-sensitive behavior. In 1891, Wilson published a report on "The Heliotropism of *Hydra*" in which he experimentally established that the polyps are most sensitive to blue light. Subsequent workers confirmed the light-sensitive migrations of *Hydra* (Hertel, 1905; Hasse-Eichler, 1931), but tended to associate it with the attraction of prey, such as *Daphnia,* which were also positively phototaxic. Haug (1933) discounted this, however, showing that *Hydra* migrates to an illuminated part of an aquarium in preference to a darker area containing small crustacean prey enclosed in a gauze bag. He also demonstrated that the apical portion of the animal was much more light sensitive than the basal region, and described in detail the complex orienting movements of *Hydra* toward a light source. These orienting motions have been described in several investigations, most recently by Passano and McCullough (1964, 1965) in their electrophysiological studies of the animal.

Factors such as the spectral composition of the light and its intensity affect migration activity of *Hydra. Hydra's* movements to a light source are accelerated by increasing the intensity of the light or moving it closer to the vessel (Haase-Eichler, 1931). However, such an increase in illumination elevates the water temperature and creates water currents that affect the animal's behavior. A study of the effect of light intensity on migration which circumvented these difficulties was undertaken by Haug (1933). He exposed *Hydra* to joint illumination from two sides of the vessel, keeping the intensity of one light fixed while making slight changes in the intensity of the opposite source. The animals migrated to the side having the highest light intensity, a difference in light intensities of as little as 0.1 m/candlepower being detected by the *Hydra* (Haug, 1933). He confirmed Wilson's earlier observation that *Hydra* is most sensitive to blue light, and was able to show slight differences in the spectral preference of two different species. Directing a spectrum 10 cm wide onto a tall cuvette he found that the green *Hydra* congregates in the blue-violet region, and brown *Hydra* in the area of the blue-green rays (Haug, 1933).

Mast (1903) studied the effect of increased temperature on the locomotory activity of *Hydra*. He heated one edge of a large flat dish containing a group of widely dispersed polyps. When the water temperature in the heated region reached approximately 31°C he observed a marked increase in the *Hydra*'s movements. The animal did not show any preference for moving out of the heated area, however, since the orientations appeared quite random. A decrease of temperature does not induce the polyp to locomote. As the temperature is lowered, the animal merely becomes more sluggish, contracting more slowly and at longer intervals, until near 0°C its movements almost cease (Mast, 1903).

When *Hydra* is mechanically stimulated, for example on the body column using a glass rod, the animal contracts. Wagner (1904) observed that the direction of extension after this contraction bears no definite relation to the side stimulated. If the mechanical stimulation is repeated, contraction and expansion occur again with no specific reference to the direction of the stimulus. If the stimulation is continued, however, the animal finally moves away using the characteristic inchworm form of locomotion.

As previously mentioned, hungry hydras are more active than recently fed ones. Wilson (1891) described the migration of starved hydras to the bottom of the pond, while more recently Lomnicki and Slobodkin (1966) reported the production of gas bubbles at the base of poorly fed polyps, aiding them to float to the surface waters. Ewer (1947a) found that the normal upward migration of freshly separated buds was inhibited by feeding. If the bud was given food it remained fixed and moved no further for at least 24 hours. Jennings (1906) emphasized the food-seeking goal of locomotion in starved *Hydra* to a considerable extent, believing that "through hunger the *Hydra* is driven to move to another region." The effect of starvation on the light response has been in dispute, however, Haase-Eichler (1931) claimed that animals starved for several days moved toward a light source faster than those that have eaten. In contrast Schulusen (1935) found that whereas a greater proportion of starved polyps move toward the light, they advance more slowly than satiated hydras.

The upward movements of *Hydra,* observed under the usual conditions employed to culture the animals in the laboratory, were usually thought to be a reaction to oxygen rather than to gravity (Wilson, 1891; Haase-Eichler, 1931; Beutler, 1933). However, Ewer (1947a) distinguished between the activities of adult *Hydra* and newly separated buds. Buds of *H. vulgaris* were observed to migrate upward toward the water surface immediately after detachment from the parent. The reaction is negative geotaxis and not a response to an increase in oxygen concentration. An increase in carbon dioxide concentration of the water had no effect on the reaction of buds, but evoked a negative geotaxis in adult animals. Normally the reaction of adult hydras to gravity is absent or very much weaker than in buds. Since hydras are photopositive in their migratory behavior, Ewer investigated the interaction of light and gravity effects on young buds. The gravity reaction was less affected by light shone from the side of the containing tank than light coming from below, which counteracted somewhat the negative geotaxic response. Ewer found that the gravity response of buds lasts for at least 3 days after separation from the parent, and acted as a distributing factor, ensuring dispersion of the buds from their parents, thus preventing local overcrowding.

III. Feeding Behavior

Feeding activities in *Hydra,* like several of the modes of locomotion, consist of a series of complex behavioral sequences. Probably the most concise description of the feeding response was given by Josephson (1967):

> First the prey strikes the polyp, usually on one of the outstretched tentacles, and becomes there attached by nematocyst discharge. The portion of the tentacle proximal to the prey then contracts, often spirally inward, which brings the prey near the mouth. As the prey nears the mouth, the surrounding tentacles concertedly flex in the oral direction. This sometimes results in adjacent tentacles contacting the prey and pushing it towards the mouth. Concerted tentacle flexion may be repeated several times during and after ingestion of the prey. Finally the mouth opens, creeps around the prey and closes about it.

The capture and engulfment of a single *Artemia salina* nauplius by a *Hydra* consists of a series of complex behavioral sequences. Such sequences may currently be enumerated as (1) nematocyst discharge; (2) tentacular movements; (3) mouth opening, creeping over the prey and closure; and (4) inhibition of endogenous tentacle and body contractions.

A. NEMATOCYST DISCHARGE

The first element in feeding behavior is the attachment of the prey to an outstretched tentacle by means of nematocyst discharge. The two types of nematocyst involved in prey capture, stenoteles and desmonemes, both discharge to the mechanical stimulation caused by prodding the tentacles with a clean glass rod. The threshold for such activation is drastically lowered, however, by the presence of food extracts. This has been shown both for the anemone *Anemonia* (Pantin, 1942) and for *Hydra* (Ewer, 1947b; Jones, 1941). The desmonemes coil around the prey, entrapping it, while the stenoteles pierce its exoskeleton in a harpoonlike fashion. The discharged nematocysts are released from the tentacle as the prey organism is enclosed by the mouth (Ewer, 1947b). The mechanisms of nematocyst discharge are considered in detail in Chapter 2 of this book.

B. TENTACULAR MOVEMENTS

On attachment of the prey organism to the tentacle with nematocyst discharge, there is a latent period before first observable movement of the tentacle. In *H. littoralis,* this time period (the tentacle reaction time) is usually between 1 and 2 seconds in duration, but sometimes the latency lasts a minute or more (Rushforth and Hofman, 1972). The tentacle movement usually consists of contraction proximal to the point of contact of the prey, but there are often bending or spiraling movements associated with this shortening, depending on the position of the attachment. These tentacular movements, bring the prey near to the mouth and precede a concerted flexion of the other tentacles (termed a "concert"). As such concerts repeatedly occur, the mouth opens and begins to creep around the prey. At this stage the concerts frequently give rise to uncoordinated, writhing activities (Ewer, 1947b; Loomis, 1955; Lenhoff, 1961a). The mouth continues to creep around the *Artemia,* finally closing about it.

Although there are different types of tentacle movements depending on the position of prey attachment, the reaction time was found to be independent of the type of movement. Thus, the times for conduction of impulses or diffusion of chemical factors from the point of prey attachment to the hypostome, where presumably coordination of the tentacle movements takes place, do not play a major role in determining the reaction time. The fact that contraction of the tentacle is limited to the portion below the attachment of the prey strongly suggests polarized conduction in the oral direction. The three forms of tentacle movement may result primarily from mechanical stimulation by the prey, but they do not occur without nematocyst discharge. If a clean glass rod is lightly touched to the tentacle, there is only slight localized contraction at the point of stimulation. However, if the stimulation is greater, causing nematocyst discharge and tentacle adhesion to the rod, then contraction below the point of attachment occurs, similar to that in the capture of an artemia.

In a study of the feeding response of *H. littoralis,* Rushforth and Hofman (1972) found that a single *Artemia* was usually engulfed within 80–100 seconds. However, concert activities initiated with the first tentacle movements, were observed to continue long after the prey had been swallowed by the *Hydra*. Concerted tentacle flexions consist of highly coordinated oral sweeping movements by all of the tentacles (Fig. 3B), or all tentacles except that involved in the movements bringing the prey to the mouth of the *Hydra*. Such concerts are quite dissimilar from uncoordinated, writhing activities (Fig. 3 C and D) which are oc-

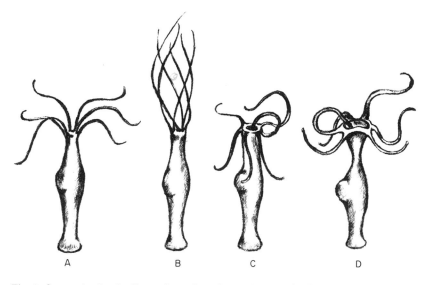

A   B   C   D

Fig. 3. Stages in the feeding reflex of *Hydra:* (A) A *Hydra* in the absence of feeding stimuli; the mouth is closed and the tentacles are outstretched and relatively motionless. (B) After the addition of reduced glutathione, the tentacles sweep inward to the central vertical axis of the animal in a concerted flexion (a concert). (C) The tentacles bend and writhe as the mouth begins to open. (D) The mouth opens widely and vigorous tentacle writhing occurs, sometimes the tips of the tentacles being observed within the *Hydra*'s mouth. (After H. M. Lenhoff, 1961a).

casionally seen following concerts when the *Hydra* feeds on a single *Artemia*. If several artemias are simultaneously captured by the polyp, initial concert activity soon gives rise to writhing movements, which continue after all the prey are engulfed. In turn, the writhing activity becomes less vigorous after ingestion and concerts return at increased frequencies. Concerts are gradually restored to base line levels, 30 to 60 minutes later.

Concerts occur spontaneously, usually in bursts, but their frequency is markedly enhanced by dilute extracts of *Artemia* or extremely small concentrations of reduced glutathione (GSH) or its analogs (i.e., below $10^{-8} M$).

Tentacle writing movements are also chemically initiated (Wagner, 1904; Ewer, 1947b; Loomis, 1955; H. M. Lenhoff, 1961a). Such chemical activation of repeated concerts at dilute concentrations, and of tentacle writhing at higher concentrations, results from stimulation via the external environment. However, a single concert may be induced if a tentacle is prodded with a clean glass rod so that nematocyst discharge occurs. The stimulated tentacle adhers to the rod and contracts below the point of attachment, and a concerted flexion of the other tentacles immediately follows. This single concert, therefore, appears to result from mechanical stimulation alone. However, additional concerts occur at frequencies not greater than prestimulation values, and writhing activity is not initiated. The coupling of this concert with the oral contraction of the stimulated tentacle appears extremely tight and suggests that these two components are internally linked in one behavioral sequence. However, further increased concert activity is undoubtedly chemically controlled.

C. Mouth Opening, Creeping over the Prey, and Closure

1. Mouth Opening

The mouth opening response is one in which chemical stimulation seems to play a key role. Wagner (1904) observed that starved hydras would open their mouths when exposed to beef extracts. Park, while testing glutathione as a antiradiation compound in regeneration experiments with *Hydra,* observed the animals to open their mouths when GSH was placed in the culture medium (in H. M. Lenhoff, 1968a). However, she did not relate this to the normal feeding response. Loomis (1955) presented evidence that GSH is the specific chemical stimulator evoking feeding responses in *Hydra.* He suggested that *Hydra*'s feeding activities were initiated by GSH released when the prey organism was pierced by discharged nematocysts. The dependence on GSH as a specific initiator of feeding in *Hydra* was questioned by Forrest (1962), who maintained that a wide range of substances unrelated to GSH produced feeding responses.

Burnett *et al.* (1963) suggested that the feeding stimulator was present in the nematocyst capsule and was released from the *Hydra* itself on nematocyst discharge. These workers observed that *H. pseudoligactis* which had terminated the mouth opening reaction to GSH would capture and ingest *Artemia* administered to them. They further pointed out that a diverse series of substances activate feeding in *Hydra,* and suggested

that such substances operate through a mechanism of inducing nematocyst discharge. Trypsin, hyaluronidase, lactic acid, NaOH, and electric
shock were found to stimulate nematocyst discharge and evoke mouth
opening. Groups of four *H. pirardi* were given an electric shock in a
single drop of water and then removed from it. Two normal hydras placed
in the drop promptly open their mouths and began a feeding response, the
response lasting for as long as 30 minutes. Similar results were obtained
when excised tentacles of this species were exposed to an electric shock.
Burnett *et al.* (1963) also found that colonies of *H. pirardi* which had remained in a GSH solution with their mouths closed for some time, re-
opened their mouths and began a feeding response if they were stimulated
by teasing their tentacles with microforceps or if they were transferred
to a slide with a pipette. Such stimulation was observed to result in the
discharge of stenoteles. These observations led Burnett and his associates
to question the uniqueness of GSH as the sole feeding stimulator in
Hydra, and to postulate the presence of activating factors in the nematocyst capsule of the animal.

Lenhoff and his co-workers have performed extensive investigations to
quantify factors involved in the mouth opening response of *H. littoralis*
to GSH (H. M. Lenhoff, 1961a, 1965; H. M. Lenhoff and Bovaird, 1959,
1960, 1961; H. M. Lenhoff and Zwisler, 1963). These studies have been
reviewed in detail by H. M. Lenhoff (1961b, 1968a; H. M. Lenhoff, 1967,
1968b) and consider (*a*) the role of various ions in influencing the feeding
response; (*b*) the properties of ionizable groups at the receptor sites on
the tentacles and mouth region, which are involved in the reversible
binding of glutathione; (*c*) the existence of a pH shell surrounding the
charged surfaces on the hydra, and its effect on the response; (*d*) the
specificity of GSH as the feeding stimulator in *Hydra*; and (*e*) the resolution of several seemingly inconsistent reports dealing with feeding behavior in the animal.

Applying concepts of enzymology, H. M. Lenhoff (1968a) proposed that
the key steps in the activation of the feeding response are the combination between glutathione and receptor sites on the hydra, and the events
initiated by the combination. He performed experiments on the equilibrium between glutathione and the receptor, determined the dissociation constant, and used it to evaluate the pK values of charged groups at
the receptor site. The equilibrium between glutathione and the receptor
was found to be attained in less than a minute, but GSH had to be constantly present at the receptor site for the response to take place (H. M.
Lenhoff, 1961a). On removal of glutathione, the response ceased within
a minute. Using a plot of the "activity" of the receptor–effector system,
i.e., the duration of mouth opening, against glutathione concentration, a

maximum response was observed at GSH concentrations of $5 \times 10^{-6} M$ and greater. The duration of the response was found to be longer in hydras starved for 2 days than 1-day starved animals.

Several environmental ions were found to affect the duration of GSH-activated mouth opening. However, since these ions bathe both the receptor and the ectodermal effector cells, which are involved in the contractile processes involved in mouth opening, it was not possible to determine their specific modes of action. The calcium ion must be present for mouth opening to occur in response to GSH. A concentration of $5 \times 10^{-4} M$ of this ion was required for a half-maximal response. Both magnesium and sodium ions, known to compete with calcium in biological systems, competitively inhibited mouth opening (H. M. Lenhoff, 1961b). The chelating agent ethylenediaminetetraacetic acid (EDTA) also inhibited the response. Such inhibition was completely reversed by calcium ions, and to some extent by the strontium ion, an ion known to replace calcium in many systems (Lenhoff and Bovaird, 1959). Potassium ions at a concentration of $10^{-4} M$ and higher were found to decrease the duration of mouth opening in response to GSH. Several anions affect the response, the order of effectiveness of such ions in increasing the duration of mouth opening was $Cl^- > Br^- > I^- = NO_3^-$ (Lenhoff and Bovaird, 1959).

Lenhoff extended a series of experiments performed by Loomis (1955) and Cliffe and Waley (1958) showing the specificity of the tripeptide backbone of GSH in eliciting feeding in *Hydra*. Loomis (1955) tested a series of compounds related to glutathione, finding that glutamylcysteine, cysteinylglycine, cysteine, and asparthione (aspartylcysteinylglycine) were not active. Additional studies using glutathione analogs and related amino acids further documented this specificity (Cliffe and Waley, 1958; H. M. Lenhoff and Bovaird, 1961). Data from these investigators was summarized by H. M. Lenhoff (1968a) as follows:

> (1) The thiol is not required for activation—because ophthalmic acid (γ-glutamylamino-n-butyrylglycine), nor-ophthalmic acid (γ-glutamylalanylglycine) and S-methylglutathione also activated feeding. (2) The hydra recognize the specific structure of the intact tripeptide backbone of glutathione because the just-mentioned analogs activated feeding, and tripeptide analogs with large and charged substituents at the sulfhydryl grouping of glutathione competitively inhibited glutathione action. (3) The receptor has a high affinity for the glutamyl part of the tripeptide—because glutamic acid and glutamine were the only amino acids to show competitive inhibition. (4) The α-amino of glutathione is probably required for the association of glutathione with the receptor—because glutamic acid competitively inhibited, while α-ketoglutaric acid did not.

The inhibitory action of glutamic acid provided evidence that GSH present in extracts of *Artemia* elicited mouth opening. Addition of glutamic acid markedly reduced the activity of such extracts, but GSH overcame this inhibition (H. M. Lenhoff, 1961b). Table II summarizes the activators and inhibitors of the feeding response in *H. littoralis*.

TABLE II

ACTIVATORS AND INHIBITORS OF THE FEEDING RESPONSE OF *Hydra littoralis*[a]

$$-O_2C-CH-CH_2-CO- \qquad \overset{\displaystyle R}{\underset{\displaystyle CH_2}{|}} \qquad $$

$-O_2C-CH-CH_2-CO-$	CH_2	
$\quad\quad\mid$	$\mid$	
$+NH_3$	$NH-CH-CO-$	$NH-CH_2-CO_2-$
A	B	C
— Glutamyl	Alanyl	— Glycine

	Inhibitors	
Activators	Tripeptide	Others
$R = -H$	$R = -SO_2H$	Glutamic acid
$R = -CH_3$	$R = -SO_3H$	Glutamine
$R = -SH$	$R = -S-COCH_3$	Cysteinylglycine
$R = S-CH_3$	$R = -S(N\text{-ethylsuccinmido})$	
	$R = -S-SG$	
	$R = -SH$	
	and	
	$A = -O_2C-CH-CH_2CO$	
	$\quad\quad\quad\mid$	
	$+NH_3$	

[a] After H. M. Lenhoff (1961b).

Further information concerning the mechanisms of GSH binding and activation of mouth opening was obtained from investigations of (1) the effect of pH on the dissociation constant K_a between glutathione and its receptor, and (2) activation of the mouth opening response by nontripeptides (H. M. Lenhoff, 1968a,b). Plots of a function of K_a against pH suggested that ionizable groups with distinct pK's at the receptor site participated in binding glutathione. The characteristic pH profiles of GSH and *S*-methylglutatione indicated the need to control and specify the pH of the medium in studying the mouth opening response. The proteolytic enzymes papain, ficin, and trypsin elicit mouth opening responses in *H. littoralis*. H. M. Lenhoff (1968a) studied the effects of trypsin in activating the feeding response as an aid in understanding the mechanism of activation of the glutathione receptor. Since addition of trypsin does not increase the duration of mouth opening elicited by saturating amounts of glutathione alone, trypsin appears to function by activating some of the same events initiated by glutathione. "That trypsin activated the feeding response in *Cordylophora* (normally elicited by proline, not glutathione) and in *Physalia* gastrozooids (normally responding to glutathione) suggests that trypsin acts on some step common to the receptor-effector system of the feeding responses of all these organisms irrespective of the natural activator involved" (H. M. Lenhoff, 1968a).

The results of experiments of trypsin-activated mouth opening in *H. littoralis* suggested the presence of an ultramicroenvironment surrounding *Hydra* (H. M. Lenhoff, 1965). The pH optimum of trypsin in evoking a feeding response in *H. littoralis* was pH 6, with only slight activation of mouth opening at pH 7.5. H. M. Lenhoff (1968a) contrasted this optimum with the alkaline pH optimum of trypsin acting on soluble proteins or on synthetic substrates, suggesting that the shift in optimum was due to the pH at the surface of the *Hydra* being more alkaline than that of the macroenvironment. He suggested that the surface of the *Hydra* at the site of trypsin action might be positively charged, thus attracting a shell of negative hydroxyl ions. "Thus, trypsin may be acting at its normal alkaline pH optimum on the surface of the hydra, although the pH measured in the macroenvironment is slightly acid" (H. M. Lenhoff, 1968a).

Lenhoff expended considerable effort to show that GSH was the feeding stimulator in *Hydra* and to resolve some of the questions arising from reported observations which conflicted with his earlier findings and those of Loomis (H. M. Lenhoff, 1965, 1968a). Several reports claimed that many compounds other than GSH, its analogs, or proteases elicit feeding responses in *Hydra*. Wagner (1904) noted that quinine would cause *Hydra* to open its mouth, while Balke and Steiner (1959) claimed that both lactic and ascorbic acids induced a feeding response. Forrest (1962) maintained that citric acid, D-glucosamine, nicotinic acid, riboflavin, sodium chloride, and urea all produce feeding activities in several species of *Hydra*. All of these compounds were subsequently tested by Loomis and Lenhoff and were found not to elicit feeding responses (H. M. Lenhoff, 1968a). Occasionally, in the presence of low calcium concentrations, quinine would cause the animal's mouth to gape open, but the response was not considered to be part of the normal feeding reaction. H. M. Lenhoff (1968a) criticized Forrest's use of filtered pond water as a medium in which to test the effects of substances as feeding initiators. Having shown the important roles of ions and the pH of the medium in the feeding response, he questioned the reliability of results using a test solution in which such parameters are unknown. Since Forrest (1962) obtained a feeding response with all the compounds she tested, Lenhoff suggested that this may be due to the glutathione present in plankton and released during filtration of the pond water. He believed such GSH contamination was responsible for the feeding response obtained with sodium chloride at the low concentrations found in soft pond water or in the culture medium frequently used for *Hydra* in the laboratory, and maintained that Forrest's observations with sodium chloride "imply that hydra always are carrying out a feeding response" (H. M. Lenhoff, 1968a).

It will be recalled that Burnett and his co-workers (1963) also questioned the uniqueness of GSH as the sole feeding stimulator in *Hydra*. They found that colonies of *H. pseudoligactis* which had closed their mouths after exposure to GSH would capture and ingest *Artemia,* and *H. pirardi* similarly adapted to GSH would reopen their mouths and reinitiate a feeding response if mechanically stimulated. Lenhoff interpreted the first result as an activation of additional GSH receptors by a reduction in the pH in the area immediately surrounding the receptors. The pH of the weakly buffered culture solution (pH 7.6) in this region could be reduced by up to 2 pH units by the fluids released from the wounds of the *Artemia,* since extracts of *Artemia* have a pH of about 6. This explanation was supported by experiments in which mouth opening in *H. littoralis* was reactivated by reducing the pH of solutions with concentrations of GSH above saturating levels in terms of the feeding response (H. M. Lenhoff, 1965). The result showing reactivation of mouth opening in *H. pirardi,* in the presence of saturating glutathione, was attributed by H. M. Lenhoff (1968a) to the intermittent feeding activity of this species. In addition, Burnett *et al.* (1963) indicated that, unlike *H. pirardi, H. littoralis* will not reinitiate feeding responses after adaptation to GSH when mechanically stimulated.

Burnett *et al.* (1963) suggest that substances other than GSH (for example, trypsin), which induce mouth opening in *Hydra,* operate through a mechanism of inducing nematocyst discharge. They postulated that the feeding stimulator, possibly GSH, is present in the nematocyst capsule and is released on discharge. H. M. Lenhoff (1968a) established that trypsin did not initiate mouth opening by causing nematocyst discharge, thereby releasing GSH into the medium.

> The clarifying experiment utilized the pH optimum curves for glutathione (broadly, from 4 to 8), and for trypsin (restricted to around pH 6). The medium around *H. littoralis* that had been treated to pH 6.0 for 1 hour with trypsin, was adjusted to a pH of either 4.6 or 7.5 and added to a fresh group of hydra. In neither case did the fresh groups of hydra give significant response, showing that trypsin does not act by releasing glutathione.

In addition, glutamic acid, a competitive inhibitor of glutathione action, did not inhibit trypsin activation of the mouth opening response, again suggesting that trypsin did not act via the release of GSH.

Additional evidence that reduced glutathione is the feeding stimulator in *Hydra* comes from the discovery of activation by GSH of other components of the feeding response. It has already been mentioned that extremely small concentrations of glutathione or various GSH analogs (less than 10^{-8} M) significantly increase concert frequency. Reduced glutathione at higher concentrations also causes tentacle writhing activities, which are also part of the normal feeding response to live prey. In subsequent sections, the role of GSH in inhibiting both spontaneous contractions of the column and tentacles, and those induced by mechanical stimulation will be discussed. Such inhibitory effects are also observed with *Artemia* or homogenates of *Artemia*. Finally, the behavioral sequence of "neck formation," discussed in Section III,C,2, occurring if *Artemia* is administered to *Hydra* 1–6 hours after previous ingestion of a large number of *Artemia,* also occurs if GSH is in the external environment. The large number of components of the normal feeding response to prey, which are also elicited by reduced glutathione, strongly suggests the specificity of this tripeptide as the feeding stimulator in *Hydra*.

2. Mouth Closure

The later stages of feeding behavior in *Hydra* consist of mouth creeping around the prey, closing about it, a reduction in the vigor of tentacle writhing, and a gradual return of coordinated concert frequencies to base-line levels. Throughout these feeding sequences the endogenous contractions of both the tentacles and the column are inhibited. They return after *Artemia* ingestion at enhanced frequencies, before they are restored to prestimulation values.

Little is known concerning the mechanisms involved in mouth closing and creeping about the prey. Creeping of the mouth may result from stimuli due to contact of the prey on the inside of the mouth. An inert object, such as a pin, will be swallowed when it is placed in the mouth of *Hydra* (Kanaev, 1952). An isolated hypostome will creep slowly up and off the shaft of a pin inserted through the mouth. The hypostome always moves in an oral direction, at a reduced speed if the tentacles are removed. Thus, by inserting the top of the pin in the lips of the mouth, the isolated hypostome can be made to creep slowly down to the bottom of the pin. The present-day description of mouth movements in the feeding response of *Hydra* go little further than those of Hartog (1880), given almost a century ago. He pointed out that the tentacles play little role in the feeding response as soon as the mouth comes into contact with the food. "The hydra then slowly stretches itself over the food in a way that recalls to some extent the manner in which a serpent gets outside its prey . . ." (Hartog, 1880).

The mechanisms responsible for mouth closure and termination of the various behavioral sequences are also not clearly understood. Burnett *et al.* (1959) show that fully fed hydras are capable of discharging nematocysts and subduing prey. But once the gastrovascular cavity of the animal is filled, the *Hydra* does not attempt to ingest the captured prey. It is difficult for the mouth to open, because of the internal pressure exerted on the walls of the gastrovascular cavity, as a result of a large intake of water during the early phases of digestion. However, during an extended period following ingestion of *Artemia* (1–6 hours) the mouth may open to engulf a single prey while the *Hydra* forms a tight constriction in the region just below the hypostome (Blanquet and Lenhoff, 1968). This neck formation was shown in *H. pirardi* to be caused by a combination of three factors (*a*) glutathione on the exterior of the *Hydra*; (*b*) distension of the wall of the *Hydra*'s body column; and (*c*) the presence of tyrosine within the gut. Tyrosine was found to be highly specific in causing neck formation. No other amino acid, including phenylalanine, was active and tryosine having either the α-amino or α-carboxyl blocked had no effect (Blanquet and Lenhoff, 1968).

D. INHIBITION OF TENTACLE AND COLUMN CONTRACTIONS

The most overt feature of the behavior of an unstimulated *Hydra* is the spontaneous production of column and tentacle contractions. Throughout the initial phases of feeding these endogenous contractions are suppressed, and are supplanted by the linked sequences of local responses. In unstimulated animals, the spontaneous activity of the tentacles consists primarily of single contractions of individual tentacles, or bursts of contractions of one or more tentacles. There is an increased frequency of such tentacle contractions before the contraction of the body column of the *Hydra* (Rushforth, 1972). During the capture and engulfment of a single *Artemia,* the endogenous tentacle contractions are supplanted by localized movements of the stimulated tentacle and concerted oral flexions of the rest of the tentacles. With greater stimulation, by multiple artemias or GSH, the tentacle activities consist of uncoordinated writhing movements, gradually giving rise to concerts. During these behavioral sequences, however, the normal spontaneous contraction activities of the tentacles are suppressed. Such contractions are gradually restored to prestimulation levels, approximately 15 minutes after *Artemia* engulfment.

Rushforth and Hofman (1972) showed that inhibition of spontaneous column contractions during feeding is chemically mediated. They observed that *Hydra* allowed to feed for a 15-minute period had significantly lower column contraction frequencies over a subsequent 90-minute period than unfed controls. However, if the culture water was changed immediately after the feeding period, then the contraction frequencies were significantly higher than the unfed *Hydra* over a similar time period. This suggested that during the ingestion of *Artemia* in the *Hydra*'s gut the column contractions were enhanced, but that a chemical substance released during the capture and engulfment of the *Artemia* inhibited the column contractions, if not removed from the medium surrounding the *Hydra*. This hypothesis was supported by the results of experiments showing a reduction in the column contraction frequency of *Hydra* exposed to extracts of *Artemia,* or 10^{-5} *M* GSH, compared with animals in culture fluid alone.

In addition to suppressing endogenous column contractions in *Hydra,* feeding stimuli, such as live *Artemia,* extracts of *Artemia,* and GSH, inhibited body contractions induced by light and mechanical stimulation. In experiments to determine the inhibition of the light-induced contractions, groups of *Hydra* were exposed to a regime of 75 seconds (or 150 seconds) of direct light stimulation followed by 75 seconds (or 150 seconds) of ambient illumination. First the hydras were exposed to a control period consisting of 5 light periods in a regime, and the numbers of animals contracting in each light period were recorded. Then GSH or other substances of known concentration were pipetted into the test dishes, and the numbers of *Hydra* contracting in subsequent light periods were recorded. Most of the *Hydra* were observed to contract in the control periods of light stimulation. In contrast, in the presence of live *Artemia,* extracts of *Artemia,* or 10^{-5} *M* GSH, the light-induced contractions were initially almost totally suppressed. The proportions of *Hydra* contracting to light gradually increased, being restored to control levels after approximately 1 hour. As a measure of inhibitory activity, the time for 50% of the animals to again contract to light ($T_{0.5}$) after exposure to GSH was determined (Rushforth, 1965a).

Using this assay system, Rushforth (1965a) discovered the following properties of GSH inhibition of light-induced contractions, using *H. pirardi* and several strains of *H. viridis*. The length of inhibition is dependent on the GSH concentration. The inhibitory effect increases with increasing concentration, and then levels off to a plateau value. A similar relationship was observed by H. M. Lenhoff (1961a) for the mouth opening response of *H. littoralis* and suggests saturation of the *Hydra*'s glutathione receptors at higher concentrations.

The nutritional state of the *Hydra,* its previous exposure to GSH, and the pH of the medium have also been shown to affect the duration of inhibition (Rushforth, 1965a). Inhibition of animals fed 24 hours previously is markedly shorter than that for 96-hour starved *Hydra*. *Hydra* adapt to 10^{-5} *M* GSH so that approximately 1 hour after exposure their light-induced contractions have returned to control levels. Fresh *Hydra* placed into the medium at this time show normal inhibitory effects, indicating that the adaptation of GSH is due to changes within the animal rather than to degradation of the glutathione molecule. Addition of 10^{-5} *M* GSH 12 hours later blocks the light response only slightly, but after 24 hours 10^{-5} *M* GSH again causes maximum inhibition. Inhibition of light-induced contractions by 10^{-5} *M* GSH is relatively short at pH 9 ($T_{0.5}$ approx. 10 minutes), but increases as the pH of the medium is reduced ($T_{0.5}$ approx. 34 minutes at pH 6). *Hydra* which have previously adapted to GSH can be reinduced into additional inhibitory activity by lowering the pH of the medium. It will be recalled that similar pH effects have been observed by Lenhoff in studies of the mouth opening response in *H. littoralis*. The mechanism of the pH reactivation of GSH effects was discussed by H. M. Lenhoff (1965) and was alluded to earlier in the present chapter.

Removal of GSH from the medium terminates the suppression of light-induced contractions. Thus, GSH must be constantly present for inhibition to occur and does not merely trigger a sequence of long-lasting inhibitory events (Rushforth *et al.,* 1964). Experiments using analogs of GSH show that the molecular configuration of reduced glutathione is quite specific for its inhibitory effects on both mechanically-stimulated and light-induced contractions (Rushforth, 1965a). However, the sulfhydryl group is not essential for inhibition since the *S*-methyl analog is active. The substitution of large groups for the sulfhydryl group produces analogs which do not inhibit contractions. Thus, neither *S*-acetyl nor oxidized glutathione block contractions stimulated by light or mechanical agitation. However, when these analogs are introduced into the medium, they compete with GSH, reducing its inhibitory effects. The results of these investigations indicate that the action of GSH in suppressing contractions appears to have similar properties to those found by other workers using the mouth opening response (Loomis, 1955; Cliffe and Waley, 1958; H. M. Lenhoff and Bovaird, 1961; H. M. Lenhoff, 1961a,b, 1965). Since in the present experiments the effects of GSH on the animal is measured independently of mouth opening, the results of such studies confirm some of the general properties of glutathione receptors in *Hydra*.

It was noted previously that inhibition of tentacle and column contractions with feeding stimuli occurs at the same time as enhanced concert frequencies and tentacle writhing activity. The joint increase in concerts and decrease in column and tentacle contractions might be explained by one or more of several mechanisms: (*a*) Concerts might be inhibitory to both column and tentacle contractions, such contractions being suppressed as a secondary effect of induced concerts with feeding stimuli;

(b) alternatively, mechanisms giving rise to contraction activity may inhibit concerts and the elevated concert frequency may be an indirect effect of the suppression of the contractions; and (c) finally, feeding stimuli could have direct but opposite effects on concerts and contractions. Efforts to distinguish between these mechanisms gave somewhat contradictory results and the major questions are not resolved (Rushforth and Hofman, 1972). In three species of *Hydra,* spontaneous concert frequencies are negatively correlated with both the frequencies of tentacle and column contractions. However, the spontaneous frequencies of all three behavioral events decrease with starvation over a period of several days. Reduced glutathione inhibits endogenous column contractions in *H. pirardi* without tentacles, but removal of the tentacles significantly reduces light-induced contractions in this animal. These results indicate that GSH inhibition of column contractions does not take place exclusively by mechanisms requiring input from the tentacles. Nevertheless the result suggests that the tentacles do contribute to GSH suppression of such contractions, and is consistent with the hypothesis that the glutathione receptors are concentrated on these structures.

Inhibition of column and tentacle contractions in *Hydra* may be an example of a more general phenomenon in coelenterates, i.e., inhibition of spontaneously reoccurring behavioral events by feeding stimuli. Long-term modifications of the rhythmic contractions of the body wall of *Metridium* have been observed with food extracts (Pantin, 1950). Suppression of the swimming response by food extracts has been reported by Ross and Sutton (1964) for *Stomphia.* The control mechanisms involved in swimming and feeding in this sea anemone appear mutually inhibitory, however, since there is also suppression of nematocyst discharge during swimming. Inhibition of the discharge of atrichous isorhizas, the nematocyst type used in the locomotion of *Hydra,* has also been found to occur with food extracts (Ewer, 1947b). In the hydroid *Tubularia,* the most obvious behavioral features are the regular concerted oral movements of the proximal tentacles, followed by a peristaltic wave originating distally in the hydranth. Such endogenous concerts are suppressed during feeding (Josephson and Mackie, 1965), and are also inhibited by food extracts (Rushforth, 1969).

Josephson (1967) has classified the feeding responses in *Hydra* as a series of linked sequences of local responses, each component being initiated by the results of the preceding one. The sequences of local responses depend solely on "appropriate effector responses to specific stimuli and morphological contiguity of the responding parts, with the linking of the components being effected through the external environment." When such local responses are taking place there is inhibition of the rhythmically recurring behavioral events of column and tentacle contractions. While considerable effort has been expended to elucidate the properties of glutathione receptors in *Hydra*, our knowledge of mechanisms occurring within the animal, controlling its sequential feeding responses, is sparse indeed.

IV. Response to External Stimulation

The previous sections of this chapter described relatively complex behavioral sequences of locomotion and feeding in *Hydra*. The range of such behavior appears quite wide, particularly since coelenterates are often thought of as simple sessile animals, not having a rich spectrum of activities. The effects of chemostimulation, in the form of reduced glutathione, in initiating various components of the feeding response have been described in some detail. This section will consider the responses of *Hydra* to other forms of stimulation. These features of the animal's behavior are seen to consist primarily of modifications of spontaneous contractions of the body column and tentacles. The effects of repeated mechanical agitation appear to satisfy many of the criteria for habituation—the simplest form of learning. Responses to joint stimulation by more than one stimulus pose several questions concerning the underlying mechanisms controlling the animal's behavior. Basically, however, the responses are all superimposed on a background of endogenously active systems. These responses will be described after a brief discussion of the spontaneously produced contraction patterns in unstimulated *Hydra*.

Most of the early descriptions of *Hydra* drew attention to the spontaneous contractions of the animal. Jennings (1906) noted that an undisturbed green *Hydra* "does not remain still, but keeps up a sort of rhythmic activity." After remaining in a given position for a short time it contracts, then bends to a new position, and reextends (Fig. 4). It remains in this

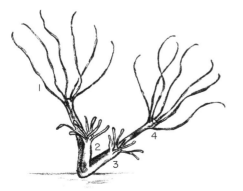

Fig. 4. Spontaneous changes of position in an undisturbed *Hydra* (side views). The extended animal (1), contracts (2), bends to a new position (3), and extends (4). (After Jennings, 1906.)

position for one or two minutes before contracting again, repeating the cycle of activity. Jennings reported that the reexpansion invariably led to a change of position, so that by this means "the animal thoroughly explores the region about its place of attachment and largely increases its chances of obtaining food." He observed that such activity was more frequent in hungry *Hydra,* a finding not substantiated by later investigators (Passano and McCullough, 1964; Rushforth and Hofman, 1972).

In a series of studies, Reis (1946a,b,c) described factors affecting the frequency of contractions and extensions in *Pelmatohydra oligactis* (*Hydra oligactis*). He found that the variable temporal and spatial patterns of extensions in the animal were more frequent when food was present in the gut, but were not affected by the presence of attached buds. Starvation appeared to modify the activity level in adult *Hydra,* by reducing the number of complete extensions while increasing the number of partial extensions. Both types of extension were more frequent in young buds during the first day after detachment.

A. EFFECTS OF SINGLE STIMULI

Inhibition of column and tentacle contractions by GSH has been discussed previously. The spontaneously produced contractions are suppressed and such activities are supplanted by the localized responses constituting feeding behavior. In the present section the responses of the animal to mechanical agitation, electrical, and photic stimulation are considered.

1. Mechanical Stimulation

The earliest recorded account of the contraction of *Hydra* to mechanical agitation was given by Trembley (1744). Wagner (1904) described the response of *H. viridis* to intermittent stimulation, observing that the animals contract when their culture dishes are tapped. If the hydras are stimulated in this manner at 1-second intervals, they first contract and then reexpand. Wagner concluded from this result that the animal adapts to intermittent, nonlocalized mechanical stimulation.

He found, however, that if the interstimulus interval is increased to allow the polyps to reexpand after each contraction, the animal does not adapt but contracts to each stimulus. Wagner assumed that the adaptation depended on the stimuli being rapidly repeated and believed that the recovery from the acclimatizing effect must be of short duration.

Rushforth (1965b, 1967) investigated the effects of repeated mechanical agitation, using both the large Belgian species *H. pirardi,* and also *H. viridis,* the species used by Wagner. In order to quantify the contraction response to intermittent mechanical stimulation, groups of *Hydra* were placed in dishes on a rotatory shaker. A timer was attached to the shaker so that a shaking pulse of short duration could be administered at fixed time intervals to the animals. The stimulus strength was measured in terms of the rotation speed of the shaker, and was calibrated in revolutions per minute. The sensitivity of the animals was represented by a response curve: a plot of the proportions of a group of hydra contracting at various rotation speeds (Fig. 5A). It is seen from such plots that the pro-

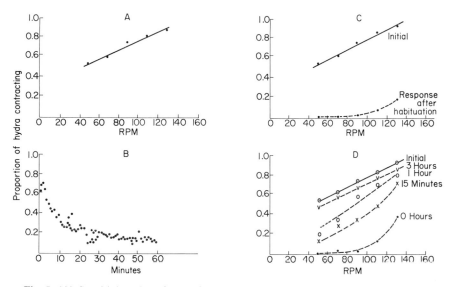

Fig. 5. (A) Sensitivity of *Hydra viridis* to mechanical stimulation: response curve. Each point represents the average proportion of hydras in five groups of 10 animals, that contracted within a 2-second period that followed a 2-second shaking period. (B) Effect of intermittent mechanical stimulation: habituation curve. Each point represents the average proportion of hydras that contracted within a 2-second period that followed a 3-second period of stimulation at 130 rpm every 30 seconds, based on three groups of 10 animals. (C) Effect of habituation on the sensitivity to mechanical stimulation: solid line response curve of hydras prior to intermittent agitation; broken line, response curve of hydras after 6 hours of intermittent mechanical agitation. These curves are based on three groups of 10 animals. (D) Decay of sensitivity to mechanical stimulation following habituation; response curves of 30 hydras prior to intermittent agitation (solid line) and at various intervals (0 hours, 15 minutes, 1 hour, and 3 hours) following habituation during which the animals were not stimulated. (After Rushforth, 1967.)

portion of contracting *Hydra* increases with increasing strength of the stimulus.

In contrast to Wagner's earlier results, Rushforth (1965b, 1967) found that *Hydra* adapts to nonlocalized mechanical agitation even when the interval between the stimuli was long enough to allow the polyps to reexpand completely. "The process of adaptation to this stimulus was not considered to be one of muscular fatigue, since contractions were readily evoked in hydras habituated to mechanical stimulation by a different stimulus, that of light. Rather, the decrease in sensitivity of the hydras to mechanical agitation was thought to be an example of habituation" (Rushforth, 1967). If the animals were exposed to intermittent stimulation at a fixed rotation speed, they were found to be less responsive to the stimulus on continued exposure. This reduced sensitivity was demonstrated by (a) a reduction in the proportion of animals contracting with an increasing number of stimulus trials, the relationship being termed a habituation curve, (Fig. 5B); and (b) a lowering of the response curve from the initial level to one taken after several hours of intermittent stimulation (Fig. 5C). It was found that following habituation, the animal's sensitivity to mechanical agitation was restored after approximately 3 to 4 hours, during which time the hydras were not stimulated (Fig. 5D).

Several parametric relations have been generally used to characterize the process of habituation (Thompson and Spencer, 1966). Rushforth (1967) investigated the response of *Hydra* to repeated mechanical stimulation, finding that it conformed with several of the criteria used to define habituation operationally. (1) Repeated applications of the mechanical stimulus result in a decreased response. The decrease is approximately a negative exponential function of the number of stimulus presentations. (2) If the stimulus is withheld, the original response recovers with time. (3) The shorter the interstimulus interval the more rapid is habituation. (4) Increasing the strength of the stimulus produces a slower rate of habituation. This result is the opposite of that expected if the process is merely one of fatigue. (5) *Hydra* habituate faster on a second exposure to intermittent stimulation, compared with the responses to the initial habituating regime. However, further successive administrations of the regime do not potentiate the habituation process further.

A characteristic feature of coelenterate behavior is that excised parts exhibit spontaneous activities similar to those observed when they are attached to the parent animal. In the literature at the turn of the century there were reports that isolated tentacles responded to mechanical and chemical stimuli much in the same way as they did before detachment (Heider, 1879; Parker, 1896; von Üxkull, 1909). The results of investigations of the behavior of excised actinian tentacles prompted Parker (1917) to suggest that "each tentacle contained a neuromuscular mechanism sufficient for its own activity and it is therefore not dependent upon the nervous control of other parts of the animal's body for the production of those movements that it ordinarily exhibits."

Rushforth (1972) has investigated the effect of removing tentacles on the behavior of *H. pirardi* and has studied the activities of the isolated tentacles. Tentacle removal reduces the frequency of spontaneous bursts of column contractions in animals of this species. There is a linear reduction in the contraction burst frequency with each successive tentacle removed. However, the reduction of contraction burst frequency by tentacle removal is not a result of merely wounding the animal.

Surgical studies also showed the importance of tentacles in the contraction response of *H. pirardi* to mechanical agitation (Rushforth, 1965b). Tentacle removal was found to inhibit contraction bursts initiated by mechanical stimulation. However, the results of experiments in which different numbers of tentacles or different lengths of each tentacle were excised, indicated that the full complement of tentacles was not essential for the response. Removal of up to half the number of tentacles had no effect, but after half of them have been excised there was an increasing suppression of contraction bursts with each successive tentacle removed. Complete blockage of the response took place when all of them were excised. The animal also responded fully to mechanical stimulation when more than 75% of each tentacle was surgically removed, leaving only the tentacle base region attached to the hypostome. If all the tentacles were excised it was found that mechanically induced contractions were virtually absent during the first hour following surgery. However, there was an increase in the proportion of *Hydra* contracting to such stimulation with time since tentacle removal. After 10 to 12 hours, the surgically treated hydras had contraction responses equivalent to those of untreated animals. At this time only approximately a quarter of the tentacle length had regenerated.

Isolated tentacles themselves contract in response to mechanical agitation. A *H. pseudoligactis* tentacle preparation held in a suction electrode contracts to weak pulses of agitation. Such contractions supplant the endogenous bursts of contractions normally exhibited by the excised tentacle. However, if repeatedly agitated once every 15 seconds the isolated tentacle adapts to the stimulation, and the normal pattern of spontaneous contraction bursts is restored.

2. Electrical Stimulation

The effects of electrical stimulation on *Hydra* have not been studied in any detail. Pearl (1901) found that *H. viridis* under weak and constant current at first bends and then turns its head to the anode, but Hyman (1932) observed that *H. oligactis* turns its head toward the cathode. This latter result was in accordance with an assumed electropolarity in most lower animals, in which the forward end has a positive charge (Hyman and Bellamy, 1922). However, the reason for the apparent polarity differences between the two species of *Hydra* has not been explained.

Passano and McCullough (1964), in their description of the spontaneous electrical activity of *Hydra,* found that in many animals complete contraction of the body column takes place in a series of partial contractions. This sequence was termed a "contraction burst" since the series of contractions were separated by relatively long intervals. Passano and McCullough found for *H. pirardi* that single electric shocks applied to various regions of the polyp induced single contractions. They found that when shocks were given 15 to 30 seconds apart, each causing single contractions, the *Hydra* rarely showed the normal pattern of bursts. Such artificially induced contractions were found to supplant the endogenous bursts of contractions for an hour or more.

3. Photic Stimulation

The influence of light in initiating locomotory activities in *Hydra* has been discussed previously. In this section the effects of photic stimulation on the animal's contraction behavior are considered. The earlier accounts of the light response (Trembley 1744; Wilson, 1891) emphasized the induced migration of the animal, and it was at a much later date that Haug (1933) reported the contraction response of *Hydra* to light. Passano and McCullough (1964) investigated the effects of ambient illumination on the frequency of spontaneous contraction bursts in *H. littoralis.* They found that the contraction-burst frequency under natural daylight was 1.5–2 times that in the dark. This diurnal variation in contraction-burst frequency was not found for a control culture under constant illumination, showing that there was no residual circadian rhythm under these conditions. Passano and McCullough (1964) suggest that the rhythm of activity imposed by the effect of natural illumination levels on the burst frequency has adaptive significance. It gives the polyps cyclic activity corresponding to that shown by their prey, mainly crustacean plankters, whose activity rhythm is synchronized to their phytoplankton food source.

Rushforth and his co-workers (Rushforth *et al.,* 1963; Singer *et al.,* 1963; Rushforth and Burke, 1972; Rushforth, 1972) investigated the contraction response to light of both intact *Hydra* and tentacles excised from the animal. Using *H. pirardi* it was found that the time between onset of the light stimulus and the completed contraction of the *Hydra* (the reaction time) was dependent on both the intensity and the wavelength of the light. Although the reaction times of individual animals were found to be quite variable, the mean reaction time was found to be inversely proportioned to the light intensity. Inspection of the spectral sensitivity of the animal indicated that the reaction time was shortest in blue light (400–450 nm), the sensitivity markedly decreasing above 500 nm (Singer *et al.,* 1963). Unlike the response to repeated mechanical agitation, *H. pirardi* does not adapt to intermittent photic stimulation. The contraction frequency was not reduced after 200 hours of exposure consisting of 1-minute periods of direct light stimulation interspersed by 1-minute periods of ambient illumination (Rushforth *et al.,* 1963). Tardent and Frei (1969) studied the reactions of *H. attenuata* to photic stimulation, observing that the response consists of a fast stepwise contraction of the entire animal including the tentacles. They found that the animal did not habituate to a regime of 2 minutes of bright light followed by 2 minutes of complete dark administered over a period of 3 hours.

Rushforth (1972) found that removal of the tentacles significantly increased the reaction time of the contraction response to light in *H. pirardi.* In making these observations the reaction time was subdivided into the induction and contraction times. The induction time was defined as the time between onset of photic stimulation and the first observed contraction in the light-induced contraction burst, while the contraction time was designated as the time between the first and last contractions in the burst. With tentacle removal it was found that whereas the contraction time was unaltered, there was a significant increase in the induction time. Rushforth concluded that while the events occurring during the contraction burst are not affected by tentacle removal, the presence of tentacles appears to shorten the time to initiate the contraction burst sequence in response to strong light. Rushforth and Burke (1972) showed that when isolated tentacles of *H. pirardi* or *H. pseudoligactis* were exposed to a regime of 2-minute periods of strong light illumination, interspersed with 2-minute periods of ambient light, contraction bursts were more frequent during the strong light periods. This finding is consistent with the observation that contraction-burst frequency is enhanced by direct illumination in tentacles attached to the hydras of the two species.

The above studies were concerned with the induction by light of contractions of various species of *Hydra.* However, the effects of photic stimulation on the animal are extremely complex and exhibit both inhibitory as well as excitatory components. In their studies of the light response Passano and McCullough (1963, 1964) found that under certain conditions light suppresses the normal endogenous contraction bursts of the body column. They observed that for dark-adapted *H. littoralis* there is a rather dramatic response to abrupt, strong illumination.

> For the first 5–10 seconds there is no behavioral response; then a seemingly smooth elongation of the column and tentacles occurs, causing the animal to become half again as extended as is typical for the species in the dark. There then ensues a period, of variable duration, but usually lasting at least 2 min., of behavior reminiscent of hydras initiating a feeding behavior sequence. The head and upper column sway from side to side, and the entire column may slowly swing around the attached base as in the photokinetic responses described by Haug. The tentacles squirm and usually show coordinated lifting movements towards the central vertical axis. Sometimes the latter

occur with asymmetrical contractions of the column just below the sub-hypostome, giving a combined nodding-tentacle sweeping movement that is very characteristic. Time-lapse motion pictures of this phase give the appearance of searching movements. Then tentacle activity increases and they tend to spread out on the surface film and attach to it, whereon a vigorous lengthy contraction burst occurs" (Passano and McCullough, 1963).

Passano and McCullough (1964) found they could halt contraction bursts already in progress by general illumination of the animal at the start of the burst. Such inhibition was occasionally effected using flashes of bright light of no more than 0.2 seconds duration. However, shorter flashes given by flashbulbs were ineffective. Reducing the intensity of the light gave rise to variable responses; some contractions were slowed down rather than halted giving abnormally long midburst intervals. In other cases inhibition was delayed, a single contraction occurring after the photic stimulation.

Using a series of interposing filters between the light source and the animal it was found that red light did not inhibit contraction bursts. However, blue light (wavelengths less than 500 nm) and blue-violet light appeared as effective as unfiltered white light stimulation in halting contractions. Passano and McCullough (1964) found that the contraction-burst frequency was increased when the contractions were blocked by light during contraction bursts. For example, dark-adapted *H. littoralis* had significantly reduced intercontraction-burst interval lengths over a 30-minute period, when an inhibiting light stimulus was given immediately after the first contraction in a spontaneous contraction burst. The reduction in intercontraction-burst lengths is successively diminished if two and three contractions are allowed to occur in the burst before exposing the preparation to the inhibitory light stimulus. However, when consecutive contraction bursts are halted in this manner, blocking thresholds gradually rise, until eventually a contraction burst occurs in spite of the inhibitory stimulus. In a 30-minute test period, about 13% of the blocking stimuli were ineffectual if administered after the first contraction in the burst, whereas only about 8% did not halt the burst if two contractions in the burst were allowed to occur. If three contractions were permitted before photic stimulation the contraction bursts were halted in all cases. The phenomenon of inhibition of later parts of contraction bursts coupled with enhanced frequency of the bursts was also found if the light stimulus was given locally to the hypostomal region rather than to the entire animal.

B. RESPONSE TO JOINT EXPOSURE TO MULTIPLE STIMULI

An example of the behavior of *Hydra* when exposed to more than one stimulus is the response of newly detached buds to light and gravity. For a period of at least three days after separation from the parent *Hydra,* buds migrate upward toward the water surface, thus exhibiting negative geotaxis. The gravity response is more strongly affected by light coming from below the animals than by light coming from the side. This is due to a partial cancelling of the gravity response by the natural positive photo-taxis of the *Hydra*.

It was previously mentioned that the contractions induced by light and mechanical stimulation in *H. pirardi* are inhibited by chemical stimulation using reduced glutathione. These are further examples of interactions

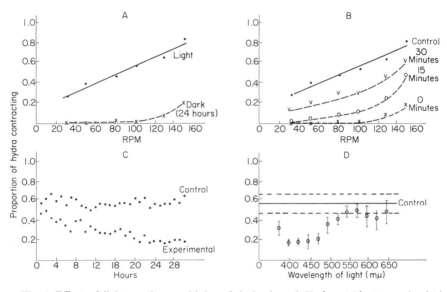

Fig. 6. Effect of light on the sensitivity of dark-adapted *Hydra viridis* to mechanical stimulation. (A) Solid line (light), response curve of 30 hydras tested in ambient light; broken line (dark 24 hours), response curve of 30 hydras dark-adapted for 24 hours and tested in ambient light. (B) Response curves of 150 hydras dark-adapted for 24 hours: solid line (control), tested in the dark; broken line (0 minutes), immediately on exposure to ambient light, and broken lines, after 15 and 30 minutes respectively in ambient light. (C) Effect of the length of dark adaptation on the sensitivity of hydras to mechanical stimula-tion. Each point represents the average proportion of a group of 60 hydras contracting to five shaking pulses at 130 rpm; the pulses were 1 minute apart and of 5-seconds duration. The experimental values were given by groups of hydras dark-adapted for different time periods and tested in ambient light, whereas the control values were given by groups of light-adapted hydras tested at the same times. (D) Sensitivity of dark-adapted hydras to mechanical stimulation when exposed to light of different wavelengths. Mean proportions and 95% confidence intervals are plotted for groups of 30 hydras dark-adapted for 24 hours, contracting to mechanical stimulation (five successive pulses of 5 seconds of shaking every minute at 130 rpm) when exposed to monochromatic light. The control values (solid line, the mean; broken lines, the upper and lower 95% confidence limits) were determined for a group of 30 hydras dark-adapted for 24 hours and tested in the dark. (After Rushforth, 1967.)

among various factors affecting behavior in *Hydra*. The results of the studies of inhibition by GSH of light-induced contractions gave information concerning the properties of *Hydra*'s glutathione receptors. In this section the joint effects of light and mechanical stimulation on the behavior of *Hydra* will be discussed.

Joint Effects of Light and Mechanical Stimulation

The influence of light on *Hydra* is quite complex, involving both excitatory and inhibitory effects on spontaneous contraction activities. Rushforth (1965a, 1967) discovered that light inhibits contractions induced by mechanical stimulation in dark-adapted *H. viridis*. He found that *Hydra* placed for 24 hours in complete darkness had significantly lower response curves to mechanical agitation when tested in light (about 70 ft-c) than animals exposed for 24 hours to light of this intensity (Fig. 6A). Other experiments showed that the former sensitivity was gradually restored. After 30 minutes the hydras had regained much of their response, and after 1 hour the response curve was not different from control values (Fig. 6B).

TABLE III

BEHAVIORAL RESPONSES OF *Hydra*

Stimulus	Response
	Tentacles
Light	Enhancement of spontaneous bursts of contractions
Mechanical agitation	Single contractions to pulses of weak stimulation supplanting endogenous contraction bursts
Reduced glutathione	Enhancement of concert frequency and initiation of tentacle writhing movements; inhibition of spontaneous contraction bursts
	Body column
Light	Inhibition of contraction bursts in progress; inhibition of mechanically induced contractions; induction of contraction bursts
Mechanical agitation	Induced contractions, but habituation to repeated stimulation
Reduced glutathione	Inhibition of spontaneous contractions, and those induced by light and mechanical stimulation

V. Summary

The behavior of *Hydra* clearly shows many examples of environmental factors interacting with endogenously active systems within the animal. Feeding responses consist of several reflexly linked behavioral sequences, together with modifications of spontaneous activity patterns. The modes of locomotion appear quite complex, and little is known concerning their underlying mechanisms.

Responses of *Hydra* to external stimuli also show modifications of spontaneous activities. The animal responds to chemical, mechanical, or light stimulation; these responses are summarized in Table III. The effect of light is particularly complex, exhibiting both excitatory and inhibitory components. Modifications of behavior in response to repeated mechanical stimulation suggest processes of habituation. However, reductions in the sensitivity to mechanical agitation of a comparable magnitude can be achieved using light or reduced glutathione. It is, therefore, necessary to study the physiological bases of such processes if distinctions are to be made between habituation and other forms of behavioral inhibition in *Hydra*.

References

Balke, E., and Steiner, G. (1959). *Naturwissenshaften* **46**, 22.
Beutler, R. (1927). *Z. Vergl. Physiol.* **6**, 473.
Beutler, R. (1933). *Z. Vergl. Physiol.* **18**, 718.
Blanquet, R. S., and Lenhoff, H. M. (1968). *Science* **159**, 633.
Burnett, A. L., Lentz, T., and Warren, M. (1959). *Ann. Soc. Zool. Belg.* **90**, 1.
Burnett, A. L., Davidson, R., and Wiernick, P. (1963). *Biol. Bull.* **125**, 226.
Cliffe, E. E., and Waley, S. G. (1958). *Nature (London)* **182**, 804.
Davis, L. E., Burnett, A. L., and Haynes, J. F. (1968). *J. Exp. Zool.* **167**, 295.
Ewer, R. F. (1947a). *Proc. Zool. Soc. (London)* **117**, 207.
Ewer, R. F. (1947b). *Proc. Zool. Soc. (London)* **117**, 365.
Forrest, H. (1962). *Biol. Bull.* **122**, 343.
Haase-Eichler, R. (1931). *Zool. Jahrb.* **50**, 265.
Hadzi, J. (1909). *Arb. Zool. Inst. Univ. Wien* **17**, 1.
Hartog, M. M. (1880). *Quart. J. Miscrosc. Sci.* **20**, 243.
Haug, G. (1933). *Z. Vergl. Physiol.* **19**, 246.
Heider, A. R. V. (1879). *Sitzungsber. Kaiserl. Akad. Wiss. Wien. Math.-Naturwiss. Kl., Abt. 1* **79**, 204.
Hertel, E. (1905). *Z. Allg. Phys.* **5**, 95.
Hyman, L. H. (1932). *Physiol. Zool.* **5**, 185.
Hyman, L. H., and Bellamy, A. W. (1922). *Biol. Bull.* **43**, 313.
Jennings, H. S. (1906). "Behavior of the Lower Organisms." Columbia Univ. Press, New York.

Jones, C. (1941). *J. Exp. Zool.* **7**, 457.

Josephson, R. K. (1967). *Symp. Soc. Exp. Biol.* **20**, 33.

Josephson, R. K., and Mackie, G. O. (1965). *J. Exp. Biol.* **43**, 293.

Kanaev, I. I. (1952). "Hydra: Essays on the Biology of Fresh Water Polyps." Sov. Acad. Sci., Moscow (English translation edited by H. M. Lenhoff, 1969).

Kepner, W. A., and Miller, L. (1928). *Biol. Bull.* **54**, 524.

Lenhoff, H. M. (1961a). *J. Gen. Physiol.* **45**, 331.

Lenhoff, H. M. (1961b). *In* "The Biology of Hydra" (H. M. Lenhoff and W. F. Loomis, eds.), pp. 203–232. Univ. of Miami Press, Coral Gables, Florida.

Lenhoff, H. M. (1965). *Amer. Zool.* **5**, 515.

Lenhoff, H. M. (1967). *In* "The Chemistry of Learning" (W. C. Corning and S. C. Ratner, eds.), pp. 341–368. Plenum, New York.

Lenhoff, H. M. (1968a). *Chem. Zool.* **2**, 158–221.

Lenhoff, H. M. (1968b). *Science* **161**, 434.

Lenhoff, H. M., and Bovaird, J. (1959). *Science* **130**, 1474.

Lenhoff, H. M., and Bovaird, J. (1960). *Nature (London)* **187**, 671.

Lenhoff, H. M., and Bovaird, J. (1961). *Nature (London)* **189**, 486.

Lenhoff, H. M., and Zwisler, J. (1963). *Science* **142**, 1666.

Lentz, T. H., and Barnett, R. J. (1965). *Amer. Zool.* **5**, 34.

Loeb, J. (1918). "Forced Movements, Tropisms, and Animal Conduct." Lippincott, Philadelphia, Pennsylvania.

Lomnicki, A., and Slobodkin, L. B. (1966). *Ecology* **47**, 881.

Loomis, W. F. (1955). *Ann. N. Y. Acad. Sci.* **62**, 209.

McConnell, C. H. (1932). *Quart. J. Microsc. Sci.* **17**, 495.

Marler, P., and Hamilton, W. J. (1968). "Mechanisms of Animal Behavior. Wiley, New York.

Marshall, W. (1882). *Z. Wiss. Zool.* **37**, 664.

Mast, S. O. (1903). *Amer. J. Physiol.* **10**, 165.

Pantin, C. F. A. (1942). *J. Exp. Biol.* **19**, 249.

Pantin, C. F. A. (1950). *Symp. Soc. Exp. Biol.* **4**, 175.

Parker, G. H. (1896). *Bull. Mus. Comp. Zool., Harvard Univ.* **29**, 107.

Parker, G. H. (1917). *J. Exp. Zool.* **22**, 95.

Passano, L. M., and McCullough, C. B. (1963). *Nature (London)* **199**, 1174.

Passano, L. M., and McCullough, C. B. (1964). *J. Exp. Biol.* **41**, 643.

Passano, L. M., and McCullough, C. B. (1965). *J. Exp. Biol.* **42**, 105.

Pearl, R. (1901). *Amer. J. Physiol.* **5**, 301.

Reis, R. H. (1946a). *Trans. Amer. Microsc. Soc.* **65**, 27.

Reis, R. H. (1946b). *Trans. Amer. Microsc. Soc.* **65**, 154.

Reis, R. H. (1946c). *Trans. Amer. Microsc. Soc.* **65**, 165.

Ross, E. M., and Sutton, L. (1964). *J. Exp. Biol.* **41**, 751.

Rushforth, N. B. (1965a). *Amer. Zool.* **5**, 505.

Rushforth, N. B. (1965b). *Anim. Behav. Suppl.* **1**, 30–42.

Rushforth, N. B. (1967). *In* "The Chemistry of Learning" (W. C. Corning and S. C. Ratner, eds.), pp. 369–390. Plenum, New York.

Rushforth, N. B. (1969). *Amer. Zool.* **9**, 1114.

Rushforth, N. B. (1972). In preparation.

Rushforth, N. B., and Burke, D. S. (1972). *Biol. Bull.* **140**, 502.

Rushforth, N. B., and Hofman, F. (1972). *Biol. Bull.* **142**, 110.

Rushforth, N. B., Burnett, A. L., and Maynard, R. (1963). *Science* **139**, 760.

Rushforth, N. B., Krohn, I. T., and Brown, L. K. (1964). *Science* **145**, 602.

Schaffer, J. (1754). "Die Armpolypen im sussen Wasser un Regensburg." Regensburg.

Schulusen, A. (1935). *Zool. Jahrb., Abt. Allg. Zool. Physiol. Tiere* **54**, 1.

Schulze, P. (1917). *Arch. Biontol.* **4**, 39.

Singer, R. H., Rushforth, N. B., and Burnett, A. L. (1963). *J. Exp. Zool.* **154**, 169.

Tardent, P., and Frei, E. (1969). *Experientia* **25**, 265.

Thompson, R. F., and Spencer, W. A. (1966). *Physchol. Rev.* **73**, 16.

Toppe, O. (1909). *Zool. Anz.* **33**, 798.

Trembley, A. (1744). "Memoires pour servir à l'histoire d'un genre de polypes d'eau douce à bras en forme de cornes." J. & H. Verbeck, Leyden, The Netherlands.

von Üxkull, J. (1909). "Unwelt und Innerwelt der Tiere." Springer-Verlag, Berlin and New York.

Wagner, G. (1904). *Quart. J. Microsc. Sci.* [N.S.] **48**, 585.

Weill, R. (1934). *Trav. Sta. Zool. Wimereux* **10/11**, 1.

Wilson, E. B. (1891). *Amer. Natur.* **25**, 414.

Zykov, W. (1898). *Biol. Zentralbl.* **18**, 270.

CHAPTER 2

Feeding and Digestion

JULIAN F. HAYNES

I. Food Capture

A. INTRODUCTION

The capture of food is the function of the nematocysts and the tentacles. Each tentacle carries localized concentrations of nematocysts called nematocyst batteries. Each battery consists of at least one large stenotele (penetrant) surrounded by desmonemes (volvents) and isorhizas (glutinants). In the *Hydra* only the desmonemes and the stenoteles participate in food capture and feeding (Ewer, 1947; A. L. Burnett *et al.,* 1960). Each nematocyst of the battery forms an intimate junction with the base of an epithelial muscle cell (Slautterback, 1967b), and with the light microscope the entire battery of nematocysts appears enclosed within an epithelial muscle cell.

43

When a small crustacean such as a *Daphnia* or an *Artemia* contacts the tentacles of a *Hydra,* the first response of the polyp is the discharge of desmonemes from the nematocyst batteries (A. L. Burnett *et al.,* 1960). The desmonemes are characterized by tubular threads with closed ends. When discharged the threads of the desmonemes form corkscrewlike coils which wrap around the bristles and appendages of the prey, drawing it into the tentacle. Shortly after it is ensnared by the desmonemes, the prey is immobilized by the discharge of stenoteles. These are penetrating nematocysts with open-ended tubular threads. The threads pierce the exoskeleton, inject a toxin into the prey, and paralyze it almost instantly. The entangled and narcotized prey is then carried to the mouth by the tentacles, where it is rapidly ingested through the open mouth.

B.   NEMATOCYST DISCHARGE

The control, the cause, and the mechanism of nematocyst discharge have been widely studied and are still not clearly understood in the *Hydra* or in any other species of coelenterate. A complete review of the work on coelenterate nematocysts can be found in Picken and Skaer (1966).

The various theories proposed to explain the discharge of nematocysts in the *Hydra* are discussed and extensively documented in Jones (1947). The most widely held theory of nematocyst discharge views the nematocyte-nematocyst complex as an independent effector discharging in response to a combination of chemical and mechanical stimulations with no direct intervention of either the nervous system or of adjacent cells. Each nematocyte possesses a small hairlike cnidocil projecting from its surface. Contact of the cnidocil by another object is essential for the normal discharge of the nematocyst. However, numerous studies have shown that mechanical stimulation of the cnidocil alone is not adequate to initiate normal nematocyst discharge. Zick (1929, 1932) noted that certain species of protozoa while colliding with the tentacles of a *Hydra* failed to cause nematocyst discharge. Other investigators (Jones, 1947; Ewer, 1947; A. L. Burnett *et al.,* 1960) have repeatedly demonstrated that the contact of the cnidocil with inert materials such as clean glass rods and cotton threads fails to bring about significant nematocyst discharge.

Similarly, most experimental evidence indicates that chemical stimulation alone is not responsible for the normal discharge of nematocysts during feeding. When extracts of food organisms or food juices are placed on a *Hydra* or on isolated tentacles they fail to elicit nematocyst discharge. There are, however, a wide variety of chemical compounds which will cause the discharge of nematocysts (A. L. Burnett *et al.*, 1960, 1963). These all involve abnormal and unusual stimuli and could not possibly play a role in the normal stimulation of discharge during feeding.

If a glass needle or some other inert object is dipped into an extract of food organisms and then touched to a tentacle, significant numbers of nematocysts are discharged. Apparently some form of synergistic action of the chemical components of the food and the physical contact of the cnidocil will bring about the normal discharge of nematocysts. While the mode of action is unknown it is probable that some chemical component of the food reduces the level of mechanical stimulation necessary at the cnidocil. Attempts have been made to identify the active material released by the food organisms (Jones, 1947). The action of the food extracts can be mimicked by surface-active agents and it is possible that the release of some agent of this sort is responsible for the depression of the threshold of the nematocyte to mechanical stimulation.

There is also evidence that the different types of nematocysts are discharged specifically and that they are not all released simultaneously in response to a single stimulus. During feeding the initial discharge is of the desmonemes. This is then followed by the discharge of the stenoteles. The isorhizas occupying the same nematocyst batteries as the stenoteles and desmonemes are never discharged during feeding. This latter type of nematocyst is discharged when the *Hydra* contacts nonfood organisms or during its somersaulting type of locomotion. The observations of Ewer (1947) further indicate that the presence of food extracts (from copepods and tubificids) actually inhibits the discharge of the isorhizas while the same extracts potentiate the release of the stenoteles.

The independent discharge of the desmonemes and stenoteles has been studied by A. L. Burnett *et al.* (1960). They have shown that the cooling of a *Hydra* to 4°C for 1.5 hours inhibits the discharge of the stenoteles while not affecting the discharge of desmonemes. Thus a chilled *Hydra* can trap and hold *Artemia* but cannot kill them.

The details of the actual discharge of the nematocyst thread from the nematocyst capsule of an appropriately stimulated nematocyte–nematocyst complex has not been determined. Some aspects of the ultrastructure of the discharging nematocyst have been described by Mattern *et al.* (1965). The appropriate chemotactile stimulation of the nematocyte causes a reaction within the nematocyte releasing the operculum of the nematocyst capsule. As the thread is discharged it is everted through the open end of the capsule. The first portion of the thread to be everted is the base which is frequently expanded and covered with spines or barbs. Slautterback (1967b) has pointed out that the discharge of the nematocyst may be analogous to secretion. He postulates that stimulation of the cnidocyte results in a fusion of the Golgi membranes surrounding the nematocyst with the plasmalemma. This extrudes the nematocyst from the cell and the naked nematocyst then spontaneously fires its thread.

C. The Nematocyst Toxin

The penetrating stenotele nematocysts contain a highly toxic material in their capsules. When the thread of the stenotele penetrates the tissues of a prey organism this toxin is injected into the prey. Initially the toxin paralyzes the prey organism and ultimately kills the prey. The toxin has not been isolated from the nematocysts of the *Hydra* so its specific identity is presently unknown. However, on the basis of properties of crude extracts of *Hydra* which are known to contain the nematocyst toxins and on the basis of comparative studies with the toxins of other coelenterates some conclusions can be drawn about the toxin of the *Hydra*. Histochemical studies of the maturing nematocysts by A. L. Burnett (1960) have shown that the functional nematocyst contains a basic protein which may be the toxic component of the nematocyst capsule. Lesh and Burnett have reported that the crude extract of *Hydra* formed by simple homogenization contains a toxic substance which is destroyed or inactivated by boiling. In other species of coelenterates where sufficient amounts of material can be isolated for actual analysis of the toxic material it has definitely been shown to be a polypeptide (Lane, 1961; Lane *et al.*, 1961).

The mode of action of the *Hydra* toxin is not specifically known. The speed with which the prey organisms are paralyzed suggests that the nematocyst toxin is some form of neurotoxin. Kline and Waravdekar (1959, 1960) and Kline (1961) have recovered a protein from the culture water following the electrically stimulated discharge of nematocysts. This protein can inhibit the activity of succinoxidase in mouse liver. However, its identity to the nematocyst toxin has not been demonstrated.

II. Ingestion of Food

A. Feeding Reaction

Within a few seconds after a food organism has been captured by a tentacle, the *Hydra* begins a characteristic series of movements called the feeding reaction (Ewer, 1947). In this reaction the tentacles of the *Hydra* move actively and those tentacles with captured food begin to shorten and coil toward the hypostome. The movements of the tentacles bring the food into contact with the mouth, the mouth opens, and the food is ingested into the gastric cavity. Frequently the food is accompanied into the gastric cavity by one or more tentacles, and these tentacles can be seen inserted into the cavity as far as the budding region. During the ingestion of food the mouth is capable of considerable extension, allowing several *Artemia* nauplii or a single *Daphnia* to pass through the mouth at one time. A complete description of the feeding reaction and the factors controlling it will be found in Chapter 1 of this volume.

B. SATIATION

Hyman (1940) reported that a fully fed *Hydra* failed to discharge additional nematocysts and thus stopped capturing food and stopped the feeding reaction. This phenomenon of satiation by which the *Hydra* stops feeding after its gastric cavity is filled with food has been studied in great detail by A. L. Burnett *et al.* (1960). They found that the presence of food in the gut does prevent the capture of additional food. In *Hydra oligactis* approximately 20–25 artemias will be ingested during a normal feeding. However, if the artemias are removed from the tentacles before they can be ingested, the *Hydra* will kill as many as 115 brine shrimp. If the hypostome and tentacles were excised from a fully fed *Hydra,* the isolated tentacles and hypostome would ingest 6 to 8 additional brine shrimp. Also, when the food was removed from the gut of a fully fed *Hydra,* the *Hydra* would kill and ingest several additional shrimp. When extracts of the gut of a fed *Hydra* or pastes made from partially digested *Artemia* were injected into the gut of test *Hydra,* the experimental animals were no longer able to capture and ingest any food. Further observations on the behavior of fully fed *Hydra* and on *Hydra* filled with glass beads rather than with food showed that the cessation of feeding did not result from a suppression of nematocyst discharge. The fully fed *Hydra* still discharged nematocysts when contacted by the potential food organism. However, they were incapable of holding on to the prey. For some reason, the nematocytes containing discharged nematocysts are squeezed out of the tentacles when the gut of the *Hydra* is full of food or when it is distended by glass beads. Thus it would appear that the distention of the gut is the factor primarily responsible for the termination of feeding and that the inhibition of feeding following the injection of a paste of brine shrimp or a partially digested brine shrimp is the result of the swelling accompanying the injection.

III. Digestion

A. EXTRACELLULAR DIGESTION

While the major portion of digestion is carried on within the cells of the gastrodermis, the initial phases occur within the gastrovascular cavity. When the food is ingested, its presence stimulates the release of the contents of the zymogenic gland cells into the gut cavity (Downing, 1902; Semal-Van Gansen, 1954). The enzymes released by these cells initiate the digestive processes and produce the small particles of food that are actively phagocytized by the digestive muscle cells (Figs. 1 and 2). According to Semal-Van Gansen (1954) the release of the digestive

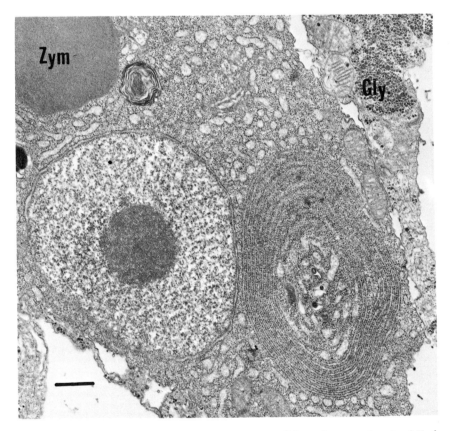

Fig. 1. Electron micrograph of a maturing zymogen cell from the gastrodermis of *Hydra viridis*. This cell shows a single zymogen granule in this section (Zym) and a highly developed endoplasmic reticulum. A small portion of a digestive cell is seen to the right of the zymogen cell. It contains large deposits of glycogen (Gly). Line indicates 1 μ.

enzymes is primarily during the first 30 minutes after the entrance of food into the gut. The first conclusive demonstration of digestive enzymes within the gut cavity of the *Hydra* was made by Beutler (1924), who introduced small sponges into the gut of a *Hydra*. The fluids absorbed by the sponge while in the gut were capable of digesting samples of protein

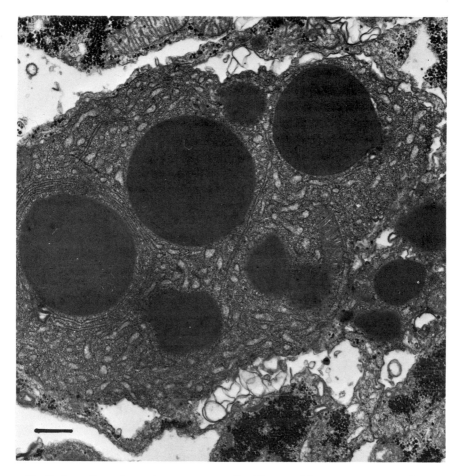

Fig. 2. A portion of a mature zymogen cell with several large zymogen granules surrounded by granular endoplasmic reticulum. Large masses of glycogen are visible in the adjacent digestive cells. Line indicates 1 μ.

and thereby definitely establishing the presence of proteolytic enzymes in the gut cavity. The function of these enzymes have been studied more completely by Lenhoff (1961), Robinson and Lenhoff (1961), and Murdock and Lenhoff (1968). They have observed the effect of *Hydra* digestive enzymes on ^{35}S-labeled mouse liver and lung and on purified hemoglobin. They found during the 6- to 7-hour period between the ingestion of the food and the egestion of the undigestible material that 90% of the ^{35}S label is transferred from the gut cavity into the gastrodermal cells of the *Hydra*. More significantly they have shown that the assimilation of the food is not in the form of free amino acids but in the form of proteins. They conclude from their studies that no appreciable degradation of proteins to amino acids occurs within the gut of the *Hydra*.

Studies of the activity of the enzymes recovered from the gastrovascular cavity and then partially purified indicate that they are proteases and are capable of digesting hemoglobin over a pH range of 2–8. The enzyme preparation shows two maxima at pH 2–3 and pH 7. This may indicate the presence of at least two different enzymes. The purified preparation possessed about 5% the activity of crystalline trypsin.

B. INTRACELLULAR DIGESTION

The digestive muscle cells actively phagocytize the small particles produced as the result of extracellular digestion (Beutler 1924; Semal-Van Gansen, 1954; Gauthier, 1963). When studied with the light microscope all the digestive cells of the gastrodermis are seen to ingest food materials. However, the phagocytic activity of the digestive cells of the peduncle and the tentacles is considerably less than those in the gastric region. Initially the food is taken up in the form of numerous small vacuoles in the apical region of the cell (Fig. 3). These vacuoles move toward the center of the cell; as they move they fuse, forming a smaller number of large digestive vacuoles. About 3 hours after feeding has begun the digestive vacuoles have coalesced to form two or three large spheres of about 20 μ in diameter. Histochemically these vacuoles contain both protein and RNA. As digestion continues these large vacuoles are broken down into smaller vacuoles (5–10 μ). As the large vacuoles break down the level of histochemically demonstrable RNA increases within the vacuoles. The contents of these smaller vacuoles transform directly into reserve granules or may divide further into even smaller granules of reserve proteins. As the smaller vacuoles containing the food materials are broken away from the larger digestive vacuoles the latter become irregular in shape and lose their ability to bind either protein stains or basic dyes. About 6 hours after feeding they have been transformed into excretory vacuoles and begin to discharge their contents into the gut cavity.

Ultrastructural studies of phagocytosis and digestion by Slautterback (1967a, 1969) indicate that the food is not being digested within large vacuoles as the earlier studies described above had concluded. He found that the presence of proteins within the gut causes cytoplasmic vesicles to add to the surface of the plasma membrane of the gastrovascular cavity and of the large primary phagocytic vesicles. The membranes of these vesicles are coated and the coating becomes extended when the vesicles are added to the plasma membrane (Figs. 4 and 5). The extended coating traps protein molecules and the vesicle reforms. The re-formed vesicle

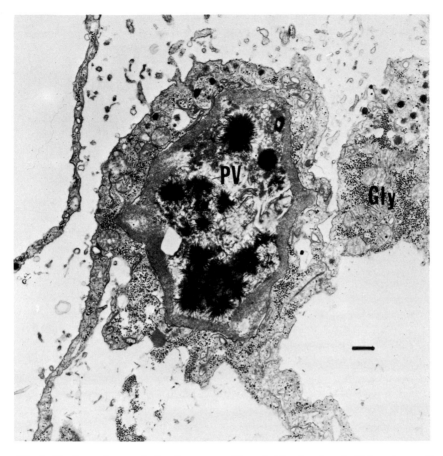

Fig. 3. Electron micrograph showing a mass of ingested food enclosed within a phagocytic vacuole (PV) of a digestive cell. Deposits of glycogen (Gly) are also clearly visible in these cells. Line indicates 1 μ.

with its trapped proteins is transported within the cell to the vicinity of the nucleus where the digestion and the absorption of the protein are completed. At the present time the relationship between the coated vesicles as a site of protein digestion and the formation of reserve materials is not understood.

The only available data on the actual chemical events of intracellular digestion come from the study of Murdock and Lenhoff (1968). They found that food initially ingested into the digestive cells was very similar to the contents of the gut. During the first 7 hours of digestion the food within the gastrodermal cells is converted from an alcohol-insoluble form to an alcohol-soluble form. The alcohol-soluble proteins were slowly

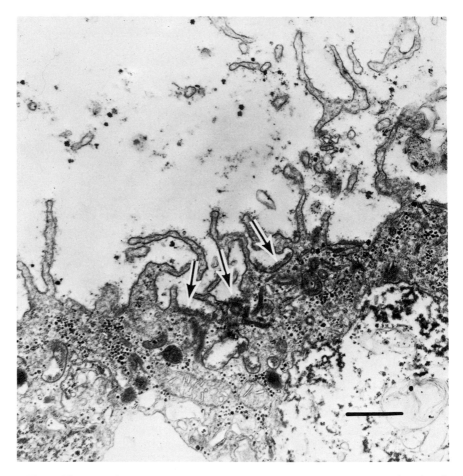

Fig. 4. Electron micrograph of the apical surface of a digestive cell. The apical surface is formed into a network of microvilli which appear to trap particulate matter (arrows). In the subapical cytoplasm are the rod-shaped vesicles which add to the membrane surface and participate in the trapping of food particles. Line indicates 1 μ.

degraded to amino acids and incorporated into alcohol-insoluble *Hydra* proteins over the 2-day period following feeding (Fig. 6). The transfer of food from the gastrodermis to the epidermis began about 24 hours after the ingestion of the food materials (Fig. 7).

C.   FOOD RESERVES AND FOOD STORAGE

The initial food inclusions are in the form of macromolecules derived directly from the food organisms. Over a period of several days the pro-

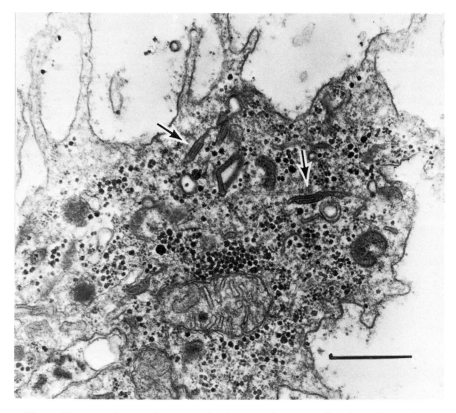

Fig. 5. Electron micrograph of the subapical cytoplasm of a digestive cell showing the cytoplasmic vesicles (arrows) which add to the membrane surface and participate in the trapping and ingestion of particulate matter. Line indicates 1 μ.

teins in these inclusions are hydrolyzed and resynthesized into *Hydra* proteins. Some of these are transported across the mesoglea to the epidermis, but in periods of ample food supplies large quantities are retained in the digestive cells as protein reserve droplets. During periods of starvation, these are rapidly depleted, and all protein reserves are usually metabolized during the first few days of starvation.

Following feeding extensive deposits of lipids including chromolipids, carotenoids, and neutral fats are also found in the digestive cells. The type of lipid material found within the digestive cells is at least in part determined by the food source. This may indicate that portions of the stored lipids are unmodified materials derived from the food organism (Semal-Van Gansen, 1954; A. Burnett, 1959). This is supported by Beutler's (1924) failure to find any lipase in the gastrovascular cavity of the *Hydra*. Gauthier (1963) has studied lipid uptake and digestion both

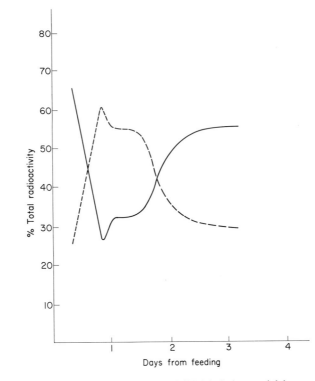

Fig. 6. A graph showing the distribution of ^{35}S-labeled material between the alcohol-soluble fraction (-------) and the alcohol-insoluble fraction(————) as a function of time. The initial alcohol-insoluble fraction represents the ingested food materials. The decrease in the alcohol-insoluble material and the parallel increase in the alcohol-soluble material represent the hydrolysis of the labeled food materials within the gastrodermal cells of the *Hydra*. The increase in the alcohol-insoluble material and the decrease in alcohol-soluble material occurring toward the end of the first day represents the synthesis of *Hydra* proteins from the derivatives of the ingested materials. (Data taken from Murdock and Lenhoff, 1968.)

ultrastructurally and biochemically. She found that emulsified lipids are absorbed directly from the gut and are contained within membrane-bound vesicles (up to 5 μ in diameter). She also found lipids in the form of nonmembrane bound droplets within the digestive cells. She interpreted these as triglycerides synthesized by the *Hydra* from the products of intracellular digestion.

The most dramatic changes following feeding involve the marked increase in glycogen that occurs within the digestive cells immediately after feeding. Glycogen begins to increase within the digestive cells during the first few hours after feeding (A. Burnett, 1959). Within 18

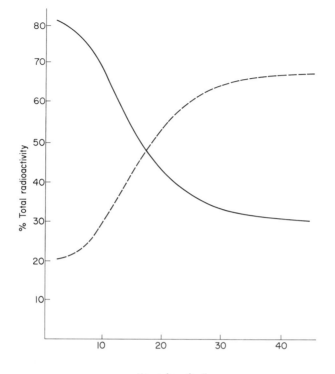

Hours from feeding

Fig. 7. A graph showing the relative distribution of ^{35}S-labeled protein between the gastrodermis (———) and the epidermis (-------) as a function of the time following feeding. At about 20 hours after feeding there is a significant transfer of the ingested food materials from the gastrodermal cells to the epidermal cells. (Data taken from Lenhoff, 1961.)

hours after feeding the glycogen is transported across the mesoglea and appears in the epidermis, and the remainder forms extensive deposits within the gastrodermis. In Gauthier's (1963) study of lipids fed to starved glycogen-depleted animals a portion of the ingested lipids was converted directly into glycogen. Thus the large quantities of glycogen appearing following feeding represent a synthetic activity of the digestive cells. This glycogen, synthesized and stored within the digestive cells, represents almost 1% of the wet weight of the *Hydra* (Gauthier, 1963) and is probably the primary reserve material of the *Hydra*.

The utilization of the different food reserves during starvation follows a definite pattern. The protein droplets are the first to be depleted and disappear in the first 4 to 5 days of starvation. Lipids are depleted next and are generally utilized within 8 days. The glycogen deposits are the last to be depleted during starvation and last for about 2 weeks. A discussion of starvation and the variability encountered during starvation can be found in Gauthier (1963).

References

Beutler, R. (1924). *Z. Vergl. Physiol.* **1**, 1–56.
Burnett, A. L. (1959). *J. Exp. Zool.* **140**, 281–341.
Burnett, A. L. (1960). *Ann. Soc. Zool. Belg.* **90**, 269–280.
Burnett, A. L., Davidson, R., and Wiernik, P. (1963). *Biol. Bull.* **125**, 226–233.
Burnett, A. L., Lentz, T., and Warren, M. (1960). *Ann. Soc. Zool. Belg.* **90**, 247–267.
Downing, E. (1902). *Science* **15**, 523.
Ewer, R. F. (1947). *Proc. Zool. Soc. London* **117**, 365–376.
Gauthier, G. (1963). *J. Exp. Zool.* **152**, 13–39.
Hyman, L. (1940). "The Invertebrates: Protozoa through Ctenophora." Macmillan, New York.
Jones, C. S. (1947). *J. Exp. Zool.* **105**, 25–60.
Kline, E. (1961). *In* "The Biology of Hydra" (H. M. Lenhoff and W. Loomis, eds.), pp. 153–168. Univ. of Miami Press, Coral Gables, Florida.
Kline, E., and Waravdekar, V. (1959). *Amer. Soc. Pharmacol. Exp. Ther.* **1**, 62.
Kline, E., and Waravdekar, V. (1960). *J. Biol. Chem.* **235**, 1803–1808.
Lane, C. (1961). *In* "The Biology of Hydra" (H. M. Lenhoff and W. Loomis, eds.), pp. 169–178. Univ. of Miami Press, Coral Gables, Florida.
Lane, C., Coursen, B., and Hines, K. (1961). *Proc. Soc Exp. Biol. Med.* **107**, 670–672.
Lenhoff, H. (1961). *Exp. Cell Res.* **23**, 335–353.
Mattern, C., Park, H., and Daniel, W. (1965). *J. Cell Biol.* **27**, 621–638.
Murdock, G., and Lenhoff, H. (1968). *Comp. Biochem. Physiol.* **26**, 963–970.
Picken, L. E. R., and Skaer, R. J. (1966). *Symp. Zool. Soc. London* **16**, 19–50.
Robinson, R., and Lenhoff, H. (1961). *Anat. Rec.* **137**, 388–389.
Semal-Van Gansen, P. (1954). *Ann. Soc. Zool. Belg., Cl. Sci.* **40**, 269–287.
Slautterback, D. (1967a). *J. Cell Sci.* **2**, 563–572.
Slautterback, D. (1967b). *Z. Zellforsch. Mikrosk. Anat.* **79**, 296–318.
Slautterback, D. (1969). *Anat. Rec.* **157**, 322–323.
Zick, K. (1929). *Zool. Anz.* **83**, 92–94.
Zick, K. (1932). *Zool. Anz.* **98**, 191–197.

PART II

ECOLOGY OF *HYDRA*

The study of *Hydra* has been so confined to the culture dish of the laboratory that investigators understandably have asked, "Does *Hydra* have an ecology?" In answer to such a question, Dr. Reisa examined evidence from hundreds of investigations, besides his own. Each study in some way provided information about *Hydra* in natural habitats. From all of these bits and pieces, he has developed a hypothetical construct that challenges traditional ideas about *Hydra* and seeks not only to answer past questions, but to provide systems in the laboratory which present new ones. Obviously, *Hydra* is a part of nature and does have an existence outside the laboratory. As behaviorists, neurophysiologists, or developmental biologists, we might realize that our findings with *Hydra* cannot be interpreted from the adaptive point of view without some knowledge of its life in natural waters.

CHAPTER 3

Ecology

J. J. REISA

I. Introduction

On one level of observation, a description of the *Mona Lisa* might consist of a composite absorption spectrum of the pigments in its oils. Few would deny, however, that much would be lost in such an interpretation.

While an analogy so hyperbolic might overwhelm the point intended, it must be admitted that most investigators now working with *Hydra* are specialists, approaching their material at levels below that of the organism. Important and exciting experimental questions are being asked by these workers, but the high resolution required in such studies usually necessitates reductions in scope. Ecological and adaptive considerations at present are a relative void in the biology of *Hydra*.

In spite of the title of this section, the discussions here presented are not an ecology of *Hydra*. Neither the author nor the field of study in question is yet ready for such a comprehensive presentation. No attempt has been made to review, or even to cite, all pertinent literature.

Rather, this section presents interacting hypotheses in a conceptual framework for considering *Hydra* in nature. Although the presentation is largely theoretical, its components are generated from evidence from many studies of the ecology, behavior, physiology, and development of these animals. It is primarily intended and hoped that the following approach to understanding *Hydra* from certain ecological and adaptive perspectives may provide new insights to investigators working at other levels. Such an objective, however, is not considered preclusive of the hope that some ecologists also might here find material of interest sufficient to instigate some productive disagreements.

To the ecology of *Hydra*, one can well apply most hackneyed remarks about the incompleteness of a given field of scientific inquiry and about the proliferation of hypotheses which often occurs when evidence is scarce. It is the author's bias, however, that as long as such hypotheses are not taken so seriously that they become counterproductive, they ought to so proliferate.

In this section, an attempt is made to state a preliminary case for considering some major revisions in thinking about *Hydra*. To guide the reader through the argumentative maze, most of the main proposals are summarized below. Later, there will be occasional references to these points, by number.

It is suggested that

1. The traditional idea, that "hydras essentially are sessile," can be misleading and has impeded the study of these animals.

2. Natural hydrid populations exhibit significant planktonic phases of great adaptive value.

3. "Surface floating" alone is inadequate to account for the mobility of hydras in nature and the many reports of subsurface plankters.

4. Hydras are adept, true plankters; there are at least two kinds of planktonic hydrid behavior; and these behavioral patterns result in some control of planktonic movement.

5. In addition to the production of basal bubbles, there are several other methods by which attached hydras become planktonic; these methods involve well-known behavioral and physiological phenomena which are seen in this context to have meaningful unity of effect; and within a natural population, planktonic synchrony is highly variable and adaptively responsive to environmental conditions.

6. Although planktonic phases provide "strategic" benefits, such mechanisms are defensively inadequate for certain kinds of environmental crises which occur in limnetic bodies successfully invaded by hydras.

7. Sexual reproduction is a mechanism which can enable a hydrid population to persist through prolonged environmental crises inescapable by plankters.

8. Some species of hydras seem to be sexually adapted to cold types of prolonged crises (e.g., winters) and other species show sexual adaptation to prolonged warm crises (e.g., droughts).

9. Unsynchronized morphogenic cycles of gonad formation in individual polyps improve chances of population survival through inadequately heralded, prolonged crises without the concomitant great energetic wastes or loss of population-level responsiveness which simpler safety mechanisms might be expected to entail.

10. In the variable conditions of limnetic habitats, temporary crises (e.g., thermal, chemical, desiccatory) occur; sexual reproduction in such crises would be an unwieldy defense and would involve great energetic waste.

11. "Depression" represents a better defense against such temporary crises; depression is a mechanism which performs two apparently distinct functions, the first being analogous to estivation, the second being a physiological aid to sexuality; although depression is a risky mechanism which may become lethal, its net effects are advantageous, and thus the phenomenon has been favored in natural selection.

12. Cycles of depression, budding, and sexuality are components of a mechanistic mosaic by which natural hydrid populations are "attuned" and adaptively responsive to variable limnetic conditions; although such mechanistic "tuning" involves gross responses on the population level, lack of *individual* phase synchrony provides adaptive variety of potential response; in such regards, understanding hydras may provide a key to

understanding the adaptive significance of at least some of the well-known variability which characterizes biological material.

13. Morphogenic and energetic considerations suggest a mechanism for sexual synchrony in hydras.

14. Although hydras may be "basically hermaphroditic" (morphogenically), some species nevertheless exhibit dioecious tendencies; in such species, the necessary spatial proximity of opposite sexes need not be left to chance; and in such populations, many sexual animals become synchronously planktonic and thus achieve aggregation.

15. The preceding considerations might provide some new insights in laboratory investigations of population energetics.

16. The preceding hypotheses are components of a conceptual framework understood best when synthesized; the interaction of such components may be seen by considering a natural hydrid population as analogous to an imaginary capitalist making investments.

II.   Some Preliminary Considerations

A.   Taxonomy and Variability

With most animals, investigators usually can determine with little difficulty the specific identities of their material. Such luck, however, is not the lot of those who work with *Hydra*.

Most hydras look alike, superficially, and closer inspection reveals that although morphological differences can be found, interspecific differences often seem not much greater than intraspecific differences. Characteristics frequently employed as taxonomic criteria are not always trustworthy. Morphological variability within single clones or natural populations is known (Hyman, 1929; Ewer, 1948; Semal-Van Gansen, 1954; Burnett, 1961; Spangenberg and Eakin, 1961; Forrest, 1963a; and others) for body color; column length; presence of stalk (peduncle); tentacle lengths and numbers; nematocyst numbers, sizes, type ratios, and shapes; separation of sexes; and other features. Intraspecific variations even in the structure of egg thecae have been reported (McConnell, 1935; Spangenberg and Eakin, 1961).

In observing such variability, it often is difficult to judge what is due solely to physiological or morphogenic responses to environmental influences and what indicates deeper genetic significance. It is certain, however, that most of these structural features do not meet normal criteria for taxonomic validity with comforting reliability. Therefore, in spite of the efforts of Schulze (1917), Hyman (1929, 1930, 1931a,b,

1938, 1940), Ewer (1948), Forrest (1959, 1963a), and others, the classification of *Hydra* has not yet become a science. It remains an art, and not many competent artists exist.

As Ewer (1948), Semal-Van Gansen (1954), and Forrest (1963a) have suggested, it is possible that the separation of hydrid species might be resolved only by cross-fertilization and grafting experiments. In any case, in *Hydra*, biologists encounter real challenges to philosophical criteria for defining the concept of "species."

One unfortunate consequence of such taxonomic uncertainty has been that many authors apparently have found attempts at meticulous classification so confusing that identification was treated cursorily or deemed unnecessary. Thus, there are many published investigations in which it is impossible to discern the species of *Hydra* studied. As will be discussed later, some kinds of hydras seem to be ecologically very different from other kinds. Therefore, taxonomic uncertainties can reduce considerably the usefulness of otherwise valuable investigative efforts.

Further, although caution obviously is advisable in making statements about "hydras in general," many authors seem to have ignored the advice.

B. IMMORTALITY AND SURVIVAL

Whether or not hydras are morphogenically "immortal" (Brien, 1953; Burnett, 1961; and others) is one question. Whether or not they show any signs of aging (Hyman, 1928; Stevenson and Buchsbaum, 1961; and others) need not be the same question. The possibility of logical equivocation on these questions is suggested since, although treated by some authors as being mutually exclusive, both questions at present seem to be answerable compatibly in the affirmative (also see Stiven, 1962; Forrest, 1963b).

The point to be made here, though, is that no matter how such questions eventually might be resolved, hydras in nature often are subjected to devastating environmental conditions against which they have little apparent structural protection. As Lenhoff (1967, p. 366) has observed, hydras, in a sense, are "naked" animals, since a significant proportion of their cells is exposed directly to the environment. Thus, survival would appear to demand that these polyps, lacking much insulation, must somehow be attuned to their environments. Mechanisms by which such adaptive "tuning" may be accomplished will be the topic of much of this section.

Although the form of *Hydra* may indeed be immortal, it is tautological (but not trivial) that such form can be "immortal" only where and when it is expressed in material that survives.

C. Ecological Background Information

No conventionally compartmentalized literature review of hydrid ecology is provided in this chapter. In other sections of this book, such as Chapter 1 by Rushforth, many studies of ecological relevance are ably reviewed. For additional background information, the reader is referred to Kanaev's (1952) *Hydra*. Although outdated, Kanaev's book contains the only existing comprehensive literature survey of studies relevant to hydrid ecology and thus treats many topics not discussed in the present volume.

Other studies of ecological significance will be considered in the following pages. However, most investigations dealing specifically with biotic relations of *Hydra* (e.g., predators, prey, commensals, parasites) are not discussed in this chapter.

Few detailed field studies of *Hydra* have been undertaken. Much information has been provided, though, by the following comprehensive attempts: Welch and Loomis (1924) and Miller (1936) studied *H. oligactis* in Douglas Lake, Michigan; Bryden (1952) described *H. oligactis* in Kirkpatrick's Lake, Tennessee; Carrick (1956) observed hydras in Lake Erie; Griffing (1965) studied *H. oligactis* and *H. pseudoligactis* in Pickerel Lake, Michigan; and Batha (1971) currently is engaged in an ambitious investigation of Lake Michigan hydrid populations. Most of these studies have been directed primarily at elucidating the factors affecting seasonal variations in observed abundance of hydras. Their findings will be considered in the following pages.

III. Planktonic Phases

Here, support will be given for the first five points proposed in Section I. The arguments necessarily are interconnected, so the sequence in which proposals are discussed will not directly conform to the order in which they were listed.

A. Traditional Reasoning and Sessile Hydras

That hydras essentially are sessile is a statement which has been made, in one form or another, in many publications describing these animals. It would appear to be a well-supported observation. It can be a misleading observation, however, as the author will attempt to show.

There is much justification for thinking of hydras as sessile animals. To begin, they are polyps. In the coelenterates, of course, it is the medusoid form that generally is associated with a motile, pelagic life, whereas the polypoid form is found in sessile species (or life cycle stages). In addition, prolonged observations of hydras in laboratory cultures have reinforced the idea that, as a rule, these polyps stay on the bottom. Their capability of substrate adhesion is obvious. Floating animals are observed, but exceptional. Further, it is well-known that if one wishes to find hydras in nature, one looks for them on submerged plants, twigs, rocks, and other substrates for attachment. Attempts to obtain these animals from open-water sampling typically are unsuccessful and might seem to represent wasted efforts, perhaps as foolish as attempts to collect rocks in surface plankton tows.

In most published field studies of *Hydra,* as well as in many laboratory studies, it seems implicitly evident that considerations similar to the preceding have influenced the investigators. Since the answers one obtains usually depend on the questions one asks, close scrutiny of the preceding logic seems warranted. Bias can be insidious.

B.   EVIDENCE OF PLANKTONIC HYDRAS

1. Some Spectacular Observations

There have been reports of planktonic hydras. Most such reports have regarded these finds as "accidentals" (tychnoplankters), but some have noted hydras in such great abundance in the plankton that minimizing comments were out of the question.

Kofoid (1908), for example, reported an occurrence of more than 5000 planktonic hydras per cubic meter in Quiver Lake, a blind branch of the Illinois River. Needham and Lloyd (1916, p. 163) observed hydras drifting in a New York stream ". . . often in such abundance that the water is tinged with red." Clemens (1922) wrote that in Lake Erie, commercial fishery pound nets spread over more than 25 km became so coated with hydras that the flow of water through the meshes was obstructed. Carrick (1956) listed other reports of hydras on nets, mostly in Lake Erie. In Lake Michigan, gill nets spanning almost 5 km were ". . . so covered with red hydra that they were literally slimy with them" (W. Koelz, as cited by Welch and Loomis, 1924, p. 215). Such occurrences reportedly were well-known to Lake Michigan fishermen. Hudgins (1931) wrote that on Lake St. Clair, intake screens of the Detroit filtration plant collected masses of hydras each year, during lake inversions. In one year, the plant's intake flow was reduced one third by the hydras. Welch and Loomis (1924) at times found *H. oligactis* abundant in Douglas Lake plankton. In a small lake in Iowa, Moen (1951) found experimental gill net meshes completely coated overnight with hydras. In plankton tows on the same lake, Moen found varying abundance of hydras, but in early June, hydras were more numerous than any other animals in the plankton.

Most reports of planktonic hydras are not as spectacular as the preceding. This is not identical to saying, however, that such other reports have less significance. In each of the detailed field studies listed under "Ecological Background Information," and in almost every less-comprehensive field report the author has found, there is evidence – direct, indirect, or probable – of the existence of planktonic hydras.

2. Colonization of Supports

One common ecologists' method of studying vertical and horizontal distribution of microscopic aquatic organisms is the suspending of artificial supports, often racks of glass or plastic slides, at various depths and locations in the body of water under study. This method was employed in field investigation of *Hydra* by Miller (1936), Bryden (1952), Carrick (1956), and Batha (1971). Each of these workers found that clean artificial supports suspended in open water for a few days (or, in some cases, a few hours) became sites of attachment of hydras. Depending on the depth, season, meteorological conditions, and other factors, numbers of animals so obtained varied greatly, but many such supports became covered with hundreds of polyps.

Although Miller (1936) and Carrick (1956) emphasized the conventional conclusion that hydras essentially are sessile and become planktonic only accidentally, Miller was moved to observe (p. 141) that "Since there was no way for hydras which collected on clean racks to get from their former supports to racks except by way of the water, it is obvious that these particular hydras became plankters for a time." Although Bryden (1952) never explored the significance of the planktonic phases of hydras, he showed more interpretive flexibility than most other authors, stating (p. 54) "The movements of hydras in Kirkpatrick's Lake must often involve them as plankters. They were not often found in plankton samples, but there is evidence of their movements through the water, such as the rapid population of plates and the long trips of the bluish-colored hydras."

The "bluish-colored hydras" to which Bryden referred were the subjects of an experiment in which he vitally stained some hydras with Nile blue sulfate and placed them on glass plates in the water. After a few weeks, these animals were found all over the lake.

Another observation made by Bryden (1952) may be of interest. The beds of *Dianthera americana* Vahl, plants on which *H. oligactis* could be found in greater density than on any other substrate in Kirkpatrick's Lake, were present only in the warmer months. These beds typically developed in June of each year. The great summer increase of Bryden's hydrid population, however, did not begin until July. Once the hydras became plentiful, transect sampling of the *Dianthera* beds revealed that all hydras were attached to plants on the edges of the beds. There were no polyps on central plants. While these data might be interpreted to mean, as Bryden suggested, that some feature of the middle of the beds was not suitable to the hydras, it is proposed here that these data more likely suggest planktonic colonization.

3. Mass Migrations

In several field studies of *Hydra* (Welch and Loomis, 1924; Miller, 1936; Marson, 1951; Bryden, 1952; Griffing, 1965; and others), investigators have observed great and rapid changes in local densities of attached hydrid populations. In such studies, the data suggest it unlikely that the observed rates of increase could be accounted for by budding of the polyps, or that the disappearances could be attributed to mortality under conditions described.

Such conclusions also were reached by some of the authors cited. Welch and Loomis (1924) mentioned the possibility of "downward migrations" during summer periods of warm surface water but made no attempt to characterize such migrations, except to note that *H. oligactis* could and did survive on the bottom and feed on mud.* Welch's student Miller (1936) later expressed doubts that migrations occurred or that significant numbers of hydras ever existed on the bottom. Rather, Miller attempted to explain observed changes in hydrid density primarily on the bases of the availablity and condition of natural supports, and essentially he begged the questions of how such rapid increases occurred or what happened to the animals during rapid decreases. Bryden (1952) reported evidence which seems to indicate planktonic migrations of hydras, but he did not pursue such general conclusions.

Finally, Griffing (1965), his advisor, Slobodkin (1965), and Łomnicki and Slobodkin (1966) considered the migratory question directly and suggested that hydras in nature may be more mobile than previously believed. Although Griffing's samplings of Pickerel Lake were limited, and although he studied only those hydras attached to vegetation in the lake, he nevertheless observed overt shifts in vertical distribution of the *H. oligactis* and *H. pseudoligactis* populations over the summer. Griffing concluded that the populations showed real mobility.

---

*Other authors, such as Wilson (1891), Goetsch (1921), Haase-Eichler (1931), and Bryden (1952) also have reported mud-feeding by hydras. In addition, hydras have been observed (see review by Forrest, 1962) to ingest bacteria, algae, protozoa, dead meat, and even other hydras. Although such observations may seem curious to those who favor the presumed role (see Part 1) of reduced glutathione as the specific feeding stimulus in hydras, the observations cannot simply be discarded. The demonstrative burden would seem to fall upon the "GSH-specific" proponents, who must show the chemical's sufficient presence in or around ingested mud (etc.). Hydras are facultative beasts.

C. SURFACE FLOATING

Although no attempts were made to observe actual hydrid migrations in Pickerel Lake, Griffing (1965), Slobodkin (1965), and Łomnicki and Slobodkin (1966) proposed that the method of migration already was known: surface floating (see Part I). Łomnicki and Slobodkin (1966) demonstrated that crowding (i.e., exposure to culture medium conditioned by budding hydras) and starvation produce an increased incidence of floaters in laboratory *H. littoralis* populations. To these observations, Griffing (1965) added the possibility that environmental "deterioration" (e.g., a change in pH or temperature) might induce floating, and he concluded that floating migrations seem to be a method by which hydras escape "local disasters." Griffing further noted that such movements essentially would be uncontrolled and random.

Although it seems likely that such floating does occur significantly in nature, in spite of Beutler's (1933) unsupported doubts, there are problems involved in such a hypothesis. An attempt will be made to show that surface floating is not the principal mechanism of planktonic mobility in hydras.

Except for one observation (Welch and Loomis, 1924), none of the many field reports of planktonic hydras cited in this section (or elsewhere) have described floating (infraneustic) hydras. Rather, such reports have indicated hydras below the surface, often well below it. Hydras have been observed off the bottom many times in nature, but when they were, they were not at the surface, either.

This lack of observation of floaters in nature also appeared to be a matter of concern to Łomnicki and Slobodkin (1966), since they mentioned the ease with which floating hydras can be dislodged from the surface film by waves and roiled water, and they commented on the absence of reports of floaters in nature. They did not consider negative evidence conclusive, however (as must be acknowledged).

Horizontal migrations seem difficult to explain by a mechanism which most evidence indicates cannot or does not reliably keep hydras off the bottom long enough for them to be transported very far, or long enough ever to have been observed. Some vertical migrations also would be included in this difficulty, since sloping lake bottoms can make horizontal transport necessary for vertical movement.

D. PLANKTONIC GLIDING

It is proposed that hydras do not have to rely on basal bubbles and floating to leave substrates and stay off the bottom long enough to be transported well. The author now will attempt to show that hydras are adept, true (subsurface) plankters.

In laboratory culture dishes, animals forming basal bubbles and rising to the surface film, or dropping from the same surface film, usually travel a vertical distance of only a few centimeters and are seen by observers merely to move up and down. However, as any glider pilot or parachutist will testify, much can happen between "up" and "down" if the descent is slowed.

1. Preliminary Observations

The author currently is studying (in *H. oligactis, H. pseudoligactis, H. littoralis,* and *H. viridis*) a phenomenon which can be observed by anyone with access to hydras. When a starved, nondepressed *Hydra* is removed from its substrate and gently dropped from a pipette at the surface of a large (e.g., 4-l) cylinder filled with undisturbed culture medium, the animal sinks. For the first 20 cm or thereabouts, the *Hydra* usually descends rapidly, but then its rate of sinking typically slows considerably. At such a time and thereafter, the animal usually is seen to assume a position in which its oral end is uppermost, its tentacles are spread widely, and its column is angled toward the horizontal plane.

In such a position, the hydra's rate of descent often is slowed so much that a 10-cm vertical drop requires a minute or more. That the positioning of its body directly influences the polyp's rate of descent seems evident. Most hydras in such a situation are seen only rarely to exhibit periodic contractions. When contractions of tentacles or column are observed, however, the rate of sinking accelerates greatly, but only during the brief performance of the contraction. The animal typically elongates quickly into the characteristic position, and descent again slows.

Nondepressed hydras with long tentacles are adept at such "braking" action, unless recently fed. Animals starved 48 hours or more, if not depressed, demonstrate the phenomenon well. In contrast, recently fed hydras often do not assume the position described at all. Rather, these usually remain partly or fully contracted and drop rapidly to the bottom. Newly detached buds are the most expert at slow descent, suggesting that their relatively high surface-to-mass ratio, as in the case of starved animals, is helpful. After the first minute of descent, the relationship of descent velocities to dry weights of individual hydras (both buds and adults) is direct and roughly linear in all four species tested, but considerable variability results, apparently from differences of individual partial contraction behavior and tentacle lengths, both difficult to quantify.

Hydras descending in such a manner capture and ingest with alacrity any introduced *Artemia* nauplius which contacts a tentacle. Carrick's (1956) denial that floating or sinking hydras can feed is challenged here. Observations of a plankter's tentacles during such feeding makes evident the fact that the same positioning which slows the animal's fall also maximizes the volume of water "fished" (sampled). While a nauplius is being ingested by a descending *Hydra,* one or more of the tentacles are used to bring the prey to the mouth and thus are unavailable for "braking" action. Consequently, during actual ingestion, the *Hydra*'s rate of sinking increases. As just mentioned, however, slowly descending polyps usually exhibit accelerated feeding behavior, often completing the abbreviated tentacle "concert" in half a minute or less. Some animals are slower about this, and these drop to the bottom of the cylinder before they have engulfed the nauplius. Even during feeding, however, tentacles not involved in manipulating a nauplius remain extended and exert some "braking" action. In planktonic feeders, the author has noted the absence of any postingestion "concerts" of the kinds exhibited (see Part I) by attached hydras. Were such to occur in feeding plankters, it would seem difficult for such animals to remain planktonic.

Any descending animal contracted completely or partially is falling faster and "fishing" less. Thus, periodic contractions which appear to aid an attached *Hydra* in exploring the water for food would seem to have the opposite effect in a planktonic animal. Full contractions are seldom observed in plankters.

2. Previous Reports

The author made most of the preceding observations unaware of the fact that Schäffer (1754, as cited by Kanaev, 1952, p. 107) previously described such slow descent in hydras. In fact, the author has found only three citings of this observation, more than two centuries since Schäffer reported it. Kanaev employed the term "gliding" in discussing the phenomenon Schäffer reported. This term subsequently will be used here. Schäffer noted that hydras loosened from some substrate near the water surface fell with partly straightened tentacles and, in effect, could "passively swim," being carried by water currents. A few other investigators, such as Wilson (1891), Bryden (1952), and Carrick (1956), more recently mentioned that in large aquaria, hydras sank slowly when dislodged from near-surface sites of attachment. None of these workers, however, pursued the kinds of considerations made by Schäffer (1754) and the present author.

E. PLANKTONIC DIRIGIBILITY

Here, it is proposed that the planktonic behavioral repertoire of hydras includes a second general method, and that with this second mechanism, hydras need not be exclusively transient plankters.

1. Preliminary Observations

Not all planktonic hydras are oriented with their head and tentacles uppermost. The author has found that if hydras floating on the surface film in a culture bowl are transferred carefully in a small petri dish to the surface film in the 4-1 cylinder previously mentioned, and if such hydras then are gently dislodged mechanically or by dropping water on their bases, the animals usually descend with their bases uppermost. Many such animals sink even more slowly than gliding polyps. In addition, tiny, glistening masses of mucus usually can be seen on the bases of dislodged floaters. On occasion, such hydras cease their descent entirely, and rise. The author has observed such animals alternately ascending and descending slowly for more than half an hour, without contact with bottom, surface, or sides of the cylinder, in less than a meter of water. In the tallest (150 × 9 cm, clear plastic) cylinder used by the author, planktonic "gliders" also have been observed on occasion to form basal bubbles before reaching bottom, cease descent, and engage in the second kind of planktonic behavior here described.

In a long, shallow trough (approximately 150 cm long, 5.0 cm wide, and 3.0 cm deep, with clear plastic sides) in which culture medium flows at the rate of 10 or 20 cm per minute in laminar fashion, hydras on the bottom usually can be induced, depending on the author's patience, by sustained irritation (bubbles from a finely drawn pipette) to form bubbles at their bases and ascend. Often, such ascent does not bring them directly to the surface, however. Many ascend part of the way toward the surface, then slow or cease their ascent and maintain their vertical position while being swept "downstream." Some have been observed to rise and fall, alternately. Such animals usually wind up either on the surface or back on the bottom before the length of the trough is traveled, but sometimes they travel a meter or more and reach the trough's drain while still suspended in medium only 3 cm deep. Closer observation shows that bubbles on the bases of these animals enlarge and shrink, respectively, as the hydras rise and fall.

Plankters hanging from bubbles have been observed to feed on introduced *Artemia* nauplii apparently as readily as do planktonic gliders.

2. A Previous Report and Suggested Explanation

Again, the author witnessed most of these phenomena before learning of a similar observation by Scourfield (1901), who noted a "remarkable appearance" of a *Hydra* suspended in mid-water. Scourfield explained that conditions prohibited close inspection, but he thought (p. 140) he saw a "very fine thread" attaching the *Hydra* to a remnant raft of mucus on the surface, ". . . but it was exceedingly faint. . . ."

An alternative explanation is suggested, however. As described by Scourfield (1901), Kepner and Miller (1928), Haase-Eichler (1931), and others, hydras floating on the surface film frequently are seen to have irregular masses of a gelatinous, water-repellent substance attached to their bases and spreading out along the water surface. Such mucus "rafts" often are ruptured remnants of the bubbles which once carried the polyps to the surface (although no normal *Hydra* is entirely without basal mucus). Since the mucus is hydrophobic, it probably facilitates the animals' adherence to the surface film.

When such a floating *Hydra* becomes dislodged from the surface film, the mucus adhering to its base adopts a shape presenting a water interface of minimum surface: a sphere. Such a ball of mucus is less dense than water and may itself provide some buoyancy. However, if air becomes trapped when the ball forms, or if the animal subsequently secretes gas into the ball (forming a bubble), descent not only can be slowed or stopped, it can be reversed.

It seems reasonable to suggest that when planktonic hydras hanging from basal bubbles repeatedly reverse their direction of vertical movement, some action of the hydras (e.g., secretion and resorption or release of bubble gas by basal disc cells) must be responsible. Although hydrostatic pressure differences varying with depth also should influence bubble size, it must be admitted that such vertical reversals of hydrid movement could not be explained by thus begging the question. There must be some kind of hydrid influence. Thus, in a limited sense, there appears to be control of planktonic movement by the hydras. Further, it is tempting to speculate that in nature, no matter what factors influence the hydras to exercise such control, the resulting overt behavioral consequences should have adaptive meaning. Thus, "planktonic dirigibility" (i.e., a term expressing analogy to controlled balloon flight) will be used here to denote this second type of planktonic behavior and to distinguish it from planktonic gliding.

F. THE MAKING OF PLANKTERS

Here will be considered ways in which hydras can depart from solid substrates and become planktonic. The formation of basal bubbles, of course, is well-known, and statements (Griffing, 1965; Slobodkin, 1965; Łomnicki and Slobodkin, 1966) to the effect that as environmental conditions become worse, more hydras make bubbles and float, seem to have justification. Once on the surface, a *Hydra* in the infraneuston then may encounter any of a number of physical influences which dislodge it into the plankton proper.

There are other ways by which hydras might become planktonic, however. Rushforth (see Chapter 1 of this volume) discussed factors influencing the substrate locomotion of hydras. Many of those same behavioral responses would have the effect, individually or in combination, of influencing hydras to climb upward on their natural supports. Hydras, for example, have been observed to move toward light. Such a response is pronounced in starved animals. Hydras seem to move in the direction of higher oxygen tension. Newly detached buds, if not recently fed, exhibit an apparent negative "geotaxis," and adults also show this phenomenon under certain conditions. Locomotion often is accelerated in warm temperatures.

It is proposed that there is a unity of effect in these movements, that the making of plankters is thereby influenced, and that these mechanisms result in adaptive population response to environmental variability.

All of these phenomena, observed in laboratories, would seem to indicate that on a natural support, such as a bulrush (*Scirpus validus* Vahl) stem in Douglas Lake (Welch and Loomis, 1924; Miller, 1936) or a *Dianthera* plant in Kirkpatrick's Lake (Bryden, 1952), for examples, a variable proportion of hydras should be climbing toward the water surface. Yet, hydras in nature are not found attached to the upper parts of emergent supports. Wave action prohibits such attachment.

Although Welch and Loomis (1924) attempted to explain the absence of *H. oligactis* from the upper several subsurface centimeters of bulrush stems in Douglas Lake by noting that hydras move away from bright light, these authors were not thereby able to explain why, in the exceptionally clear water of their lake, this would result in a sharp discontinuity of vertical hydrid distribution on bulrushes. The authors, in fact, noted their lack of a critical study of this phenomenon.

In the same lake, Miller (1936) later noted that hydras usually were absent from the upper 8 or 10 subsurface cm. On calm days, however, these animals could be found on bulrushes within 2 or 3 cm of the surface. Also in Douglas Lake, Young (1945) observed that although hydras are dislodged by waves less readily than many other animals in the periphyton, *H. oligactis* nevertheless was not found near the water surface on natural supports.

Bryden (1952) found that the top subsurface meter of *Dianthera* plants in Kirkpatrick's Lake bore far fewer hydras than did the second meter (the zone of greatest density). Only in serene weather did the top half-meter hold any hydras at all. Below the second meter, hydras again were scarce. Bryden reported that, in a large aquarium, hydras occupied the entire length of *Dianthera* plants when first introduced, but when the water in the aquarium was agitated for an hour by an electric fan (simulating wave action), the upper few centimeters of the plants were swept clean of hydras.

But if waves keep the upper subsurface regions swept clean of hydras, it is obvious that the polyps must be swept somewhere, and that means potential plankters. Winds and waves are variable factors, and such variability easily could add to the effect. During lulls and quiet times, hydras can ascend their supports. When waves come again, plankters result.

Here, it seems advisable to point out that one should expect considerable variation in the making of plankters. During certain unfavorable environmental conditions, a relatively large proportion of attached hydras would be predicted by these arguments to become planktonic. If food is in low supply, for example, laboratory behavior discussed previously would indicate that hydras not only ascend faster on supports, but that they show greater tendencies to produce bubbles and float. If surface waters become too warm, it is expected that nondepressed hydras would show increased locomotion and also use up more energy in maintenance, so that hydras in warm water might be "starving" in conditions of food availability adequate for animals in cooler water. All of this, of course, is in addition to any effects which temperature might have on the adhesivity of mucus or on the cells which produce it.

The preceding considerations might help to explain such mass disappearances of hydras from surface-water supports in summer as those observed by Welch and Loomis (1924), Miller (1936), and Griffing (1965), as well as the simultaneous increases in planktonic and bottom hydras reported by the same authors (with the exception of Griffing, who did not sample for plankters) and, for plankters only, by Moen (1951). Wilson's (1891) observations that starvation increased "cycles of movement" in aquarium hydras, and that in foul water, more hydras lingered near the surface (as any laboratory observer knows), also would seem to lend support. Animals near the surface are potential plankters.

Even when mass migrations are not occurring, however, it seems certain that plankters still are produced in a fairly continuous process. When favorable conditions prevail, hydras generally stay where they are. As Łomnicki and Slobodkin (1966) have observed, it would appear to be a strategic blunder were hydras to give up a good thing. Nevertheless, as these authors also noted, there is a long-term "strategic advantage" to the invasion of new environments or habitats. Or, in other words, these "naked" polyps cannot afford to be "complacent" with regard to any habitat.

Even when environmental conditions are good, some hydras still locomote. Light still affects them, and newly detached buds still climb (Ewer, 1947). Such buds would seem to make excellent potential planktonic colonists. As noted earlier, they are adept planktonic gliders, and as

Stevenson and Buchsbaum (1961) have reported, their rate of bud production, once they begin, seems to be higher than that of older members of the population. These would be good criteria for animals charged with reaching favorable sites and establishing new "colonies."* In addition, Bloom (1963) reported that by placing a homemade plankton net in the current of an Indiana stream, he could collect hydras in every season. He never collected many at a time, but they appeared reliably. About these animals so obtained, Bloom made the interesting observation (p. 352) that at the time of collection, ". . . the hydras are quite small and possess fewer tentacles than the typical adults." This observation, of course, could indicate damaged or depressed hydras. But it also might indicate that he was collecting newly detached, planktonic buds.

G. THE PAUCITY OF OBSERVED PLANKTERS

We must here consider possible reasons why planktonic hydras have been found relatively seldom in nature. In the first place, not many investigators have searched for them, possibly for some of the reasons given earlier as "evidence" for thinking of hydras as sessile animals. In addition, it must be realized that when one dilutes part of a population of tiny animals from two-dimensional, discontinuous supports into three-dimensional open water, one should expect these animals to be considerably more difficult to find.

To further obscure such plankters, natural bodies of water have tendencies to produce discontinuous distribution of suspended microscopic biota. One exciting set of problems being investigated today by limnologists and marine ecologists deals with the aggregations of plankton produced by currents and by more subtle physical events (caused by wind and thermal phenomena). If a million planktonic hydras were suspended in a million-liter pond, one could not expect to obtain five polyps by taking five random one-liter samples. Wind-driven and thermal currents, upwellings and downwellings, wind rows, and other water-mass boundary events all apparently have great influence on planktonic distribution. A somewhat similar point, in reference to floating hydras, has been made by E. Baylor (cited in Łomnicki and Slobodkin, 1966). In fact, it was Drs. Baylor and Slobodkin who first made the author aware of some of these physical phenomena, during a series of fascinating lectures at the Marine Biological Laboratory, Woods Hole, Massachusetts.

* A "colony" here refers to a local group of individual hydras attached to a single support. Hydras, of course, are solitary, not colonial, coelenterates. An alternative term, "microdeme," might be proposed, but ecological jargon is being avoided here, and such a term also might bring unintended genetic connotations.

H. Discontinuous Planktonic Distribution and Some Proposed Consequences

There is no apparent reason why the same factors which produce aggregations of other members of the plankton could not do so also for hydras. If so, one immediate conclusion might be that these planktonic hydras would be placed in proximity with prey. As noted earlier, planktonic hydras seem to feed as well as do attached animals. And although it has been discussed that starved animals appear to have a better-than-average chance of becoming planktonic in one way or another, Batha (1971) has made the interesting observation that when planktonic hydras in Lake Michigan are collected on suspended plastic supports, the animals usually appear well-fed.

Although many planktonic hydras may reach new supports quickly, what about those (e.g., dirigibles) who do not? Since they can feed and seem to be able to influence their level in the water, what about the well-known diurnal vertical migrations of other plankters? Could hydras follow them? Although diel rhythmicity in locomotor behavior is known for other (medusoid) coelenterates (see Thorpe, 1956; Robson, 1965), such considerations here will remain interrogative.

A speculation probably safer, however, is that those currents and other aquatic physical phenomena mentioned also should have some effect on where most planktonic hydras eventually do come to rest, on supports or on the bottom. It seems likely that plankters would tend to settle more in areas where other suspended things also are being deposited. Such would indeed be fortunate, since some of these other things probably would be edible. Thus, although many planktonic hydras may meet disastrous ends, those which survive the journey and find a suitable new habitat might receive dietary assistance in their missions of establishing new colonies by budding.

Even those animals which settle on the bottom, as opposed to other supports (e.g., plants, twigs, rocks), might be in luck for similar reasons. In general, muck bottoms indicate areas of deposition, and sandy bottoms usually indicate scouring action by currents. There are a number of reports of hydras collected from muddy or leaf-covered bottom areas (Welch and Loomis, 1924; Bryden, 1952; and others), and if no better (i.e., living) food is available, hydras, as mentioned earlier, have been known to eat mud. As far as the author knows, no benthic hydras have been collected on sand. Of course, sand certainly would not seem to be the sort of thing a *Hydra* might eat.

It is well-known that locations of the aquatic physical phenomena mentioned, as well as of areas where suspended debris (and organisms) tend to settle, often are variable. Thus, a new colony, or an old one, for that matter, may find its food supply suddenly reduced. As Griffing (1965) noted, the food of hydras in nature does not arrive with the regularity enjoyed by laboratory animals. Rather, natural food tends to come in irregular bunches. It appears (Shostak *et al.,* 1968), though, that hydras fed irregularly produce about as many buds as those receiving the same amount of food regularly (within limits, of course). Once the development of a bud is well underway, it usually is completed even if the parent obtains no subsequent food (Rulon and Child, 1937).

Besides, if things get too bad with regard to food supply or other factors, hydras have the options of climbing to the wavy zone, forming bubbles, or possibly even simply detaching and permitting local currents to take charge (in other words, dispatching new colonists to find better pastures).

I. HYDRAS AND HERMITS

A rather counterconventional view of hydras in nature and the significance of their planktonic phases has been proposed here. That hydras are sessile is not suggested to be an erroneous statement, of course, as long as it is placed in reasonable perspective. The general observations which might lead to such a statement, summarized earlier, must be scrutinized again.

Medusae are pelagic and polyps sessile, but there are exceptions to most rules. *Gonionemus* medusae, for example, bear adhesive pads on their tentacles, and they use them to attach periodically to substrates (see Thorpe, 1956). Hydras, of course, do not have a medusoid phase, and complete sessility of "naked" polyps in limnetic habitats should not seem appealingly adaptive.

Field investigations reporting only attached hydras no more justify ignoring the possibility of significant planktonic phases than would, for example, the presence in air of "invisible" particulate matter be made to seem unlikely by the fact that it only is noted when it accumulates on windowsills and automobiles. Field and laboratory observations of sessile hydras do not demonstrate that hydras "essentially are sessile." They demonstrate only that observers were looking where sessile hydras were.

In the preceding discussions, the author has refrained from citing most of the unwieldy and unproductive interpretations made by workers who hesitated to challenge the sessility of hydras. But perhaps the following allegory might be useful.

A hermit who by chance comes upon a small airfield notices some large, quiescent, winged objects. Each time he returns, the curious objects are reliably there, still unmoving. The few airborne specimens observed occasionally are dismissed as "accidentals" (possibly wind-dispersed).

After all, in his wanderings (which usually are not conducted below heavily used flight paths), he seldom sees any in the air. Besides, when he visits the airfield late at night and drags one of the winged objects into his cave, he is able to confirm the object's immobility under prolonged observation. Therefore, he concludes that these objects essentially are sessile, and he is not entirely unbiased in subsequent study.

IV. Environmental Crises and Hydrid Defenses

A. SOME BENEFITS OF SEXUAL REPRODUCTION

To justify the sixth and seventh points proposed in Section I of this chapter, it is observed that although mechanisms of planktonic dispersal and colonization may improve chances of hydrid success in the variable conditions of most freshwater environments, the effectiveness of such mechanistic aids depends on the accessibility to plankters of sufficient favorable areas. Field data on hydras indicate, however, that these animals have successfully invaded limnetic bodies in which sometimes occur crises during which most, or all, local areas become unfavorable. Thus, success would seem to have demanded mechanistic defenses other than planktonic evasion.

It is well-established that sexual reproduction can help in such regard. Hydras obtain much benefit from reproducing sexually. Obviously, one such benefit is the opportunity for genetic exchange, providing a greater potential variety of material with which hydras can face natural selection. With both asexual and sexual abilities in the reproductive repertoire of these animals, such an exchange feature becomes especially attractive, since any phenotypic advantages obtained sexually can be favored in asexual proliferation.

In addition, however, sexual reproduction in hydras produces encysted embryos which most authors (Burnett and Diehl, 1964; Griffing, 1965; and others) agree can be resistant to hardships that occur even in the worst natural crises. The eggs of *H. oligactis,* for example, have been reported (McConnell, 1938a) to withstand even the desiccation involved in being stored out of water for 20 days, hatching normally when returned to water.

As are the gemmules of freshwater sponges and the statoblasts of ectoprocts, the eggs of hydras seem to be forms which can persist even through the worst of times in nature.

B. INITIATION OF SEXUALITY

In order to be of value to natural populations, resistant eggs must be present, of course, at the same times crises are occurring. For this reason, and because of morphogenic significances, consideration of factors which might influence the initiation of sexuality in hydras is important and has been the subject of many investigations.

In the next few discussions, the author will attempt to supply credence to the eighth and ninth proposals listed in Section I.

1. A Few Enigmas

In general, the many studies of sexual initiation in *Hydra* have not yielded simple answers. Environmental factors implicated (see discussions by Kanaev, 1952; Itô, 1952a,b,c; Burnett, 1961; Burnett and Diehl, 1964; Park *et al.,* 1964, 1965) as stimuli for gonad formation have included temperature, photoperiod, pH, oxygen tension, carbon dioxide tension, starvation, overfeeding, stagnation of medium, endogenous cyclic phenomena, and others. Although manipulations of these variables have been shown, under certain conditions and in certain species of hydras, to result in sexuality, the basic ecological questions involved still appear to be far from satisfying resolution.

Some species of *Hydra* remain in the asexual condition in laboratory cultures for years. Other species exhibit occasional "spontaneous" inductions of the sexual state. In some species, all animals in a culture develop gonads following appropriate manipulation of one of the environmental variables previously mentioned. For other species, there is no such reliable procedure. Additonal confusion has resulted from tendencies of certain workers to argue that their favorite gonad inducer was the specific sexual evocator in *Hydra*.

Burnett (1961; Burnett and Diehl, 1964) has presented a hypothesis which considers sexuality and its control in hydras on the cellular level. Burnett's hypothesis, stated briefly, proposes that there need not be a specific, universal environmental evocator of hydrid sexuality, but rather that anything which interferes properly with neurosecretion and, henceforth, growth, will result in gonad formation. Such a proposal does not require resolution of ecological questions for its consideration and testing. In the present discussions, however, *Hydra* and sexuality will be considered from ecological perspectives. The knotty task of bridging the interpretive level gap largely will be left to the reader.

Of all the sexual stimuli implicated, temperature has been the most thoroughly studied and appears to be the most reliably successful. Even temperature, however, does not produce the same kinds of sexual effects in all kinds of *Hydra*. In some species of *Hydra,* such as *H. fusca, H. oligactis, H. parva, H. pirardi, H. pseudoligactis,* and *H. robusta,* gonads develop reliably (see Itô, 1954b, 1955b; Burnett and Diehl, 1964; Park *et al.,* 1965) when the temperature of the medium is reduced to a sufficiently low level. In other species, such as *H. attenuata, H. japonica,*

H. littoralis, H. magnipapillata, H. paludicola, and *H. viridis,* the effects of temperature are more cryptic.

As known by anyone who has maintained cultures of the latter group of species, sexual animals occur with periodic mystery in asexual cultures. Proportionately more such sexual animals appear, however, when temperatures are raised or maintained at high levels (see Itô, 1952c, 1953; Burnett and Diehl, 1964; Park *et al.,* 1965).

Itô (1954b, 1955a) and Burnett and Diehl (1964) have suggested that the former group of species just mentioned consists of "cold types," with regard to the initiation of sexuality, and that the latter group might be described as "warm types," since these animals more frequently develop gonads in warm temperatures. Such descriptions are consistent with data from most investigations, but there are a few difficulties to be considered.

Why, for example, have asexual representatives of cold-type species been found (Hyman, 1930; Miller, 1936; Carrick, 1956; and others) in icy water in nature? Why do not elevations of temperature influence all polyps in a warm-type culture to develop gonads? Why do some warm-type sexual animals occur even in relatively cool water? Why have sexual cold types been seen (Hyman, 1928; Burnett and Diehl, 1964; and others) in warm laboratory cultures? What about the reported effects of stimuli other than temperature?

2. Cold-Crisis Hydras

A few authors have considered one or more of the preceding apparent discrepancies to be evidence sufficient to cast doubt upon hypotheses that identify temperature as a principal stimulus for sexuality in hydras. It is suggested, however, that such judgments miss a few important points, and that the first step in resolving such problems is to understand that environmental variables which signal the approach of a crisis are not necessarily identical to the unfavorable conditions which make the crisis critical.

The postulated role of temperature as a major sexual stimulus requires only that it act as an "indicator" or "timer." Such a hypothesis does not require that temperature be one of the reasons why sexuality might be necessary for hydrid survival in certain situations. Shortening day length, for example, certainly is not harmful to birds, but it consistently announces the coming of conditions (i.e., in winters) which might be unfavorable, if certain species failed to migrate south. A robin can survive easily in an 8 L : 16 D photoperiod, if warm and well-fed. Observations of cold-type hydras in icy waters would seem to indicate that such low temperatures, of themselves, challenge the survival of these animals not much more than short-day photoperiods harm a robin. Although entomostracan food supply may be low in icy waters, so are the metabolic rates and energetic maintenance requirements of hydras.

However, falling water temperatures herald winters. In winters, especially in upper latitudes, an ice cover may form on the surface of the water. Under prolonged ice cover, a number of undesirable events may occur, even in the epilimnion (in smaller limnetic bodies). Oxygen may become depleted; carbon dioxide tension may increase; pH may fall; and hydrogen sulfide, methane, ammonia, and other toxic materials may build up.

In short, it seems that selection for reliance on consistent *indicators* of the approach of such crises might be expected. Sexual reproduction can increase a population's chances of persisting through winters. However, the formation of gonads and the successful completion of the sexual process take time. In cold-type species (hereafter termed "cold-crisis" hydras), gonad initiation usually requires a week or two after administration even of a sharp chilling stimulus (Burnett and Diehl, 1964; and many others). And, as the evidence of Itô (1955a) and others suggests, the initiation of gonads in the gradual temperature declines common in nature probably would require even more time than is observed when temperatures are rapidly lowered in the laboratory.

Advance notice of winter may not always be given with sufficient reliability by temperature alone, but there is at least one other well-known harbinger: day length. Burnett and Diehl (1964), for example, observed that during an unusually warm autumn, *H. pseudoligactis* collected from a lake near Cleveland in late October bore gonads, even though the water temperature had not yet declined below 20°C. These authors then demonstrated that in laboratory cultures of these same animals, an artificial photoperiod could markedly affect the incidence of sexual specimens (at temperatures normally resulting in the asexual condition).

It is not difficult to appreciate the potential adaptive value of such additional influence. Unusually warm autumns do occur. Under such conditions, sole reliance on temperature as an indicator might not provide sufficient time for successful completion of the sexual process. It is probable, of course, that when a belated (and probably more rapid) temperature drop finally does occur in such anomalous cases, gonads are produced by hydras more rapidly than in the usual natural situation. Such would be nicely compensatory. Accommodation seems to produce a negative correlation between rate of temperature drop and length of time required for the initiation of gonads. Dr. Paul Brien (1970), in fact, has managed even to maintain asexual cultures of Belgian *H. fusca* at 8°C., by cooling them gradually over a 6-month period.

Supplementary photoperiodic control of gonad initiation also might reduce the frequency of energetically wasteful sexual responses to "false alarms." In nature, hydras can be subjected to temperature drops which are not indicative of season. Many lakes stratify, and even in some of the warmer months, a wind or current change, the relocation of an upwelling area, a planktonic descent, or any of a number of other events could cause cold-crisis hydras to experience sudden, significant declines in temperature.

The formation of gonads, while protective in end result, is an expensive energetic investment, and adaptive considerations would not favor thoughts of wasteful hydrid sexual responses to commonplace events through which asexual hydras could persist. Therefore, additional control by photoperiod, possibly mediated through neurosecretory processes (Rushforth et al., 1963) seems likely, and reports such as that by Burnett and Diehl (1964) of sexual animals appearing in the autumn in relatively warm laboratory cultures of cold-crisis species would tend to lose mystery, since most laboratories have windows. In fact, reports of such hydras developing gonads in the spring might also be explained, if sexual responses are geared to absolute photoperiods which approximate natural autumn day lengths.

3. Warm-Crisis Hydras

Northern winters are not the only situations in which serious natural crises might threaten the survival of a hydrid population. Another type of crisis suggested for consideration is that resulting from prolonged periods of drought. In ponds and streams, especially in the lower latitudes, droughts often are seasonal, but occasionally they result from anomalous meteorological conditions (here naively considered random). In these situations, conditions devastating to hydras can be produced. In fact, many of the same unfavorable conditions (regarding O_2, CO_2, pH, etc.) listed earlier as selecting factors in cold crises can occur also in warm, stagnant ponds or backwaters of streams.* In addition, hydras in such warm crises would suffer prolonged exposure to elevated temperatures, with obvious metabolic implications (or perhaps not so obvious, as will be discussed later).

As in the case of winter crises, water temperature also would seem to be one of the best available indicators of the approach of drought-

---

*Most ecologists seem to agree that any stream plankter also must be a pond, slough, or backwater plankter. By definition, plankters cannot make significant locomotor progress against a current, so there is no apparent way such animals could maintain distribution in a stream unless regularly "fed" into its currents from quieter waters continuous with the stream. Hydras, of course, are not typical plankters. They attach. Nevertheless, there has been no evidence of their substrate locomotion against a current.

related crises. In droughts, the water in a pond usually warms somewhat before the advent of other, unfavorable conditions. Studies by Itô (1954a) and Park (1961; Park *et al.,* 1965) have provided much of the foundation for such a suggestion. In laboratory cultures of *H. magnipapillata* or *H. littoralis* (both listed earlier as warm-type species, hereafter termed "warm-crisis" hydras), Itô and Park, respectively, found greater proportions of sexual animals at higher temperatures than at lower ones. A temperature rise produced a high incidence of sexuality. A temperature drop resulted in few or no sexual animals.

Such results seem to support the proposal that these warm-crisis hydras, in effect, use temperature as an indicator of the probability of approach of a drought-related crisis. If the water gets warmer, more animals take some of the energy they might otherwise have spent on budding and invest it in the sexual process. The more imminent the crisis "appears" to the hydras (i.e., the higher the absolute temperature or the greater or more rapid the rise), the larger the proportionate energetic investment in sexuality made by the population.

At this point in the argument, however, we must appreciate a serious difference between droughts and winters, a difference which seems to present a dilemma to warm-crisis hydras. Cold-crisis hydras generally are well provided with thermal and photoperiodic cues, by which relatively straightforward mechanisms would seem to be able to reduce chances either of great sexual energetic wastes in false alarms, or of inadequate preparedness for winters. Warm-crisis hydras, however, often are not given such reliable warning.

Although the formation of gonads seems (Itô, 1954a; Burnett and Diehl, 1964; Park *et al.,* 1965; and others) to occur more rapidly in warm-crisis hydras than in cold-crisis animals (at the temperatures involved, of course), a sexual morphogenic time lag still is evident in the former types. And successful completion of the sexual process entails more and requires more time than does the mere first appearance of gonads. Although one can not rule out the possible assisting influence of photoperiod in those geographic areas where droughts occur with seasonal regularity, it should be evident that even in seasonal drought situations, thermal cues are not nearly as reliable in providing supplementary warning as they are for winters. Besides, many droughts are not seasonal at all.

A simple solution to this problem might be for warm-crisis hydras to form gonads whenever they receive any apparent indication of the approach of such crises. Much energetic waste would result from such a solution, however.

A *Hydra* in nature frequently may experience brief elevations of temperature. Although habitat conditions often are considered in terms of averages, aquatic microhabitat conditions can vary considerably and quickly. On summer days, for example, surface waters at the windward side of a pond or lake often are cooler than those at the leeward side. This occurs because the wind pushes the warm surface water before it. Net upwelling occurs at the windward side, and the warmest water collects at the lee side. Thus, hydras attached to supports near the surface or in shallow water could be acutely affected by a mere change in wind direction lasting a few hours or a few days. This effect would be enhanced by any abrupt weather-related changes in air (and surface-water) temperatures, such as during the passing of a weather front. Of course, such weather changes often are accompanied by wind changes. And, as noted earlier, there are additional ways by which hydras can experience brief temperature fluctuations, such as by the temporary shift of a current or the movements of plankters.

It would seem a waste of energy were a major proportion of a warm-crisis population to enter sexuality in rapid response to such ephemeral (or thereabouts) events which generally would not be accompanied by the other unfavorable conditions which characterize serious, prolonged, drought crises, survivable only by encysted hydrid embryos. In many small ponds, such wasteful practice would seem to require that warm-crisis hydras did little else but make gonads. Such populations understandably would find it difficult to maintain a decent asexual foothold.

Thus, we see the sexual dilemma of warm-crisis hydras. How can an adaptive, mechanistic balance be achieved, between not wasting energy on false alarms and not being caught unprepared by poorly heralded droughts? A possible answer to this dilemma will be proposed next.

4. Sexual Cycles

It is suggested, as stated in the ninth point listed in Section I, that the sexual dilemma described for warm-crisis hydras is mechanistically resolved in large part by cyclic morphogenic phenomena.

Such "rhythms" of sexual differentiation in warm-crisis hydras have been studied in detail by some investigators (Itô, 1952c, 1953, 1954a; Park, 1961; Park et al., 1965; and others, reviewed by Kanaev, 1952) and are well-known to laboratory culture observers, who note in such animals "mysterious" appearances and disappearances of gonads. Sexual periodicity has been shown (Itô, 1955a) to occur also in a cold-crisis Hydra, H. robusta.

Unlike cold-crisis hydras, however, warm-crisis animals continue budding and feeding while developing gonads (Brien and Reniers-Decoen, 1949, 1950, 1951; Itô, 1956; Burnett, 1961; Burnett and Diehl, 1964). The interstitial cell supply in the latter type of animals does not become totally devoted to the sexual process. Nematocysts still are made. And, as Burnett and Diehl (1964) have observed, morphogenic cell movement in polyps which bud while they are sexual results in the relatively transitory presence of gonads, which become sloughed eventually at the base.

Thus, the ability of warm-crisis hydras to drift repeatedly in and out of the sexual condition (without the necessarily high probability of irrevocable commitment found in cold-crisis hydras) might be thought of as a mechanistic safeguard against the possibility of insufficient forewarning of a prolonged warm crisis. Authors reporting cyclic sexuality in warm-crisis hydras have noted that within a population, the individuals are not phase synchronized. If any common environmental influence were capable of entraining such cycles in nature, it probably would do so. That no such phase synchrony seems to exist, however, probably results in adaptive temporal variability on the population level.

Except under the least "alarming" (i.e., cool) conditions, a population of hydras thereby would include at least some animals capable of producing energetically expensive, encysted embryos on short notice. This becomes even more important when it is realized that when temperatures and metabolic rates are high, energy is at a premium. Thus, the population could persist through an inadequately heralded crisis. Similarly, polyps in other phases of the cycles would retain the morphogenic inertia necessary to reduce the chances of their being wastefully "fooled" by brief temperature rises.

Upon inspection of the careful observations of sexual rhythmicity reported by Itô (1952c, 1953, 1954a), Park (1961), and Park et al. (1965), it appears that the higher proportions of such gonadic polyps observed at any point in time in warm cultures or after temperature rises might really represent, or be interpreted as, a sort of "gapers' block" effect in the cyclic processes. Under such conditions, each animal, repeatedly drifting in and out of sexuality, seems to develop gonads more frequently and linger longer each time in the sexual condition. In a culture or population, this would result in a greater incidence of sexual animals at any single moment in such conditions. In cooler conditions, or after temperature declines, the reverse occurs.

As an analogy, it might be considered that the probability one will find that the compressor motor of an air conditioner is working at any given moment depends mostly on the temperature of the room and the setting of the thermostat. Although the compressor works in cycles, the opening of a nearby window on a hot day will cause the compressor to work most of the time. If the room contains a dozen such air conditioners, an observer would see an increased incidence of functioning compressors if the window were opened. Here, the presence of gonads in warm-crisis hydras is represented by functioning compressors. For each species, adaptation has set the thermostats.

5. Sexual Stimuli Other Than Temperature and Photoperiod

In the preceding arguments, it is not denied that factors other than temperature and photoperiod also can induce sexuality in hydras. However, some of these other reported factors (crowding, stagnation, "halos" in soft agar, etc.) probably have more meaning in confined laboratory cultures and in morphogenic investigations than they do in natural limnetic situations.

Additional effective factors (regarding O_2, CO_2, pH, etc.), on the other hand, seem to include some of those unfavorable phenomena previously listed as selecting factors for sexuality in hydras. But, in considering this latter group of factors, one might paraphrase the cliché which observes that it is not the best practice to delay closing a barn door until some of the livestock already have been lost. Natural selection usually results in organisms "wiser" than that.

6. Adaptation vs. Distribution

Adaptation, of course, does not by itself specify distribution. Rather, it is lack of adaptation which determines the inability of a species to successfully invade certain environments.

The hypotheses here presented deny neither the ability of cold-crisis hydras to exist in many ponds and streams, even southern ones, nor the ability of warm-crisis populations to succeed in certain northern lakes. What is predicted by these arguments is that cold-crisis species generally would be excluded from limnetic bodies subject to long, warm, drought-related crises in which conditions in all accessible locations became lethal, and that warm-crisis populations would be unsuccessful in northern ponds and lakes in which unviable situations, inescapable by plankters, occur under winter's cover of ice. Such predictions are consonant with all field reports of which the author is aware.

Hydras adapted to one type of situation may succeed but seem to behave curiously in another. A few authors (see review by Park et al., 1965), for example, have reported that sexual specimens of warm-crisis hydras have been found in nature in the spring, during conditions not at all like those of drought crises. In the spring, however, pond-water temperatures generally rise. A warm-crisis population using temperature as an important sexual cue might have difficulty discriminating between a vernal warm-up and an impending drought.

One can speculate about many methods by which hydras might become dispersed. Rivers empty into lakes. Lakes are drained by rivers.

Eggs or polyps may cling to parts of snails, crayfish, birds (etc.) or be ingested and thus be transported to new environments. Whether such hydras achieve success in such new environments, however, depends on local crises and hydrid defenses.

C. DEPRESSION

Here, arguments will be presented to support the tenth, eleventh, and twelfth proposals listed in Section I.

1. Temporary Warm Crises

We must now consider certain kinds of temporary natural crises for which the hydrid mechanisms discussed previously do not, by themselves, seem to supply adequate defenses. Earlier, situations were described in which hydras can be exposed to relatively brief elevations of temperature which, while not drought-related, can last a day or more. Such elevated temperatures, even though accompanied by no other critical phenomena, would be expected to produce metabolic consequences detrimental to hydras.

As Slobodkin (1964a) has suggested, for example, the tendencies of various species of hydras to exhibit different characteristic body sizes is evidence that, for a particular species of *Hydra*, being somewhat larger or smaller is advantageous. Although the length and weight of hydras is highly variable, it is obvious upon inspection that, other conditions being equal, hydras of certain species simply are bigger than others. If there is selection for body size in a species (such as the need to be large enough to engulf certain kinds of prey), then it would seem that such polyps, exposed for several days to elevated temperatures, might be in some difficulty. The expectedly high metabolic rates would cause the animal to shrink.

In cases where elevated temperatures persist long enough, planktonic escape would seem to be one kind of adaptive response. This option has been discussed earlier. In many similar crises, however, planktonic escape would not appear possible. In shallow water, for example, the possibility of planktonic descent to cooler water might be eliminated. Also, on the warm, lee side of a pond in summer, planktonic transport against the wind-driven water movement could not occur. In addition, mass hydrid departure from normally favorable attachment sites would not seem to be a strategically adaptive response to the more temporary warm crises.

Yet, no other defense against such crises has been mentioned here for cold-crisis hydras such as *H. oligactis*. In the case of warm-crisis polyps, sexuality might seem to be a possible answer, since the persistence of elevated temperature for more than a day or two would, by earlier arguments, influence a significant proportion of the population to become sexual, as more and more individual morphogenic cycles came around to the gonadic phase. The thought, however, of a warm-crisis population or "colony," spending so much energy and time on the sexual process, in response to any temperature rise lasting a couple of days or more (often resulting from little more than a random wind change and survivable by asexual polyps) should not have great appeal to those who study adaptive mechanisms in nature.

In an attempt to answer these kinds of problems, an additional defense mechanism of hydras will be suggested next.

2. Deprestivation

It is proposed that "depression" in hydras is a process which can reduce energetic expenditures in temporary 'warm" crises, that in cold-crisis hydras it represents the only warm-crisis defense other than planktonic escape, that in warm-crisis species it brings many more polyps through temporary misfortune than sexual reproduction possibly could (and does not entail the loss of potentially precious postcrisis time which otherwise would be required for embryonic development), and that chances of hydrid persistence through certain temporary crises other than thermal also are improved by this mechanism.

When temperatures rise, most poikilotherms demonstrate the well-known logarithmic increase in standard metabolic rate, usually up to a temperature level close to the lethal one. As known by anyone who cultures hydras, however, a sufficient temperature rise, especially a rapid one, often has the result that most, or all, of the polyps in a culture become depressed.

As Hyman (1928) first demonstrated, and as a number of other authors (Turner, 1950; Burnett, 1961; and others) have discussed, a depressed *Hydra* is an animal exhibiting reduced metabolism. Hyman demonstrated this by observing the length of time required for low concentrations of potassium cyanide to produce death in depressed (versus nondepressed) *H. ogligactis*. The depressed animals survived the chemical crisis longer, and their better resistance to the cyanide was interpreted as evidence of their lowered metabolic rates.

There has been occasional speculation that depression, as first suggested by Hyman (1928), may represent a form of senescence in hydras. In view of the present arguments, however, it is proposed that depression, in temporary crises, would be described better as a functional analog of estivation. A depressed hydra is less vulnerable and is wasting less metabolic energy during a temporary crisis than is a nondepressed animal. Thus, the term "deprestivation" is used here to distinguish such a defensive role from a second kind of function apparently performed by depression, to be discussed shortly.

In addition to being aided through temporary thermal crises, a depressed *Hydra*, as Hyman (1928), Burnett (1971), and others have found, generally is more resistant to a number of other potentially harmful environmental factors than is a nondepressed animal. Crowding, stagnation, anoxia, noxious chemicals, brief desiccation, and other factors, all of which seem unfavorable, can elicit depression, and a healthy polyp placed in a noxious culture dish containing deprestivating animals often dies within 1 hour. As was suggested for factors influencing sexuality, some of these effects may have important significance in nature, others may have meaning primarily in the artificial confinement of a culture bowl or in investigations on the cellular level.

It is the general observation of the author that in the case of temperature and a few other variables of probable ecological significance, relatively rapid, acute onsets of conditions here judged unfavorable tend to produce more deprestivating than sexual animals in warm-crisis species. The converse is true when onsets of such conditions are somewhat more gradual. Of course, rapid onsets would seem more characteristic of the types of temporary crises previously described than of prolonged drought situations. Both deprestivation and sexuality, however, can be produced in warm-crisis hydras by both categories of stimulus.

Crisis onsets which are too rapid can not be handled even by deprestivation. In fact, the author currently is employing deprestivation features and death as assay criteria in an attempt to develop simple procedures by which *H. oligactis* may be employed in field-station or in-plant rapid bioassays of certain trace metals to which these animals are hypersensitive.

If the unfavorable conditions (thermal, chemical, or desiccatory) producing deprestivation persist long enough (depending on degree of crisis), a deprestivating polyp shows other features besides reduced metabolism. First, the tentacles become reduced or lost. In overcrowded or noxious culture dishes, as well as in the lowest effective metal concentrations in the bioassays mentioned above, it frequently is observed that reduction of tentacles begins at the tips and moves proximad. This results in shortened tentacles bearing large balls of sloughing cells, commonly called "clubs." At certain higher metal concentrations (varying between metals), quick tentacle autotomy is observed. Here, tentacles constrict proximally and are pinched off the animal, usually within 1 hour after exposure to a medium containing an effective metal concentration.

It is proposed that an effect of such tentacle clubbing or autotomy is the reduction of that surface of the polyp in contact with an unfavorable environment *without* the metabolic rate requirements which would be involved in muscular contraction. Similarly, if those conditions producing deprestivation are sufficiently acute or persist long enough, a *Hydra*'s body column begins to exhibit a feathery floc, and the animal eventually recedes into a small lump. Furthermore, the mucus which previously had covered the entire, healthy animal becomes much thicker when covering only the small, depressed lump (Burnett, 1971), thus furnishing additional apparent protection.

Another attractive feature of deprestivation, however, is that if the environmental situation improves, a *Hydra* can recover rapidly from such deprestivation and begin budding, without loss of time which may be precious in variable habitats. Deprestivating animals can recover more quickly than can sexual animals, and, of course, there is no fair contest between recovery times of deprestivating hydras and encysted embryos. Furthermore, it has been observed (Burnett, 1971) that a polyp in the lumplike advanced stage of deprestivation shows a high cell density and contains all cell types necessary to begin budding, often without additional feeding, once conditions improve.

Thus, deprestivation in hydras would appear to be a mechanistic answer to temporary crises.

3. Sexual Depression

Sexual hydras, of both warm- and cold-crisis species, typically also are depressed hydras. Depression in the latter kind of species in icy water, of course, could not represent deprestivation. Rather, a second functional role of depression, that of aiding the sexual process, is seen in hydras.

The mechanism is a risky one. Brien and Reniers-Decoen (1949) have called sexuality in cold-crisis hydras a "metabolic crisis," meaning that a sexual animal is a sick animal. Burnett and Diehl (1964) have postulated that "complete sexuality" means death for hydras. These authors, of course, were referring to the entire sexual process, which includes not only the morphogenesis of gonads, but also the onset of depression. Cold-crisis hydras usually do not feed in the cold. Tentacles shorten, and stenoteles do not discharge effectively. Few or no nematocysts are formed (since interstitial cells are forming gametes). Many such animals enter advanced stages of depression and die.

In spite of the risk, however, a reasonable amount of depression might be expected to help the sexual process in hydras, as is implicit in the discussions of Burnett and Diehl (1964). The resultant metabolic rate reductions in sexual animals, both warm- and cold-crisis types, seem to have the morphogenic side effect of slowing rates of cell movement, thereby giving the gonads more time to develop and perform their function before they are sloughed at the base of the animal.

In short; there may be good reasons for depression to accompany sexuality. The observed frequent association of these two phenomena probably can be considered good evidence of adaptive value to such an association. And there is no apparent reason why a physiological process, such as depression, might not be used for more than one good purpose (sexual depression as well as deprestivation).

By analogy, a tense hospital patient may be helped by taking one sedative, or even two or three, but there comes a point at which too much "help" is lethal. "Complete sexuality," as described by Burnett and Diehl (1964), would seem to represent an overdose.

4. Physiological Cycles

Even in asexual hydras, there appear to be cycles of depression. Turner (1950) studied this in detail, a number of authors have since commented upon it, and those who culture hydras are not strangers to the "mysterious" appearances and disappearances of depressed polyps. It seems possible that a suitably adjusted version of the air-conditioner analogy used earlier for sexual cycles might also be illustrative here, with respect to the relation between depression cycles and point-in-time observations of the incidence of depressed animals in cultures.

There appear also to be cycles in rates of bud production in hydras, other influences being controlled as much as possible. Such cycles have been studied by Turner (1950) and Itô (1956) and should be obvious from the simple fact that even under the best conditions, budding hydras do not overwhelm lakes or laboratories.* It seems entirely possible that in such budding cycles, one may witness physiological events which, if expressed in greater amplitude, better synchrony, or, simply, other ways, might result in cycles of depression, or even of sexuality.

On the level of the population, the reported lack of phase synchrony of such cycles between individual animals seems adaptive. If any obvious environmental variable were capable of synchronizing the phases of individuals, then populations of these animals, or large segments of populations, would be denied the variety of potential response that seems to give such populations the capacity to survive any type of crisis (or series of temporary crises) encountered. Although the proportions of planktonic, budding, deprestivating, and sexual hydras in a population seem

---

* Were an asexual hydrid clone under ideal conditions to double itself even every 3 days (a rate slower than reported in some short-term studies), a single *Hydra* should be expected to give rise to more than 1 million polyps within 2 months! Beyond that, expectations would be staggering. The author knows of no one who has experienced such luck in raising hydras.

to be adaptively attuned, through mechanisms proposed earlier, to environmental conditions, it is the variety which seems to provide security against mistakes.

An asexual, deprestivating, warm-crisis polyp, for example, might find it difficult to develop gonads, at least while deprestivating. If the population were synchronously deprestivating, and if the warm crisis turned out to be a long one, chances of survival would be low. Similarly, if planktonic dispersal turned out to be the best way to meet a particular crisis, neither deprestivating nor sexual animals would be able to contribute as much as would asexual animals. Also, a sexual animal is not able to recover and bud as quickly and prolifically as a polyp recently out of deprestivation. In any case, should such a warm crisis turn out to be temporary, the less gonad-formation energy expended on that crisis by the population, the better. After all, there are important planktonic colonists to be produced; there are new gonads to be made for possible future crises; and in terms of metabolic maintenance energy, who knows when the next meal is coming?

Therefore, although such variety in hydrid responses may complicate the tasks of investigators, it seems to be of great value to the animals in nature. And in hydras, at least, some of the well-known variability which characterizes biological material thus seems to have adaptive significance.

Such general considerations need not be limited to hydras. Although hydras may seem more "naked" than most animals, all animals are naked (vulnerable) in one way or another. When biologists study behavioral and physiological responses of animals to their environments, interpretive emphasis typically is given to phenomena seen in most of the individuals studied. Often, attempts then are made to describe the apparent advantages of such phenomena. However, unless a given mechanistic response is *always* advantageous under eliciting conditions, variability of response within a population becomes adaptive. Without such variability, a single anomalous situation in which a normally advantageous response has lethal results, for example, could result in population extinction. Thus, although 95% confidence tests are useful to investigators, it seems that "the other 5%" may provide "insurance" for natural populations.

D. PROXIMITY, A SEXUAL IMPERATIVE

Under this heading, the task of justifying proposals 13 and 14 will be undertaken.

1. The Problem of "Dioecious Hermaphrodites"

Most taxonomic publications on hydras, as well as many experimental reports, have included information about the separation, or lack of separation, of sexes in the hydrid species described. Some species of *Hydra,* such as *H. carnea, H. parva,* and *H. viridis,* for examples, show obvious hermaphroditism (see Itô, 1955b,c; Forrest, 1963a; Burnett and Diehl, 1964). Within a single clone containing sexual animals of these species, one may observe some polyps bearing testes, others with ovaries, and still others bearing both types of gonads.

However, there are other well-studied species, such as *H. littoralis, H. oligactis,* and *H. pseudoligactis,* in which it has been observed that the animals in a single clone tend to be all of one sex (Hyman, 1929; Forrest, 1963a; Burnett and Diehl, 1964). Such species usually have been considered "dioecious."

Loomis' statement (1959, p. 148) that ". . . males and females are quite distinct in most species of hydra, all the buds of a male becoming males, and all the buds of a female becoming females" has been shown by several authors [see discussions by Forrest (1963a) and Burnett and Diehl (1964)] to be unjustified. Rather, even in supposedly dioecious species, animals of both sexes have been obtained from asexual offspring of a single animal, usually by appropriate manipulation of culture conditions.

Burnett and Diehl (1964, p. 245) contended, on these and other (morphogenic) grounds that ". . . all species of hydra are basically hermaphroditic . . ." In morphogenic considerations, such an outlook seems to be the only view consonant with the evidence.

Whether or not such an outlook, by itself, is productive in ecological considerations, however, is another matter. Few reports of sex reversal in so-called dioecious species have noted spontaneous reversals. In order to produce reversals in such animals, some environmental condition (e.g., temperature, ions, day length, crowding, food, etc.) had to be altered, either by the investigators or by independent events.

It seems that although *Hydra* may be basically hermaphroditic, the sex displayed depends, at least in large part, on the environmental history of the animal. Such a point was implicit in the considerations of Burnett and Diehl (1964). No matter what past event or mechanism causes members of a dioecious clone to tend toward one sex or the other, the animals do show such real tendencies. Under identical culture conditions, they display them.

Successful sexual reproduction, of course, requires temporal and spatial proximity of opposite gametes. With dependable hermaphrodites, this presents no problem. In species with dioecious tendencies, however, polyps which are together in time and space in nature would seem likely to experience similar environmental influences. Thus, members of male "colonies" (see earlier footnote, Section III,F) usually would become males. Members of female colonies would tend to become females. Consequently, some new questions must be raised about the successful meeting of hydrid eggs and sperms in nature.

2. Sexual Proximity in Time

In considering the requisite "togetherness" in the making of zygotes, one first may consider questions about synchrony of available, viable gametes. In these regards, several gonadic features of hydras are noteworthy.

Almost invariably, hydras of a particular species, whether hermaphroditic or dioecious, bear more testes than ovaries (Hyman, 1938; Kanaev, 1952; and others). It is not difficult to understand why such a situation might be beneficial. Much effort and energy goes into the production of an ovary, and each ovary bears only one yolk-endowed egg. A hydrid egg, furthermore, is a very perishable cell. Its period of viability lasts only about a day after loss of its epidermal covering exposes it, and in some species, this period of viability is measured only in hours (Hyman, 1929; McConnell, 1938b; and others). If not fertilized within this time, the ovum perishes, wasted.

Each testis, on the other hand, contains a large number of sperms. Each sperm represents a considerably smaller energetic investment than does an ovum. The male gametes have been reported functional (see Kanaev, 1952) as long as 3 days after their release, although this time probably varies greatly with species and conditions. In addition, while a mature testis releases most of its sperms soon after rupturing, a significant number of the gametes can be observed to linger for a time within the testicular sac, trickling out slowly. Testes generally are produced in spiral sequence on the column of a *Hydra* (Burnett, 1961; Park *et al.,* 1964; and others), and as they move proximad, their maturation and subsequent release of sperms occurs in temporal sequence.

Thus, it seems from the preceding considerations that gametic synchrony in a colony of *Hydra* might involve fairly continuous elaboration of sperms, blanketing the times when susceptible ova become locally available.

Although most time-series studies of sexuality in hydras have included observations only of the times of initial appearance of gonads, the sexual cycles described by Itô (1954a) and Park (1961) also provide information about the duration of the gonads. Itô, moreover, carefully recorded the *functional* periods (i.e., intervals of sperm release or viable ovum availability) within each phase of cyclic gonad formation in isolated *H. magnipapillata* (a warm-crisis *Hydra,* considered dioecious) cultured identically and simultaneously. Inspection of these data, especially those of Itô (1954a), reinforces the previous suggestion that times of sperm availability greatly exceed and "surround" times of ovum availability. In fact, had all of Itô's isolated "male" and "female" hydras been in the same bowl, and behaved in the same way, not a single egg in all of his observations would have gone unfertilized.

These considerations suggest an adaptive value to Burnett's (1966) placement of testes above ova in the morphogenic hierarchy proposed in his model of growth in *Hydra*. In this model, testes are considered to result from a higher "stimulator-to-inhibitor" ratio (see Chapters 4 and 5 of this volume), and a generally higher metabolic state, than do ovaries. Here we encounter a conclusion, reached in morphogenic considerations, which makes ecological sense.

As environmental conditions worsen or otherwise mechanistically indicate the increasing probability of an approaching crisis, more hydras make gonads. The first gonads formed are testes. Were the gonads' hierarchical positions reversed, ova often might be produced when no sperms were present, resulting in great energetic waste. Data from the field observations of Miller (1936) in Douglas Lake show that his *H. oligactis* population must have "realized" this. As winter approached, the water got colder and the days grew shorter. At first, all sexual animals Miller found bore testes. Only after functional testes were well-present were any ovaries seen in the population. Adshead *et al.* (1963) reported similar observations in Canadian *H. pseudoligactis*.

At the population level, the production and availability of hydrid ova seem to be precious events, temporally surrounded by those of sperms.

3. Sexual Proximity in Space

It was argued earlier that although dioecious hydras may basically be hermaphroditic, they nevertheless show definite dioecious tendencies, environmental experiences being equal. To this, one may add the observation that some of the most successful (i.e., widely distributed) hydras, such as *H. littoralis, H. oligactis,* and *H. pseudoligactis,* show such dioecious tendencies.

On a single natural support, attached polyps of dioecious species, close enough in space to be considered for potential sexual interaction, are experiencing similar environmental conditions. But the buds of a polyp of this type (perhaps the former planker who started the colony) tend, under similar conditions, to be of one sex. Therefore, it might seem that it largely would be left to chance that animals with opposite sexual tendencies will settle or have settled on, or moved to, the same part of the same support.

Such a possibility should not be appealing to anyone who ever has heard of a salmon, a catadromous eel, or a palolo worm. Spatial proximity of opposite sexes certainly is as necessary for successful sex as is synchrony. One might hope to find a mechanism more reliable than mere chance to achieve this.

But, to borrow from an old phrase, when more adaptive organisms are possible, nature usually produces them. It is taught even in elementary biology courses that hermaphroditism suits sessile organisms and that dioecious organisms generally move around (unless they have the energetic resources to attempt near saturation of the local environment with gametes). When dioecious hydras are considered, this rule ought to cause some pondering.

As discussed earlier in this section, however, hydras are not always sessile. The comprehensive field studies (Welch and Loomis, 1924; Miller, 1936; Bryden, 1952; Griffing, 1965) of *H. oligactis,* cited throughout this section, reported mass summer disappearances here previously described as planktonic migrations. Except for the Welch and Loomis (1924) study, which was conducted only in summer months, these reports also described other mass disappearances, even more pronounced than those in summer. Such occurred in autumn. And in the studies of Miller (1936) and Bryden (1952), artificial supports suspended in midwater showed relative maxima of planktonic hydrid abundance occurring concurrently with the autumnal disappearances of *Hydra* from plant supports.

It is proposed that such autumn migrations can result in sexual aggregations of *H. oligactis.*

Any of a number of behavioral, physiological, or physical events can cause hydras to leave supports and become planktonic. Since the winds and currents affecting planktonic aggregation and settling areas are variable, it would appear that in times of favorable environmental conditions, a slow, steady output of plankters would be the strategic practice. Such a slow output might lessen intraspecific competition and, more probably, would increase the number of new locations settled by colonists.

During the autumn migrations, however, it would seem important that a maximized proportion of the dioecious population becomes planktonic almost simultaneously, so that these animals will tend to settle together. In addition to any possible behavioral or physiological mechanisms which might be of influence here, three autumnal planktonic synchronizers are suggested. First, many plant supports, such as the bulrushes and *Dianthera* plants which were the principal summer supports of *H. oligactis* in Douglas and Kirkpatrick's lakes, respectively, die soon after the first frost. This would produce a considerable number of plankters in a relatively short time interval. Second, as noted in *H. vulgaris* by Mast (1903), hydrid adhesion to substrates may be markedly reduced in cold temperatures. Third, autumn frequently is a time of storms and generally foul weather. Such weather can produce violent wave action. Waves make plankters.

It is not suggested in these arguments that cold-crisis hydras involved in such autumn movements do all of their aggregating on the bottom. Evidence of bottom hydras at any time of year is scarce. It should be realized, however, that two of the same reasons previously suggested for the paucity of observed planktonic hydras might also apply here. First, very few bottom samples have been taken. Second, if there are aggregations, there would be discontinuous benthic distribution. An additional factor also is suggested: Considering sexual depression and unfavorable conditions, there probably is high mortality in such hydras. A dead *Hydra* quickly becomes a decomposed *Hydra*.

Bryden's (1952) largest autumn and winter collections, on the other hand, were from willow twigs and roots in undercut areas along the shore, places where *H. oligactis* was not significantly present in summer. Bryden also found no sexual animals, but he was studying a cold-crisis *Hydra* in a lake that had no real cold crises. Kirkpatrick's Lake, in Tennessee, does not freeze over in the mild southern winters.

In dioecious, warm-crisis hydras, any migrations and aggregations of major sexual significance would, of course, require methods of synchronous plankter production which differ from those suggested above specifically for cold-crisis hydras. No specific suggestions are made here in such regard. Once plankters or floaters are produced, however, hydras in streams, at least, should have no trouble being aggregated. As Łomnicki and Slobodkin (1966) observed, large numbers of *H. littoralis* have been found below areas of roiled water in streams.

It should be evident that there are possibilities for sexual isolation and speciation implicit in the preceding arguments. Hydras with behavioral and physiological differences, proliferated asexually, might be isolated spatially during sexuality as a result of these differences. Griffing's (1965) demonstrations of differential movements of *H. oligactis* and *H. pseudoligactis* populations in Pickerel Lake show this possibility nicely.

The sexual process in hydras represents their only hope of persistence through certain kinds of crises, and it represents a considerable investment of energy. It would be less than adaptive were either to be wasted. By whatever mechanisms, the temporal and spatial proximity necessary for successful sexual reproduction is achieved.

E. THE EMPATHETIC APPROACH

Teleological devices may have been detected by mechanistic purists reading the preceding arguments. Such devices, of course, have been employed carefully. Slobodkin (1964a) has suggested that while teleological discussions may not themselves be rigorous, they certainly can be considered logically defensible if resolved into two components: (1) a description of the phenomena observed to occur when the animal encounters certain situations; and (2) a statement relating such phenomena to the organism's chances of survival. In this section, the author is attempting to convey a large number of ideas in a relatively brief treatment. Such tactics save words.

Basically, though, the approach taken here has been to propose that when hydras are known to survive certain crises, it almost is tautological that they must possess mechanisms which enable them to do so. Empathy can be heuristic.

V. Energetic Capital Investments of Hydrid Populations

In the preceding discussions of this chapter, several considerations have been made about energetics. A few things still need to be mentioned, however, regarding hydras and energy. Here will be discussed the last two points proposed in Section I.

A. STUDIES OF POPULATION ENERGETICS

1. Population Efficiency

In attempts to investigate ecosystem energetics, the approaches taken by ecologists have included studies of the energetics of specific components of such systems. Thus, "population energetics" has received much attention. One such approach, briefly stated, involves the idea that the food energy ingested per unit of the population may be used for two purposes: metabolic energy to maintain the organisms, and energy used for growth of the population.

In certain simple situations, such as with asexual hydras in laboratory cultures, the former (input) energetic quantity often is considered to equal the sum of the latter two (investment) quantities, per unit of the population. "Population efficiency," or the "ecological efficiency" of a population, may represent either "the ratio of growth rate to ingestion rate of a population" (Schroeder, 1969), or "the percentage of energy consumed as food that is converted into new protoplasm" (Slobodkin, 1962), or "the ratio of yield to a predator to the portion of input utilized in producing that yield" (Slobodkin, 1960). These are specific (i.e., perunit) quantities, often expressed as percentages. Most authors label well which of these definitions they are using, but the three are somewhat similar anyway, since the basic difference between the former two and the latter one lies only in whether some predator is considered to eat what the population has grown. Of course, when the laboratory investigator acts as a "predator," equilibrium densities in cultures are affected.

With most kinds of animals, these population efficiency quantities seem to be reliably on the order of 10 to 15%. Thus, if the predator is considered, one sees basis for the well-known observation that there usually is a one-order-of-magnitude loss in energy at each trophic level in a "simple food chain." Feeders at each level use about 85 or 90% of what they eat for metabolic maintenance.

With hydras, the situation is not as simple. Ecological efficiencies of hydrid populations in laboratory cultures have been reported (Slobodkin, 1964b; Stiven, 1965; Schroeder, 1969; and others) to vary widely, ranging from 7 to 37% in various species of brown hydras (and over 60% in green hydras).

In considering steady-state densities in confined laboratory hydrid populations, however, certain authors (Slobodkin, 1964b; Stiven, 1965; Griffing, 1965; Schroeder, 1969) apparently were unaware of, or chose not to consider, the possible influences of a growth-inhibitory substance (see Burnett, 1961, 1966; Davis, 1966; and chapters 4 and 5 of this volume) which is produced by asexual hydras and which affects confined culture media. In fact, the authors attempted to interpret equilibrium densities in the cultures on the bases of food, temperature, and maintenance energy, when the steady-state levels involved several animals per milliliter. Thus, one might expect some confusion.

These criticisms should not be taken as a suggestion that data from such studies should be discarded. Rather, one simply needs to exercise care in their interpretation.

2. Strategic Self-Denial

In the preceding laboratory studies, asexual hydras seemed to produce buds almost "foolishly" at times, at the cost of much energetic self-denial. As Griffing (1965) and Stiven (1965) observed, elevated temperatures and starvation both have the effect of reducing the sizes of these animals. Griffing remarked that smaller animals have less surface area and lower maintenance requirements. However, it should be realized that per gram, such animals have higher requirements and greater surface. At any rate, the plausible arguments of Slobodkin (1964a), cited earlier, suggest that it is adaptive for polyps to maintain a certain size. Yet, in the higher temperatures employed by Griffing and Stiven, their shrinking animals continued to deny themselves considerable maintenance energy and invest it in the forming of buds. In fact, in these hydras, rates of bud production generally were higher in elevated temperatures. Recently, Park and Ortmeyer (1972) have corroborated such observations and have shown also that in *H. littoralis,* an abrupt temperature rise produces a temporary overshoot in budding rate, as compared with that of animals acclimated to the new, higher temperature. An abrupt temperature drop has the opposite effect.

It is suggested that such findings of Griffing (1965), Stiven (1965), and Park and Ortmeyer (1972) support the hypothesis of strategic planktonic dispersal in hydras. In nature, buds can become planktonic colonists which represent increased survival probability for the population. Were these buds to remain in nature in the immediate vicinity of the parent, such self-denying budding activity would seem curious. Considering the buds as colonists, however, it seems most adaptive.

An additional hydrid response, observed regularly by the author in the trace-metal bioassays mentioned earlier, seems pertinent here. At certain metal concentrations, usually the same as those eliciting tentacle autotomy, most mature (tentacled) *H. oligactis* buds detach from their parents within 1 or 2 hours after exposure to test media. Such a response not only effects an additional quick surface reduction for the animals, but it also seems consonant with the hypothesis that newly detached buds are planktonic colonists in a hydrid population and, in this case, represent a possible method for evading a chemical crisis.

Griffing (1965) and Stiven (1965) observed that, in general, the larger the parent polyp, the larger the buds produced. Such observations fit with arguments presented here. If the parent can afford it, it is a good idea to endow a potential colonist with as much energy as possible. If times are bad, however, one does as well as one can. Many planktonic colonists will die, of course, but those which survive and succeed would seem to make the asexual energetic investment worthwhile, if the population is to persist. Such arguments, of course, imply group selection (cf. Łomnicki and Slobodkin, 1966).

3. Population Maintenance Energy

It is proposed that when energetic quantities are considered by ecologists, the simpler models lose applicability to certain kinds of animals, such as hydras. There is more to "maintenance" than that energy used metabolically by the organisms. A "population maintenance energy" term might be thought about in such cases. All animals sacrifice some potential maintenance energy to produce offspring, so that the population can persist. In asexual hydras, however, this expenditure gains additional meaning, since such offspring seem to be of paramount importance to the persistence of these "naked" polyps. In the simpler kinds of energetic considerations described previously, this population maintenance energy term is hidden in the population's more conventional growth term. The

task of adding apples (metabolic energy) and oranges (population maintenance energy), however, will not be undertaken here.

B. POPULATION CAPITALISM

Now that most of the basic pertinent arguments have been presented,
it should be evident to the reader that there is considerable interaction
among hypotheses proposed in this work. To illustrate such interaction,
an extended analogy will be employed. The following analogy may be
amusing, but it seems remarkably consistent with hypotheses proposed
in this chapter. Slobodkin (1964a; and other publications) has found
heuristic value in "playing the game" of evolution. With hydras, the
author prefers to "play the market."

One might consider an imaginary investor in control of a natural population of hydras. The investor's name is "A. Daptive Mechanisms." The
investor has a variable amount of capital resources (total population
energy) to invest. The amount of his capital depends both on market
fluctuations (environmental conditions) and his investment decisions.
While his ultimate goal (Slobodkin, 1964a) is not the maximizing of profit,
but rather the avoidance of losing all of his capital (population extinction),
the two goals are not always easily separable (with naked polyps).

The investor wants to maximize his capital gains (population growth)
in a bull market (favorable environmental conditions), if and only if this
does not leave him vulnerable to losing all of his capital, should the advent
of a bear market (a crisis, temporary or prolonged) catch him unaware.

To minimize risk, therefore, he diversifies, He has the options of de-
ploying his resources into blue chip stocks (attached, asexual, parent
polyps), with somewhat limited growth potential but proved ability to
produce dividends; glamor issues (planktonic colonists), which involve
greater risk but may, if a fortunate decision has been made (favorable
area colonized), show spectacular capital gains per successful unit; cash
reserves (deprestivating animals), which are not productive but are good,
liquid assets with which to wait out temporary market setbacks; and
bonds (encysted embryos), which are safe from stock market disasters,
are less liquid than cash, and yield only on maturity.

All of our investor's holdings are convertible, and he continuously
appraises the market outlook, in order to make the best of any financial
climate and retain a certain amount of security. He is a wise investor and
has learned (through natural selection) to recognize many of the danger
signs (temperature, photoperiod, etc.) of an approaching bear market.
Further, he usually, though not always, is able to predict whether such
will be a big bear market (winter or drought) or a little bear market (temporary crisis). If he thinks the latter is coming, he tends to stop buying

glamor issues and accumulates cash reserves. If he anticipates the former kind of crisis, he will pull capital out of his blue chips and glamor issues and purchase bonds. If a bull market looks very likely, he will put much of his capital into diverse glamor issues. In all market conditions, however, he maintains a balanced portfolio (population variability), or tries to.

The analogy could be carried further, but its heuristic value probably lies most in its creative use by the reader. There are few general phenomena discussed in this section which cannot be incorporated into the analogy. Perhaps this might lead one to wonder whether mutual fund managers, for example, might be wise, in making investment decisions, to study data not only from computers, but from *H. littoralis* populations as well. And, considering the ecological havoc wrought by *Homo sapiens* in quest of the quick profit, one wonders whether human capitalists also might benefit from the example of hydrid capitalists (the latter have been in business much longer).

It is primarily hoped, however, that "population capitalism" might be an analogy useful in attempts to understand hydras.

VI. Conclusion

This section has included a rather lengthy presentation of a hypothetical construct attempting to describe hydras in nature. Its length was considered necessary because it suggests some revisions in thinking, as well as the synthesis of many phenomena which gain significance when assembled and viewed as interacting components.

Every laboratory observer witnesses a number of curious phenomena from time to time. Under various conditions, some hydras move, some do not; some climb and float, some do not; some bud prolifically, some do not; some become depressed, some do not; some develop gonads, some do not; and so on.

The arguments here presented in preliminary form attempt to add meaning to such observations. It is acknowledged, not apologetically, that no topic has been covered with high resolution. One of the *raisons d'être* of ecologists is the identification of broad problems which then can be studied in detail by workers with more specific interests and talents. Thus, these hypotheses have been presented for general scrutiny by biologists (i.e., ecological jargon was avoided), who, it is hoped, might wish to participate in their testing and analysis.

These hypotheses may be accurately descriptive of hydras in nature, or they may not. However, they seem to fit, and were in fact generated from, data from many investigations. The proposals are testable, and it is hoped that they may prove productive.

Almost a decade ago, Burnett (1962, p. 27) noted the wisdom of Aristotle's remark that ". . . the object of philosophy is not the material elements, . . . but their combination and the totality of form . . . ." Burnett since has shown that such an outlook can be a productive stimulus if employed on the cellular level. It seems to have value at any level. Individually, most pieces of evidence employed in the preceding discussions cannot acquaint one with hydras in nature. Put together in a certain way, however, they seem to show how these simple animals, without much going for them structurally, have been able to achieve success through a beautiful mosaic of adaptive mechanisms.

The *Mona Lisa* is appreciated best from a bit of a distance.

References

Adshead, P., Mackie, G., and Paetkau, P. (1963). *Bull. Nat. Mus. Can.* **199**, 1.
Batha, J. V. (1971). Personal communication.
Beutler, R. (1933). *Z. Vergl. Physiol.* **18**, 718.
Bloom, W. (1963). *Proc. Indiana Acad. Sci.* **72**, 351.
Brien, P. (1953). *Biol. Rev.* **28**, 308.
Brien, P. (1970). Personal communication.
Brien, P., and Reniers-Decoen, M. (1949). *Bull. Biol. Fr. Belg.* **83**, 293.
Brien, P., and Reniers-Decoen, M. (1950). *Ann. Soc. Zool. Belg.* **81**, 33.
Brien, P., and Reniers-Decoen, M. (1951). *Ann. Soc. Zool. Belg.* **82**, 285.
Bryden, R. (1952). *Ecol. Monogr.* **22**, 45.
Burnett, A. L. (1971). Personal communication
Burnett, A. L. (1961). *J. Exp. Zool.* **146**, 21.
Burnett, A. L. (1962). *Symp. Soc. Stud. Develop. Growth* **20**, 27–52.
Burnett, A. L., and Diehl, N. (1964). *J. Exp. Zool.* **157**, 237.
Burnett, A. L. (1966). *Amer. Natur.* **100**, 165.
Carrick, L. (1956). Ph.D. Dissertation, Ohio State University, Columbus.
Clemens, W. (1922). *Science* **55**, 445.
Davis, L. (1966). *Nature (London)* **212**, 1215.
Ewer, R. (1947). *Proc. Zool. Soc. London* **117**, 207.
Ewer, R. (1948). *Proc. Zool. Soc. London* **118**, 226.
Forrest, H. (1959). *Amer. Midl. Natur.* **62**, 440.
Forrest, H. (1962). *Biol. Bull.* **122**, 343.
Forrest, H. (1963a). *Trans. Amer. Microsc. Soc.* **82**, 6.
Forrest, H. (1963b). *Ecology* **44**, 609.
Goetsch, W. (1921). *Biol. Zentralbl.* **41**, 414.
Griffing, T. (1965). Ph.D. Dissertation, University of Michigan, Ann Arbor.
Haase-Eichler, R. (1931). *Zool. Jahrb., Abt. Allg. Zool. Physiol. Tiere* **50**, 265.
Hudgins, B. (1931). *J. Amer. Water Works Ass.* **23**, 435.
Hyman, L. (1928). *Biol. Bull.* **54**, 65.
Hyman, L. (1929). *Trans. Amer. Microsc. Soc.* **48**, 242.
Hyman, L. (1930). *Trans. Amer. Microsc. Soc.* **49**, 322.
Hyman, L. (1931a). *Trans. Amer. Microsc. Soc.* **50**, 20.
Hyman, L. (1931b). *Trans. Amer. Microsc. Soc.* **50**, 303.

Hyman, L. (1938). *Amer. Mus. Nov.* **1003**, 1.
Hyman, L. (1940). "The Invertebrates. Protozoa through Ctenophora." Macmillan, New York.
Itô, T. (1952a). *Mem. Ehime Univ., Sect. 2* **1**, 33.
Itô, T. (1952b). *Mem. Ehime Univ., Sect. 2* **1**, 45.
Itô, T. (1952c). *Mem. Ehime Univ., Sect. 2* **1**, 53.
Itô, T. (1953). *Mem. Ehime Univ., Sect. 2* **1**, 333.
Itô, T. (1954a). *Jap. J. Zool.* **11**, 287.
Itô, T. (1954b). *Mem. Ehime Univ., Sect. 2, Ser. B* **2**, 51.
Itô, T. (1955a). *Sci. Rep. Tohoku Univ., Ser. 4* **21**, 78.
Itô, T. (1955b). *Bull. Mar. Biol. Sta. Asamushi, Tohoku Univ.* **7**, 120.
Itô, T. (1955c). *Mem. Ehime Univ., Sect. 2, Ser. B* **2**, 205.
Itô, T. (1956). *Mem. Ehime Univ., Sect. 2, Ser. B* **2**, 293.
Kanaev, I. (1952). "Hydra. Essays on the Biology of Fresh Water Polyps." Sov. Acad. Sci., Moscow (English translation edited by H. M. Lenhoff, 1969).
Kepner, W., and Miller, L. (1928). *Biol. Bull.* **54**, 524.
Kofoid, C. (1908). *Bull. Ill. Lab. Natur. Hist.* **8**, 1.
Lenhoff, H. (1967). *In* "The Chemistry of Learning" (W. C. Corning and S. C. Ratner, eds.), pp. 341–368. Plenum, New York.
Łomnicki, A., and Slobodkin, L. (1966). *Ecology* **47**, 881.
Loomis, W. (1959). *Sci. Amer.* **200**, 145.
McConnell, C. (1935). *Wilhelm Roux' Arch. Entwicklungsmech. Organismen* **132**, 763.
McConnell, C. (1938a). *Zool. Anz.* **123**, 161.
McConnell, C. (1938b). *Zool. Anz.* **124**, 321.
Marson, J. (1951). *Microscope* **8**, 144.
Mast, S. (1903). *Amer. J. Physiol.* **10**, 165.
Miller, D. (1936). *Trans. Amer. Microsc. Soc.* **55**, 123.
Moen, T. (1951). *Proc. Iowa Acad. Sci.* **58**, 501.
Needham, J., and Lloyd, J. (1916). "The Life of Inland Waters." Cornell Univ. Press, Ithaca, New York.
Park, H. (1961). *In* "The Biology of Hydra" (H. M. Lenhoff and W. Loomis, eds.), pp. 363–372. Univ. of Miami Press, Coral Gables, Florida.
Park, H., and Ortmeyer, A. (1972). *J. Exp. Zool.* **179**, 283.
Park, H., Mecca, C., and Ortmeyer, A. (1964). *Biol. Bull.* **126**, 121.
Park, H., Sharpless, N., and Ortmeyer, A. (1965). *J. Exp. Zool.* **160**, 247.
Robson, E. (1965). *Anim. Behav., Suppl.* **1**, 54.
Rulon, O., and Child, C. (1937). *Physiol. Zool.* **10**, 1.
Rushforth, N., Burnett, A. L., and Maynard, R. (1963). *Science* **139**, 760.
Schäffer, J. (1754). "Die Armpolypen im sussen Wasser um Regensburg." Regensburg (as cited in Kanaev, 1952).
Schroeder, L. (1969). *Ecology* **50**, 81.
Schulze, P. (1917). *Arch. Biontol.* **4**, 39.
Scourfield, D. (1901). *J. Quekett Microscop. Club* [2] **8**, 137.
Semal-Van Gansen, P. (1954). *Ann. Soc. Zool. Belg.* **85**, 187.
Shostak, S., Bisbee, J., Ashkin, C., and Tammariello, R. (1968). *J. Exp. Zool.* **169**, 423.
Slobodkin, L. (1960). *Amer. Natur.* **94**, 213.
Slobodkin, L. (1962). *Advan. Ecol. Res.* **1**, 69.
Slobodkin, L. (1964a). *Amer. Sci.* **52**, 342.
Slobodkin, L. (1964b). *J. Anim. Ecol.* **33**, Suppl., 131.
Slobodkin, L. (1965). *Amer. Sci.* **53**, 347.
Spangenberg, D., and Eakin, R. (1961). *J. Exp. Zool.* **147**, 259.

Stevenson, J., and Buchsbaum, R. (1961). *Science* **134,** 332.
Stiven, A. (1962). *Ecology* **43,** 173.
Stiven, A. (1965). *Res. Popul. Ecol.* **7,** 1.
Thorpe, W. (1956). "Learning and Instinct of Animals." pp. 168–172. Methuen, London.
Turner, C. (1950). *Biol. Bull.* **99,** 285.
Welch, P., and Loomis, H. (1924). *Trans. Amer. Microsc. Soc.* **43,** 203.
Wilson, E. (1891). *Amer. Natur.* **25,** 413.
Young, O. (1945). *Trans. Amer. Microsc. Soc.* **64,** 1.

PART III

POLARITY IN *HYDRA*

Probably more attention has been given to this area of *Hydra's* biology than any other. The same would be true of planarians or annelids. This is because the subject of polarity is innately tied in with the question of regeneration. Why does an animal, when excised through its body column, invariably regenerate a head at the most distal tip and a foot at its most proximal tip? The question alone is over two hundred years old.

In the following section the first discussion is on the one cell type, thought by many to control polarity. To investigators not working with *Hydra,* the cell would be called a neoblast, that is, a cell which never differentiated during normal embryogeny but remains as an embryonic reserve in the adult. In coelenterates, in *Hydra,* the cell is the interstitial cell or I-cell.

Finally, the question of polarity is examined from the holistic point of view. That is, organismic polarity is discussed.

CHAPTER 4

The Developmental Significance of Interstitial Cells during Regeneration and Budding

FRED A. DIEHL

I. Introduction

A. THE CONCEPT OF THE INTERSTITIAL CELL

The primary objective of this chapter is to examine the contribution of interstitial cells to the regenerative process in *Hydra*. (Also the role of interstitial cells in budding will be discussed briefly.) Two possible sources of the tissue comprising the regenerate have been suggested Some investigators stressed the role(s) played by differentiated cells such as epitheliomuscular cells and gastrodermal digestive cells in forming the regenerate, while others argued that interstitial cells alone participate in regeneration. The lack of information concerning the capacity of interstitial cells to differentiate into the specialized cell types of adult *Hydra* during normal growth has further confused the issue. Let us at this point examine in some detail the historical and current concepts regarding this one cell type which has been at the center of many discussions of cnidarian regeneration.

Visualized originally as the precursors of *Hydra* gametes, interstitial cells have occupied a dominent position in studies of coelenterate development. Kleinenberg (1872), who is given credit for the first description of these small, epidermally located cells, noted their morphological similarity to the precursor, or stem, cells of other animals and referred to them as embryonic. This was in order to contrast them to the other types of specialized cells of *Hydra* which carry out definite physiological functions such as digestion and secretion. These small, darkly staining cells with a prominent nucleus and nucleolus (Fig. 1) lie in the epidermis

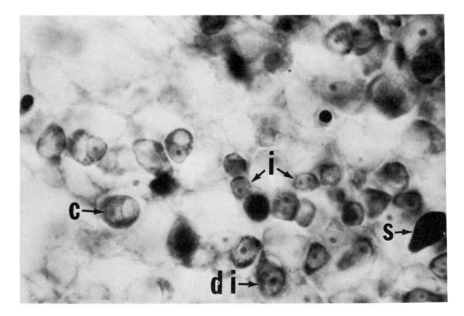

Fig. 1. Interstitial cells (i) of *Hydra* as revealed by whole mount staining with toluidine blue at pH 8. A differentiating interstitial cell (di), cnidoblast (c), and stenotele type of nematocyst (s) are also seen.

of *Hydra* and have been traced histologically as they differentiated into gametes (Kleinenberg, 1872; Schulze, 1918; Kanajew, 1930; Brien and Reniers-Decoen, 1950). Nussbaum (1887, 1907) was the first investigator to suggest that in addition to their role in perpetuating the germ cell line, interstitial cells may represent a reserve supply of somatic embryonic elements capable of transforming (differentiating) into adult cell types whenever needed during the processes of growth.

B. TOTIPOTENT EMBRYONIC CELLS AND THE I-CELL THEORY

Many specialized cells of *Hydra* are exhausted regularly by their activities. Digestive cells, gland cells, and stinging (cnidoblast) cells must be replaced periodically if the animal is to retain its size and integrity. Therefore Nussbaum's theory of an embryonic reserve of unspecialized cells which could constantly produce new elements seemed to explain the dynamics of tissue replacement. Brauer (1891) traced the development of interstitial cells as they differentiated into cnidoblast cells and as the latter in turn produced within their cytoplasm a stinging organelle, the nematocyst. This discovery added impetus to the notion that interstitial cells are uniquely responsible for growth and maintenance in the sense of cellular replacement and tissue repair. The I-cell theory, in essence, says that interstitial cells continually differentiate into all other cell types of the organism and in fact are the only vegetative elements active in the processes of growth. In addition to Nussbaum and Brauer, this view was championed by various authors including Lang (1892, 1894), who studied growth phenomena as depicted in the budding process, Hadzi (1910), and others. One of the major supporting arguments for the I-cell theory centered around the lack of mitoses in cells other than interstitial cells. In order to continually grow, bud, or regenerate, *Hydra* must replenish its stock of cells from some source and these early investigators concluded that only the interstitial cells seemed to divide in sufficient rates to account for cellular replacements. A few cellular divisions were noted in differentiated cells by Schneider (1890), Downing (1905), and Kanajew (1930), but these observations were not considered to be of great significance and were offset by the discoveries of Gelei (1924), who showed that gland cells can arise from I-cells. Other similar reports tended to reinforce the idea that I-cells are the primary progenitors of differentiated cells. Schulze (1918) carried arguments for the I-cell theory to the greatest extreme, stating that interstitial cells localized in various parts of the *Hydra* possess unique form-determining properties, being capable of forming, or restoring (in the case of regeneration), particular regions of the body. Accordingly, some I-cells are destined to give rise to the adult cells which make up one part of the animal such as the hypostome, other cells form the gastric region, and other special groups of interstitial cells are responsible for production of each distinct morphological area.

In summary, a dichotomy of opinion grew out of early histological studies as to the role of interstitial cells and the role of differentiated cells in the growth process of *Hydra*. One group of investigators favored the interstitial cells as the source of all new cells and tissues; the other group concluded from their work that differentiated somatic cells can divide and replace themselves and that the major role of interstitial cells is the production of gametes and cnidoblasts.

C. THE ORIGIN OF NEW CELLS DURING REGENERATION

The problems raised previously regarding the cellular dynamics of normal growth were also explored in the context of regeneration. Whenever an animal replaces a missing part it is assumed that new cells and tissues must arise through cell replications, and the problem becomes one of identifying those dividing parent cells which give rise to the regenerate.

We have already mentioned some of the major investigators who advocated the primary role of interstitial cells in providing new material for the regenerate. As late as 1930 Schlottke definitively stated that interstitial cells comprise the only autoreproductive elements in *Hydra* and therefore inferred that they are the major, if not only, source of regenerating tissues. This period in history (1900–1930) seemed to be one of confusion on the interstitial cell issue. Some investigators such as Gross (1925) concluded that although interstitial cells may not be the only cells participating in regeneration, they are certainly very important and necessary. Investigations of Tannreuther (1909), showing movement of parent tissue toward the asexual offspring during budding, and of Gelei (1924) and Nussbaum (1907), demonstrating actual movement of parent body wall on to the bud, were used as further evidence that cells other than interstitial cells can play a major role in growth processes. A few years later McConnell (1933a,b) did a lengthy study of mitoses in *Hydra* and concluded that numerous cells other than interstitial cells show divisions of sufficient quantity to be important in growth phenomena such as budding and regeneration. Thus, the original interstitial cell theory, which rested not on experimental evidence but instead mainly on the failure of investigators to locate mitoses in cells other than interstitial cells, was greatly weakened. As in similar cases of scientific effort further clarification of this question as to the origin of new cells for the various growth processes awaited new approaches and new techniques.

D. Regeneration in Irradiated Animals

It had been known for some time that X rays of appropriate dosage destroy rapidly dividing cells when Zawarzin (1929) and Strelin (1929) utilized this technique to remove interstitial cells, which were known to have a high mitotic rate, from *Hydra*. This treatment eliminated the regenerative potential of the animals and the authors interpreted these results as giving support to the interstitial cell theory. They argued that if interstitial cells are responsible for regeneration, then lack of regeneration when interstitial cells are not available provides proof of their primary role in the regeneration process.

Even though some of Strelin's X-rayed animals showed a slight tendency to regenerate small hypostomes or other abortive distal structures, many investigators were convinced that Zawarzin and Strelin's work had again placed the interstitial cell theory on firm footing by this new and dramatic experimental evidence. Others such as Kanajew (1930) were not convinced either way and spoke of the interstitial cells as important but not exclusive components of regeneration.

Evlakhova (1946) also subjected *Hydra* to an X-irradiation dosage of about 5000 r and subsequently assayed the animals for regeneration of distal parts. This author claimed complete repression of regeneration and concluded that since this coincided with the loss of interstitial cells, the latter must be essential for the regeneration process. However, the possibility should be mentioned that regeneration may have been suppressed because of the generally poor condition of the animals and not directly as the result of lack of interstitial cells. (Careful histological processing of treated tissues was not carried out and the state of the animals at intervals following irradiation was not described in detail in his paper.) Evlakhova carried these experiments further and grafted healthy normal pieces of *Hydra* onto irradiated pieces a few days after treatment. In some cases there was regeneration of part, or all, of the distal structure which had been amputated previously. The conclusion was drawn that the regenerate resulted from migration of interstitial cells from the normal tissue into irradiated parts where they played an active role in regeneration. However, no direct evidence was presented which supported this conclusion.

Irradiation experiments reported by Brien and Reniers-Decoen (1955) were an extension of Brien's previous investigations into the cellular dynamics of normal growth and regeneration in *Hydra*. Through his numerous histological studies Brien (1953) concluded that the interstitial cells of *Hydra* constitute "polyvalent reserve elements." These elements, or cells, are able to differentiate into other cell types including epitheliomuscular cells, gland cells, cells of the nerve plexus, sensory cells, nematocysts, and gametes. Their major function, according to his theory, is the production of nematocysts, but since they can replace other adult cell types they actually comprise the major elements of growth. But this is not the complete story, as Brien pointed out, because cells other than interstitial cells had been shown to divide in numbers sufficient to be easily observed and therefore adult cells may also be involved in growth and regeneration. Thus, Brien (as well as other workers in the field) had arrived at an impasse on the interstitial cell controversy when he performed his experiments with Reniers-Decoen in 1955.

These investigators (Brien and Reniers-Decoen, 1955) treated hydra with 5000–6000 r of X irradiation over a period of 14 minutes and subsequently observed gross and histological changes in the animals as well as their regenerative and budding potentials. Their animals invariably died, and this was taken as evidence that the interstitial cells are necessary for continued survival of the animals but that some regeneration of oral structures and budding can occur after interstitial cell elimination. Their work was not quantitative, however, and it is somewhat difficult to glean from their data the amount of regeneration and budding or the time intervals involved. Two major technical objections can be made of the X-ray technique when used on hydras to destroy interstitial cells. Hydras never appear normal after treatment but exhibit degenerative changes which terminate in disintegration of tissues and eventual death. In addition, some animals retain a small number of interstitial cells after treatment and it is not certain whether or not these cells can divide and repopulate the animal. These objections made it desirable to search for other means of eliminating the interstitial cells from *Hydra* if this general approach was to be followed in future experimentation.

Further analysis of the role of interstitial cells in regeneration (and budding) was carried out by Diehl and Burnett (1964, 1965a,b). The experimental removal of interstitial cells was accomplished in this study by chemical means rather than by short-wave radiations. The technique, along with pertinent results, will be discussed in Section II.

E. REGENERATION FROM PORTIONS OF *Hydra* NORMALLY
    LACKING INTERSTITIAL CELLS

Investigators have noted that not all isolated regions of *Hydra* and other coelenterates are equally capable of regenerating missing parts. Tentacles and peduncle-base regions were described as nonregenerating parts of *Hydra* (Goetsch, 1919, 1920; Issajew, 1926; Weimer, 1928). Burnett (1961) minced pieces of peduncle from richly fed hydras, mixed the pieces from several animals, and in 12 of 12 cases obtained small reorganization masses which regenerated a hypostome and 2–3 tentacles. The animals grew into normal hydras if fed immediately after completion of regeneration. Bases of hydras prepared in the same manner regenerated to a lesser extent. Only 3 of 12 fusion masses comprised of bases regenerated into complete animals. These animals captured and ingested food but were not able to digest the prey. It was assumed that gland cells were absent from the gastrodermal cell layer. Tentacles were also isolated and minced into small pieces which were subsequently placed in contact with tentacle pieces from 5 other hydras. The tentacle fragments fused into plates but failed to reorganize into whole animals in all cases. Disintegration occurred after 1 day. These experiments, coupled with earlier observations on regeneration of isolated hypostomal and gastric tissues, suggested to the author that all regions of *Hydra*, with the exception of the tentacles, are capable of reorganizing and regenerating into complete animals from a tissue mince. In this paper Burnett (1961) did not attempt to link regeneration with interstitial cell presence but did point out that interstitial cells are found to some degree in all regions of *Hydra* with the possible exception of the tentacles.

Tardent (1952, 1954, 1963) also examined the regenerative potential of different regions of *Hydra* and attempted to correlate regenerative potential with interstitial cell distribution along the distal–proximal axis of the animal. Earlier Burt (1934) had examined regeneration of distal and proximal structures at various levels along the body column and found that the potential for forming distal structures (hypostome and tentacles) decreased in a proximal direction, whereas peduncle base-forming potential increased as the cut was made further and further toward the proximal end of the animals. In his experiments Tardent examined microscopic, stained sections of *Hydra* taken at fixed intervals along the axis and calculated the number of interstitial cells at each level. He concluded that there are more interstitial cells in the distal third of the body than in the middle third which in turn contains more than the proximal one third. When the curve of values for the average number of interstitial cells in the three regions of the body column is compared to a curve showing rate of regeneration, there is a high degree of correlation. However, as Tardent points out clearly in the 1954 paper, and later in a review article (Tardent, 1963), the problem is to unequivocally ascertain whether the presence of large numbers of interstitial cells in regions of high regenerative potential and low numbers in poorly regenerating areas is coincidental or whether there is a direct causal relationship. Furthermore, if a causal relationship can be verified there remains the question of the role of the interstitial cells in the regeneration process. Are they mainly participating as building blocks for the new tissues of regeneration; do they act as inductive agents for regeneration; or do they play some other roles? We shall examine these questions in some detail in Section III.

More recent attempts to study developmental phenomena in *Hydra* by looking at the quantities of various cell types distributed throughout the animal and divisions of these various cell types (Campbell, 1967; Macklin, 1968) have led to some interesting results and ideas which will be discussed elsewhere in this book.

II. Experimental Analysis of Regeneration and Budding in *Hydra* Treated with Nitrogen Mustard to Selectively Eliminate Interstitial Cells

A. INTRODUCTION

There are two general methods of studying the importance and role(s) of any cell type in a living organism. One of these is to follow in some manner the fate of a cell as it progresses through its lifetime, from origin via cell division, through differentiation, physiological function, and on to death, or division, as the case may be. This is probably the ideal or preferred way to look at the role of a single cell or a population of cells, but unfortunately it is very difficult technically to trace living cells in this manner. Therefore, it is often more feasible to adopt a method whereby the cell, or cells, in question are eliminated from the organism and the developmental or physiological potential of the organism, minus the cells in question, is examined.

As mentioned earlier, Zawarzin (1929), Strelin (1929), Evlakhova (1946), and Brien and Reniers-Decoen (1955) utilized X irradiation in experiments designed to elucidate the importance of interstitial cells for the life and cellular dynamics of *Hydra*. Although the technique described by Brien and Reniers-Decoen (1955) for removing interstitial cells proved valuable, it is laborious and time consuming, especially if large numbers of animals are required for experimentation. In addition, as was pointed out earlier, some interstitial cells are not destroyed and the animals appear to be in very poor condition after treatment.

In 1962 the present author and A. L. Burnett undertook a series of experiments designed to investigate the role of interstitial cells in the maintenance of form in *Hydra,* specifically their role(s) in regeneration and budding, using a chemical means of selectively eliminating the interstitial cells (Diehl and Burnett, 1964, 1965a,b).

B. TECHNIQUES: GROSS APPEARANCE AND HISTOLOGY OF TREATED ANIMALS

The special techniques used in regeneration and budding studies will be described in detail elsewhere but mention should be made of the agent used to destroy the interstitial cells. In seeking to find a substitute for X irradiation, which was known from previous experiments to be rather unsatisfactory, attention was drawn to the class of chemicals known as the nitrogen mustards. These are powerful gases developed originally as war tools, but since World War II synthesized as hydrochloric salts and used for research and cancer chemotherapy. One of the nitrogen mustards was known to be effective in preventing mitoses in larval ectodermal cells of the amphibian *Ambystoma punctatum* (Bodenstein, 1947) and it was reasoned that it might also selectively affect the embryoniclike interstitial cells of *Hydra*. Consequently, dosage-response curves were run on a number of animals using a commercially available nitrogen mustard, methyl bis (β-chloroethyl)amine hydrochloride (Merck and Co.). Treatment for 10 minutes with a 0.01% solution yielded animals which lost all of their interstitial cells by 6–8 days and could be used for 30–40 days after treatment for analysis of regeneration and budding.

Immediately following treatment with nitrogen mustard and rinsing, the hydras often appeared depressed. That is, their body columns and tentacles were contracted, and some of the tentacles were knobbed. The depressed condition lasted from 12 to 24 hours, after which the animals regained their normal form and resumed feeding activities. No explanation of this temporary depression is available.

The animals appeared to remain in a healthy condition for 10–12 days. At that time it was observed that prey animals which had been captured were not ingested although some feeding movements of the tentacles toward the mouth did occur. Once feeding ceased, the animals gradually became smaller, their tentacles shortened, and body movements were less frequent and less pronounced. Death of the animals always occurred in 40–50 days at 18°C. At 4°C some of the animals remained alive for over 50 days.

Histological examination of randomly selected animals was carried out at regular intervals in order to determine what cellular changes, if any, were occurring. No change in any cell types were observed until 1 day following treatment. At this time a slight increase in the size of some interstitial cells and their nuclei (Fig. 2) was seen but other cells appeared unchanged. By the second day most of the interstitial cells were greatly enlarged and both sections and whole mount preparations revealed that some of these enlarged cells had become spindle-shaped. Other cell types still appeared unchanged in histological detail.

Three days after treatment with nitrogen mustard all the interstitial cells in the hydra showed an increase in size. In some of the enlarging spindle-shaped cells vacuoles appeared as clear areas between the large nucleus and extended cytoplasm forming "tails" extending out from the main cell body. A continued increase was noted in the length of the cyto-

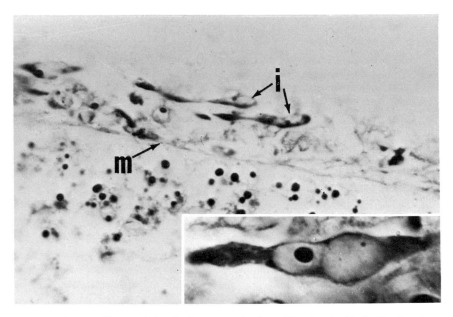

Fig. 2. Elongated interstitial cells (i) are seen in the epidermis of a *Hydra* fixed and sectioned 6 days after mustard treatment. The mesoglea (m) separates the epidermis and gastrodermis in this longitudinal view. An enlargement of one such elongated cell appears in the inset at lower right.

plasmic extensions, and in some cases the long dimension of the enlarged cells reached more than 100μ. The only interstitial cells detected at 5 days after mustard treatment were enlarged to twice or more their original size and most (75%) had elongated tails. In some enlarged cells nuclear pyknosis had occurred. There was a decrease in the concentration of interstitial cells in the growth, gastric, and budding regions as compared with normal animals. The mustard-treated animals differed from normal forms in another respect: Interstitial cells always appeared singly in the mustard-treated animals and never in clusters. Differentiation of the giant interstitial cells into cnidoblasts or other known cell types was not observed.

Gland and mucous cells persisted at this stage with no apparent change in their structure or concentration. The number of cnidoblasts appeared to be diminishing in some animals. No intermediate stages of differentiation of interstitial cells into cnidoblasts were observed.

No interstitial cells were detected in over 90% of the animals examined at 7 days; in the remainder only a few giant cells with a lightly staining cytoplasm were seen scattered throughout the body column. Gland and mucous cells remained in large numbers and their persistence around the mouth–hypostomal area was evident.

After 7 days the changes observed in cell types were more gradual, and assigning specific time sequences to cellular phenomena was difficult. There were no interstitial cells in any animals at day 9 (Fig. 3); pre-

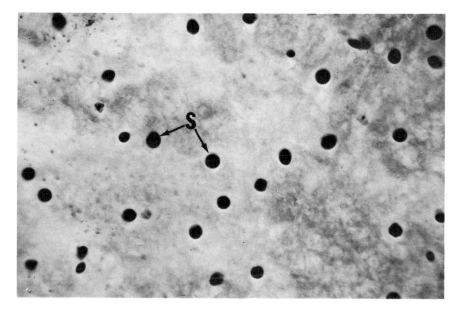

Fig. 3. Whole mount of *Hydra* 8 days after mustard treatment. No interstitial cells are present but stenoteles (s) and other nematocyst types persist.

sumably their disappearance was completed between 7 and 9 days. No stages which could be interpreted as a dedifferentiation of other cell types into interstitial cells were ever seen in these studies. Nematocysts declined gradually in numbers, both in the body and in the tentacles. Also, no cnidoblast cells containing developing nematocysts were observed. Whole mounts and sections stained with toluidine blue revealed a decrease in basophilia over the entire organism. Epitheliomuscular cells and digestive cells which previously exhibited good cellular integrity began to show some degeneration at 23–30 days. Mucous cells declined gradually in number. This was especially noticeable in the hypostomal region. However, by the time final sections were prepared (23–25 days after mustard treatment), this decrease was never more than 25% of the original, and in most cases, less.

In light of these observations several points can be made. The depression exhibited by the *Hydra* immediately after immersion in the mustard solution lasted a relatively short time. Once this period was past the animals again appeared normal and remained so for 10–12 days. Brien and Reniers-Decoen (1955) reported a more pronounced and rapid change in the *Hydra* following treatment with X rays. This suggests that nitrogen mustard is either a more gentle treatment than X irradiation, or that it has a different mode of action. In either case nitrogen mustard appears equally effective in selectively destroying interstitial cells and is much easier to administer. At the present there is no evidence of secondary effects of nitrogen mustard; we can only postulate that its primary, and perhaps only, effect is the destruction of interstitial cells. The mechanisms responsible for interstitial cell growth, elongation, nuclear changes, and the subsequent death of these cells following nitrogen mustard treatment are not clearly understood at the present.

It appears, therefore, that *Hydra* can survive without interstitial cells, but only for a limited time. The question remains as to whether its eventual death is caused by the absence of other cell types in the organism or by the specific absence of interstitial cells. Of course, the possibility also exists that the nitrogen mustard has harmful or lethal effects on cell types other than interstitial cells. The latter is rather doubtful; two facts substantiate the view that other cells types are not irreversibly harmed. First, it has been shown that interstitial cells can repopulate and revitalize the tissues of mustard-treated animals (Diehl and Burnett, 1966). Both Evlakhova (1946) and Brien and Reniers-Decoen (1955) demonstrated this in X-rayed animals. Second, other cell types do not exhibit cytological changes for several weeks after treatment.

Cells with a spindle or comma shape similar to the enlarging interstitial cells of mustard-treated animals have been reported by Burnett (1959). They are seen during normal growth processes and are regarded as differentiating interstitial cells. Intermediate stages in their differentiation to cnidoblast cells and possibly to gland cells can be detected in the normal animals. However, there appear to be major differences between the differentiating cells of normal animals and the enlarging cells of mustard-treated animals. Normal transforming cells never reach the giant proportions of the comparable cells in treated animals, nor are the giant cells histologically similar to known intermediates in the differentiation pathway of other cell types.

The number of cnidoblasts decreased rapidly after 7–9 days from the time of nitrogen mustard treatment, indicating they were no longer being replaced. Since there is good evidence from previous studies (Chapman, 1961; Slautterback, 1961) that interstitial cells differentiate directly into cnidoblast cells which form the nematocysts, it can be assumed that a depletion of interstitial cells resulted in a corresponding decrease in nematocysts. The observation on gland and mucous cells lining the hypostome and gut were contrary to what was anticipated. They did not disappear rapidly and there were still many present at the time of death. It has been proposed that interstitial cells differentiate into gland cells (Gelei, 1924), but the fact that mustard-treated animals were able to feed, digest their food, and still maintain a normal population of gland cells casts doubt on this conclusion. The possibility exists that gland and mucous cells are autoreproductive; thus one would not necessarily expect to find depletion when the interstitial cells are destroyed. However, division of these cells was not observed in our studies.

In line with our results on interstitial cells, Bodenstein (1947) reported that after treating various larval stages of the amphibian, *Ambystoma punctatum,* with nitrogen mustard, division of the ectoderm cells did not occur, even though there was a large increase in size. Similar results were obtained by Brewer *et al.* (1961), who treated mouse fibroblasts *in vitro* with nitrogen mustard. Any mechanism which interferes with the early steps in formation of the mitotic configuration could give such results. In any case, what may happen after nitrogen mustard treatment is this: Cells continue to synthesize RNA and protein and the size of the cells increases. But since the mitotic cycle is interrupted the cells cannot divide and as a consequence they grow to gigantic proportions.

C. REGENERATION OF HYPOSTOME AND TENTACLES IN ANIMALS TREATED WITH NITROGEN MUSTARD TO REMOVE THEIR INTERSTITIAL CELLS

The nitrogen mustard technique described previously was used to answer several questions concerning the role of interstitial cells in regeneration. Can *Hydra* whose interstitial cells have been selectively destroyed regenerate excised head regions (tentacles and hypostome)? If so, how long after elimination of interstitial cells does *Hydra* retain the capacity to regenerate? How many times can the animals regenerate after the loss of interstitial cells? Does feeding affect regeneration of animals without interstitial cells? Is the level of excision of the body column important in determining the amount of regeneration in animals without interstitial cells? Except for interstitial cells, is the regenerate morphologically and histologically similar to the normal animal? Do cells divide during regeneration of mustard-treated animals? Is remolding of tissues (morphallaxis) important in regeneration?

The major premise underlying the experiments designed to answer these questions was the following: If regeneration does occur in animals lacking interstitial cells then it can be assumed that they are not essential in initiating or maintaining the regenerative process. Conversely, if animals without interstitial cells fail to regenerate then the interstitial cells can be considered essential to the process.

Asexually propagated clones of three species of *Hydra*, (*H. pseudoligactis, H. fusca,* and *H. pirardi*) were used in the experiments. Animals of each species were treated with the nitrogen mustard, and normal, untreated animals of the same species were set up as controls. Neither group of animals was fed throughout the duration of the experiment.

Animals were allowed to relax and stretch out in a petri dish and then excised just proximal to the tentacle bases with a sharp scalpel. Tentacle development as witnessed at the gross level was used as an index of regeneration. Preliminary experiments were conducted on normal animals and it was determined that the number of tentacles regenerated by each animal in a given length of time was relatively constant. *Hydra pseudoligactis,* which were used for most of these experiments, were bisected proximal to the tentacle bases at 10 days after mustard treatment and fixed at regular intervals, sectioned, and then stained. A control series of normal regeneration animals was prepared in the same way.

1. Regeneration at Various Intervals after Mustard Treatment

Distal structures were severed from groups of *H. pseudoligactis* at 1, 5, 8, 10, 15, 20, and 25 days after mustard treatment. The control

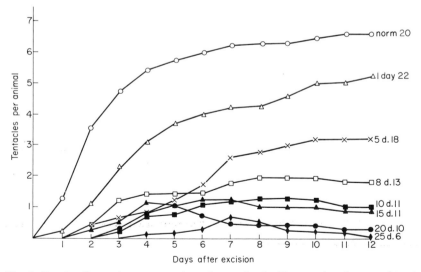

Fig. 4. Graphs illustrating regeneration of tentacles in 22 normal and mustard-treated *H. pseudoligactis.* Animals were severed at various times after mustard treatment and allowed to regenerate 12 days. Daily observations were made and the number of tentacles regenerated per total number of animals in the sample was plotted against time. The numbers at the right indicate the number of animals which regenerated any tentacles.

animals were normal untreated hydras which had been fed 24 hours previous to excision. The animals were allowed to regenerate for 12 days and daily recordings were made of the total number of tentacles regenerated. From this data the number of tentacles per animal was calculated. The number of animals in each group showing regeneration of tentacles during the 12-day period was also recorded.

Some tentacle regeneration was observed in all mustard-treated animals, provided they were excised not later than 25 days after treatment (Fig. 4). However, there was a gradual decline in the number of tentacles produced per animal tested, as the interval after mustard treatment increased. This was especially noticeable in animals challenged 20 and 25 days after treatment.

The number of regenerating animals, as well as the amount of regeneration per animal, varied for each group. For example, in the group excised at 1 day all of the animals exhibited tentacle regeneration as compared to 27% regenerating at 25 days.

Tentacles regenerated by mustard-treated animals were shorter than controls and tentacle size diminished as the time between mustard treatment and excision increased. Tentacles on 20- and 25-day hydras were less than one fourth the normal length. The regeneration of a single median tentacle was observed in several normal and mustard-treated groups (Fig. 5).

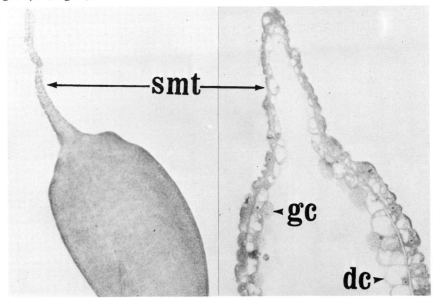

Fig. 5. Whole mount view on the left and longitudinal section on the right illustrating the single median tentacle (smt) regenerated by some normal and mustard-treated animals. Gland cells (gc) and digestive cells (dc) are seen in the sectioned *Hydra*.

2. Repeated Regeneration

Animals (*H. pseudoligactis*) were allowed to regenerate for a given number of days and were then excised again to see if repeated regenerations would occur. This was repeated until a total of 12 excisions had been made on each animal. Twenty mustard-treated animals were excised for the first time 1 day after treatment and allowed to regenerate for 4 days between subsequent excisions. A total of 5 excisions were made on these animals. Four repeated excisions were made on another group of 20 animals excised 5 days after mustard treatment, but otherwise the procedure was identical to that for animals excised after 1 day.

Controls (normal, untreated *H. pseudoligactis*) regenerated tentacles 12 times within a period of 38 days (Fig. 6A). Both the rate of regeneration and the number of animals regenerating in the allotted time of 3 days decreased with repeated excisions. However, 27 days after the last feeding 11 of the original sample of 25 animals exhibited some regeneration and 33 days after feeding 7 animals (28% of the total) still regenerated.

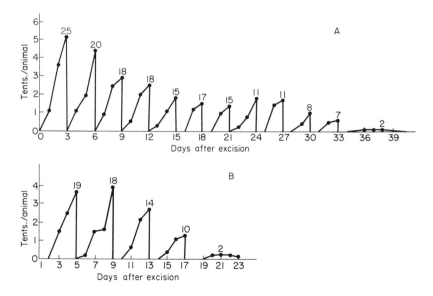

Fig. 6. (A) Repeated tentacle regeneration in 25 normal *H. pseudoligactis*. Untreated animals were severed 1 day after feeding, allowed to regenerate 3 days and severed again in the same subhypostomal region. This procedure was repeated 10 times. Verticle lines on the chart indicate excisions. The number of tentacles regenerated per total number of animals in the sample is plotted against days after initial excision. The numbers at the top of the vertical lines indicate the number of animals which regenerated in the alloted time. (B) Repeated tentacle regeneration in 20 *H. pseudoligactis* severed for the first time 1 day after mustard treatment. The procedure was essentially the same as for normal animals except that 4 days elapsed between excisions.

Whole mounts prepared at the termination of the experiment revealed the presence of nematocysts in the regenerated tentacles and interstitial cells in the epidermis.

Animals excised 1 day after mustard regenerated five times (Fig. 6B). The animals severed 5 days after treatment regenerated four successive times (Fig. 7A). There was a decline in the number of regenerated tentacles per animal in a mustard-treated group first excised at 10 days (Fig. 7B); in addition the rate of tentacle formation was lower in this group than those described previously.

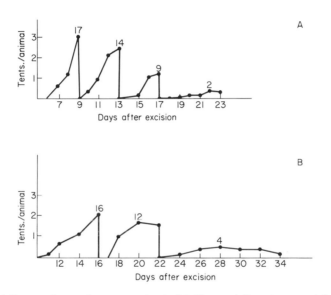

Fig. 7. (A) Repeated tentacle regeneration in 20 *H. pseudoligactis* severed for the first time 5 days after mustard treatment. Four days elapsed between successive excisions. (B) Repeated tentacle regeneration in 20 *H. pseudoligactis* severed for the first time at 10 days after mustard treatment. Six days elapsed between successive excisions.

3. Effects of Feeding on Regeneration

A third experiment was designed to test the effects of feeding on regeneration of animals lacking interstitial cells. Animals in one group were fed *Artemia* larvae every day for a period of 10 days after treatment. Samples were tested for anterior regenerating capacity by severing just proximal to the tentacle bases at 5, 10, 15, 20, and 25 days after treatment. The animals to be bisected were starved for 24 hours prior to excision in order to ensure that there was no partially digested food in the gastrovascular cavity which might contaminate the culture medium. The other group of animals from the same mustard-treated population were not fed during the course of the experiment. Samples of these animals were similarly tested for regeneration at 5-day intervals.

Starved animals severed below the tentacles 5 days after mustard treatment behaved similarly to fed controls in that about the same number of animals regenerated in both groups (16, 17). However, the regeneration rate and number of tentacles formed per total number of animals were lower in the fed group (Fig. 8).

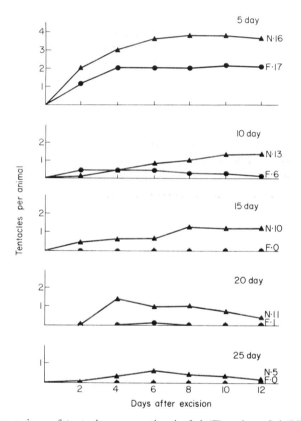

Fig. 8. A comparison of tentacle regeneration in fed (F) and nonfed (N), or starved, *Hydra pseudoligactis* severed 5, 10, 15, 20 and 25 days after mustard treatment. The sample size (*n*) was 20 in all cases. On the chart tentacles regenerated per total number of animals in the sample is plotted against days after excision. The numbers at the right indicate the number of animals which regenerated in the fed (F) and starved (N) groups.

There was less regeneration in the fed animals than in the starved ones tested at 15, 15, 20, and 25 days after mustard treatment (Fig. 8).

These results with *Hydra* substantiate previous reports which indicate that starved amphibians regenerate at a faster rate than those which are well fed. A satisfactory explanation for these observations of normal as well as nitrogen mustard-treated animals is not available but one can postulate that cells packed with food and/or involved with intensive metobolic activities are ill prepared for participation in the developmental events (mitosis, differentiation, migration) of regeneration.

4. Trauma as a Stimulus of Regeneration

Some excised, mustard-treated animals simply healed over at the distal end and no tentacles or well-formed conical hypostome developed. Ten such animals which were excised 8 days after mustard treatment and showed no regeneration after 4 days were isolated for this study. They were traumatized at the original wound surface by tearing the epidermis with glass needles. Any regeneration which subsequently occurred in these animals was noted and compared with regeneration occurring in ten nontraumatized animals from the same 8-day mustard-treated group.

The first day after trauma the wound surface was healed, but no tentacle regeneration was observed. On the second day, however, 1 animal developed a short anteriolateral tentacle. After 3 days this animal had developed 2 additional tentacles but no hypostome. Another animal formed a single, short, median tentacle after 3 days. No further regeneration occurred.

No regeneration of tentacles was noted in the nontraumatized, mustard-treated animals serving as controls, although they were observed for a total of 13 days.

5. Histological Observations

The most obvious histological difference in regeneration of normal (see Mattes, 1925; Kanajew 1926a,b, 1929, 1930; Burnett, 1961) and mustard-treated animals was the complete absence of interstitial cells in the treated animals. Otherwise the regenerative process appeared similar in both groups (Fig. 9). Wound healing occurred by the stretching of epitheliomuscular cells over the gastrodermal cells. Later the tentacles began as outpushings of both layers. A large accumulation of nematocysts at the wound site was seen in the early stages of tentacle formation in normal animals. In regenerating mustard-treated hydras there were few nematocysts in the entire column at 10 days and consequently few, if any, nematocysts migrated to the presumptive tentacle site.

A conical hypostome was not evident in all regenerating hydras but in the experimental animals there was an area between the tentacles composed of the kinds of cells normally found in the regenerated hypostome. Epithelio-muscular cells in this area were flattened and contained large vacuoles. A normal mesoglea was present and mucous cells were concentrated in the gastrodermis. Invaginations occurred in the gastrodermal layer and extended almost to the mesoglea, but no mouth opening formed.

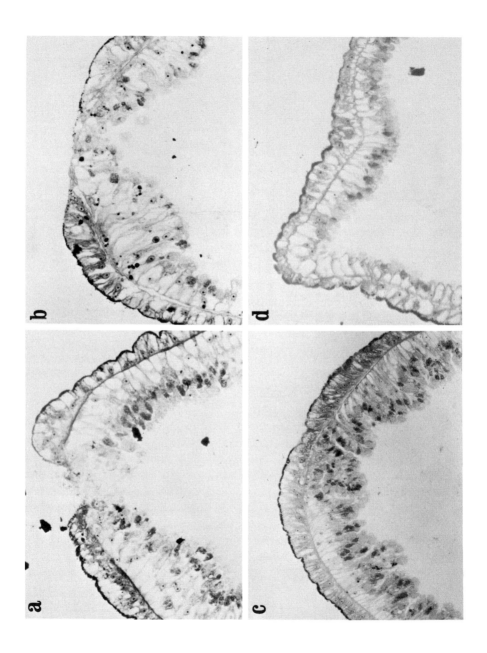

Whole mounts and sections were examined for mitotic activity. Interstitial cells were absent in mustard-treated animals so they can be disregarded. Gland and mucous cells persisted for long periods but we did not observe mitotic activity in these cells, even in normal animals. They probably represent a stock of long-lived cells able to recharge their cytoplasm several times after secretion. Thus, they did not disappear at a rapid rate from feeding hydras. However, at the level of the lower gastric region and peduncle these cells showed degenerative changes. The secretory material was clumped and the cytoplasm became vacuolated. There was a substantial decrease in the numbers of these cells in the most proximal areas of the column, although a few were present at the level of the basal disc.

Thousands of digestive cells were examined in animals in all stages of regeneration but no mitotic figures were observed. Epidermal epitheliomuscular cells, on the other hand, continued to divide after mustard treatment. Although the number of divisions was one half that of normal forms, some of these cells were seen in division 20 days after treatment.

6. Discussion of Regeneration Experiments Utilizing Mustard-Treated Animals

These results demonstrated that animals without interstitial cells can regenerate excised anterior structures. In some instances, (animals excised 1 day after mustard treatment), regeneration in the absence of interstitial cells equaled that of untreated controls in both rate and number of tentacles regenerated per animals. (Although it is implied, interstitial cells are not actually absent in 1- and 5-day animals. In *H. pseudoligactis* they do not all disappear for 8 to 10 days but interstitial cells persisting until this time become greatly enlarged and eventually die. They were never observed to differentiate into other cell types. Therefore, interstitial cells were considered nonfunctional after treatment with nitrogen mustard.)

Of the three species used in these experiments *H. pseudoligactis*

Fig. 9. Regeneration of *H. pseudoligactis* treated 10 days previously with nitrogen mustard. Animals were severed just below the tentacle region and fixed at various intervals to show different stages in the regenerative process. (a) An animal 10 minutes after excision. The contracted epidermis is beginning to seal the cut surface and the gastrodermal cells are starting to form a wound plug. The state of regeneration after 1 hour is depicted in (b). Note the thin, stretched epidermal epitheliomuscular cells. The gastrodermis is continuous but the mesoglea has not re-formed. Ten hours after excision, as seen in (c), the epidermis is thickened except in the center of the original wound area. The mesoglea is re-formed and the gastrodermis appears normal. Many darkly staining secretory cells are evident, especially in the distal region. Tentacles are beginning to form after 18 hours of regeneration, as seen in (d). No nematocyst accumulations are seen in the tentacle region.

seemed to regenerate better without interstitial cells than did *H. pirardi* and *H. fusca*. The reason for this difference is not readily apparent but some variations in morphological and cytological details do exist in these species.

The presence of nematocysts (in the regenerated tentacles) and interstitial cells in starved, control animals severed 11 times over a period of 33 days indicates that interstitial cells are able to persist for long periods in starved animals and retain the capacity to differentiate into cnidoblasts.

A noteworthy feature of the regeneration of 1- and 5-day mustard-treated animals was the cessation of regeneration at about 17 days. In 1-day animals four cuts were made prior to 17 days, while in 5-day animals only three excisions were made during this period. Apparently regeneration after mustard treatment depends on the number of times the animals have regenerated and also on the interval between treatment and excision.

Tardent (1954) found differences in regenerative capacity at various levels of the body column and correlated the differences with distribution of interstitial cells. Tardent's experiments should be repeated using hydras without interstitial cells in order to determine whether or not differences in regenerative capacity persist after the interstitial cells disappear. In our previous investigation (Diehl and Burnett, 1965a) we showed that developmental potential is not equal along the column in animals devoid of interstitial cells, since buds which originate on animals after mustard treatment always form in the normal budding region. Therefore, even though interstitial cells are absent, the animals still retain a higher growth potential in certain regions of the body column. The appearance of buds at specific sites, and differences in regenerative potential at various levels of the column probably result from an unequal rate of division and/or migration of differentiated cells. With this interpretation the concentration of interstitial cells in particular areas is not responsible for initiating budding or regeneration or for determining rates of development at various levels.

During regeneration, a hypostome and tentacles appear at the distal excised surface. This indicates that polarity is maintained in mustard-treated animals. Other evidence substantiates this observation: if proximal portions of *Hydra* containing interstitial cells are grafted to distal portions lacking these cells, the mid-gastric region of this animal when excised regenerates a head at the distal cut surface and a base proximally. In this experiment interstitial cells are absent at the distal end of the excised portion and cannot determine the nature of the structure elaborated at the cut surface. This suggests that polarity of *Hydra* depends on other factors, possibly a growth-stimulating agent and an inhibiting agent, which diffuse along the body column from the hypostomal region (Burnett, 1966).

D. BUDDING IN ANIMALS TREATED WITH NITROGEN MUSTARD TO REMOVE THEIR INTERSTITIAL CELLS

Biologists have studied the process of asexual reproduction in *Hydra* for more than fifty years (Braem, 1894, 1910; Lang, 1892, 1894; Hadzi, 1910; Tannreuther, 1909; Goetsch, 1919; Gelei, 1924; Kanajew, 1930). Lang, Tannreuther, and Hadzi reported that interstitial cells accumulated at the presumptive budding site and, after dividing, caused the outpushing of the body column which ultimately produced the bud. The differentiated cells of the developing bud were thought to be derived primarily from these interstitial cells.

Braem (1894, 1910) and Gelei (1924) objected to the conclusions of Lang (1892, 1894) and stated that the materials of the bud are derived predominantly from the epitheliomuscular cells of the epidermis and the digestive cells of the gastrodermis. They agreed that interstitial cells were present but felt they were not especially important in the budding process. Later, Kanajew (1930) concluded that dividing epitheliomuscular cells and digestive cells of the parent, and not interstitial cells, were responsible for bud formation.

Brien and Reniers-Decoen (1955), in their study which employed X irradiation to selectively destroy the interstitial cells of *Hydra*, observed that irradiated animals continued to bud for a short period. This evidence supports the theory that interstitial cells are not the primary elements of bud formation and are not necessary for the growth of buds.

By employing nitrogen mustard (Diehl and Burnett, 1965a) to remove the interstitial cells and no other cells from large groups of animals, it was possible to compare budding in normal and mustard-treated hydras and to answer the following questions. Does development of existing buds continue after removal of interstitial cells? Do these buds show a normal pattern of development? Do buds arising before and after mustard treatment detach in the same time as normal, untreated buds? Are any new buds initiated after the destruction of interstitial cells?

Our results show that buds continued to originate from the column of the parents for 9 days following mustard treatment (Fig. 10). Data from several experiments revealed that buds never arise after 8–10 days from the time of treatment. In the first 9 days 39 new buds were produced by 46 mustard-treated animals, as compared to 93 new buds by 48 normal, untreated controls and 37 new buds by 48 starved, untreated controls. The time required by animals, which are at stages I, II, III, and IV (Bur-

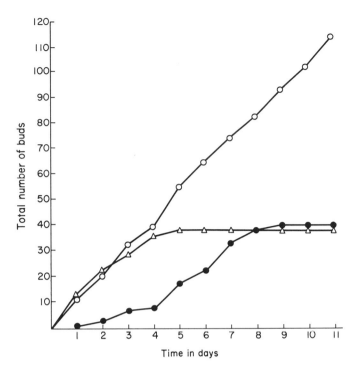

Fig. 10. Budding in normal, fed hydras (O) compared with budding in normal, starved animals (Δ) and mustard-treated animals (●). This graph shows the total number of buds produced by 48 fed, untreated controls; 48 starved, untreated controls; and 46 mustard-treated animals. Counts were made daily and all detached buds removed from the culture dishes.

nett, 1961) at the time of treatment, to complete their development and detach was calculated (Table I). Buds which originated after mustard treatment eventually detached but only after a much longer period of time. The mean detachment time was 13.5 days, but this represents a minimum because in some instances the animals were sacrificed for histological studies before they actually detached. Buds present at the time of the treatment and buds arising after treatment showed no significant differences in the time required to complete their development and detach.

Buds of the experimental group which remained attached to the parent animal for periods longer than 10 days after reaching stage IV were seen to have small connecting bridges of tissue between the most proximal portion of the bud and the parent column. In addition some mucus accumulation was also seen in the same area but this material was removed with forceps in several animals and the bud still failed to detach. The processes involved in bud release during normal budding of untreated hydra have not been investigated in detail and therefore the failure of buds to detach from mustard treated animals is difficult to interpret.

TABLE I

TIME NEEDED FOR BUDS TO COMPLETE DEVELOPMENT AND DETACH

	Buds present on parents at time of mustard treatment				Buds originating on mustard animals after treatment[b]
	Stage I[a]	Stage II[a]	Stage III[a]	Stage IV[a]	
Sample size	23	9	5	13	30
Mean in days	8.4	8.1	8.6	7.2	13.5
Standard deviation	3.6	2.9	0.9	2.4	2.4

	Normals, fed	Normals, starved (Stage I) (days after last feeding)		
	Stage I	2	3	4
Sample size	50	10	10	10
Mean in days	5.6	6.5	7.8	8.4
Standard deviation	0.8	0.9	1.1	1.7

[a] Stage of development at time of mustard treatment.

[b] No significant difference between buds originating at various days after mustard treatment.

Some data was gathered on the incidence of mitosis in normal and mustard-treated animals (Fig. 11). Epidermal epitheliomuscular cells in all stages of division were observed in both normal and mustard-treated animals. Mitotic figures were abundant in the subhypostomal growth region and budding region and scarce in the gastric region and hypostome. It is interesting to note that a few epitheliomuscular cells in division were observed in animals 20 days after mustard treatment. This is taken as evidence that although mustard specifically eliminates interstitial cells, it probably does not seriously injure other epidermal cell types.

Mitotic figures were not observed in any gastrodermal cell types after treatment with mustard. In normal animals, 75 digestive cells in division were sighted after examining 1500 cells. An examination of more than 50,000 digestive cells in mustard-treated animals failed to reveal a single mitotic figure. In some cases, a digestive cell which appeared to be in early prophase was observed, but it was impossible to determine whether

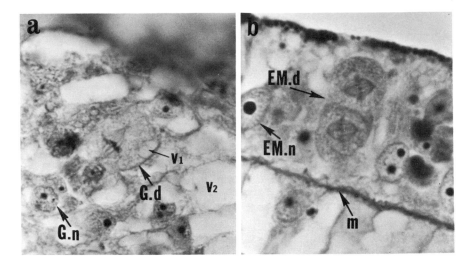

Fig. 11. Mitoses in normal and mustard-treated *H. pseudoligactis*. In photograph (a) at the left normal gastrodermis has been sectioned and stained with toluidine blue at pH 8. A gastrodermal digestive cell is seen in metaphase (Gd) and can be compared to a non-dividing cell of the same type at the lower left (Gn). Note the small vacuole (V_1) in the dividing cell and the large vacuole (V_2) of a similar cell in interphase. In photograph (b) at the right the telophase stage of division is depicted in the epidermis of *H. pseudoligactis* treated 20 days previously with nitrogen mustard. In addition to the dividing epithelio-muscular cell (EMd), a nondividing cell of the same type (EMn) is also seen. The mesoglea (m) separates the epidermal and gastrodermal layers.

this was due to cell division or a clumping of chromatin material due to fixation or other artifacts. In any case, metaphase and anaphase stages, prevalent in normal animals, were not observed after mustard treatment.

The results presented in the foregoing section answer the questions posed in the introduction as to whether or not these buds show a normal pattern of development.

Once buds were initiated in mustard-treated animals their development proceeded at a normal rate until stage IV. This continued growth of buds is not surprising if one considers that divisions of epidermal epithelio-muscular cells continues after mustard treatment. It will be remembered that Kanajew (1930) stressed the importance of epithelial cells in bud formation. One fact is certain: The form of the bud does not depend upon the presence of interstitial cells. Although the processes of form regulation may differ in normal and mustard treated animals the end result is the same, i.e., the formation of a young *Hydra* with a mouth, tentacles, gastric column, peduncle, and basal disc. It was thought that if interstitial cells were not present to contribute to the cellular pool of the bud and if part of the parent column was experimentally removed by severing it just above and below the budding region, the new buds might be deficient in some respect from the normal ones. Another possibility was that the entire mass of tissue present would reorganize into a single large *Hydra* Our results indicate that in all cases the buds which were separated 1 day after treatment from the rest of the parent column became normal polyps as evidenced by the appearance of tentacles, hypostome, peduncle, and basal disc. In only one case did a rearrangement of all the tissues into a single polyp occur and this was from a bud at early stage I. Thus, the mechanism responsible for bud formation appears to reside in the budding region and is not dependent upon other regions of the animal for its expression.

Do buds arising before and after mustard treatment detach in the same time as normal buds? Buds present at the time of mustard treatment showed some retardation in detachment but in only two cases did buds remain attached for more than ten days after reaching stage IV. The mean time at stage IV for 50 animals was about five days. This figure was obtained by summing the number of days at stages I–III and then subtracting this value from the total time required for development and detachment. This corresponds closely to the time required by 4-day, starved normal animals to complete stage IV. This latter fact indicates that any inhibition of the normal growth pattern of the animal, such as that produced by starvation, is reflected as a retardation in budding. This is particularly noticeable at stage IV, which includes detachment. The formation of a basal disc occurred more slowly in starved, normal animals than in well-fed controls and it is most probable that the inhibition occurs at this point. It will be remembered that a depression period occurs in mustard-treated animals just after treatment. Later the animals feed and regain a healthy appearance. Such a metabolic shock could possibly produce the slight delay in detachment time observed in animals with buds attached at time of treatment, but the loss of interstitial cells to buds initiated after treatment produced a more significant change, for there was considerable delay in the detachment of buds. This was probably due to the growth of the previously mentioned slender column of tissue between the parent column and the most proximal portion of the bud.

Are any new buds initiated after the destruction of interstitial cells? Budding activity was definitely affected in animals which had their interstitial cells destroyed by treatment with nitrogen mustard. Most noticeable was the slower rate and eventual cessation of bud production in these animals. The fact that no buds were produced on the first day after mustard treatment can be explained by the temporary state of depression exhibited by the *Hydra* during the first day (Diehl and Burnett, 1964).

On the second day after mustard treatment the animals had recovered and began producing buds. Asexual reproduction continued for 9 days and then ceased. This halt in budding was permanent and new buds did not arise after this time.

It is very unlikely that lack of food was the direct cause of the cessation of budding in the mustard-treated animals, although food is without doubt important in the budding process of normal animals. Untreated control animals which were starved continued to produce new buds for a period of only 5–6 days after the last feeding, indicating that starvation does have an effect on budding. Mustard-treated animals continued to ingest food for 12 or more days after treatment but budding ceased 9 days after mustard treatment. Protein reserve droplets (Burnett, 1959) were observed in gastrodermal digestive cells of these animals after budding ceased. It was concluded from these observations that ingestion and digestion of food was normal in the animals and their nutrition should have been adequate to maintain the budding process.

The data collected from buds arising 1–9 days after mustard treatment demonstrates clearly that stage IV is the period of development most altered following destruction of interstitial cells. Time required to reach stage IV was about the same in mustard-treated and control animals, but total time for development and detachment in treated animals was more than twice as long.

The histological observations of budding substantiate the results from forementioned experiments. The presence of interstitial cells is not essential for buds to be initiated although some interstitial cells are seen in the budding region of stage I normal animals. These findings are in general agreement with Braem's theory (1894) that interstitial cells are not responsible for the production of buds.

III. Theoretical Aspects of Regeneration and Budding in Animals Devoid of Interstitial Cells

Even though interstitial cells are present in large quantities in all species of *Hydra,* experiments show that they do not play an indispensable role in regeneration and budding. Animals which have their interstitial cells experimentally removed eventually die, but between destruction of interstitial cells and death they produce numerous buds and regenerate hypostome and tentacles. One alternative to interstitial cells as the source of raw materials for regeneration and budding has been suggested earlier, namely, adult cells such as epitheliomuscular and gastrodermal digestive cells. Divisions of these cells occur in normal animals and even though there is some question as to their rates of division, presumably they can contribute significantly to the pool of cells which comprise the growing adult *Hydra*. Unfortunately, however, there is no work which clearly correlates their presence and their mitotic activity with the events of regeneration and budding.

In any case, it appears that epitheliomuscular cells are the only cells which continue to divide after mustard treatment. This suggests that if cell divisions are essential, the epidermis alone can support regeneration. Gastrodermal cells are attached to the epidermal layer by the mesoglea and as the epidermis moves they are pulled along toward the regenerating area. Some stretching of epidermal and gastrodermal cells occurs during initial stages of regeneration, but it is postulated that divisions and migrations of epidermal epitheliomuscular cells are mainly responsible for formation of the regenerate and bud in the absence of interstitial cells. (More discussion of this theory will be presented later.)

Our results (Diehl and Burnett, 1964, 1965a,b) confirmed the report of Brien and Reniers-Decoen (1955) that epitheliomuscular cells divide after destruction of interstitial cells. Cell divisions are important in regeneration but, in addition, migration of cells also contribute to the formation of the lost part. In regenerating mustard-treated animals epitheliomuscular cells and gastrodermal digestive cells assume a flattened, squamous appearance. This flattening and stretching of cells which appears to be directly correlated with their role in regenerating is seen in normal *Hydra* only during the first stages of regeneration when the cut surface heals.

In addition to their capacity for division it has been suggested (Brien and Reniers-Decoen, 1955) that some epitheliomuscular cells dedifferentiate into interstitial cells. This suggestion was based on the observation of condensation of cytoplasm around the nucleus in epitheliomuscular cells of regenerating hydras containing no interstitial cells. The condensed cells were regarded as interstitial cells, capable of redifferentiation into other cell types. We have never observed dedifferentiation of any cell types following removal of interstitial cells by nitrogen mustard, although dedifferentiation can occur when cell layers are separated and allowed to regenerate (Haynes and Burnett, 1963; Davis *et al.*, 1966).

In *Hydra* the question of cell competence is central to a discussion of the cellular dynamics of regeneration and budding but unfortunately this question has been only partially answered. Interstitial cells differentiate into cnidoblasts, gametes, and nerves (Slautterbach and Fawcett, 1959; Brien and Reniers-Decoen, 1949; Burnett and Diehl, 1964) but there is no evidence to support the view that these cells are totipotent. Our recent observations of mitosis in epidermal epitheliomuscular and gastrodermal digestive cells of normal animals confirm similar reports by McConnell (1933a). This is taken as evidence that interstitial cells are not needed for the production of all other cell types. If the cell layers of *Hydra* are separated, the endoderm alone regenerates a complete polyp (Haynes and Burnett, 1963); gastrodermal digestive cells differentiate into epitheliomuscular cells and interstitial cells are formed by dedifferentiation of gland cells. However, during normal regeneration gastrodermal digestive cells have never been seen to differentiate into another cell type nor has dedifferentiation of gland cells been observed.

Once the involvement of interstitial cells as building blocks for the regenerate or bud has been ruled out through the studies of nitrogen mustard-treated animals and once it has been established in the same studies that interstitial cells do not differentiate into other cell types essential for elaboration of normal structures such as tentacles and hypostome, the question can be raised as to whether or not they play some other, less direct role in the processes of budding and regeneration of normal animals. Burnett (1966) proposed both a growth-stimulating principle and a growth-inhibiting principle to explain the observed pattern of growth in normal budding and in regenerating hydras. It is evident that controlling factors continue to influence regeneration and budding after interstitial cells are destroyed. Buds continue to be produced on the parent column in a normal pattern and normal regenerates are formed which maintain the original polarity of the organism. If stimulating or controlling principles were absent in animals without interstitial cells one would expect to find lack of regeneration and budding or else deviations from the normal patterns of growth. Since this is not the case it can be concluded that neither the growth-stimulating principle nor the growth-inhibiting principle is produced solely by interstitial cells; also their effects are not mediated exclusively through interstitial cells.

Recent work has shown (Burnett and Diehl, 1964) that nerves of *Hydra* directly affect regeneration. It remains to be seen whether the secretory product of nerves is actually a growth-initiating principle but it should be noted that nerves persist in mustard-treated hydras for 30 days and could continue to stimulate regeneration and budding even in the absence of interstitial cells.

In order to explain regeneration and budding in normal animals and those lacking interstitial cells it is suggested that adult cells (mainly epitheliomuscular cells), under the influence of growth-regulating substances, divide and establish the general form of the regenerate or bud. Migrations of the epidermal cells pull the gastrodermis along and the structures characteristic of the adult *Hydra* take shape. [Cnidoblast cells of normal hydras and interstitial cells of sexual animals migrate extensively according to Jones (1941) and Brien and Reniers-Decoen (1949), but the extent of structural cell, i.e., epitheliomuscular and gastrodermal digestive cell, migration has not been established.] Haynes and Burnett

(1963), in studies of dissociated cell layers of *Hydra,* found that epidermal epitheliomuscular cells were formed prior to the elaboration of the regenerate and Diehl (1969) found similar results in the brackish-water hydroid, *Cordylophora.* This evidence, along with our present work, supports the view that in *Hydra* the epidermal cells control the form of the organism. Interstitial cells function largely as a source of certain additional cells which differentiate according to the needs of the new structure. Their primary pathways of differentiation are the formation of cnidoblast cells and nerves. Both these cell types are important in the life of the animal, but we have shown (Diehl and Burnett, 1964) that *Hydra* can survive for 2 months or longer without a new supply of these cells. Cnidoblasts are essential for the production of nematocysts which are continually required for prey subduction. Nerves act to integrate the behavior of the animal and to supply neurosecretory materials.

It is possible that a certain number of specialized cell types in addition to digestive cells and epidermal epitheliomuscular cells must be present before the normal form of the animal can be attained through regeneration or budding. After interstitial cells have been specifically eliminated from the animal there is a sufficient reserve of gland cells, mucous cells, and cnidoblasts to contribute to the regenerate or bud. However, as growth continues the number of gland cells and mucous cells diminishes, and cnidoblasts are almost entirely lacking. In addition, digestive cells, which appear to cease dividing after mustard treatment, also decline in numbers. The ratio of these specialized cell types necessary for regeneration or budding has not been determined but there is presumably a lower limit; whenever this is reached these developmental processes stop. However, in spite of the necessity of maintaining a certain minimal number of other cell types, epitheliomuscular cells, under the influence of some growth-controlling factors, appear to be at the heart of the developmental events leading to the production of the adult form through either budding or regeneration.

This theory combines limited division of "adult" cells and the remolding of existing tissues (morphallaxis) as the bases of regeneration and budding in *Hydra.* It excludes any obligatory role of interstitial cells and relegates to them the task of differentiating into cells required for long-term survival and physiological efficiency, namely, nerve cells, cnidoblasts, gametes, and possibly gland and mucous cells.

Acknowledgment

The author wishes to express his gratitude to the Wistar Press for granting him the use of the figures which appear in this chapter. They originally appeared in the Journal of Experimental Zoology, Volumes 155, 158, and 163.

References

Bodenstein, D. (1947). *J. Exp. Zool.* **104,** 311.

Braem, F. (1894). *Biol. Zentralbl.* **14,** 140.

Braem, F. (1910). *Biol. Zentralbl.* **30,** 367.

Brauer, A. (1891). *Z. Wiss. Zool.* **52,** 169.

Brien, P. (1953). *Biol. Rev.* **28,** 308.

Brien, P., and Reniers-Decoen, M. (1949). *Bull. Biol. Fr. Belg.* **82,** 283.

Brien, P., and Reniers-Decoen, M. (1950). *Ann. Soc. Zool. Belg.* **81,** 3.

Brien, P., and Reniers-Decoen, M. (1955). *Bull. Biol. Fr. Belg.* **89,** 259.

Brewer, H. B., Comstock, J. P., and Aranow, L. (1961). *Biochem. Pharmacol.* **8,** 281.

Burnett, A. L. (1959). *J. Exp. Zool.* **140,** 281.

Burnett, A. L. (1961). *J. Exp. Zool.* **146,** 21.

Burnett, A. L. (1966). *Amer. Natur.* **100,** 165.

Burnett, A. L., and Diehl, N. (1964). *J. Exp. Zool.* **157,** 217.

Burt, D. R. (1934). *J. Exp. Zool.* **68,** 59.

Campbell, R. D. (1967). *Develop. Biol.* **15,** 487.

Chapman, G. B. (1961). *In* "The Biology of Hydra" (H. M. Lenhoff and W. F. Loomis, eds.), pp. 131–151. Univ. of Miami Press, Coral Gables, Florida.

Davis, L. E., Burnett, A. L., Haynes, J. F., and Mumaw, V. R. (1966). *Develop. Biol.* **14,** 307.

Diehl, F. A. (1969). *Wilhelm Roux' Arch. Entwicklungsmech. Organismen* **162,** 309.

Diehl, F. A., and Burnett, A. L. (1964). *J. Exp. Zool.* **155,** 253.

Diehl, F. A., and Burnett, A. L. (1965a). *J. Exp. Zool.* **158,** 283.

Diehl, F. A., and Burnett, A. L. (1965b). *J. Exp. Zool.* **158,** 299.

Diehl, F. A., and Burnett, A. L. (1966). *J. Exp. Zool.* **163,** 125.

Downing, E. R. (1905). *Zool. Jahrb., Abt. Anat. Ontog Tiere* **21,** 379.

Evlakhova, V. F. (1946). *C. R. Acad. Sci.* **53,** 369.

Gelei, J. V. (1924). *Z. Zellforsch. Mikrosk. Anat.* **1,** 471.

Goetsch, W. (1919). *Biol. Zentralbl.* **39,** 289.

Goetsch, W. (1920). *Biol. Zentralbl.* **40,** 458.

Gross, J. (1925). *Naturwissenschaften* **13,** 580.

Hadzi, J. (1910). *Arb. Zool. Inst. Univ. Wien* **18,** 61.

Haynes, J., and Burnett, A. L. (1963). *Science* **142,** 1481.

Issajew, W. (1926). *Wilhelm Roux' Arch. Entwicklungsmech. Organismen* **108,** 1.

Jones, C. S. (1941). *J. Exp. Zool.* **87,** 457.

Kanajew, J. (1926a). *Zool. Anz.* **65,** 217.

Kanajew, J. (1926b). *Zool. Anz.* **67,** 305.

Kanajew, J. (1929). *Zool. Anz.* **81,** 89.

Kanajew, J. (1930). *Wilhelm Roux' Arch. Entwicklungsmech. Organismen* **122,** 736.

Kleinenberg, N. (1872). "Hydra. Eine Anatomische-Entwicklungsgeschichtliche Untersuchung." Engelmann, Leipzig.

Lang, A. (1892). *Z. Wiss. Zool.* **54,** 365.

Lang, A. (1894). *Biol. Zentralbl.* **14,** 682.

McConnell, C. H. (1933a). *Biol. Bull.* **64,** 86.

McConnell, C. H. (1933b). *Biol. Bull.* **64,** 96.

Macklin, M. (1968). *J. Cell. Physiol.* **72,** 1.

Mattes, O. (1925). *Zool. Anz.* **62,** 307.

Nussbaum, M. (1887). *Sitzangsber. Niederrhein. Ges. Natur.-Heilk.* **44,** 10.

Nussbaum, M. (1907). *Biol. Centralbl.* **27,** 651.

Schlottke, E. (1930). *Z. Mikrosk.-Anat. Forsch.* **22,** 493.

Schneider, K. C. (1890). *Arch. Mikrosk. Anat.* **35,** 321.

Schulze, P. (1918). *Sitzungsber. Ges. Naturforsch. Freunde Berlin* pp. 252–277.

Slautterback, D. B. (1961). *In* "The Biology of Hydra" (H. M. Lenhoff and W. F. Loomis, eds.), pp. 77–129. Univ. of Miami Press, Coral Gables, Florida.

Slautterback, D. B., and Fawcett, D. W. (1959). *J. Biophys. Biochem. Cytol.* **5,** 441.

Strelin, G. S. (1929). *Wilhelm Roux' Arch. Entwicklungsmech. Organismen* **115,** 27.

Tannreuther, G. W. (1909). *Biol. Bull.* **16,** 210.

Tardent, P. (1952). *Rev. Suisse Zool.* **59,** 247.

Tardent, P. (1954). *Wilhelm Roux' Arch. Entwicklungsmech. Organismen* **146,** 593.

Tardent, P. (1963). *Biol. Rev.* **38,** 293.

Weimer, B. R. (1928). *Physiol. Zool.* **1,** 183.

Zawarzin, A. A. (1929). *Wilhelm Roux' Arch. Entwicklungsmech. Organismen* **115,** 1.

CHAPTER 5

Expression and Maintenance
of Organismic Polarity

GEORGIA E. LESH-LAURIE

Polarity defines an asymmetrical organization exhibited throughout living systems. It is discernible, for example, within an unfertilized egg from the position occupied by yolk material, the nucleus, and cytoplasmic inclusions. Asexual reproductive processes, as budding, are often characterized by a rigorous maintenance in the new individual of the polar axes manifested in the parent. Irrespective of the widespread expression of the phenomenon, however, the morphological features by which it is recognized represent the result, not the cause, of polarity. Numerous detailed descriptive studies of polarity have failed to define the mechanisms by which this organization is expressed and/or maintained within an organism.

The freshwater polyp *Hydra* represents a model system for the experimental analysis of the causal factors underlying the expression and maintenance of a polarized form. Structurally *Hydra* is a bipolar animal, possessing a limited number of cell types. Its distal hypostome is separated from a proximal basal disc by the body column. Each region of the animal may be individually characterized at the levels of gross morphology, tissue, cellular, and molecular constitution (Burnett, 1959). These facts, coupled with the *Hydra's* consistent growth pattern and extensive regenerative capacity enable one to analyze the development and maintenance of a polarized form at all levels of biological organization.

In this chapter, significant evidence accumulated at each level of biological organization will be reviewed. The material presented has been selected for its relevance in the development of testable theories that propose mechanisms for the control of polarity in *Hydra*. Using this foundation of information, several existing theories analyzing the expression and maintenance of polarity will then be considered. No detailed review of the historical literature on hydroid polarity has been attempted. Excellent accounts of this material are already available (Kanaev, 1952; R. P. Davis, 1964).

I. Review of Evidence Accumulated at Various Levels of Biological Organization

A. Investigations at the Level of Gross Morphology

Three areas of investigation using observations made on whole animals are relevant to an understanding of the expression and maintenance of organismic polarity in the *Hydra:* (1) the occurrence and explanation of spontaneous heteromorphosis; (2) the effects of induction in determining axial polarity; and (3) the experimental alteration of polarity. Each of these phenomena was explored initially as an individual problem. Yet, each includes within its parameters a transformation from the normal polarized configuration to an abnormal heteromorphic condition. It is hoped, therefore, that by reviewing what is known of hydroid polarity at the gross morphological level of organization, and later at the histological and molecular levels, to define some unifying concepts of polarized form, a prerequisite to an analysis of its control and direction within an individual.

1. Occurrence and Explanation of Spontaneous Heteromorphosis

Spontaneous heteromorphosis among hydroids has often been reported in association with recovery from depression (Hyman, 1928; Hand and Jones, 1957). A general decline in metabolism accompanies physiological depression, which Hyman believed resulted in decreased hypostomal control of the body column. Therefore, as a more uniform metabolism existed throughout the animal, any regeneration which occurred did so at more than one growing point.

An additional example of spontaneous heteromorphosis occurs if hydras in the early stages of gonad formation are removed from the stimulus initiating sexual development. A common stimulus for sexuality in *Hydra* is cold temperatures. Consequently, hydras (specifically *Hydra pirardi* or *H. pseudoligactis*) removed from a pond in the fall and brought into the laboratory often develop supernumerary hypostomes at varying positions along the body column. Burnett and Diehl (1964b) attributed this heteromorphosis to the absence in sexual animals of any growth inhibitory materials that may be derived from rapidly proliferating tissue. In the absence of inhibitors, any residual growth stimulatory substances could act unabated, leading to the development of supernumerary hypostomes.

2. Effects of Induction in Determining Axial Polarity

Tissues constituting the apex of an asymmetry often exhibit high inductive potency when apposed to other somatic tissue. Browne's classic experiments in 1909 delimited three regions of inductive capacity within the *Hydra:* (1) hypostomal tissue of the tentacle ring; (2) the most distal portion of a bud which had not yet developed tentacles; and (3) regenerating hypostomes. Significant among these observations was the fact that all of these regions represented areas of hypostome differentiation. No other tissue elicited this response. By using graft combinations between green and bleached animals she demonstrated that the outgrowth formed did not arise solely from the grafted material but was largely organized from host tissue around the graft site. These findings have been confirmed by Koelitz (1911a,b), Issajew (1926), Rand *et al.* (1926), Tripp (1928), Mutz (1930), Li and Yao (1945), and Yao (1945).

Following the inductive effects of hypostome but not of basal disc grafts in *H. oligactis (fusca),* Rand *et al.* (1926) first theorized that the hypostome is the

seat of formative agencies which may act: (1) to initiate or control development of structures appropriate in relation to itself, or (2) to inhibit the operation of a developmental mechanism where such operation would result in structures inconsistent with the attainment of a form normal in relation to the dominant head region.

Yao (1945) reported that the inductive capacity of hypostomal grafts was not drastically modified after treatment with "low molecular weight concentrations" of either respiratory inhibitors (e.g., potassium cyanide, lithium chloride, or sodium fluoride) or respiratory catalysts (e.g., methylene blue). He also rejected the idea that inductive potency in hydroids was directly related to a physiological gradient. If this were the case, Yao argued, transplantation experiments should reveal this gradient in terms of the relative frequency of induction. He found no inductive ability outside the hypostome, and hence concluded that induction was confined to the cells of that region.

By grafting with varying orientation annuli of tissue from each body region to stock animals from which the hypostome and basal disc had been excised, Burt (1925, 1934) also tested the capacity of regeneration to follow an axial gradient. He discovered that in addition to hypostomal material, the anterior margin of the budding zone also possessed a high potential for hypostome formation.

Evidence relating the development of organizational (or inductive) centers with a polar gradient in *Hydra* was also demonstrated in reconstitution masses by Weimer (1928, 1932, 1934). He obtained an increase in bipolar and multipolar reaggregates as the material of the mass was taken from increasingly more distal regions. Reconstitutes from pieces allowed to heal 24 hours, and then exposed to dilute potassium cyanide solution, exhibited disintegration patterns paralleling reaggregation polarities. From this data he indicated that the form of the reconstituted piece was established within 24 hours, before any apical differentiation had occurred.

Although he failed to speculate on the controlling mechanism involved, Chalkley (1945) reported that in *H. vulgaris* a logarithmic relation existed between the volume of tissue one included in the reconstituting mass and the number of hypostomal organization centers developing in the re-aggregate.

Similar inductive phenomena have been observed in the colonial hydroids *Cordylophora lacustris* and *Corymorpha* sp. Child (1929) discovered he could induce the development of new axes by grafting naked distal stem pieces into lateral cuts in the stalk of *Corymorpha*. Neither the size nor original polarity of the implanted piece influenced its inductive ability. Injury alone at the oral end also occasionally yielded new axes. From these experiments Child reaffirmed his belief that the inducer or organizer was not a particular tissue entity, but rather a physiological condition. Incisions, like grafts, induced because they initiated a localized region of increased cellular activity.

Hypothesizing that Child's physiological gradients may represent more the result than the cause of organization, Beadle and Booth (1938) examined reorganization masses of minced *Cordylophora*. They found only oral cone tissue capable of inducing hydranth formation when grafted into the mass. Such grafts overcame the inhibition to reconstitution exerted by calcium and magnesium deficiencies, cyanide, and phenylurethane, but not that caused by a potassium lack. Therefore, they suggested that the ". . . action of the grafted oral cone is in the nature of a nonspecific stimulus which releases organizing potentialities already present in the mass" mediated either by diffusion of a chemical substance or the establishment of some form of metabolic gradient.

3. Experimental Alteration of Polarity

Wetzel (1895, 1898) described the initial experimental alteration of polarity in *Hydra* by removing the basal discs of two animals and grafting their aboral ends together. Excision of one of the hypostomes resulted in a basal disc developing in its place. Burnett (1961a,b, 1962), seeking evidence for the existence of a diffusible growth stimulatory material in the hypostomal area, succeeded in inverting polarity by inducing tentacle formation in former peduncular tissues. Here, after tandem grafting the growth region of one species of *Hydra* to the peduncle of another species (basal disc removed), the vacuolated tissue of the peduncle began to resorb food material, interstitial cells invaded the region, and eventually a complete hypostome differentiated. Burnett was also able to collect and concentrate a hypostomal growth substance in agar blocks, which induced hypostome formation at a proximal surface after application.

Heteromorphosis was also accomplished through grafting in R. P. Davis's (1964) system. He achieved 100% reversal in regenerating gastric regions following a 45-hour inversion within the body column of an intact animal. Removal of the host hypostome after the grafted region was in place decreased the amount of reversal in these grafts. A regenerating hypostome (cut 8 hours before the inversion), however, still yielded 100% reversal.

More recently Lentz (1965) and Lesh and Burnett (1964, 1966) have achieved an experimental alteration of the normal polarized configuration in *Hydra* through the use of extracts prepared from homogenates of hypostomal material. These extracts are capable of directing supernumerary hypostome and tentacle development all along the body axis of regenerating annuli of tissue. Animals possessing over 45 tentacles have been described. These organisms exhibit none of the typical axial polarity exhibited in *Hydra*.

Polarity appears more easily altered in *Tubularia* than in *Hydra*. Peebles (1931) increased the proportion of aboral hydranths by merely ligaturing regenerating stem pieces. She attributed this result to the removal of an apical dominance existing at the distal end.

Hydroid polarity is clearly, therefore, a dynamic, not a static, condition. Although rigorously maintained in normal and regenerating animals, it can be altered experimentally. A dominant role for the hypostomal area in determining and maintaining this phenomenon is also outlined by these studies. Once this dominance is suppressed or redirected, heteropolarity develops. Also a correlation between the apex of polarity and the occurrence of high inductive potency is suggested, as it is only hypostomal material that possesses the ability to organize surrounding tissue.

B. TISSUE AND CELL STUDIES

Histological studies define another anatomical condition common to polar apeces of hydroids, a concentration of nervous elements. Hadzi (1909) initially described the "nerve net" of *Hydra,* showing the greatest accumulation of nervous material in the hypostome. Later, using methylene blue reduced to its leuco form with Rongalit and thus rendering it specific for nerves, McConnell (1932) and Burnett and Diehl (1964a) confirmed and extended Hadzi's findings. Recently several investigators have succeeded in demonstrating the presence, and dominant role in controlling regeneration and growth, of neurosecretory material which collects primarily within the ganglionic elements of the hypostome and growth region (Lentz and Barnett, 1963; Burnett *et al.,* 1964; L. Davis *et al.,* 1968).

Role of Interstitial Cells

Cytological investigations provide evidence of a recurrent cellular pattern also common to axial polarity and inductive systems in the hydroids. The apex of polarity and primary inductive region is generally characterized by an absence of the small, basophilic interstitial cells (or I-cells). Areas immediately proximal to this region, however, contain excessive concentrations of them. If grafting procedures are employed these cells collect at the site of implantation prior to any morphological expression of the inductive event (Singer, 1952; Tardent, 1954, 1960; Burnett *et al.,* 1962).

Tardent showed that the gradient in interstitial cell distribution in *H. vulgaris* corresponded directly to the axial gradient in regenerative capacity exhibited by this animal. In *Tubularia,* however, the interstitial cell population was more evenly distributed throughout the coenosarc, and polarity was easily altered in this organism. He asserted, therefore, that it was this cellular relationship that determined the polarized form of *Hydra.*

Lehn (1953), however, correlated polarity with the presence of gastrodermal "gland tissue." Wherever hypostomal gland cells came to lie following centrifugation of a reaggregate, a mouth and tentacles formed. Correspondingly a basal disc developed where basal disc "gland tissue" was located during wound healing.

It has now been established that both nerves and gland cells represent types of interstitial cell differentiation in *Hydra* (Haynes and Burnett, 1963; Burnett and Diehl, 1964a; L. Davis *et al.,* 1966; L. Davis, 1969). This, coupled with Tardent's conjecture that I-cells were the sole determinant of a polarized form, and Diehl and Burnett's (1965) demonstration that those cells were not directly required for regeneration of form, suggested the necessity for further exploration of the function of this cell type in the expression and maintenance of polarity in *Hydra.*

Recently, Lesh (1970) succeeded in demonstrating that quantitative differences in a crude preparation of hypostomal inductive materials influenced the direction of interstitial cell differentiation. This observation provided a basis for explaining the asymmetrical distribution of interstitial cells and interstitial cell derivatives along the body column in *Hydra.* How this cellular polarity is reflected in the form expressed at the organismic level, however, has not been clearly established.

C. STUDIES AT THE MOLECULAR LEVEL OF ORGANIZATION

Axial gradients in *Hydra* can also be illustrated by both physical and chemical means. Some of the agents utilized in these investigations affect a destruction of living tissue; the rate at which lethality is accomplished reflecting the metabolic activity of the material being tested. Employing UV light and photolysis of eosin-yellow stained animals with visible light Hinrichs (1924–1925) found the tentacles destroyed first. Before disintegration reached the base of the tentacles, however, it was observed in the hypostome. Electrical current also influences organismic polarity in some marine hydroids. Regenerating *Obelia* stems deflected their axis of growth toward the anode, whereas regeneration at the cathode was inhibited (Lund, 1924–1925). Alternatively, using electrophoretic measurements, Macklin (1971) found that *Hydra* exhibited no relation between electrical current and either the rate of regeneration or the expression of polarity.

Child discovered that body regions maintaining the highest rate of oxidative metabolism coincided directly with those areas exhibiting rapid cytolysis upon treatment with cyanide, ether, and alcohol. Testing lethal susceptibility to these substances, he observed that reactions occurred first in the tentacle tips and subhypostomal growth region, and then proceeded proximally. The pattern of oxidation and reduction of the indicator dyes potassium permanganate, methylene blue, Janus green, and neutral red followed a similar apical–basal gradient. These observations reinforced those established with physical agents. Further supporting evidence was derived from studies with colonial hydroids (*Obelia, Gonothyria, Bougainvillia*) in which the actively metabolizing hydranth growing tips concentrated the above-mentioned stains most rapidly (Child, 1919, 1946, 1947; Child and Hyman, 1919).

Polar abnormalities have also been produced using mitotic inhibitors. Colcemid and colchicine both normally inhibit hypostome regeneration in hydra (Webster, 1967; Corff and Burnett, 1969). Webster (1967), however, also observed the development of supernumerary hypostomes following the exposure of regenerating hydras to 20 mg/ml colcemid. Shostak and Tammariello (1969) described similar heteropolar animals following a 1-hour incubation in 0.1% colcemid. They attributed this abnormal development to an interference by the colcemid of basal disc formation, and consequently bud detachment, rather than as an overt stimulation of hypostome development.

Low concentrations of colchicine, conversely, have been shown to have only a suppressive effect on hypostome and tentacle formation in regenerating hydras (Sturtevant *et al.,* 1951; Ham and Eakin, 1958; Corff and Burnett, 1969). Corff and Burnett (1969) achieved a true polar reversal, inducing peduncle and basal disc development at the distal surface of a regenerating *Hydra* after varying periods of exposure to colchicine concentrations of between 0.01 and 0.025%.

In addition to the investigations with mitotic inhibitors, Hicklin *et al.* (1969) described polar reversals similar to those obtained by Corff and Burnett, using approximately 2×10^{-4} M dithiothreitol (DTT), a protective agent for sulfhydryl groups.

It is evident from these experiments that *Hydra* manifests regional differences in physiological activity. In all cases the areas sensitive to metabolic and growth modifiers, by the methods employed (e.g., hypostome, hydranth growing tips, and regeneration of these structures) correspond to those regions representing the apex of polarity within the system. The existence of a direct correlation between metabolism and the development and control of the polarized state remains to be proved, however.

II. Growth Patterns

Regulation of growth and form among coelenterates represents an additional area in which studies relating to polarity have been undertaken. Tripp (1928) initially hypothesized a growth model for *Hydra* which was later confirmed by Brien and Reniers-Docoen (1949) through vital staining techr.:ques and by Burnett and Garofalo (1960) employing algal marked cells. Beneath the hypostome of *Hydra* a growth region exists in which cell proliferation presumably exceeds that exhibited elsewhere in the animal. Divisions in this area force adjacent cells distally to the tentacle tips and proximally to the basal disc. When cells reach the extremities of the body column they slough off and die. Thus, the animal is capable of continual growth without a change in form.

More recently the autoradiographic evidence of Campbell (1965, 1967a–d) has disputed the existence of regions of differential growth in *Hydra*. He has shown that cell divisions occur somewhat "uniformly" throughout the body column of the animal. The form of the animal, therefore, is the reflection of a steady-state type of growth. The biochemical data of Clarkson (1969) on ^{3}H-thymidine incorporation during hypostomal regeneration also revealed neither an axial gradient in DNA synthesis nor any regional localization of growth.

In Chapter 15 of this volume, the process of cell division in *Hydra* will be discussed in depth. The information in that chapter will resolve the conflict existing here in a manner that explains both of the forementioned theories. Both theories, however, contain information and implications that can be employed in developing testable models to explain polarity.

SUMMARY

Therefore, regardless of the approach utilized to investigate the problem of the development and maintenance of polarity in *Hydra,* one relationship is consistently repeated. In *Hydra,* as well as other representative hydroids, the correlation and possible interdependence of polarity, high inductive potency, and a concentration of nervous elements are evident. Analyses that satisfactorily explain the capacity of these phenomena to regulate the form of an individual could define the mechanisms inherent in the expression and maintenance of organismic polarity in *Hydra.*

III. Theories Analyzing the Control of Polarized Form

Theories exploring mechanisms for the control of polarity in *Hydra* fit into two categories. One proposes that polarity in *Hydra,* and other hydroids, is the result of activity originating at each end of the animal. The other category suggests that polarity derives from the activity of only one end of the animal. This latter activity, however, may involve a two-component mechanism.

A. Polarity Resulting from Activities Originating at Each End of the Animal

1. Antagonistic Gradients

Goetsch (1929) initially proposed that polarity in *Hydra* is the result of two antagonistic gradients. According to his interpretation, when an isolated portion of the animal is free to regenerate each of its ends, undifferentiated cells accumulate at the wound sites. These cells are exposed to a higher concentration of hypostome-determined cells at the distal end and to a similar higher concentration of basal disc-determined cells at the proximal end of the regenerating piece. As a result of the influence of these determined elements, the differentiation of the undifferentiated elements is directed toward either hypostome or basal disc formation.

The evidences on which Goetsch developed his theory were principally the grafting experiments of Wetzel (1895, 1898), Peebles (1900), King (1901, 1903), and Browne (1909), plus a variety of experiments in which he also obtained heteromorphic regeneration by employing grafting techniques (Goetsch, 1929). He found hypostomes regenerated from the proximal ends and basal discs from the distal ends of pieces prepared in diverse graft combinations. In addition, Goetsch discovered that he could graft between the basal disc and hypostome of an animal an inverted *"mittelstuck"* of another animal, and in some cases these inversions became incorporated into a normal-appearing animal. While Goetsch failed to state what body region served as the *mittelstuck,* his diagrams suggest that he used the gastric region and the distal portion of the budding region.

Goetsch attempted to determine whether an incorporated *mittelstuck* was truly reversed by observing its regeneration following reexcision after a period of time. He prepared four grafts, using *H. viridis* in which the inverted piece was either bleached or green and the associated hypostome and peduncle of the contrasting type. Using the color of the various parts of the graft combination as a marker he excised the inverted regions after they had been in place for 5 days. In order to distinguish between the two ends of the inverted region he had left a piece of the base of an amputated bud attached to the originally proximal end of two of the inversions. The remaining two inversions were left unmarked. He found that both of the excised inversions on which a basal disc marker had been left formed hypostomes at the original distal end and thus failed to show a reversal. One of the two unmarked *mittelstucks* formed a hypostome at each end and the other failed to regenerate at all.

Of the results obtained, the specimen that showed a bipolar development was the most significant. Here, the developmental capacity of each end of the piece upon isolation was identical. This suggests strongly that at the moment of excision this piece was not polarized. This single case, in which one of the two hypostomes formed was heteromorphic, is the first instance in which a polar reversal was produced in a piece permitted to regenerate free from the influence of any other components of the prepared graft combination. Although heteromorphosis occurred, however, a complete reversal of polarity was not obtained since the original distal end of the inverted piece still reflected its origin by forming a hypostome.

2. Bipotential Gradient

Extending Goetsch's observations and those of Burt (1934), Sinha and his co-workers (Sinha, 1966; Mookerjee and Sinha, 1967; Mookerjee and Bhattacherjee, 1967) also believe that organismic polarity in *Hydra* derives from the activity of two opposing potencies, potencies that extend along the body column from their point of origin. Distally, one finds a hypostome-forming potency; proximally a basal disc-forming potency. The result is a cylinder with two unipolar ends (a hypostome and a basal disc) and a bipotential middle region that possesses the capacity to elaborate a hypostome and/or a basal disc.

The supportive evidence on which this theory was formulated also involved grafting experiments. Here, grafts were performed principally in two ways. Body column pieces of varying length were excised from different regions of the animal and then replaced in reverse order. (This is similar to Goetsch's *mittelstuck* grafts.) When these "bipotential" middle pieces were excised, Sinha (1966) recorded two alternative types of development: (1) the achievement of diverse degrees of polar reversal; or (2) the retention of the original polarity of the piece. The relative frequency of polar reversal or retention of existing polarity varied with the length of the implanted piece and its original location within the *Hydra*.

In a second series of experiments, hypostomes were grafted in the vicinity of basal discs. These hypostomes successfully induced new axes of polarity. Basal discs placed in the hypostomal region, however, were eventually sloughed.

Histological investigations revealed a marked parallel between changes in the interstitial cell distribution in inverted pieces and successful experimental reversals of polarity (Sinha, 1966). This observation led Sinha to extend his polarity theory to the cellular level. Although his experiments provided no means to determine whether a division and/or migration of interstitial cells achieved the redistribution, he suggested that a migration in interstitial cells may have served as a "basic act of differentiation" — an act that could ultimately be involved in the expression of polarity in the animal.

One major question the bipotential gradient theory fails to solve is the problem of what causes any portion of a bipotential region to become unipotential. To answer this question Sinha evokes the possibility of a specific inhibitor. This inhibitor could then act as an "epiphenomenon" to convert an originally equipotential system into unique distal–proximally determined systems. Sinha provides no direct evidence consistent with this conclusion. However, he cites numerous examples of inhibitory phenomena described in the hydroid polarity literature as support for his beliefs.

Unfortunately, this theory was proposed almost simultaneously with those of Burnett (see Section III,B,2) and Webster (see Section III,B,3). Consequently, there have been no realistic attempts to integrate the concepts presented here with those proposed by Burnett and Webster. Yet, as will become evident, areas of both continuity and discontinuity exist between all three of these theories. Critical experiments testing the points of discrepancy between the existing theories remain to be performed.

3. Basal Disc Differentiation

One final investigation that must be interpreted as supporting the existence of unique hypostomal and basal disc activities in the expression and maintenance of organismic polarity in *Hydra* is the recent work on basal disc differentiation by MacWilliams *et al.* (MacWilliams and Kafatos, 1968; MacWilliams *et al.,* 1970). Rather than explain the differentiation of basal disc in terms of gradients emanating from the hypostome, these investigators explored the possibility that both the regeneration of a basal disc and the normal replacement of basal disc cells are controlled by mechanisms "directly responsive to the basal disc itself." Through grafting experiments they established that the presence of a basal disc suppressed the normal regeneration of a disc. This observation supported the contention of an inhibition to basal disc differentiation by basal disc (MacWilliams and Kafatos, 1968).

The experimental results of Corff and Burnett (1969) and Hicklin *et al.* (1969) are also consistent with the suggestion that basal disc formation may be an autonomous process. In both systems hypostome development was suppressed through the use of inhibitors, yet basal disc formation proceeded normally.

Later, MacWilliams *et al.* (1970) grafted basal discs of varying sizes (whole basal discs, half-basal discs, quarter-basal discs, no basal discs) to animals already in the process of regenerating these structures. These experiments allowed them to measure the frequency of basal disc inhibition in the host with respect to disc size and the time of host regeneration. They discovered that in such grafts information did pass from the grafted basal disc to the host. This finding led to the formulation of a mathematical model consistent with the hypothesis that the basal disc controls both its own differentiation and the continuous replacement of its cells through a negative feedback system. Furthermore, the feedback system exhibits a "continuously variable intensity," which is a function of disc size. Interestingly, despite being developed using a different differentiation system (basal disc differentiation), the mechanisms of inhibition proposed by MacWilliams *et al.* coincide directly with those developed by Webster for the control of hypostome differentiation (see Section III,B,3).

4. Summary

Although the alternative theories explaining polarity in *Hydra* (see Section III,B) do not require the existence of separate hypostome and basal disc gradients, no experiments exclude the possibility that both the distal and proximal ends of the organism are actively involved in establishing the conditions leading to the regeneration of the appropriate structure at the appropriate end of a system in which both ends are regenerating simultaneously.

B. POLARITY RESULTING FROM THE ACTIVITY OF ONLY ONE END OF THE ANIMAL

Alternative schemes suggest that polarity results from the activity of only one end of the animal. In many of these theories however, a two-component mechanism appears to be involved. The first component is that, while either end of the regenerating system is able to form a given structure, e.g., a hypostome, one end can accomplish this more rapidly than the other. The second component is that the end enjoying the developmental advantage inhibits regeneration of the same structure at the opposite end of the system.

1. Interstitial Cell Gradient

Differences in the rate of hypostome regeneration at various levels of the *Hydra* have been demonstrated by Weimer (1928), Rulon and Child (1937), Spangenberg and Eakin (1961), and Mookerjee and Bhattacherjee (1967). They have shown that hypostome regeneration occurs more rapidly at distal levels of the animal than it does at more proximal levels. This observed proximal to distal increase in regeneration rate appears related to polarity.

Utilizing this information Tardent (1954, 1960, 1963) proposed that this gradient in regeneration rate was a product of (1) physiological gradients such as those studied and described by Child (1947), and (2) a distoproximal gradient of decreasing interstitial cell concentration along the body column (Tardent, 1954). He claimed that development was favored at more distal levels because of their greater metabolic activity and the presence of more undifferentiated cells as a source for regenerative materials.

Therefore, by combining the two components described above: a distoproximal gradient in regeneration rate and inhibition between competing ends, polarity in hydroids has been explained by Tardent (1954, 1960, 1963) in the following manner. If an animal is cut in half the cut surface of the proximal half is freed from inhibition by the hypostome and regenerates that structure. However, the cut surface of the distal half is inhibited from regenerating a hypostome by the hypostome present on the piece and is instead directed toward the "alternative possible realization," a peduncle. In the case of a length of the animal with both distal and proximal regions amputated, the distal end acquires a dominant position as the result of the gradient in regeneration rate and by the production and release of an inhibitor which blocks the development of a similar primordium at the proximal end. Due to this inhibition, regeneration at the proximal end is directed toward the organization of a peduncle.

Two problems arise, however, in accepting Tardent's analysis of the establishment and expression of organismic polarity in hydroids. Initially, the significance of physiological gradients is open to question since it has been shown that the *Hydra,* at least, does not possess a single, continuous gradient. Instead, there are three points of relatively high metabolic activity: the hypostome, the budding region, and the basal disc. Between these are two regions of lower metabolic activity: the gastric region and the peduncle. If metabolic activity alone were sufficient to determine where a hypostome should form, one would anticipate that on an excised piece of the body column extending from the middle of the gastric region to the middle of the budding region a hypostome should be formed at the proximal end rather than the distal end. This does not happen.

In addition, Tardent's methods of demonstrating an interstitial cell gradient are open to criticism. He determined the average number of interstitial cells per 6400 μ^2 for each third of the body: a distal third extending from the growth region down to the lower part of the gastric region; a middle third including the lowest portion of the gastric region, all of the budding region and the uppermost portion of the peduncle; and a proximal third composed of most of the peduncle and the basal disc. However, in doing so, he averaged the figures obtained for various levels within a given third. Treating the data in this manner he found that the distal third had the highest concentration of interstitial cells, the proximal third had the lowest, and the middle third was intermediate. However, while these figures suggest a continuously decreasing distal to proximal interstitial cell gradient they do not prove that such is, in fact, the case. It is possible that the concentration of interstitial cells follows the same pattern as does the physiological gradient and shows a secondary increase in the budding region. Tardent's methodology to obtain an average count for each third of the animal would obscure this, since the region where a secondary increase in interstitial cell number may occur is averaged with the surrounding areas which might have a decreased interstitial cell concentration.

Recently R. P. Davis and Burnett (1969) tested further the validity of an interstitial cell gradient in the establishment of organismic polarity in *Hydra*. Using nitrogen mustard treatment, hydras devoid of interstitial cells were obtained (Diehl and Burnett, 1964). In these preparations distal halves of nitrogen mustard-treated animals were grafted to the proximal portions of normal, untreated hydras. Once the grafts were securely established, the hypostomes and basal discs were excised. Therefore, the regenerating graft combinations consisted of distal regions lacking interstitial cells and proximal regions containing normal populations and distributions of this cell type (Fig. 1). Within 2.5 days hypostomes formed

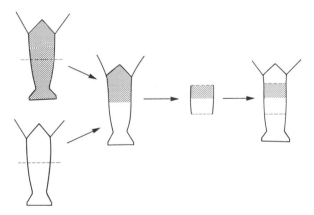

Fig. 1. Diagrammatic representation of grafting experiments performed to test the role of an interstitial cell gradient in the expression of polarity in *Hydra*. Initially, the distal halves of nitrogen mustard-treated animals (▦) were grafted to the proximal regions of normal, untreated hydras (☐). Once these grafts were securely established, the extremities of the grafts were excised, as shown, leaving isolated gastric regions. These isolates consisted of distal portions lacking interstitial cells as a result of nitrogen mustard treatment, and proximal regions containing normal populations and distribution of this cell type. Regeneration always occurred as indicated in the last illustration, with hypostomes forming the original distal cut surface. Reciprocal grafts also resulted in hypostome development at the original distal end.

at. the original distal cut surface, despite the histologically demonstrable absence of interstitial cells in that area. Reciprocal grafts (distal portion, normal; proximal portion, nitrogen mustard-treated) also resulted in hypostome development at the distal cut surface. These data strongly indicate the requirement for a reevaluation of the role of interstitial cell gradients in the actual expression of polarity in *Hydra*.

2. Stimulator/Inhibitor Ratios

Burnett (1961a,b, 1966) envisions the hypostomal region as the sole organization center of the *Hydra*. It produces and contains the highest concentrations of a diffusible inductive (or "growth stimulatory") material. Quantitative variations in this material result in qualitative differences in the direction of interstitial cell differentiation (Lesh and Burnett, 1966; Lesh, 1970). Burnett believes further that dividing cells along the body column of the animal produce a "growth inhibitory" material, which is also diffusible. According to his theory, therefore, the balance between inductive (or growth stimulatory) material and growth inhibitory material ultimately determines the cellular and morphological form of that region (Fig. 2) (Burnett, 1966).

Although the result of grafting and regeneration experiments initially led to the development of this theory, additional evidence has recently been obtained by the isolation and characterization of the materials presumably involved in the expression and maintenance of polarized form. Burnett (1961b) originally provided evidence that the inductive (or growth stimulatory) material could be collected in agar blocks. Application of these blocks to the cut aboral surfaces of test animals resulted in polar reversals in these hydras. Later, Lesh and Burnett were able to concentrate a low-molecular-weight, trypsin-sensitive material from homogenates of whole hydras. This material, when applied to regenerating annuli induced supernumerary hypostome and tentacle development in the animals. Cell count analyses have documented that the asymmetry of interstitial cell differentiation exhibited along the body column in *Hydra* is in part the result of the exposure of these cells to quantitative differences in inductive material (Lesh and Burnett, 1964, 1966; Lesh, 1969, 1970).

If Burnett is correct that dividing cells produce an inhibitor of division, it might be possible to initiate abnormal growth along the body column of a *Hydra* by suppressing cell division. This may be accomplished in *H. pirardi* and *H. pseudoligactis* by culturing these animals at 8°–10°C for extended periods (Burnett and Diehl, 1964b). When they were returned to room temperature, supernumerary hypostomes formed throughout the gastric region.

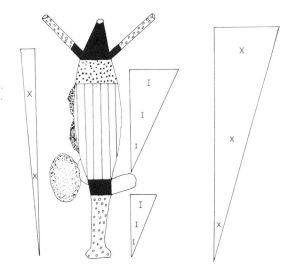

Fig. 2. Schematic diagram of how Burnett's stimulator to inhibitor ratios could control cellular differentiation in the various body regions of the *Hydra*. In the illustration X represents the postulated gradient in inductive or growth stimulatory material, and I the distribution of growth inhibitor. Burnett (1966) explains the model as follows:

In the extremities (open circles), no cell divisions occur and interstitial cells are rare or lacking. Dark areas (hypostome and junction of budding region and peduncle) indicate where interstitial cells differentiate into nerve. This can only occur where there is excess stimulator in proportion to inhibitor. Solid circles show the growth region which, because of its proximity to the hypostome, is an area high in cell division. The gastric region (lined area) is where interstitial cells complete their divisions forming nests of several cells which then differentiate into cnidoblasts. Those interstitial cells which don't differentiate into cnidoblasts in the gastric region differentiate into nerves at the junction of the budding region and peduncle. On the left-hand side of the model is the gradient of stimulator that occurs during sexuality. Stimulator production is reduced or ceases entirely. Interstitial cells in the presence of reduced stimulator differentiate into sperm (testes indicated as dotted protuberances on left side of animal) and in areas where stimulator is lacking or present in trace amounts into ova (below testes at level of bud).

From Burnett (1966). *Amer. Natur.* **100,** 165–190. Reproduced by permission.

This observation led to the prediction that the growth inhibitory material was released from the animal into the culture solution. Consequently, it would soon be lacking in the tissues of animals whose growth was retarded. Residual amounts of inducer or growth stimulator could then initiate supernumerary hypostome development. Recently, considerable progress has been made in purifying and crystallizing the growth inhibitory material from the culture solution (D. Reisa, unpublished observations).

Finally, Haynes (1967) has shown that when various species of *Hydra* are examined, it is apparent that, although they conform to the same general polarized form, no two species express identical growth patterns. If the growth stimulator/growth inhibitor model for the control of polarized form is valid, it should be possible to explain these variations as modifications of this model. To accomplish this, Haynes developed a way to quantify the stimulator/inhibitor ratio of a species. Direct measurement was impossible, so he evaluated their relative amounts through their biological effects. Burnett stated in 1966 that metabolic gradients were a function of the relative levels of stimulator/inhibitor present. Therefore, by examining a product of metabolic activity in different species, one should be able to establish a stimulator/inhibitor ratio for each species. Using a histochemical demonstration of succinic dehydrogenase activity, Haynes found a positive correlation between what would be postulated stimulator/inhibitor ratios from Burnett's growth experiments and the gradient in succinic dehydrogenase activity.

However, despite the additional fact that one can explain differences in polarity and metabolic gradient in terms of stimulator/inhibitor ratios, concrete information regarding the mechanisms by which these growth materials affect the cellular or organismic polarity of *Hydra* is only now being established. Until the inductive (or growth stimulatory) material has been further purified the critical experimental tests of this model cannot be made.

3. Time–Threshold Theory

Webster (1966; Webster and Wolpert, 1966) also views the hypostome as the principal organization center within the *Hydra*. He, however, prefers to explain polarity solely as an inhibitory phenomenon. According to his time–threshold theory, three interacting factors result in the organization of a *Hydra* into distal hypostomal regions and proximal non-hypostomal regions. These factors include (1) the time period required for hypostome determination; (2) the level of inhibition to hypostome formation present in a given region; and (3) the threshold for inhibition possessed by a specific region of the organism. All of these factors are distributed in gradients along the body column of the animal.

In an intact *Hydra,* therefore, the hypostome is constantly producing an inhibitor, which is subsequently lost from or destroyed by the animal. Because of this steady state, the level of inhibition maintained decreases as one moves away from the hypostome. The threshold required for inhibition of hypostome formation in any region is, therefore, determined by the position of that region relative to a hypostome. As a result of these interactions, the presence of a hypostome inhibits the formation of another hypostome nearby. Removal of the hypostome causes the level of inhibition to fall; regeneration of it restores this level (Webster, 1966).

Webster's theory also draws support principally from the results of regeneration and grafting experiments. Initially Webster (Webster and Wolpert, 1966) investigated whether regional differences existed in the rate of hypostome determination in *Hydra*. Following excisions in different regions of the body column, he measured the time required for hypostome determination in those regenerates, and also the time necessary for hypostome determination in similar-sized annuli isolated from similar regions of the animal. As a result of these experiments, he concluded that the hypostome was the "dominant" region of the animal (i.e., that it exerted the organizing influence). Furthermore, the time required for its determination depended upon the original position of the hypostome forming region along the distoproximal axis of the animal, a conclusion consistent with Sinha's findings (see Section III,A,2).

From an additional series of induction grafts carried out either in the presence or absence of the original oral hypostome he concluded that the existence of a hypostome inhibited the formation of another hypostome. Furthermore, the threshold for inhibition declined as the distance from the existing hypostome increased. This led to the concept that "inhibition is a threshold phenomenon," i.e., that regions of a *Hydra* "differ in the amount or level of inhibition required to prevent hypostome formation." As Webster (1966) states, an

> . . . interaction between threshold and level of inhibition is believed to control hypostome formation. If the level of inhibition is above the threshold of a region, then the formation of a hypostome will be prevented. Conversely, if a region is released from inhibition as a result of a fall in level of inhibition below the threshold, then a hypostome will be formed.

Several unanswered questions also remain with respect to Webster's theory. As Webster admits, no information is available defining the change in the level of inhibition present throughout the column following excision of the hypostome. Is the entire column released from inhibition by hypostome removal? Alternatively, is only a restricted area released from inhibition? Also, does hypostome formation initiate only in the "presumptive hypostomal area," or elsewhere in the column as well?

An additional unproved assumption of the theory is that the threshold for inhibition is a more stable feature of a piece of tissue than is its level of inhibition. Consequently, when one transplants a piece of tissue Webster's theory assumes that its level of inhibition drops precipitously to the level of the graft site. The original threshold, however, persists for a considerable period. No direct evidence to support this contention exists, to date.

Finally, one must consider the fact that a clear distinction between the theories of Webster and Burnett lies in their explanation of hypostome differentiation. Burnett views hypostome formation as a result of "stimulation." Alternatively, Webster believes it derives from a "removal of inhibition." This represents a subtle but definitive difference. In an attempt to design an experiment whose outcome would exclude one of these proposals, R. P. Davis (unpublished observations) performed the following triple grafts.

Three gastric regions from *H. viridis* were excised and grafted together in the manner designated in Fig. 3A. After grafting, hypostomes always developed at the position indicated in Fig. 3B. If one then examined these grafts from the perspective of gradients, these gradients (whether gradients of "inhibition" or of "stimulation"), would appear as shown in Fig. 3C.

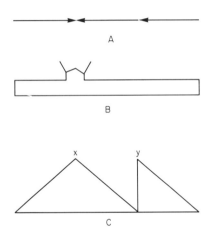

Fig. 3. Triple grafting experiment designed to distinguish whether hypostome differentiation was the result of stimulation or of a removal of inhibition. A. Three isolated gastric regions of *H. viridis* were grafted together as indicated. The arrow heads represent the original distal region of the isolate. B. Results of the grafting experiments illustrated in Fig. 3A. Hypostome formation always occurred at the position shown. C. Diagrammatic representation of the gradients existing in the experiment illustrated.

Because the hypostomes of the grafted organisms were removed in the experiment, Webster's theory would presume that a release from inhibition had occurred. If one assumes the threshold for inhibition remains somewhat constant, the level of inhibition should fall more quickly at position *y* than at position *x* because of the relative steepness of the gradients at these points. Webster's theory, therefore, would predict hypostome formation at position *y*. Yet, it occurred at *x*.

Alternatively, Burnett would consider that stimulation, not inhibition, was responsible for hypostomal development. This viewpoint would result in points x and y being in developmental competition for the initiation of hypostome formation. Because the gradients are less steep at point x, and because two regions of high activity come together here, the concentration of stimulation should be greater at point x than at point y. Hypostomes formed at point x.

IV. Prospectus

At present, it is apparent that the mechanisms controlling the determination, expression, and maintenance of a polarized form in the *Hydra* remain enigmatic. Despite the successes achieved by Goetsch, Sinha, MacWilliams, Tardent, Burnett, and Webster in placing the phenomena associated with asymmetry in an acceptable conceptual framework, very little is actually known of the mechanisms directing this morphogenesis. Hopefully, other sections of this text will shed some light on the very basic questions concerning polarity.

In addition, the resolution of three obviously problematical areas could provide information salient to a clearer understanding of organismic polarity in *Hydra*. These areas include (1) the occurrence and/or the production of heteromorphosis and its relevance to the question of polarity; (2) a meaningful integration and critical evaluation of the existing theories to explain the control of polarized form in *Hydra;* and (3) the exploration of presently untested parameters (e.g., environment) that may influence the asymmetry of an organism.

A. PRODUCTION OF HETEROMORPHOSIS AND THE QUESTION OF POLARITY

Initially, one must confront realistically the question of what information the spontaneous or experimental production of a heteromorphosis actually conveys with respect to the control of polarity in *Hydra*. For example, if one compares the polarity expressed in excised gastric regions that have previously been experimentally inverted in the organism with similar inversions in which only the imposed distal end of the inversion is amputated, a seemingly paradoxical result ensues. After 16 hours in an inverted position the preparations which were completely excised still expressed their original polarity: A hypostome regenerated at the original distal end. Those pieces from which only the imposed distal end was amputated after 16 hours, however, behaved as though their polarity were reversed. They regenerated a hypostome at the amputation site, which was, of course, the original proximal end (R. P. Davis, 1964).

On the basis of these results it appears that the simple production of a heteromorphic regenerate does not necessarily provide the investigator with any definitive information about the developmental hierarchy that exists within the piece. While 16 hours in the inverted position failed to produce a change in the polarity expressed by pieces free to regenerate at both ends, similar pieces, in which regeneration was restricted to a single end, behaved in an opposite manner. The latter type of preparation is directly comparable to the bulk of those experiments used to obtain the polar reversals described in the literature. These involved joining pieces of oppositely oriented polarity and then cutting away most of one of the components. This leaves a small piece attached to a larger, oppositely oriented segment under whose influence the reversal occurs. In these preparations the reversal of polarity appears to result from, rather than cause, the quality of the regenerate formed.

In turn, the quality of the regenerate formed at the amputation site could be a function of what structures the entire preparation lacks or possesses at the time of amputation. Since these preparations lack a hypostome the regeneration site would be free of any hypostomal inhibition and would regenerate that structure. However, in the completely excised pieces both ends were free to regenerate and under these circumstances the original developmental hierarchy was expressed by the formation of a hypostome at the original distal end.

B. Integration and Evaluation of Existing Theories

Points of convergence and divergence, confirmation and contradiction exist among all of the theories proposed to explain organismic polarity in *Hydra*. Overt coincidence in the interpretation of experimental data is only occasionally perceived. The imaginative analysis and confirmation of Webster's data by MacWilliams, Kafatos, and Bossert probably represents the best example of this type of recognition. More often, reported experimental observations are easily consistent with more than a single existing theory. Yet, the experiments performed are usually not sufficiently definitive to allow the investigator to eliminate or to select between these theories.

For example, if one uses the same type of *in situ* gastric region inversion technique described above, one can compare excised inversions from intact animals with inversions excised from animals whose hypostomes have been amputated. This experiment will show that removal of the hypostome reduces the percentage of reversals obtained in a given time.

According to Burnett, amputation of the hypostome removes the source of inductive or growth stimulating material, thus delaying the establishment of a new concentration gradient of this material in the inverted piece. Thus, the result obtained agrees with what would be predicted by Burnett's scheme.

However, the observed decrease in reversal rate occurring with removal of the hypostome can also be explained by Tardent's hypothesis that an interstitial cell concentration gradient is involved in hydroid polarity. The amputation of the hypostome of the inversion-containing animal may deplete the interstitial cell population at the distal end of the animal since some of these would become involved in the regeneration of a new hypostome. As a result, there would be fewer interstitial cells available to migrate proximally into the inverted piece to bring about the establishment of a new interstitial cell gradient. Therefore, both Tardent's and Burnett's theories of polarity in *Hydra* could readily explain the results of the experiment described.

Yet, what fundamental information is derived from either this experiment or the "philosophical meanderings" that could be involved in its interpretation? Very little! Clearly additional theoretical considerations to explain each new piece of evidence are not required. Rather, additional critical evaluation and testing of the points of discontinuity between the existing theories would prove fruitful.

C. EXPLORATION OF UNTESTED PARAMETERS

Additional areas that could potentially yield significant information relative to the expression and maintenance of an asymmetrical condition are investigations of previously untested or uncontrolled parameters that may influence polarity. One such parameter is the effect of population density. R. P. Davis (1964) demonstrated that crowded cultures, when thinned to population densities of 400–500 animals per bowl, showed a marked increase in the rate at which an experimental reversal of polarity could be achieved. This suggests that factors involved in the normal maintenance of polarity are influenced by environmental conditions. In animals from the crowded cultures no excised gastric regions showed a reversal of polarity after being inverted 24 hours *in situ*. Animals from the same cultures, after thinning the population, produced 78% reversals after the same period of time.

What may be a related effect of crowding on *Hydra* has been reported by Lenhoff and Loomis (1957). They observed a decrease in budding rate in association with increases in the population density of cultures. They suggested that this might be the result of the animals releasing some substance(s) into the water which could interfere with tentacle and cnidoblast differentiation. A factor acting in this manner would seriously interfere with the ability of the organism to catch and devour food and so cause a depression in budding rate. If Lenhoff and Loomis are correct, and the effect of crowding on budding primarily occurs through an interference with the feeding capacity of the animal, it would be interesting to study the effect of the nutritional state of the animal in any experimental analysis of polarity.

It would also be interesting to determine if the effect of crowding is a relatively generalized one, or if certain body regions are affected more than others. For instance, if one were to place on an animal from a crowded culture the hypostome of an animal from an uncrowded culture, would the rate at which a polar reversal occurs in an inverted gastric region in such a preparation be characteristic of that of animals from crowded, or uncrowded cultures, or lie somewhere between the two? The existing theories would not agree on either the predicted result, nor the interpretation, of such an experiment.

Acknowledgment

The author would like to express her sincerest thanks to Dr. R. P. Davis, who has for years served as a sounding board for her ideas regarding hydroid polarity, and who made substantial amounts of unpublished information available for use in this chapter.

References

Beadle, L., and Booth, F. (1938). *J. Exp. Biol.* **15**, 303–326.
Brien, P., and Reniers-Docoen, M. (1949). *Bull. Biol. Fr. Belg.* **82**, 293–386.
Browne, E. (1909). *J. Exp. Zool.* **7**, 1–23.
Burnett, A. L. (1959). *J. Exp. Zool.* **140**, 281–342.
Burnett, A. L. (1961a). *J. Exp. Zool.* **146**, 21–84.
Burnett, A. L. (1961b). *In* "The Biology of Hydra" (H. M. Lenhoff and W. F. Loomis, eds.), pp. 425–440. Univ. of Miami Press, Coral Gables, Florida.
Burnett, A. L. (1962). *Symp. Soc. Study Develop. Growth* **20**, 27–52.
Burnett, A. L. (1966). *Amer. Natur.* **100**, 165–190.
Burnett, A. L., and Diehl, N. (1964a). *J. Exp. Zool.* **157**, 217–226.
Burnett, A. L., and Diehl, N. (1964b). *J. Exp. Zool.* **157**, 237–250.
Burnett, A. L., and Garofalo, M. (1960). *Science* **131**, 160–161.
Burnett, A. L., Diehl, N., and Mutterperl, E. (1962). *Biol. Bull.* **123**, 489–490.
Burnett, A. L., Diehl, N., and Diehl, F. (1964). *J. Exp. Zool.* **157**, 227–236.
Burt, D. R. (1925). *Arch. Mikrosk. Anat. Entwicklungsmech.* **104**, 421–433.
Burt, D. R. (1934). *J. Exp. Zool.* **68**, 59–93.
Campbell, R. D. (1965). *Science* **148**, 1231–1232.
Campbell, R. D. (1967a). *Develop. Biol.* **15**, 487–502.
Campbell, R. D. (1967b). *J. Morphol.* **121**, 19–28.
Campbell, R. D. (1967c). *J. Exp. Zool.* **164**, 379–391.
Campbell, R. D. (1967d). *Trans. Amer. Microsc. Soc.* **86**, 169–173.
Chalkley, H. (1945). *J. Nat. Cancer Inst.* **6**, 191–195.
Child, C. M. (1919). *Biol. Bull.* **36**, 133–147.
Child, C. M. (1929). *Physiol. Zool.* **2**, 342–374.

Child, C. M. (1946). *Physiol. Zool.* **19**, 89–148.

Child, C. M. (1947). *J. Exp. Zool.* **104**, 153–195.

Child, C. M., and Hyman, L. (1919). *Biol. Bull.* **36**, 183–223.

Clarkson, S. G. (1969). *J. Embryol. Exp. Morphol.* **21**, 33–70.

Corff, S., and Burnett, A. L. (1969). *J. Embryol. Exp. Morphol.* **21**, 417–443.

Davis, L. (1969). *J. Cell Sci.* **5**, 699–726.

Davis, L., Burnett, A. L., Haynes, J., and Mumaw, V. (1966). *Develop. Biol.* **14**, 307–329.

Davis, L., Burnett, A. L., and Haynes, J. (1968). *J. Exp. Zool.* **167**, 295–331.

Davis, R. P. (1964). Ph.D. Thesis, Cornell University, Ithaca, New York.

Davis, R. P., and Burnett, A. L. (1969). Unpublished observations.

Diehl, F., and Burnett, A. L. (1964). *J. Exp. Zool.* **155**, 253–260.

Diehl, F., and Burnett, A. L. (1965). *J. Exp. Zool.* **158**, 299–318.

Goetsch, W. (1929). *Wilhelm Roux' Arch. Entwicklungsmech. Organismen* **117**, 211–311.

Hadzi, J. (1909). *Arb. Zool. Inst. Univ. Wein* **17**, 46–65.

Ham, R., and Eakin, R. (1958). *J. Exp. Zool.* **139**, 33–54.

Hand, C., and Jones, M. (1957). *Biol. Bull.* **112**, 349–357.

Haynes, J. (1967). *J. Embryol. Exp. Morphol.* **17**, 11–25.

Haynes, J., and Burnett, A. L. (1963). *Science* **142**, 1481–1483.

Hicklin, J., Hornbruch, A., and Wolpert, L. (1969). *Nature (London)* **221**, 1268–1271.

Hinrichs, M. (1924–1925). *J. Exp. Zool.* **41**, 21–31.

Hyman, L. (1928). *Biol. Bull.* **54**, 65–108.

Issajew, W. (1926). *Wilhelm Roux' Arch. Entwicklungsmech. Organismen* **108**, 1–67.

Kanaev, I. I. (1952). "Hydra. Essays on the Biology of Fresh Water Polyps" Sov. Acad. Sci., Moscow (English translation edited by H. M. Lenhoff, 1969).

King, H. D. (1901). *Arch. Entwicklungsmech. Organismen* **13**, 135–178.

King, H. D. (1903). *Arch. Entwicklungsmech. Organismen* **16**, 200–242.

Koclitz, W. (1911a). *Arch. Entwicklungsmech. Organismen* **31**, 191–297.

Koelitz, W. (1911b). *Arch. Entwicklungsmech. Organismen* **31**, 423–455.

Lehn, H. (1953). *Wilhelm Roux' Arch. Entwicklungsmech. Organismen* **146**, 371–402.

Lenhoff, H., and Loomis, W. (1957). *Anat. Rec.* **127**, 429–430.

Lentz, T. (1965). *Science* **150**, 633–635.

Lentz, T., and Barnett, R. (1963). *J. Exp. Zool.* **154**, 305–328.

Lesh, G. (1969). *Amer. Zool.* **9**, 610–611.

Lesh, G. (1970). *J. Exp. Zool.* **173**, 371–382.

Lesh, G., and Burnett, A. L. (1964). *Nature* **204**, 492–493.

Lesh, G., and Burnett, A. L. (1966). *J. Exp. Zool.* **163**, 55–78.

Li, H. P., and Yao, T. (1945). *J. Exp. Biol.* **21**, 155–160.

Lund, E. (1924–1925). *J. Exp. Zool.* **41**, 155–190.

McConnell, C. H. (1932). *Quart. J. Microsc. Sci.* **75**, 495–510.

Macklin, M. (1971). *J. Cell Physiol.* **77**, 83–92.

MacWilliams, H., and Kafatos, F. (1968). *Science* **159**, 1246–1247.

MacWilliams, H., Kafatos, F., and Bossert, W. (1970). *Develop. Biol.* **23**, 380–398.

Mookerjee, S., and Sinha, A. (1967). *Wilhelm Roux' Arch. Entwicklungsmech. Organismem* **158**, 331–340.

Mookerjee, S., and Bhattacherjee, A. (1967). *Wilhelm Roux' Arch. Entwicklungsmech. Organismen* **158**, 301–314.

Mutz, E. (1930). *Wilhelm Roux' Arch. Entwicklungsmech. Organismen* **121**, 210–271.

Peebles, F. (1900). *Arch. Entwicklungsmech. Organismen* **10**, 435–488.

Peebles, F. (1931). *Physiol. Zool.* **4**, 1–35.

Rand, H. W., Bovard, J. F., and Minnich, D. E. (1926). *Proc. Nat. Acad. Sci. U.S.* **12**, 565–570.

Rulon, O., and Child, C. M. (1937). *Physiol. Zool.* **10,** 1–13.

Shostak, S., and Tammariello, R. (1969). *Nat. Cancer Inst., Monogr.* **31,** 739–750.

Singer, J. (1952). *Quart. J. Microsc. Sci.* **93,** 269–288.

Sinha, A. (1966). *Wilhelm Roux' Arch. Entwicklungsmech. Organismen* **157,** 101–116.

Spangenberg, D. C., and Eakin, R. E. (1961). *J. Exp. Zool.* **147,** 259–270.

Sturtevant, F. M., Sturtevant, R. P., and Turner, R. C. (1951). *Science* **114,** 241–242.

Tardent, P. (1954). *Wilhelm Roux' Arch. Entwicklungsmech. Organismen* **146,** 593–649.

Tardent, P. (1960). *Symp. Soc. Study Develop. Growth* **18,** 21–43.

Tardent, P. (1963). *Biol. Rev.* **38,** 293–333.

Tripp, K. (1928). *Z. Wiss. Zool.* **132,** 476–525.

Webster, G. (1966). *J. Embryol. Exp. Morphol.* **16,** 105–141.

Webster, G. (1967). *J. Embryol. Exp. Morphol.* **18,** 181–197.

Webster, G., and Wolpert, L. (1966). *J. Embryol. Exp. Morphol.* **16,** 91–104.

Weimer, B. (1928). *Physiol. Zool.* **1,** 183–230.

Weimer, B. (1932). *J. Exp. Zool.* **62,** 93–107.

Weimer, B. (1934). *Physiol. Zool.* **7,** 212–225.

Wetzel, G. (1895). *Arch. Mikrosk. Anat. Entwicklungsmech.* **45,** 273–294.

Wetzel, G. (1898). *Arch. Mikrosk. Anat. Entwicklungsmech.* **52,** 70–96.

Yao, T. (1945). *J. Exp. Biol.* **21,** 147–155.

PART IV:

GASTRODERMAL REGENERATION IN *HYDRA*

Although *Hydra* regeneration after the excision of the hydranth or basal disc has been observed for two hundred years, it is mainly within the past decade that regeneration from a single cell layer has been studied in detail. In this type of regeneration metaplasia is most easily observed and one learns more of the factors controlling regeneration. In the following section, the problems of dedifferentiation and redifferentiation from a single cell layer are discussed in detail at the ultrastructural level. Attention is also paid to the type of ionic media that is necessary to maintain isolated gastrodermal explants.

CHAPTER 6

Ultrastructural Changes during Dedifferentiation and Redifferentiation in the Regenerating, Isolated Gastrodermis

LOWELL E. DAVIS

I. Introduction

The regenerating isolated gastrodermis of *Hydra* is a remarkable system in which to examine such processes as differentiation, dedifferentiation, redifferentiation, and transformation. Haynes and Burnett (1963) presented histological evidences that the isolated gastrodermis, consisting of only two cell types (gland and digestive cells), could regenerate into a complete animal. Later, ultrastructural studies of the various stages of regeneration of the gastrodermal explants revealed that the gland cells at the periphery of the explant underwent striking morphological and physiological changes — dedifferentiation (Davis *et al.*, 1966). These changes resulted in the formation of interstitial cells which were indistinguishable from similar cells of normal animals. The resulting interstitial cells were then capable of dividing and even forming nests of eight to sixteen cells (Davis *et al.*, 1966; Davis, 1970a). Thus, a gastrodermal explant containing no interstitial cells is capable of forming them from gland cells.

The interstitial cells are then capable of redifferentiating into cell types other than that from which they were derived. Cnidoblasts arise initially from these interstitial cells, and some of these cnidoblasts, under the conditions of the culture medium, are capable of dividing and giving rise to other cnidoblasts (Davis *et al.*, 1966; Davis, 1968, 1970a,b). It is important to recognize that these cells do not divide in normal animals. Nerve cells (presumably the three types of nerves) (Davis *et al.*, 1968) and germ cells (Burnett *et al.*, 1966) also originate from these interstitial cells.

Digestive cells of the gastrodermal explant — those at the periphery of the explant — also reveal extensive changes during regeneration. They degrade their algal symbionts, form mucous droplets typical of epitheliomuscular cells, elaborate basal longitudinal myonemes, and, presumably, participate in the formation of the mesoglea. The final result is the complete transformation of peripheral digestive cells (gastrodermal) to epitheliomuscular cells (epidermal). As in normal animals, these epitheliomuscular cells are also capable of division, which process aids in the growth of the regenerating explant.

The various ultrastructural changes during dedifferentiation and redifferentiation, as well as transformation, will be presented in this chapter. It should be mentioned that *Hydra viridis* was selected for these studies because the gastrodermal cells contain algal symbionts. These symbionts act as excellent markers for isolating the gastrodermis from the epidermis. More significant, however, is the fact that this peculiarity permits an accurate observation of the various changes during transformation of the digestive cells. Moreover, the gastrodermis of this species contains only three types of cells — gland cells, digestive cells and mucous cells — each of which has been identified histochemically (Haynes and Burnett, 1963). The gastric region used in all studies contains only two cell types: gland and digestive cells. Mucous cells are restricted to the hypostome. In addition, this species lacks neoblasts and mature cnidoblasts in the gastrodermis (Haynes and Burnett, 1963).

II. Epidermal Differentiation — Dedifferentiation and Redifferentiation

A. INTERSTITIAL CELLS

Before describing the ultrastructural changes during the dedifferentiation of peripheral gland cells into intersitial cells, it seems appropriate to define the term dedifferentiation. Dedifferentiation, as employed in these studies, means the process by which a fully specialized cell loses all of its morphological and physiological characteristics, thus reverting to an embryonic cell which is then capable of redifferentiation into a cell type other than that from which it was derived. If a gland cell, for example, reverted to an embryonic cell and then differentiated into another gland cell, such a process would not be considered dedifferentiation in the light of the present definition. The dedifferentiation of peripheral gland cells into interstitial cells and their ultimate redifferentiation into other fully specialized cell types represent a spectacular series of cellular reorganization. Gland cells (Fig. 1) are characterized by the presence of several large, dense secretory droplets, an extensive system of granular endoplasmic reticulum, and numerous free ribosomes. In the isolated mass, however, the peripheral gland cells, triangular in shape, are oriented in such a manner that their bases (containing the secretory droplets) border the periphery of the explant. The release of secretory droplets and the breakdown of the endoplasmic reticulum apparently occur concurrently, although not at the same rate. Figure 2 reveals that most of the droplets have been released, and the endoplasmic reticulum is being degraded. The exact mechanism of release of these droplets is uncertain. It is assumed, however, that the droplets merely diffuse from the cell. This assumption is based on the fact that intact droplets in various stages of release have not been observed, although tissues from short-time sequences ranging from zero hour isolation to several days after isolation have been examined. Also, as Davis et al. (1966) have shown, gland cells which have completely dedifferentiated into interstitial cells and some which have begun redifferentiation still contained small droplets of extremely low density and intact, empty, evaginated plasma membranes. Finally, since the droplets are not membrane bounded (Haynes and Davis, 1969) and the gland cells are undergoing such a massive cellular reorganization during this process, it seems entirely plausible that the droplets could be degraded easily and transported intracellularly for subsequent reutilization during redifferentiation.

The mechanism by which the highly organized system of endoplasmic reticulum becomes degraded remains equally as obscure. It seems, however, that two processes are involved. First, the membranes of the endo-

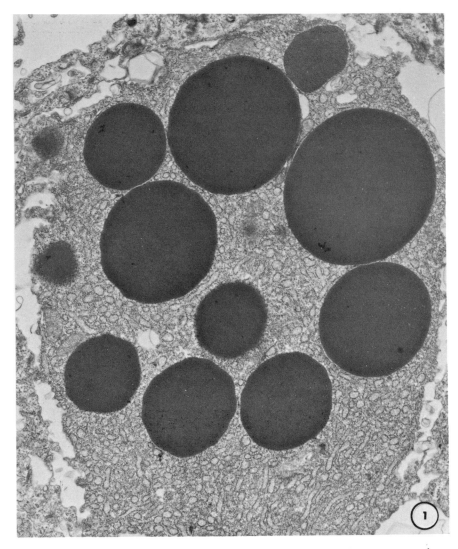

Fig. 1. Portion of a gland cell from a normal animal showing large, dense secretory drop-lets, extensive granular endoplasmic reticulum, and free ribosomes (× 11,550).

plasmic reticulum appear to be discontinuous or ruptured in several regions as evidenced by the accumulation of small particles in those regions. Second, isolation bodies associated with Golgi complexes are formed in several parts of the cell (Figs. 3 and 4). These bodies are enclosed entirely within isolation membranes which are derived presumably, from the Golgi complexes, as evidenced by the direct continuity of the

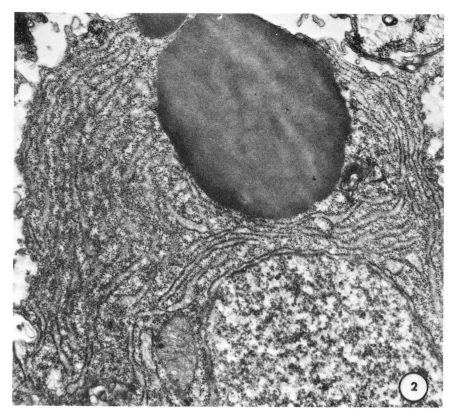

Fig. 2. Part of a gland cell at the periphery of the isolated tissue. Most of the characteristic secretory droplets have been released. Although much of the endoplasmic reticulum still persists, some has begun to degenerate (× 22,200).

Golgi membranes and the isolation membranes (Fig. 3). The isolation membranes segregate free ribosomes, fragments of endoplasmic reticulum, and mitochondria, in some cases. The latter mechanism has some support in studies involving insect fat bodies during metamorphosis (Locke and Collins, 1965). According to these authors, isolated regions of endoplasmic reticulum are located within paired membranes derived from Golgi vesicles. Several isolation bodies coalesce to form a storage body for both protein and RNA. The authors also suggested the possibility that some ribosomes may be actually reserved as an RNA pool that will be utilized in adult development of the insect.

Further dedifferentiative changes are seen in Figs. 5 and 6. Figure 5 shows that all secretory droplets have been released, most of the extensive endoplasmic reticulum has disappeared, and there is an increase

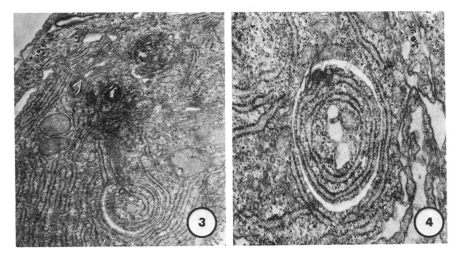

Figs. 3 and 4. Isolation bodies found in dedifferentiating gland cells. These contain elements of endoplasmic reticulum and mitochondria in some cases. Note in Fig. 3 the close association of the Golgi membranes and the isolation body (Fig. 3: × 18,000; Fig. 4: × 35,300).

in free ribosomes. It should be borne in mind, however, that although this plane of section revealed no droplets or isolation bodies, such structures in various stages of morphological modifications persist even as late as during redifferentiation. Figure 6 represents the final stages of dedifferentiation. The cytoplasm is completely packed with free ribosomes and polysomes, and a few mitochondria are also observed. Two membrane-bounded vacuoles are also present, one of which contains deposits resembling digested materials.

Returning to the discussion of isolation bodies, it is believed that the vacuolar structures (Fig. 6) represent the final stages of the original isolation bodies. The digested contents indicate that the organelles segregated earlier (endoplasmic reticulum, ribosomes, and mitochondria) have been almost or completely degraded. In many instances, empty or partially empty vacuoles are observed within the interior of the cytoplasm as well as fused to the plasma membrane (Figs. 6 and 7). In other cases, the fused membranes rupture, discarding the residual material into the extra-cellular spaces. It is suggested, therefore, that whatever other functions isolation bodies may provide intercellularly, they furnish, through local autolysis, usable materials for the dedifferentiating (or dedifferentiated) cells and possibly for dividing and redifferentiating cells. The discarded cellular debris may also serve as sources of raw material during the regenerative process.

A newly formed interstitial cell shown in Fig. 7 resembles typical

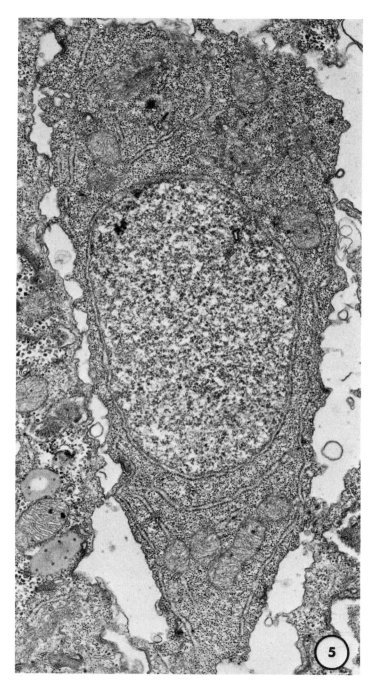

Fig. 5. Dedifferentiating gland cell from which all secretory droplets have been released and most of the endoplasmic reticulum degraded. A few mitochondria, short segments of endoplasmic reticulum, and numerous ribosomes are the principal organelles at this stage (× 21,000).

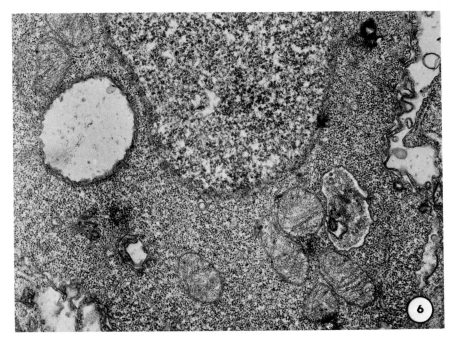

Fig. 6. Portion of a dedifferentiated gland cell during the formation of an interstitial cell. Ribosomes represent the most conspicuous organelles at this stage. Note the two vacuoles, one of which still contains degenerated materials. These probably represent the final stages of the original isolation bodies ($\times$ 23,000).

interstitial cells in normal *Hydra*. These cells are characterized by a centrally located nucleus containing a prominent nucleolus, numerous free ribosomes, and few small mitochondria. Occasionally, an inconspicuous Golgi complex and sparse segments of endoplasmic reticulum are observed.

Division of interstitial cells occurs some time after their formation. Figure 8 shows two interstitial cells (ic), one of which is undergoing mitosis and contains almost twice the number of mitochondria and significantly more endoplasmic reticulum than the interphase interstitial cell. Ribosomes are the most abundant organelles in both cells. Division apparently occurs rapidly throughout the explant as indicated by the presence of nests of up to sixteen interstitial cells (Davis *et al.*, 1966). As in normal animals, newly formed interstitial cells give rise to a variety of cell types which will be considered presently.

B. CNIDOBLASTS

The fine structure of developing and mature cnidoblasts has been the subject of several investigations (Chapman, 1961; Hess, 1961; Slautter-

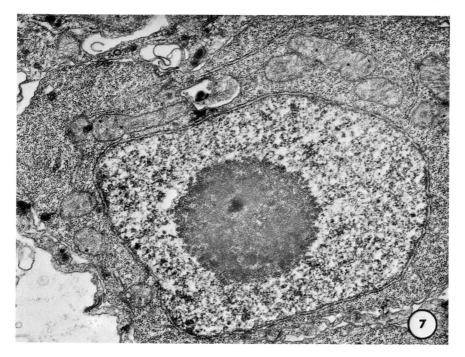

Fig. 7. A newly formed interstitial cell derived from a gland cell. Except for a few short segments of endoplasmic reticulum, this cell is morphologically identical to normal interstitial cells (× 18,200).

back, 1967a; Davis *et al.*, 1966; Davis, 1969, 1970b). These studies, considered collectively, have shown that cnidoblasts originate from interstitial cells. Furthermore, the ultrastructural changes from the onset of differentiation to the mature cnidoblast as well as the structure of different types of nematocysts have been well authenticated. The development of cnidoblasts in this experimental system is identical to that in normal animals. The description of their development presented in this chapter will be limited, therefore, to a few cellular profiles in an attempt to demonstrate that interstitial cells, derived from gland cells, represent one source for cnidoblast development and that such developmental stages are identical to comparable stages in normal animals.

The earliest stages of cnidoblast development are recognized by the appearance of scattered vesicles which subsequently coalesce to form elements of granular endoplasmic reticulum. Figures 9 and 10 show early stages in which the endoplasmic reticulum is being formed. Numerous ribosomes are still present at this stage. Concurrent with these activities is the development of a Golgi complex (Fig. 11). Both organelles participate in the formation and development of the structurally complicated

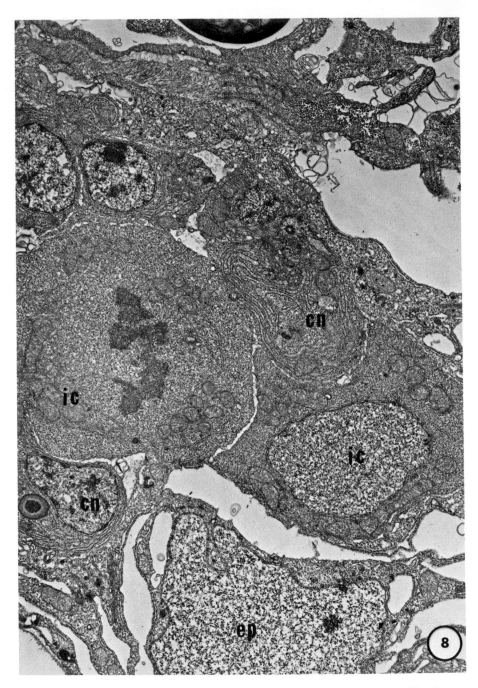

Fig. 8. Two interstitial cells (ic), one of which is undergoing division. The dividing interstitial cell contains numerous ribosomes, several mitochondria, and segments of granular endoplasmic reticulum. The nondividing interstitial cell also contains numerous ribosomes and fewer mitochondria. Both cells are indistinguishable from similar cells in normal animals. Two cnidoblasts (cn) and a portion of an epitheliomuscular cell (ep) are also observed (× 10,900).

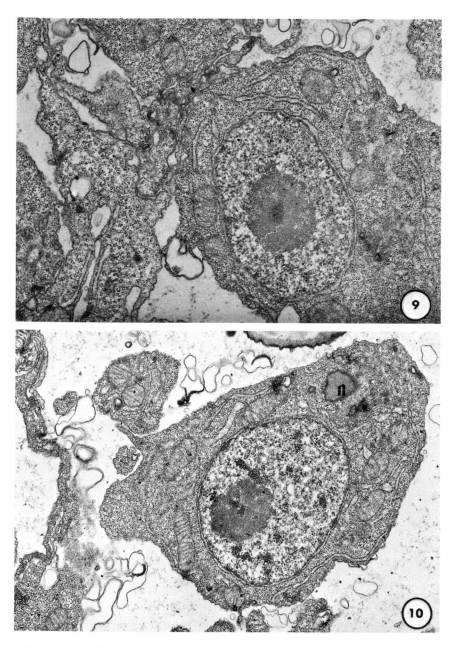

Figs. 9 and 10. Sections of two cnidoblasts in early stages of development. The nuclei are somewhat centrally located and the cytoplasm contains long developing segments of endoplasmic reticulum, few mitochondria, and numerous ribosomes. A portion of a nematocyst (n) is seen in Fig. 10 (Fig. 9: × 18,900; Fig. 10: × 12,750).

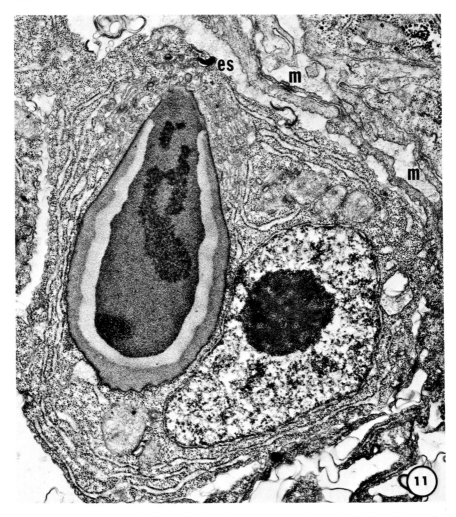

Fig. 11. Developing cnidoblast showing its nematocyst in longitudinal section and a nucleus (with its conspicuous nucleolus). Note the long strands of endoplasmic reticulum, few mitochondria, the persistence of many ribosomes, and the membranes and vesicles of a Golgi complex surrounding the apical portion of the nematocyst. Note also the similarity of contents in the forming mesoglea (m) and the extracellular space (es) (× 18,900).

nematocyst. The latest stage of differentiation is seen in Figs. 12 and 13. The nucleus is displaced to the periphery of the cell, the nematocyst develops in size and complexity, and the segments of endoplasmic reticulum have increased to the extent that they occupy most of the cytoplasm. In addition, the cisternae of the endoplasmic reticulum have become distended, with a simultaneous increase in the quantity of the moderately

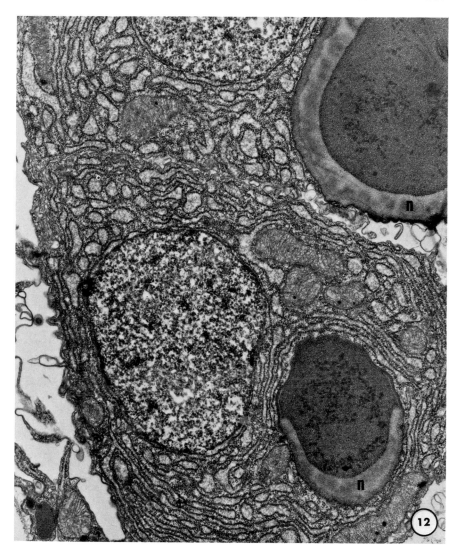

Fig. 12. Two cnidoblasts in a later stage of development showing nematocysts (n), nuclei displaced to the periphery of the cell, mitochondria, and an elaborate system of endoplasmic reticulum. See longitudinal section of a nemotocyst in Fig. 13 ($\times$ 16,500).

dense secretory product, indicating that the cnidoblast is nearing, or has reached, its height of synthetic activity. The membranes of the Golgi complex have also increased and surround the apical portion of the nematocyst (Fig. 13). At the same time, numerous ribosomes which once dominated the cytoplasm have decreased considerably.

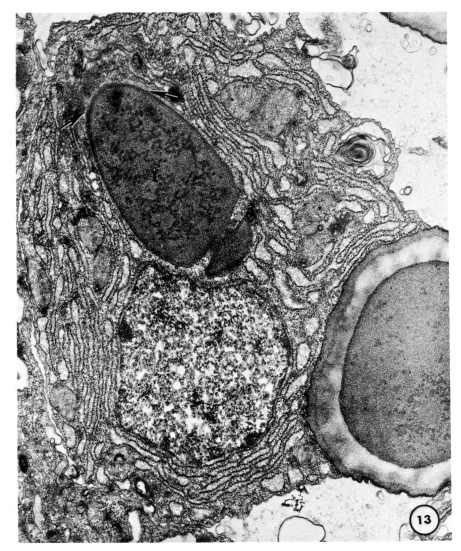

Fig. 13. Section of a developing cnidoblast similar to those shown in Fig. 12, except that a portion of the cytoplasmic tube (t) is also present. Surrounding the tube are microtubules (arrows) and Golgi membranes (× 18,200).

The continuation and completion of cnidoblast differentiation involve a greater size increase in the nematocyst, a dramatic increase in complexity of intracapsular structures, and the formation of a cnidocil. Once the nematocyst has been formed completely, and consequently the synthetic activities of the endoplasmic reticulum and Golgi complex no longer are required, these organelles undergo a state of regression. The endoplasmic reticulum acquires a vesiculated form and much of it diminishes, while the Golgi complex becomes smaller and inconspicuous and most of the free ribosomes disappear (Slautterback, 1961; Lentz, 1966).

One of the most significant aspects of cnidoblast development in the regenerating isolated gastrodermis is shown in Fig. 14. Three cnidoblasts are in exactly the same stage of development, with nematocysts (seen in two cells), a few small mitochondria, and endoplasmic reticulum located toward the periphery of the cell, while dividing nuclei occupy their centers. A careful inspection reveals that the cnidoblasts are in an early stage of development. It is not known whether nematocyst synthesis is interrupted until the completion of nuclear division or whether both activities occur simultaneously. It is known, however, that except for one instance in which a binucleated degenerating cnidoblast was reported, nuclear and cytoplasmic divisions are completed. According to Davis (1970b), the daughter cell containing the nematocyst develops normally, but the fate of the other cell remains questionable. On the basis of several arguments, it was suggested that the latter cell should be considered a cnidoblast, in which case it would be able to synthesize a nematocyst.

These structural observations indicate that, at least in the system under discussion, cnidoblasts may arise through one of two different routes: (1) from interstitial cells, and (2) from preexisting cnidoblasts. Regardless of their initial origin, their ultimate source must be considered as the peripheral gland cells.

The question invariably arises concerning the reasons for the appearance of dividing cnidoblasts in the regenerating isolated gastrodermis and the absence of such cell divisions in the normal animals. It has been assumed that the experimental conditions (ionic medium) in which the isolated tissue was cultured are partially responsible for cnidoblasts acquiring the capacity to undergo mitosis while maintaining their usual functions of synthesizing nematocysts (Davis, 1968, 1970a). This assumption is supported by previous results of Macklin and Burnett (1966), who cultured a portion of the gastric column of *Hydra* in a medium containing specific concentrations of sodium and calcium ions. Gland cells transformed directly into mucous cells and all interstitial cells differentiated into cnidoblasts. In interpreting the results, these authors suggested that the structural growth-promoting substance concentrated in the hypostome of normal animals (Lesh and Burnett, 1964, 1966), which is probably produced by nerves (Lesh and Burnett, 1964, 1966; Davis *et al.,* 1968; Davis, 1969) may operate at the cell membrane level to control the entry of ions or substances into the cell. The results concerning the dividing cnidoblasts, therefore, may also represent another example of the influence of ions.

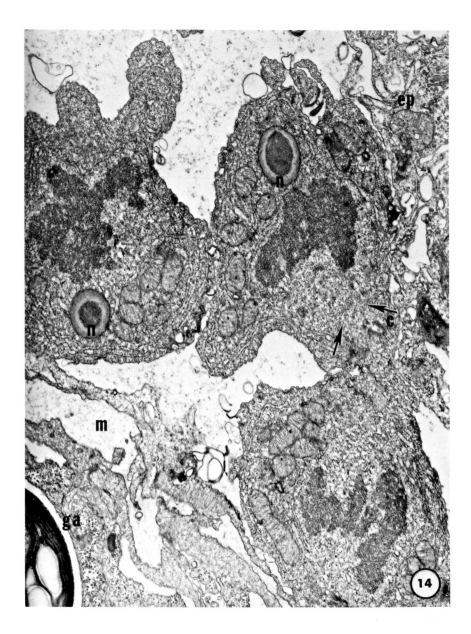

Fig. 14. Three cnidoblasts undergoing nuclear division. Developing nematocysts (n) observed in two cnidoblasts, mitochondria, and long narrow strands of endoplasmic reticulum are located toward the periphery of the cells. Note the centriole (c) and spindle fibers (arrows) in one of the cnidoblasts; epitheliomuscular cell (ep), mesoglea (m) still being formed, and the gastrodermis (ga) (× 12,300).

C. NERVE CELLS

Several histological and ultrastructural studies have indicated the existence of three types of nerve cells in *Hydra,* namely, neurosensory, ganglionic, and neurosecretory cells (Burnett and Diehl, 1964a,b; Lentz and Barrnett, 1965; Lentz, 1966; Davis *et al.,* 1968). In addition to describing the structure of mature nerve cells, other recent investigations have shown that neurosensory and ganglionic cells arise solely from interstitial cells and, presumably, neurosecretory cells follow a similar pattern (Lentz, 1965; Davis, 1969, 1971).

The complete ultrastructural differentiation of neurosensory and ganglionic cells as well as various structural aspects of mature neurosecretory cells will be presented in Part VI of this volume. The brief ultrastructural descriptions of nerve cells presented here are intended to demonstrate that interstitial cells derived from gland cells are also capable of redifferentiating into nerve cells.

1. Neurosensory Cells

Figures 15–17 show various profiles of neurosensory cells. Some of the first signs of neurosensory cell development include the elongation of the originally rounded or oval-shaped interstitial cell. The cytoplasmic elongations eventually form neurites and there may be two or more per cell (Fig. 15). The most distinguishing structural feature of these developing cells is the presence of numerous ribosomes and the formation of a ciliary apparatus from an existing centriole (Fig. 15). A Golgi complex is usually located near the developing cilium. The cells at this stage, and even throughout their development to the mature cell, contain little endoplasmic reticulum. Figure 16 shows a portion of a mature neurosensory cell. The rootlets of the cilium (not included in micrograph) are striated, and there are few secretory droplets and many glycogen particles. The cell body of a mature cell is seen in Fig. 17. The nucleus is displaced peripherally and there are several secretory droplets ranging from 600 to 1500 Å in diameter. The arrows indicate areas in which neurosecretory release occurs. The insets show two different planes of the mature cilium. As will be discussed in Chapter 12, the cilium contains the typical $9 + 2$ arrangement of internal tubules. Although there is evidence to suggest that more than one cilium begins development in the young neurosensory cell (Fig. 18), only one cilium has been seen in mature cells (Davis, 1969). Golgi complexes which appear to be primarily responsible for the production of secretory droplets, strands of endoplasmic reticulum, microtubules, mitochondria, and droplets (approximately 1100 Å in diameter) are also present.

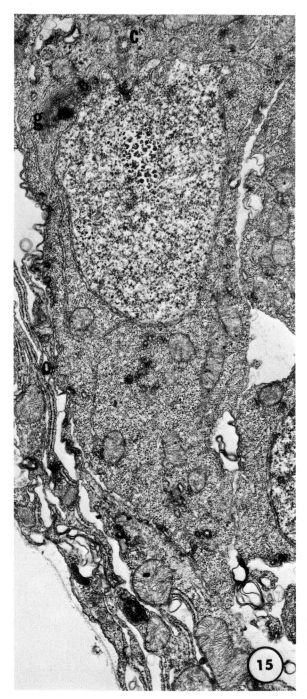

Fig. 15. Early stage of a differentiating neurosensory cell which has assumed an elongated shape. The centriole (c), which is located at one end of the cell, will give rise to a cilium. A Golgi complex (g) is located characteristically near the developing cilium. The cytoplasm contains numerous ribosomes ($\times$ 15,000).

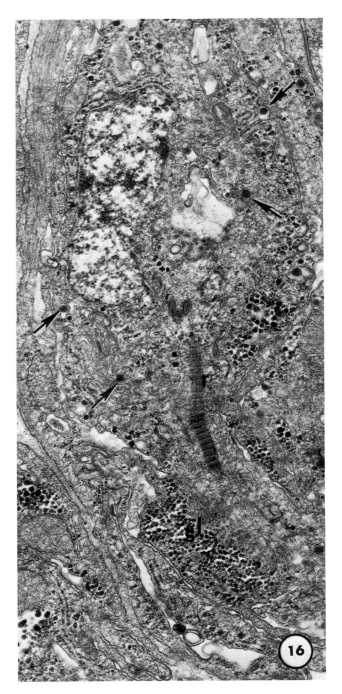

Fig. 16. Portion of a mature neurosensory cell showing striated rootlets (r) of the ciliary apparatus, a few secretory droplets (arrows), glycogen deposits (gl), and an elongated nucleus located toward the periphery of the cell (× 25,750).

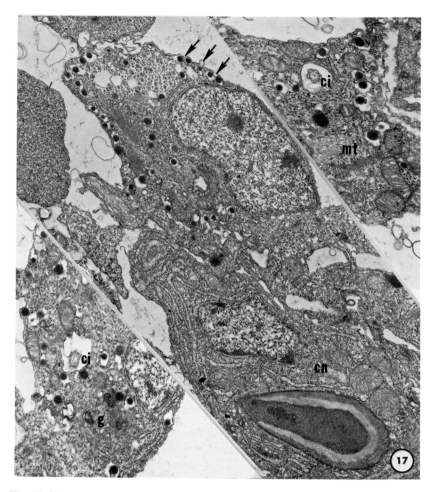

Fig. 17. Mature neurosensory cell with dense secretory droplets (ranging from 600 to 1500 Å in diameter) in the cell body and portion of the neurite shown (upper left). Arrows indicate areas of neurosecretory release. Note the developing cnidoblast (cn) in longitudinal section (× 11,000). Insets: Portions of mature neurosensory cells showing the cilium (ci) in two different planes, neurosecretory droplets, microtubules (mt), Golgi complex (g), and short fragments of endoplasmic reticulum (both insets: × 17,600).

2. Ganglionic Cells

In studying ganglionic cell development, as is the case with other types of *Hydra* nerve cells, it is imperative that serial sections be examined to determine accurately the specific type of nerve cell. One of the cells in Fig. 18 is identified as a developing ganglionic cell. The cytoplasm extends into the extracellular spaces forming two or more long neurites.

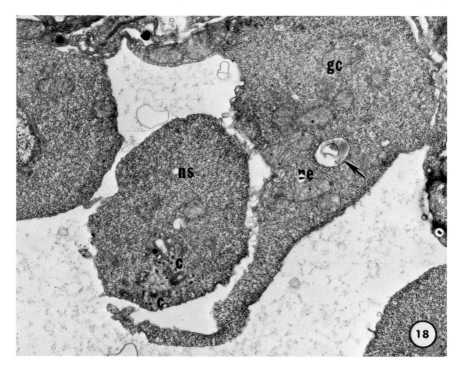

Fig. 18. Portion of a cell believed to be a young ganglionic cell (gc). The cytoplasm at this stage contains mainly free ribosomes. Mitochondria accumulate characteristically at the base of the developing neurite (ne). Note the structure (arrow), which represents the final stage of an isolation body, and an early stage of a developing neurosensory cell (ns). Note especially that there are two sets of centrioles (c) and small dense aggregates surrounding them (× 16,500).

The base of the neurites usually contains several mitochondria, short segments of endoplasmic reticulum and a small Golgi complex (not shown in this figure). Note that there are numerous ribosomes and a vacuolated structure (arrow) believed to be the final stage of an isolation body.

The structure of the fully differentiated ganglionic cell will be presented in Chapter 13 of this volume. It may be indicated here, however, that most of the structures observed in Fig. 18 are replaced as differentiation progresses. The neurites of the mature cell, for example, except for a few mitochondria and ribosomes, are completely occupied by microtubules. Such mature ganglionic cells have been observed in the regenerating isolated gastrodermis.

3. Neurosecretory Cells

A mature neurosecretory cell is shown in Fig. 19. The nucleus contains clumps of scattered chromatin material and there are at least two neurites

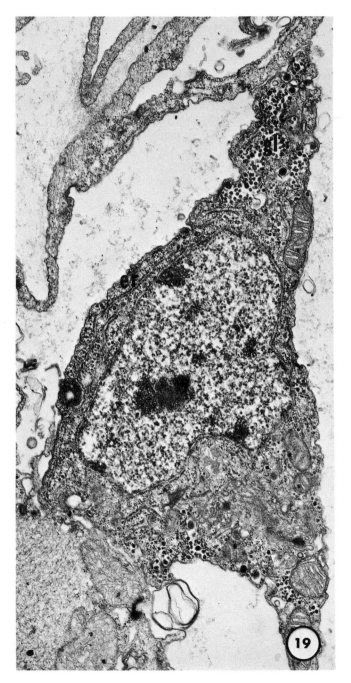

Fig. 19. Mature neurosecretory cell with nucleus containing clumps of scattered chromatin material, two neurites (top and bottom), a few neurosecretory droplets (900 Å in diameter), mitochondria, endoplasmic reticulum (er), and glycogen droplets (gl) (× 20,900).

(top and bottom). The cytoplasm contains segments of endoplasmic reticulum, a few mitochondria, glycogen, and dense droplets (approximately 900 Å in diameter).

As far as we are aware, the ultrastructural stages of development have not been studied. It has been assumed, however, that neurosecretory cells also originate from interstitial cells. This assumption seems reasonable in view of the fact that ultrastructural studies reveal the sequential stages of neurosensory and ganglionic cell differentiation and also indicate an independent development from a similar source — interstitial cells (Davis, 1969, 1972).

The foregoing description of the three types of nerve cells is not intended to be a detailed account of their structural development and final formation. Instead, it is designed to focus on the fact that nerve cells in general arise from interstitial cells which themselves have originated from dedifferentiated peripheral gland cells.

D. GERMINAL CELLS

The dedifferentiation and redifferentiation of gland cells described above refer specifically to the formation of somatic cells, that is, one type of somatic cell (gland cell) has been shown to be capable ultimately of producing several different types of somatic cells (cnidoblasts, neurosensory, ganglionic, and presumably, neurosecretory cells). Burnett *et al.* (1966) reported that complete animals which had regenerated from isolated gastrodermis could be induced into sexuality. The animals in mass cultures initially formed sperm and, subsequently, under more crowded conditions, hermaphroditic animals appeared.

Spermatozoa

Although ultrastructural investigations of developing and mature sperms and eggs are proceeding currently, the present literature is conspicuously limited concerning these aspects of *Hydra* development. In the system under discussion, however, it is known that, during the development of the testes, interstitial cells form spermatogonia. The spermatogonia are located immediately adjacent to the mesoglea; extending peripherally are primary spermatocytes, division area, secondary spermatocytes, division area, spermatids, and finally the mature flagellated spermatozoa (Burnett *et al.*, 1966).

Figure 20 shows a nest of seven cells which have already begun to differentiate into spermatozoa. They are located at precisely the same area (immediately adjacent to epithelial myonemes) as are nests of interstitial cells. The nuclei are usually finely granular and each nucleus reveals a conspicuous nucleolus. The cytoplasm, except for a few mito-

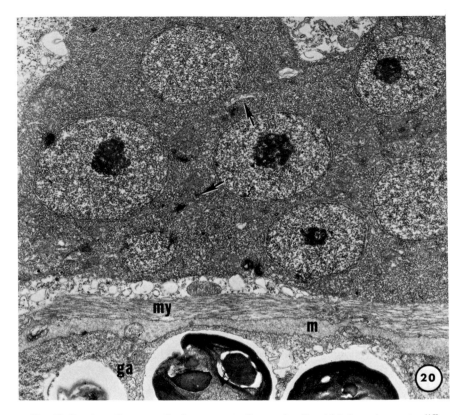

Fig. 20. Portion of seven cells from a nest of several cells which have begun to differentiate into sperms. The cells contain mostly ribosomes; few mitochondria are also present. Plasma membranes (arrows) are recognized in a few places; therefore the cells essentially form a syncytium. The epithelial myonemes (my) are immediately adjacent to the developing cells; mesoglea, m; gastrodermis, ga ($\times$ 5800).

chondria, is occupied completely with ribosomes. Portions of the plasma membranes are barely recognizable in certain areas, indicating that the nest is essentially a syncytium.

Cross-section of a testis with cells in a later stage of development is seen in Fig. 21. Most of the cells are isolated, but in some cases two or three cells remain connected by cytoplasmic bridges. The nuclei are small, rounded, and compact. As the cells become more differentiated, the nuclear material acquires greater density, until it becomes a dense, concentrated, homogeneous mass. At the same time, the nucleus with its thickened, receding membrane is displaced to the periphery of the cell immediately adjacent to the plasma membrane.

The cytoplasm also undergoes certain drastic changes (Fig. 21). Small

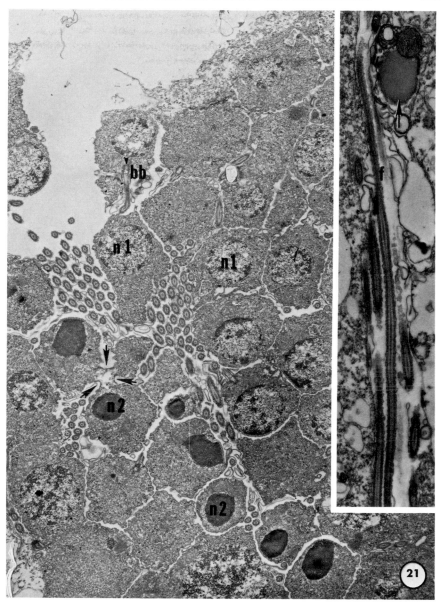

Fig. 21. Low magnification electron micrograph of the testis showing cells in different stages of differentiation. Several of the cells are still connected by cytoplasmic bridges (arrows), mitochondria are in close proximity to the nuclei. Note the diffuse nuclear material (n 1) in younger cells and the condensed nuclei (n 2) in the more mature cells, basal body (bb) of the flagellum, and several sections of flagella in the extracellular space (× 5800). Inset: A mature sperm revealing a condensed nucleus (arrow) surrounded by a thick membrane, basally located mitochondria and a flagellum (f) in the extracellular space (× 11,550).

myelinlike structures appear in the cytoplasm. These are almost always associated with the developing flagellum. The flagellum, connected to the base of the cell by a kinetosome, gradually elongates; several of these structures are observed in the extracellular spaces. Three mitochondria later appear between the condensing nucleus and the kinetosome. As the cytoplasm diminishes during later development, the mitochondria become lodged in small pockets of the nucleus. The mature sperm (Fig. 21) reveals a small, dense, homogeneous nucleus surrounded by a thick membrane, basally located mitochondria, and a long flagellum.

The information presented above concerning spermatozoa shows that a fully specialized cell, a gland cell, maintains the ability to undergo meiosis and also to differentiate into other fully specialized cells such as cnidoblasts and nerve cells. Whatever the course of redifferentiation may be, the gland cell first dedifferentiates into germinal or somatic cells. A discussion of the factors which influence or control differentiation of interstitial cells will be presented in Chapter 4.

III. Epidermal Differentiation — Transformation

The discussion up to this point has been focused on the dedifferentiation of gland cells and the redifferentiation into somatic and germinal cells. In short, we have accounted for all cell types of the newly formed epidermis, except the most prevalent type of cells — the epitheliomuscular cells. The formation of epitheliomuscular cells involves certain cellular changes of the peripherally located digestive cells in the isolated gastrodermis. These changes, however, require a different set of cellular activities than those prescribed for gland cells. The conversion of a digestive cell to an epitheliomuscular cell is a direct one, without the reversion to an embryonic cell stage. We shall refer to this process as transformation.

EPITHELIOMUSCULAR CELLS

Following the isolation of the gastrodermis, two cellular activities occur at the surface of the explant. Reference has already been made to one of these activities, that is, the release of secretory droplets from gland cells. The second is the formation of pseudopodialike structures of the digestive cells which extend and cover the entire surface. Except for the first few hours immediately following gastrodermal isolation when gland cells actually border the explant, they (the gland cells) are invariably surrounded distally by a narrow strip of digestive cell cytoplasm. Figure 22 shows a digestive cell at the periphery of the explant approximately 2 hours after isolation. The external surface contains apical projections

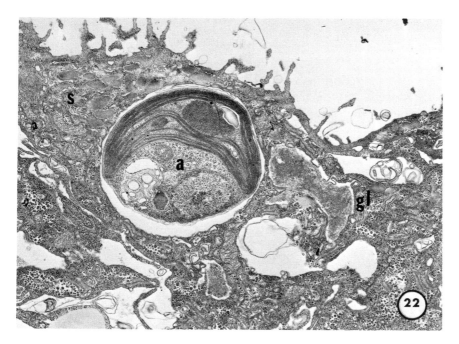

Fig. 22. Portion of a digestive cell at the periphery of the explant shortly after isolation. The external surface contains projections which normally would be inserted into the mesoglea. Note the alga (a), which is still morphologically normal, secretory droplets (s), glycogen particles (gl), and the rod-shaped crystalline structures typical of digestive cells (× 13,900).

extending into the surrounding medium. These projections would normally be inserted into the mesoglea. There are several small secretory droplets, a morphologically normal alga, several glycogen granules that decrease as differentiation proceeds, and rod-shaped structures peculiar to digestive cells. Although all the structures described are present also in the apical portion (facing the digestive cavity) of digestive cells in the interior of the explant, there is no possibility of confusing these cells (compare Fig. 31).

As transformation continues, a thin layer of mucus is formed and there is a corresponding decrease in glycogen granules (Fig. 23). Algae still persist but they are in various stage of degeneration — from complete disintegration to intact forms that show obvious signs of disintegration. The apical surface of a fully transformed cell is seen in Fig. 24. This portion of the cell is indistinguishable from the same region of similar cells in normal animals. A thick mucous covering and mucous droplets

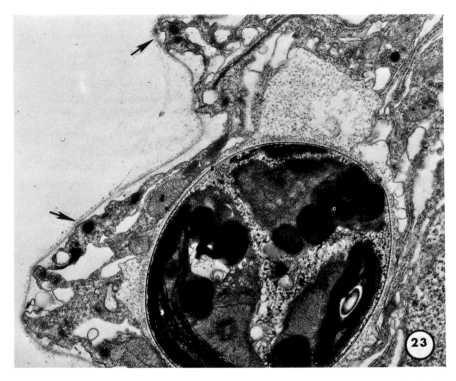

Fig. 23. Portion of a digestive cell at the periphery of the explant a few days after isolation. A mucous border (arrows) is being formed and the alga is being degraded (× 13,900).

are completely formed, large inclusions representing the final stages of algal degeneration are still present, and there are several ribosomes, polysomes, and vacuoles typical of epitheliomuscular cells.

While the apical portion of the epitheliomuscular cells is being formed, certain conspicuous changes are also occurring at the base of the cell (immediately adjacent to the forming mesoglea). Figure 25 shows the nucleus and the basal portion of a transforming cell. Only a narrow strip of cytoplasm (containing a few ribosomes and a segment of endoplasmic reticulum) borders the incompletely formed mesoglea. Cells in a similar stage of development occasionally contain a much thicker basal cytoplasm, many ribosomes, and polysomes. In any case, during these early stages of transformation, few if any developing longitudinal myonemes are observed. The first appearance of the myonemes does not occur throughout the entire basal cytoplasm, as evidenced by the fact that some areas are lacking myonemes (Fig. 26). Several ribosomes, polysomes, fragments of endoplasmic reticulum, and mitochondria are usually located close to the developing myonemes, indicating possible participation

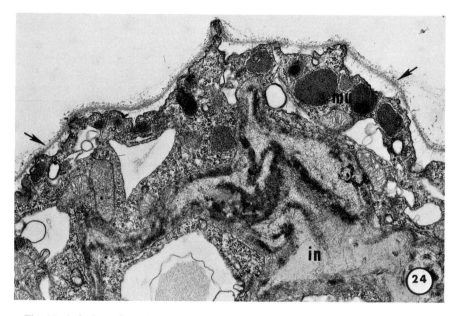

Fig. 24. Apical portion of a newly formed epitheliomuscular cell which is identical to normal epitheliomuscular cells. The mucous border (arrows) and mucous droplets (mu) are completely formed. A large inclusion (in), which may represent the final stage of algal degeneration, is also observed (× 16,650).

of these organelles in myoneme synthesis. Figure 26 also shows microtubules, a thin mucous covering suggesting that its formation is still in progress, and an incompletely formed mesoglea.

Completely differentiated longitudinal myonemes are observed in Fig. 27. Although not all myonemes are as large as those shown in this micrograph, their development is indicative of the tremendous synthetic activities which occur in the basal cytoplasm. Note that the myonemes are composed of thick and thin filaments, as described recently by Haynes *et al.* (1968). It is also apparent that the mesogleal fibers are also completely formed at this stage.

Reference has been made to division of interstitial cells and cnidoblasts in the regenerating isolated gastrodermis. Division of the former cells occurs in normal animals and therefore would be expected to take place in the regenerate. The latter cells have not been observed in division in normal animals and the appearance of such mitoses represents an unusual structural phenomenom. Epitheliomuscular cells in the mid-gastric region of normal animals usually engage in mitosis (Burnett, 1966). The presence of dividing epitheliomuscular cells in this system (Fig. 28) was regarded, therefore, as a natural sequence to their formation. Such divisions are

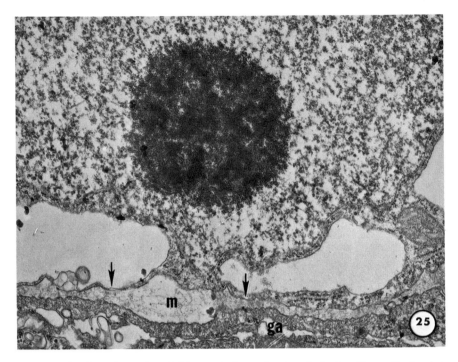

Fig. 25. Portion of a nucleus (with a typical prominent nucleolus) and base of a developing epitheliomuscular cell. The base (arrows) contains none of the characteristic myonemes and the mesoglea (m) is still being formed; gastrodermis, ga (× 20,300).

obviously necessary if additional epitheliomuscular cells are to be provided and also for ultimate growth of the regenerate.

The question concerning the origin of epitheliomuscular cells deserves some consideration. Lentz (1966) in his studies on various aspects of differentiation has suggested that epitheliomuscular cells arise from interstitial cells. As indicated earlier, these cells also undergo mitosis. The suggestion, therefore, is that epitheliomuscular cells are derived from two sources: interstitial cells and preexisting epitheliomuscular cells. What factors influence the production of cells from one mechanism as against the other has not been determined. Although it is entirely possible that epitheliomuscular cells may arise from interstitial cells, no stages of such cell developments have been observed in our laboratory, and the interstitial cell's origin has been questioned (see Slautterback, 1967a). Besides, the regenerating isolated gastrodermis represents an ideal system in which to study cell differentiation. Even in this system, where one might expect to see such cellular events, interstitial cells have not been observed to differentiate into epitheliomuscular cells. In short,

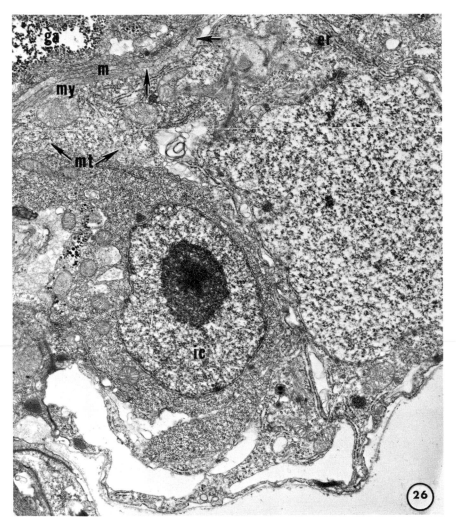

Fig. 26. Developing epitheliomuscular cell. Myonemes are still lacking in some areas of the base (arrows) while in other parts of the base myonemes (my) have begun to appear. Note the ribosomes and polysomes near the myonemes, segments of endoplasmic reticulum (er), microtubules (mt), inclusion (left of nucleus), narrow mesogles (m), and the gastrodermis (ga) containing large amounts of glycogen; interstitial cell (ic), thin mucous coat (bottom, right) (× 12,800).

it appears that epitheliomuscular cells are derived exclusively from pre-existing epitheliomuscular cells.

This description of epitheliomuscular cell differentiation and subsequent proliferation accounts for the presence of all cell types in the nor-

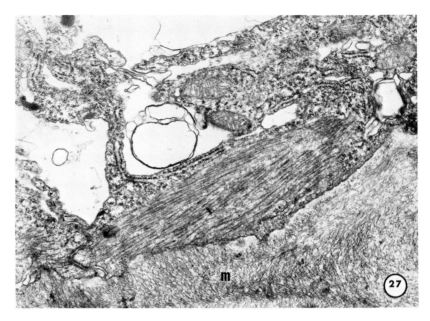

Fig. 27. Base of epitheliomuscular cells showing fully developed myonemes. The meso-glea (m) is also completely formed at this stage (× 17,600).

mal epidermis: interstitial cells, cnidoblasts, nerve cells (neurosensory, ganglionic, and neurosecretory), germinal cells, and epitheliomuscular cells. That two types of cells (gland and digestive) can give rise to such a heterogeneous group of highly specialized cells indicates a phenomenal degree of cellular reorganization of the two cell types involved. Further-more, these results indicate that fully mature cells are not irreversibly fixed, but that under "appropriate" conditions they can form not only other fully specialized somatic cells, but also can be geared to undergo meiosis.

IV. Gastrodermis

Gland and digestive cells in the gastrodermis of the regenerating (or regenerated) animal represent a stock of cells from the original gastro-dermis. Since they undergo little cellular changes, they will be discussed only briefly. There must be some degree of reorganization, however, such that, for example, the bases of the digestive cells will orient toward the future mesoglea. Also, the presence of mucous cells must be accounted for — whether they are of epidermal or gastrodermal origin.

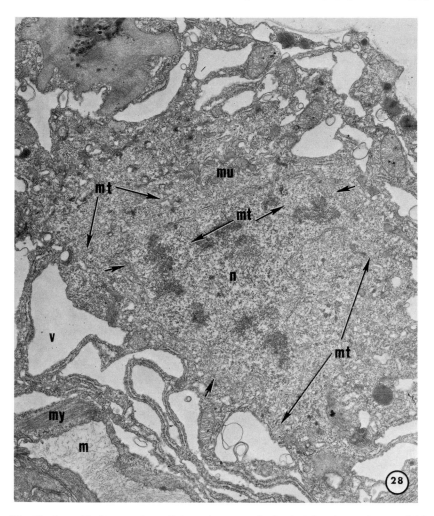

Fig. 28. An epitheliomuscular cell in early stage of mitosis. The chromatin material is scattered throughout the nucleus (n), and the nuclear membrane is ruptured in several areas (arrows). This cell extends from the external mucous border (extreme top right), where mature mucous droplets are located, to the mesoglea (m). Note the small mucous droplets (mu), microtubules (mt), vacuoles (v), and myonemes (my) at the base of the cell (continuation between myonemes and the remainder of the cell is not shown) (× 11,000).

A. GLAND CELLS

A normal gland cell is shown in Fig. 29. It is characterized by the presence of an extensive system of endoplasmic reticulum, numerous free ribosomes, and dense, spherical, secretory droplets located toward the

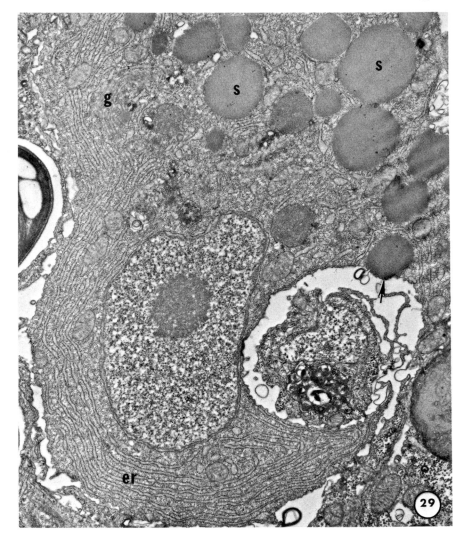

Fig. 29. Normal gland cell of the original isolated gastrodermis. The nucleus (containing a conspicuous nucleolus) is located at the base of the cell. The secretory droplets (s) are located mainly in the apical region (adjacent to the gastric cavity). The cytoplasm also contains an extensive system of endoplasmic reticulum (er), numerous free ribosomes, several mitochondria, and a Golgi complex (g). Note the droplet (arrow) which seems to be in the process of being released and the cell (lower right) almost completely engulfed by the gland cell (× 12,750).

gastric cavity. Some of these droplets fuse, producing even larger droplets. A Golgi complex is also observed, but whether this organelle participates significantly in the production of secretory droplets is not known.

This micrograph also shows part of another cell almost completely surrounded by the gland cell. From this evidence, as well as the appearance of what seems to be materials in various stages of digestion, it is suggested that gland cells in this system (if not generally) engage in phagocytic activities. The phagocytized cell is identified as a digestive cell that has begun disintegration. It contains several glycogen granules and a large mass typical of food inclusions of digestive cells. Immediately adjacent to the space surrounding the phagocytized cell is a secretory droplet which seems to be in the process of being released, presumably for digestion of the engulfed material.

B. DIGESTIVE CELLS

Figures 30–32 show three different regions of normal digestive cells in the gastrodermis. The nucleus, containing a prominent nucleolus, is located in the central portion of the cell and is surrounded by a narrow strip of cytoplasm (Fig. 30). Elements of endoplasmic reticulum, glycogen granules, mitochondria, vacuoles of various sizes, food inclusions, and morphologically normal algae are also observed.

The apical regions are easily recognizable by the appearance of many cytoplasmic extensions which extend from the free surfaces into the gastric cavity (Fig. 31). These projections, or microvilli, and the entire surface membranes are usually coated with a fibrillar material which may be of a mucous nature. The cytoplasm of the apical region contains many glycogen granules, mitochondria, small, dense secretory droplets, and rod-shaped structures. Lentz (1966) has shown that these structures arise from the invaginated plasma membranes, and suggested that they may contain digestive or proteolytic enzymes which aid in digestion of food materials. Slautterback (1967b) has indicated their involvement in selective absorption and transport of materials from the gastric cavity, and their possible participation in digestion. The most conspicuous structure in these cells is the presence of one large vacuole or several small vacuoles containing food material. In the present system, digestive cells contain algae in various stages of degeneration (Fig. 31). These degraded algae apparently provide the major source of food for the growing regenerate.

The basal region of the digestive cells contains normal algae, glycogen granules, mitochondria, and vacuoles of various sizes (Fig. 32). Circular myonemes are located immediately adjacent to the mesoglea. Although the myonemes are well developed, they do not reveal thick and thin filaments as seen in epithelial myonemes. Note that the mesoglea is densely packed with typical mesogleal fibers, some of which appear to be attached to the plasma membrane of the circular myonemes.

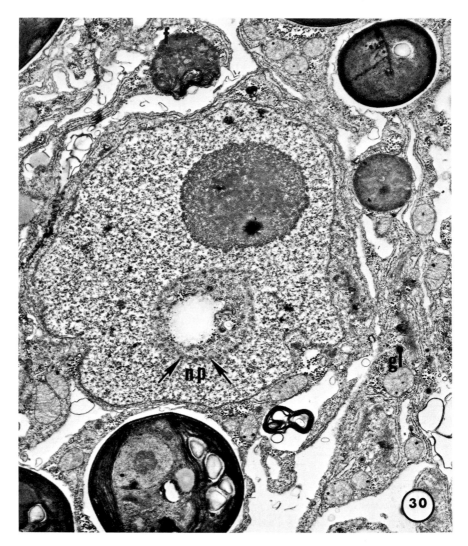

Fig. 30. Nucleus of a normal digestive cell of the original isolated gastrodermis. Note mitochondria, nuclear pores (np), glycogen granules (gl), food inclusions (f), and algae (a) (× 10,400).

C. Mucous Cells

Ultrastructural studies on the origin and development of mucous cells in normal animals are surprisingly limited. Even in the present system, which provides an ideal system for such investigations, this cell type is unfortunately neglected. In their studies on hypostomal regeneration,

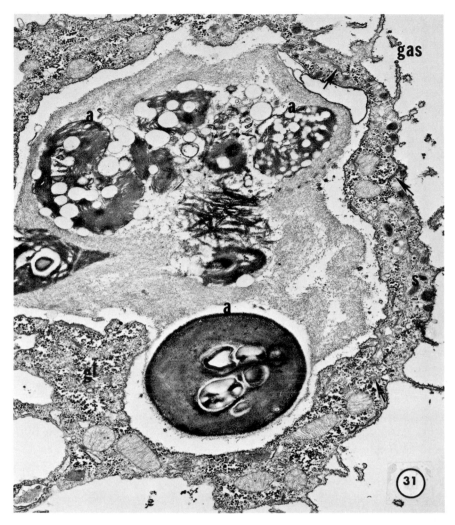

Fig. 31. Apical portion of a normal digestive cell. The surface is covered with a flocculent material and contains several cytoplasmic extensions which project into the gastric cavity (gas). Note the small, dense secretory droplets (s), typical rod-shaped structures (arrows), glycogen particles (gl), and algae (a) undergoing digestion (compare Fig. 22) ($\times$ 12,000).

Rose and Burnett (1968a) suggested that gland cells and basophilic cells transformed into mucous cells. The authors pointed out, however, that the ultrastructural events during transformation of gland cells to mucous cells and the origin of basophilic cells were unknown. Later studies by these investigators showed that in regenerating animals which had been transected in the mid-gastric region, the gastrodermal basophilic cells

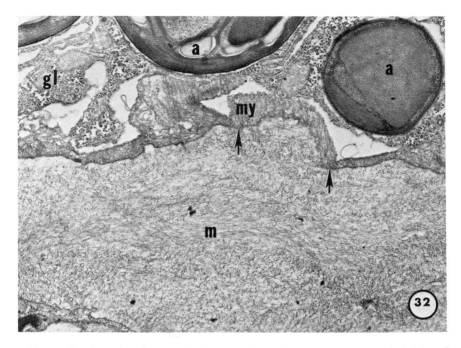

Fig. 32. Basal portion of a normal digestive cell showing myonemes (my), algae (a), and glycogen particles (gl). The mesoglea (m) contains well-developed fibers; some of these fibers seem to be "attached" to the plasma membrane of the myonemes (arrows) (× 13,600).

were the primary source of new mucous cells. Furthermore, the basophilic cells were derived from epithelial interstitial cells (Rose and Burnett, 1968b; 1970).

The processes involving the formation of mucous cells in the regenerating isolated gastrodermis are not clear. It is possible that both origins suggested by Rose and Burnett may be applicable to mucous cell formation in this system. The superficial evidence that exists, however, tends to favor the gland cells as at least the primary source. This is because the original isolated explant consisted of gland cells and digestive cells only, and at no time during the course of these studies were basophilic cells observed.

Evidence for the above suggestion is seen in Fig. 33. There are two cells which contain two types of droplets. One type of droplet is slightly dense, compact, and almost completely homogeneous. The other type of droplet is larger and, in addition to containing components of the previously mentioned droplets, contains fibrillar elements of low density. These cells are tentatively identified as gland cells which are in the process of transforming into mucous cells.

Fig. 33. Cells which appear to be in the process of transformation from gland cells to mucous cells. Some of the droplets (arrows) appear identical to those of mature mucous cells (× 14,200).

V. Gastric Cavity

While the epidermis and the gastrodermis are being reconstructed, some of the digestive cells in the interior of the explant degenerate, thus releasing their algal symbionts. Figure 34 shows whole and partially degenerated algae extruded into a large extracellular space—the future gastric cavity of the animal. In some instances, large portions of digestive cells and several bacteria are also observed. Thus the gastric cavity is

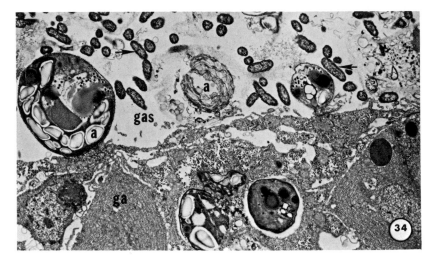

Fig. 34. Portion of the gastrodermis (ga) and gastric cavity (gas). The cavity is formed in the center of the isolated tissue and involves the degeneration of many cells. Free algae (a) in various stages of digestion and bacteria (arrows) are commonly observed in the cavity (× 4900).

formed in a similar manner as during embryogenesis, that is, by cell death in the interior of the stereoblastula, and not by invagination of cells from a single pore (Davis *et al.,* 1966).

VI. Formation of the Mesoglea

Our final consideration concerns the mesoglea. Although Chapter 16 of this volume will deal with the various ultrastructural components of the mesoglea from several species (see also Davis and Haynes, 1968) this section will be focused primarily on the possible origins of mesogleal fibers.

Some of the ultrastructural events which have occurred so far are seen in Fig. 35. The apical regions of the epitheliomuscular cells seem to be completely formed, contain mucous droplets, and are covered with an external mucous coat. The bases of these cells show developing longitudinal myonemes in some areas, while in others they are completely lacking. The central region (not shown in Fig. 35) closely resembles similar structures of typical epitheliomuscular cells. Interstitial cells and cnidoblasts in various stages of differentiation are located in a large extracellular space between the developing myonemes and the apical portion of epitheliomuscular cells. Numerous small granules and fibrillar materials of low density are located in the extracellular spaces.

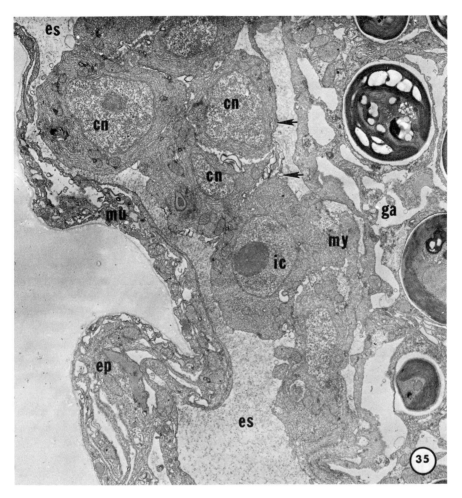

Fig. 35. Low magnification electron micrograph showing complete formation of the apical region of epitheliomuscular cells (ep) with mucous droplets (mu) and external mucous coat, several developing cnidoblasts (cn), interstitial cells (ic), myonemes (my) present in some areas and lacking in others (arrows), and large extracellular spaces (es) containing granular deposits. Note especially that although the limits of the mesoglea are demarcated and some deposits are present, typical mesogleal fibers are lacking; gastrodermis, ga (× 6300).

The basal regions of the gastrodermal cells seem normal in every respect, except that in certain areas their circular myonemes still maintain a close contact with the developing epithelial myonemes which, significantly enough, were once parts of digestive cells also. In other regions, there are no structural connections, but the two sets of myonemes are closely apposed to each other. The result is that although the limits of the future mesoglea seem to be clearly demarcated, there are periodic structural barriers. The mesoglea at this point, although truly not a mesoglea, contains membranous cellular debris and elements of fibrillar material similar to those in the large extracellular spaces.

In attempting to explain the initial location of the mesoglea and the possible origin of the mesogleal fibers, it is necessary to return to a consideration of some of the initial events in the explant. Immediately following isolation, the gastrodermis assumes a spherical and compact mass, thus eliminating the original digestive cavity. Since gland cells and digestive cells do not clump selectively, but are scattered uniformly throughout the explant, both types of cells are found along the periphery as well as in the interior. In the interior some of the digestive cell myonemes, in addition to maintaining their end-to-end orientation, undergo a type of folding. The events that occur immediately after this phase are not clear. It is known, however, that some of the original digestive cells are reorganized such that the usual tubelike gastrodermis is formed. The complete formation of this new gastrodermis requires that the circular myonemes be located immediately adjacent to the future mesoglea. At the same time the epithelial longitudinal myonemes are being synthesized. In several instances, these two sets of myonemes are observed immediately adjacent to each other, separated by a narrow extracellular space (Fig. 36). It is within this space that the mesoglea later forms.

As the extracellular space for the future mesoglea increases in width, small granules of moderate density appear. The granules are identical to those observed in the large, distal extracellular spaces (Figs. 35 and 37). Those in the extracellular spaces are believed to be derived, in part, from the mucous droplets. Figure 37 shows areas of release to both the external mucous coat and the large extracellular spaces. Since this single source may not explain the presence of so many granules, it seems likely that other origins must be involved. Such sources could include products of (1) degraded algal symbionts during transformation of digestive cells to epitheliomuscular cells, (2) degraded secretory droplets "released" from gland cells and the discharged residual contents of original isolation bodies during dedifferentiation, and (3) digestion of dead cells during and after the formation of the gastric cavity. The presence of the granules, therefore, in both the large epidermal extracellular spaces and the forming mesoglea may be a result of direct continuity with one another. This is due to the absence of developing or formed myonemes in several areas of the epithelium (Figs. 35 and 38).

As the development of the mesoglea proceeds (Fig. 39) until its final formation (Fig. 40), the granular component decreases drastically or even completely. At the same time, the identical granules, although de-

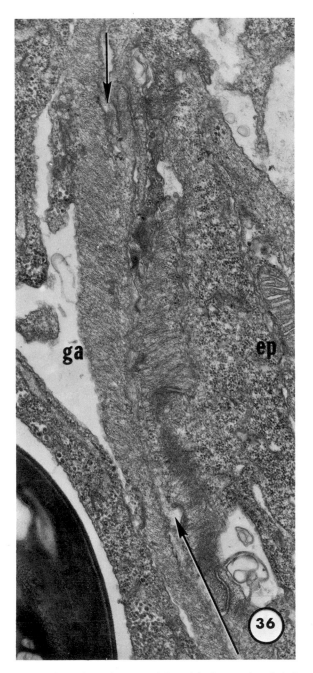

Fig. 36. The developing epidermis (ep) and the original gastrodermis (ga) are in very close contact. Arrows indicate the region in which the mesoglea will be formed ($\times$ 27,100).

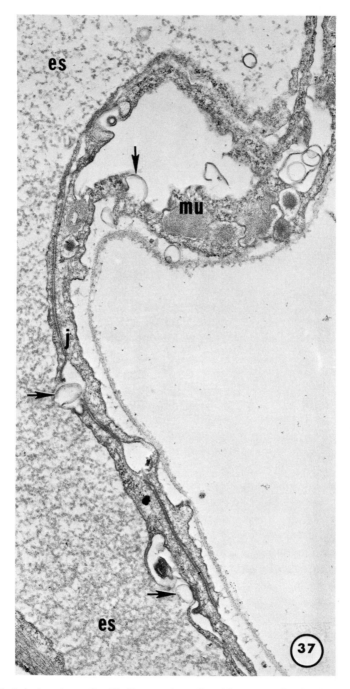

Fig. 37. Apical regions of epitheliomuscular cells with mucous droplets (mu). Close to these droplets are other mucous droplets in the process of being released to form the mucous covering. Membranous elements (arrows), from which mucus may have been released, are located adjacent to the extracellular space (es). Numerous granules are found in the extracellular space; septate desmosomes (j) (× 24,400).

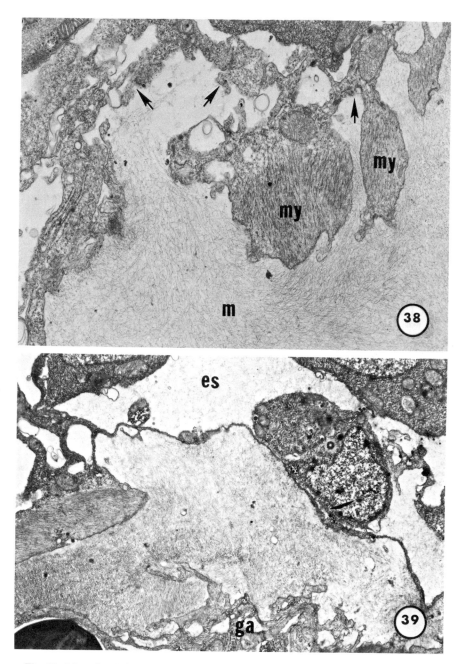

Fig. 38. Mesoglea (m) containing typical fibers which seem to accumulate especially near the epithelial myonemes (my). Note that there are few or no fibers in areas lacking myonemes (arrows); instead these areas contain small granules similar to those seen in the extracellular space in Figs. 32 and 34 (× 15,300).

Fig. 39. Micrograph similar to that in Fig. 35, except that most of the granules which accumulated in the extracellular space (es) have disappeared. The remaining deposits resemble those present in the initial stages of mesogleal formation (see Fig. 32); gastrodermis, ga (× 6600).

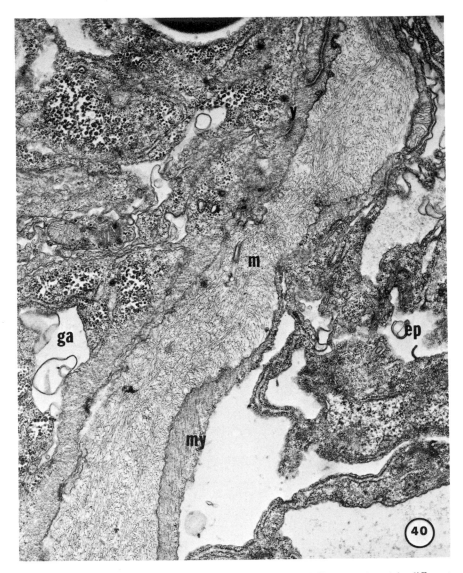

Fig. 40. Completely formed mesoglea (m) showing typical fibers sectioned in different planes and oriented in different directions. The myonemes (my) of the gastrodermis (ga) and epidermis (ep) are well developed if not completely formed. Note the small droplets and fibrillar materials in the epithelial extracellular spaces (× 17,700).

creased in number, are still observed in some of the large epidermal extracellular spaces (Fig. 40). Since the function of these droplets in mesogleal synthesis is unknown, the suggestions offered here are highly speculative. It is possible that the granules are digested and resynthesized for the formation of the amorphous matrix into which the fibers are embedded. On the other hand, they may be used in some manner for the synthesis of the fibers themselves.

As far as the mesogleal fibers are concerned, the present ultrastructural evidence strongly suggests that both the epithelial and gastrodermal myonemes are involved in their formation (Davis *et al.*, 1966). Figure 35 shows that the gastrodermal myonemes are mostly undeveloped, and the mesoglea consists merely of granular and fibrillar deposits (see also Figs. 25 and 26). The appearance of developed gastrodermal and epidermal myonemes is later accompanied by dense bundles of mesogleal fibers. In some areas where the myonemes are missing, there are few, if any, fibers (Figs. 32, 38, and 39). A close examination of the developed myonemes and associated dense mesogleal fibers indicate that the fibers seem to be attached to the plasma membrane surrounding the myonemes (Figs. 28, 32, 38, and 40). It is tempting to suggest that the myonemes are responsible for the synthesis of the mesogleal fibers. Whether they are or not has not been determined. It is apparent, therefore, that although much is known about the structure of the mesoglea, its origin and formation of structural components remain obscure. It may be added that the regenerating isolated gastrodermis is probably the most ideal system in which to pursue such investigations.

VII. Summary and Conclusions

Several aspects of cell development on the ultrastructural level were considered in this chapter. Specifically, such processes as dedifferentiation, redifferentiation, and transformation were presented as they occur in the regenerating, isolated gastrodermis of green *Hydra* (*H. viridis*). It was shown that gland cells located at the periphery of the explant undergo dedifferentiation and revert to embryonic cells (interstitial cells) which are indistinguishable from interstitial cells of normal animals. The resulting interstitial cells are then capable of division, forming nests of up to 16 cells. Subsequently, interstitial cells redifferentiate into several types of fully specialized somatic cells, other than that from which they were derived. Such cells include cnidoblasts and nerve cells—neurosensory, ganglionic, and neurosecretory. In addition to the formation of somatic cells, germinal cells are also formed from interstitial cells.

The peripheral digestive cells undergo a direct transformation to epitheliomuscular cells, without an intervening embryonic cell stage. The resulting epitheliomuscular cells then divide and contribute to the growth of the regenerate.

The gastric cavity is formed as a result of cell death in the interior of the mass. It is noted that the cavity is formed in a similar manner as during embryogenesis, that is, by cell death in the interior of the stereoblastula and not by invagination of cells from a single pole. The remaining cells in the interior of the mass form the gastrodermis of the regenerated animal. The origin of a third cell type—mucous cells—in the gastrodermis is not clear. It appears that they are derived directly or indirectly from existing gland cells.

Evidence concerning the origin of the mesoglea and the formation of its components is limited. It seems that both gastrodermal and epidermal layers must be completely formed prior to the synthesis of mesogleal fibers. The close association of the fibers to the myonemes possibly indicates a particular participation of these structures.

The reappearance of all the cell types (including germinal cells) as in normal animals from two somatic cells represents a phenomenal degree of cellular reorganization. Although most of the material presented is limited to cytoplasmic changes, it must be realized that such changes require equally significant changes in the nucleus. The morphological aspects of nuclear changes, however, are not nearly as dramatic as cytoplasmic changes and therefore were not considered extensively.

Finally, it is recognized that many questions have not been answered and that the material presented raises many other questions. In other cases, we have had to resort to mere speculations. It is believed, however, that the regenerating, isolated gastrodermis is a superb system in which to study a wide spectrum of problems in developmental biology.

Acknowledgment

Some of the material presented in this section was obtained as a result of a National Science Foundation Grant (No. GB-8384). The author is indebted to Linda M. Bookman for her technical assistance.

References

Burnett, A. L. (1966). *Amer. Natur.* **100**, 165–190.
Burnett, A. L., and Diehl, N. A. (1964a). *J. Exp. Zool.* **157**, 217–226.
Burnett, A. L., and Diehl, N. A. (1964b). *J. Exp. Zool.* **157**, 237–250.
Burnett, A. L., Davis, L. E., and Ruffing, F. E. (1966). *J. Morphol.* **120**, 1–9.
Chapman, G. B. (1961). *In* "The Biology of Hydra" (H. M. Lenhoff and W. F. Loomis, eds.), p. 131. Univ. of Miami Press, Coral Gables, Florida.
Davis, L. E. (1968). *Exp. Cell Res.* **52**, 602–607.
Davis, L. E. (1969). *J. Cell Sci.* **5**, 699–726.
Davis, L. E. (1970a). *Exp. Cell Res.* **60**, 127–132.
Davis, L. E. (1970b). *Z. Zellforsch. Mikrosk. Anat.* **105**, 526–537.

Davis, L. E. (1971). *J. Exp. Zool.* **176,** 107–128.

Davis, L. E. (1972). *Z. Zellforsch. Mikrosk. Anat.* **123,** 1–17.

Davis, L. E., and Haynes, J. F. (1968). *Z. Zellforsch. Mikrosk. Anat.* **92,** 149–158.

Davis, L. E., Burnett, A. L., Haynes, J. F., and Mumaw, V. R. (1966). *Develop. Biol.* **14,** 307–329.

Davis, L. E., Burnett, A. L., and Haynes, J. F. (1968). *J. Exp. Zool.* **167,** 295–332.

Haynes, J. F., and Burnett, A. L. (1963). *Science* **142,** 1481–1483.

Haynes, J. F., and Davis, L. E. (1969). *Z. Zellforsch. Mikrosk. Anat.* **100,** 316–324.

Haynes, J. F., Burnett, A. L., and Davis, L. E. (1968). *J. Exp. Zool.* **161,** 283–294.

Hess, A. (1961). *In* "The Biology of Hydra" (H. M. Lenhoff and W. F. Loomis, eds.), p. 1. Univ. of Miami Press, Coral Gables, Florida.

Lentz, T. (1965). *Z. Zellforsch. Mikrosk. Anat.* **67,** 547–560.

Lentz, T. L. (1966). "The Cell Biology of Hydra." Wiley, New York.

Lentz, T., and Barrnett, R. (1965). *Amer. Zool.* **5,** 341–356.

Lesh, G. E., and Burnett, A. L. (1964). *Nature (London)* **204,** 492–493.

Lesh, G. E., and Burnett, A. L. (1966). *J. Exp. Zool.* **163,** 55–78.

Locke, M., and Collins, J. (1965). *J. Cell Biol.* **26,** 857–884.

Macklin, J., and Burnett, A. L. (1966). *Exp. Cell. Res.* **44,** 665–668.

Rose, P., and Burnett, A. L. (1968a). *Wilhelm Roux' Arch. Entwicklungsmech. Organismen* **161,** 281–297.

Rose, P., and Burnett, A. L. (1968b). *Wilhelm Roux' Arch. Entwicklungsmech. Organismen* **161,** 298–318.

Rose, P., and Burnett, A. L. (1970). *Wilhelm Roux' Arch. Entwicklungsmech. Organismen* **165,** 177–191.

Slautterback, D. B. (1967a). *Z. Zellforsch. Mikrosk. Anat.* **79,** 296–318.

Slautterback, D. B. (1967b). *J. Cell Sci.* **2,** 563–572.

Slautterback, D. B. (1961). *In* "The Biology of Hydra" (H. M. Lenhoff and W. F. Loomis, eds.), p. 77. Univ. of Miami Press, Coral Gables, Florida.

PART V

EPIDERMAL REGENERATION IN *HYDRA*

In some species of coelenterates the epidermis has been shown to regenerate a whole animal. In other forms, as seen in Chapter 6, the gastrodermis has performed this feat. However, only in the *Hydra* has it been demonstrated that either cell layer can replace the missing layer. In the following sections, we will use a different format to demonstrate our findings because no one to date has observed epidermal regeneration in a *Hydra*. Thus, there is no substantial reference list to rely on. We have decided to present this material as a series of "experimental" papers, not only because they are novel, but because they offer a new system for developmental studies on the animal. We will begin with one method of removing whole epidermal pieces by simple chemical means. This will be followed by methods for removing epidermal tubes free of interstitial cells, cnidoblast cells, and nerve cells. Then we will attempt to show how many specialized cell types are necessary to restore the morphology of the *Hydra* (see Chapter 5), and finally and most important, how cell layers of *Hydra* may be recombined in various species-specific and interspecific grafts.

CHAPTER 7

Regeneration from Isolated Epidermal Explants

RALPH LOWELL AND ALLISON L. BURNETT

I. Introduction

The regenerative properties of the coelenterates are well known and have been investigated by many workers. However, the limits of this ability are not known, and one approach to determining such limits has been to separate the cell layers and culture them individually.

Gilchrist (1937) and Steinberg (1963) reported the ability of isolated epidermis from *Aurelia* scyphistomae to regenerate complete polyps. Zwilling (1963) found that isolated pieces of epidermis from *Cordylophora* would regenerate complete polyps, but that isolated gastrodermis disintegrated.

Papenfuss and Bokenham (1939) reported that neither cell layer in *Hydra* would regenerate, but later work has shown that the gastrodermis of both brown and green *Hydra* can regenerate whole animals. Normandin

(1960) reported complete polyp regeneration from gastrodermal explants of *Hydra oligactis,* and Haynes and Burnett (1963) obtained similar regeneration from the isolated gastrodermis of *Hydra viridis.* In 1969 Lowell and Burnett showed that isolated epidermis from *H. oligactis* and *H. pseudoligactis* would also regenerate complete hydras.

II.   Methods

A.   Cell Layer Separation by Perfusion

The separation of epidermis from gastrodermis is accomplished by perfusing the gastrovascular cavity with Haynes' solution (0.1% NaCl, 0.2% CaCl₂, 0.03% MgSO₄, 0.01% KHCO₃ in distilled or deionized water). During perfusion the animals are kept in dishes filled with standard culture water (Loomis and Lenhoff, 1956) arranged beneath the perfusion apparatus (Fig. 1). Each perfusion unit (Fig. 2) consists of a

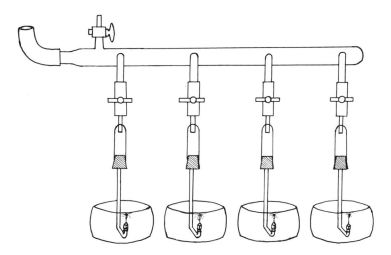

Fig. 1. Perfusion apparatus (see text for explanation).

specially perforated #33 hypodermic needle mounted on the end of a J-shaped glass tube suspended from a perfusion manifold by a short piece of rubber tubing fitted with an adjustable clamp. A transparent monitoring chamber is inserted in the unit to provide a visible check on flow rate. The end of the perfusing needle is sealed with epoxy, and another opening made about half way down the needle.

The *Hydra* is threaded on the needle and positioned so the perfusion

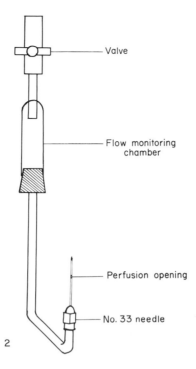

Fig. 2. Perfusion unit.

opening is in the gastrovascular cavity. The animal is held in position by a small piece of Parafilm placed above it on the needle (Figs. 3 and 4). The temperature of the perfusion dishes is brought down to 10°–12°C with crushed ice at the start of perfusion.

Once the epidermis has separated, the lower part of the perfusion unit (still immersed in its dish of culture medium and with the *Hydra* still on the needle) is detached from the monitoring chamber and mounted in a clamp under a dissecting microscope. Then, by using fine forceps and iridectomy scissors, large pieces and frequently entire cylinders of epidermis can be cut away from the animal.

B. REGENERATION TESTS

Epidermal explants free from gastrodermis are tested for regeneration by placing them in small (6 cm) petri dishes containing standard culture water to which 3–5% Haynes' solution has been added and maintaining them at room temperature. They are changed daily and the Haynes' solution eliminated after the second day. Culturing is continued until regeneration is complete, differentiation ceases at some intermediate stage, or the tissue disintegrates. Sterile procedures are not necessary; bacterial growth is not a problem so long as the tissue is alive.

Fig. 3. *Hydra* on perfusion needle showing epidermal separation ($\times$ 66).

III. Results

A. Perfusion Results

Once perfusion is begun the *Hydra* swells like a miniature balloon until the mouth opens and allows the perfusate to escape. Separation of cell layers first appears as a blister in the epidermis, and may stop with this. Frequently, however, it continues proximally or distally, or both, and

Fig. 4. *Hydra* on perfusion needle showing spontaneous eversion. (× 66).

also around the animal, until a large fluid-filled space is formed between the inner and outer cell layers. At maximum separation the entire epidermis between tentacles and basal disc appears as a nearly transparent sphere inside which the gastrodermis may be seen as a spindle around the needle (Figs. 3 and 4). Ordinarily separation does not occur at the hypostome or tentacles or at the basal disc and frequently only partial separation occurs in the peduncle. There is no separation around the projecting portion of a developing bud.

Separation occurs during the first 2 hours of perfusion, and usually during the first half hour. Often maximal separation will occur in the first 5 minutes. If perfusion is continued for 3 to 6 hours in a separated animal, tears occur in the epidermis exposing blisters of mesoglea; in a maximally separated *Hydra* the tears encircle the animal and the epidermis retracts or sloughs away, leaving behind a fluid-filled sac of naked mesoglea.

Successful separation with the perfusion technique ranges from about 25% in *H. fusca* and *H. viridis* to about 50% in *H. oligactis* and *H. pseudoligactis*, including all degrees of separation. Highest separation frequencies are obtained at temperatures between 10° and 15°C with animals starved 24–48 hours during the fall and winter months.

The line of separation is in the mesoglea. Stained sections of whole animals in which separation has occurred show most of the mesoglea attached to the epidermis. This would be expected from the fact that the fluid-filled mesoglea is exposed following retraction of the epidermis on prolonged perfusion.

B. REGENERATION RESULTS

About 20% of epidermises of *H. oligactis, H. pseudoligactis,* and *H. fusca* show regenerative ability when the piece of epidermis tested exceeds approximately one eighth of the body column. Frequency and degree of regeneration increase with increasing size of the explant until the piece equals about one-half the body column epidermis. Pieces larger than this show no greater frequency or degree of regeneration. Pieces less than one-eighth body column size uniformly disintegrate when cultured as decribed above.

In most cases regeneration stops short of complete polyp formation, only 2% becoming fully differentiated hydras.

In a regenerating explant visible changes appear in the first 24 hours. Morphogenesis continues actively during the second day, after which the rate of change declines over the next four or five days. Morphogenetic events may be grouped as follows:

1. Stage I: Cavitation

Depending on the size of the explant one or more small cavities become visible with a dissecting microscope within 6 to 20 hours. Examination of sectioned material fixed at 6 and 12 hours indicates that these cavities arise through the coalescence of intercellular spaces appearing early in the regenerative process. At the end of this stage there is no gastrodermal layer, although the cavities may show partial bordering by a mesoglealike membrane, and scattered cells may be present inside the membrane as well as lying free within the cavity. Zymogenlike cells may be found occasionally near the cavity or along the recesses ramifying from it (Fig. 5). During this stage the regenerate begins to show contractile movements.

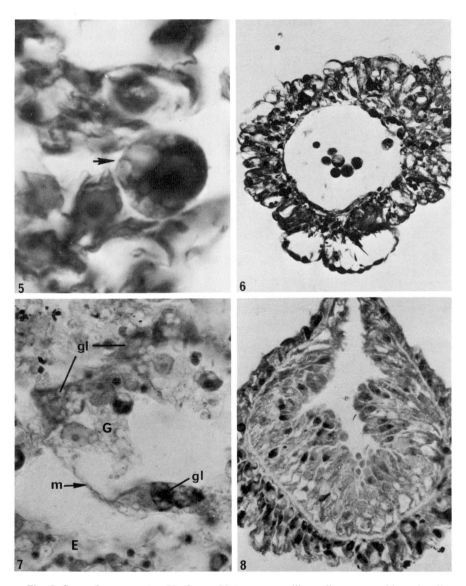

Fig. 5. Stage I regenerate, *H. fusca*. Note zymogenlike cell among epidermal cells (arrow). Toluidine blue, pH 8 (× 2700).

Fig. 6. Stage II regenerate, *H. pseudoligactis*. Note flattened layer of gastrodermal cells lining coelenteron. Toluidine blue, pH 8 (× 1100).

Fig. 7. Stage II regenerate, *H. pseudoligactis*. E, epidermis; G, gastrodermis; m, mesoglea; gl, gland cell. Toluidine blue, pH 8 (× 1120).

Fig. 8. Stage III regenerate. *H. pseudoligactis*. Note fully differentiated gastrodermis. Toluidine blue, pH 8 (× 450).

2. Stage II: Body Column, Hypostome, and Tentacle Formation

Further morphogenesis depends to some extent on the region from which the epidermis has been taken. When the explant comes from the subhypostome and gastric regions a hypostome and/or tentacle buds are the next structures to appear. When the explant includes basal disc epidermis the regenerate may form a basal disc instead of a hypostome. Concomitantly there is a lengthening of the regenerate as a body column is formed. During this period extension and fusion of the stage I cavities occur forming a coelenteron. The mesogleal layer is completed between the epidermis and a developing gastrodermis (Fig. 6). Early gastrodermal cells appear on the inner surface of the mesoglea as a lining of flattened epithelium (Fig. 6), which later becomes thickened and contains presumptive digestive and gland cells (Fig. 7). In this stage there is a noticeable increase in the rate and extent of spontaneous contractions.

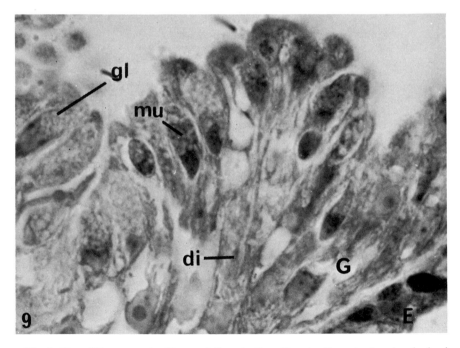

Fig. 9. Stage III regenerate, *H. pseudoligactis*. E, epidermis; G, gastrodermis; gl, gland cell; mu, mucous cell; di, digestive cell. Toludine blue, pH 8 (× 1530).

3. Stage III: Mouth and Basal Disc Formation

With the appearance of a mouth the regenerate becomes a potentially independent organism. Histologically such completed polyps show fully organized epidermal, mesogleal, and gastrodermal layers (Fig. 8), in which the gastrodermis contains fully differentiated digestive, gland, and mucous cells (Fig. 9).

IV. Discussion

The epidermal cell type or types which give rise to the gastrodermal layer are not known. Nevertheless it is likely that interstitial cells play a prominent role in the process. Gastrodermal regeneration in *Hydra* may be analogous to gastrodermal regeneration in *Cordylophora* which Diehl (1969) has reported. He has followed regenerative stages in epidermal explants from *Cordylophora* in which interstitial cells move to the base of the epitheliomuscular cells soon after the epidermis is isolated. These cells become elongate, vacuolated, and differentiate directly into normal digestive cells. Rose (1970), also working with *Cordylophora,* has combined epidermis labeled with tritiated thymidine with the gastrodermis from a "cold" animal and studied the regeneration of new feeding hydranths at different time periods. He finds basophilic and secretory cells in the gastrodermis labeled, strongly implying that the labeled epidermal interstitial cells migrate to the interior of the regenerating explant and differentiate into the zymogen and mucous secretory cells.

One of the most interesting facts regarding regeneration in *Hydra* is that each cell layer alone can give rise to the other. Details of the regeneration of epidermis from gastrodermis have been worked out by Davis *et al.* (1966). The fact that these complementary regenerations occur in media of different ionic concentrations supports the view that ionic environment is an important factor in the control of cell differentiation *in vivo* (Burnett, 1966; Macklin and Burnett, 1966).

V. Summary

A method of obtaining living, undamaged, sheets or cylinders of epidermis from *Hydra oligactis, H. pseudoligactis, H. fusca,* and *H. viridis* is presented. This is a perfusion technique by which about 50% of perfused animals show separation of epidermis from gastrodermis under optimum conditions.

Isolated epidermal explants, of *H. fusca, H. oligactis,* and *H. pseudoligactis* show some regenerative ability, and in about 2% of cases regenerate complete hydras. It is proposed that interstitial cells of the epidermis have a prominent role in the formation of new gastrodermis.

Since it has been demonstrated that isolated gastrodermis in *H.*

oligactis and *H. viridis* can regenerate complete hydras, similar regeneration from isolated epidermis makes *Hydra* the first animal in which it has been shown that each layer alone can give rise to the other.

References

Burnett, A. L. (1966). *Amer. Natur.* **100,** 165–190.
Davis, L. E., Burnett, A. L., Haynes, J. F., and Mumaw, V. R. (1966). *Develop. Biol.* **14,** 307–329.
Diehl, F. A. (1969). *Wilhelm Roux' Arch. Entwicklungsmech. Organismen* **162,** 309–335.
Gilchrist, F. G. (1937). *Biol. Bull.* **72,** 99–124.
Haynes, J., and Burnett, A. L. (1963). *Science* **142,** 1481–1483.
Loomis, W. F., and Lenhoff, H. (1956). *J. Exp. Zool.* **132,** 555–574.
Lowell, R. D., and Burnett, A. L. (1969). *Biol. Bull.* **137,** 312–320.
Macklin, M., and Burnett, A. L. (1966). *Exp. Cell Res.* **44,** 665–668.
Normandin, D. K. (1960). *Science* **132,** 678.
Papenfuss, E. J., and Bokenham, A. H. (1939). *Biol. Bull.* **76,** 1–6.
Rose, P. G., and Burnett, A. L. (1970). *Wilhelm Roux' Arch. Entwicklungsmech. Organismen* **165.** 192–216.
Steinberg, S. (1963). *Biol. Bull.* **124,** 337–343.
Zwilling, E. (1963). *Biol. Bull.* **124,** 368–378.

CHAPTER 8

Epithelial-Muscle Cells

JULIAN F. HAYNES

The epidermis of a *Hydra* is basically a simple columnar epithelium made up of epithelial-muscle cells. These cells along with a similar epithelial cell in the gastrodermis (the digestive-muscle cell) form the bulk of the body of any hydroid polyp. Ultrastructurally they reflect their complex role in the structure and the function of the polyp. They are physiologically and developmentally polarized cells extending from the mesoglea to the free outer surface of the organism. The basal ends of the cells at their contact with the mesoglea form the muscular system of the *Hydra* while the apical ends are highly active secretory cells producing the extracellular coat and forming the integument of the polyp. The central regions of the epithelial-muscle cells usually contain a large vacuole separating the muscular and integumental-secretory portions of the cell.

The apical surface of the epithelial-muscle cell forms the contact of the polyp with its environment and controls the interaction of the polyp with its surroundings. This surface of the epithelial-muscle cell is an active secretory surface and produces the well-developed extracellular coat. This extracellular material plus the apical portions of the epithelial-muscle cells form the integument. This integument must provide protection from physical abrasion, prevent the loss or entry of excessive water or salts, and still allow free respiratory exchange.

The apical rim of cytoplasm (Fig. 1A) contains varying numbers of large secretory droplets which appear to be precursors of the extra-cellular coat. While there have not been adequate studies between species or even of different regions within a species it is clear that there are major differences within a species and between species. These differences affect both the amount of secretory material and the ultrastructural characteristics of the material. In the hypostomal region of *Hydra fusca* the apical portion of the cell is filled with closely packed, large, secretory droplets. In the gastric region of *Hydra viridis* the secretory droplets are smaller, less dense, and less numerous. The most distinctive secretory materials are found in the epithelial cells of the basal disc where the specialized materials by which the *Hydra* adheres to the substrate are synthesized and released.

The cytoplasm of the cells immediately surrounding the secretory droplets contains empty vesicles and larger numbers of free ribosomes. Mitochondria are found scattered throughout the apical region. Strands of endoplasmic reticulum and well-developed Golgi regions are frequent in the apical portion of the cell. Frequently the single strands of endo-plasmic reticulum are very closely applied to the Golgi. The cisternae of the endoplasmic reticulum are sometimes distended with a flocculent material. This material is of a somewhat lower density than that found in the secretory droplets.

The base of each epithelial-muscle cell is formed into a series of branched processes or extensions. According to Mueller (1950) the exact number of major processes per cell cannot be determined, but some cells possess at least four processes. Within each of these extensions is found a contractile element, the myoneme. These are cylindrical threads about 1 to 2 μ in diameter and 20 to 50 μ long (Fig. 2). The myoneme contain-ing processes of each cell contact similar processes of adjacent cells and form a web or a net of contractile tissue along the mesoglea of the polyp. Within this meshwork the myonemes are all oriented parallel to the long axis of the polyp and their contraction causes the *Hydra* to shorten. The fine structure of the myonemes of the tentacle have been described by Slautterback (1967) and that of the gastric region by Haynes *et al.* (1968).

The myonemes are a form of smooth muscle made up of larger numbers of parallel filaments. These filaments are of two sizes (50 and 200 Å in diameter) and are apparently actin and myosin. The thick and thin fila-ments show no particular relationship to each other (Fig. 2) as do the similar fibrils in striated muscle.

The surfaces of contact between adjacent myoneme containing processes are regions of lateral specialization (Fig. 1B). The membranes of apposing processes are differentiated into structures resembling the

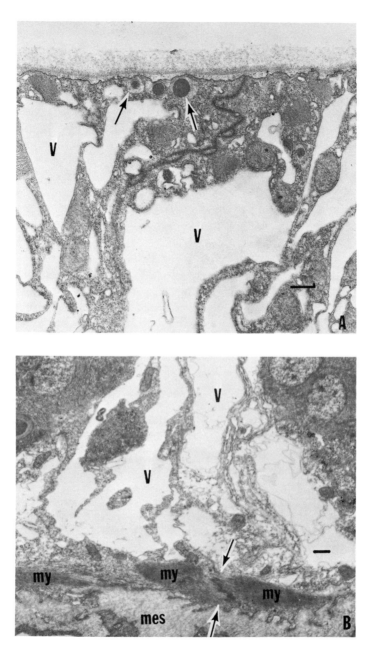

Fig. 1. The apical and basal regions of typical epithelial muscle cells. A. The apical region with the thick extracellular coat secreted by this region. This coat consists of a broad band of diffuse material on the external surface and a relatively thin band of very dense material closer to the cell surface. In some regions the dense band is separated from the surface of the cell by a third region of lesser density. Droplets which appear to be the precursors of the extracellular coat are seen just under the apical surface of the cell and are indicated by arrows. Portions of the extensive vacuolar system can be seen within the cells just under the apical surface. B. The basal region of the cell and is cut parallel to the long axis of portions of three myonemes (my). Where two myonemes contact each other a specialized junction can be seen (arrow). The basal portions of the vacuoles can be seen (V). Directly under the myonemes is the mesoglea (mes). Lines indicate 1 μ.

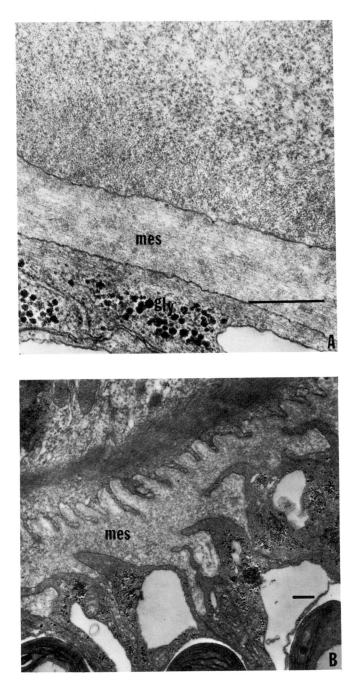

Fig. 2. Electron micrograph through the bases of two epithelial muscle cells. A. A myoneme in cross-section and the two filaments (thick and thin) can be seen. Directly under the myoneme is the fibrous mesoglea (mes). Glycogen deposits (gly) can be seen in the base of the gastrodermis. B. A myoneme in longitudinal section. The folds in the base of the cell indicate that the myoneme is not attached along its length to the plasma membrane. The individual fibers of the myoneme can be seen. The mesoglea (mes) separates the epidermis from the gastrodermis. In the gastrodermal cells deposits of glycogen can be seen. Lines indicate 1 μ.

intercalated discs of vertebrate cardiac muscle. These regions appear to be the only points at which the fibers of the myonemes are attached to the lateral walls of the cell and are the points at which the tension developed during contraction is transmitted to the mesoglea, thus effecting the shortening of the polyp. Additionally, it is possible that they represent regions for the transmission of an impulse from one epithelial cell to another. Thus they may be responsible for the phenomenon of epithelial conduction of an impulse.

One of the most distinctive features of the muscle processes of the epithelial cells is the fact that they form a highly organized system. Because of their extensive branching and close contact an actual sheet of muscle is formed along the mesoglea of a *Hydra*. By the simple modification of the bases of the epithelial cells a true muscle tissue has been formed in these organisms.

The apical secretory region and the basal contractile region occupy only 20–25% of an average epithelial-muscle cell. They are separated by an intermediate region containing a large branched vacuole. This region occupies as much as 60–70% of the volume of an epithelial-muscle cell. The major exception to this condition is in specialized regions such as the tentacles where the cells become more cuboidal in shape and the intermediate region is reduced in size.

The vacuole pushes the cytoplasm of the cell closely against the lateral plasma membranes. There are strands of cytoplasm crossing the vacuole and the nucleus is frequently contained within one of these strands or is suspended by a strand of cytoplasm into the vacuole. The cytoplasmic strands very often have long segments of granular endoplasmic reticulum running through them parallel to their longitudinal axes.

The relationship between the individual epithelial cells is complex. The contact at the basal ends where the myoneme-containing processes form specialized junctions have been referred to previously. In the apical regions of the epidermis the cells are physically attached by septate junctions joining the outer leaflets of the cell membranes of adjacent cells (Wood, 1959). In addition the cells are highly interdigitated by irregular, fingerlike lateral processes. This interdigitation is found along the entire length of the lateral surface but is most pronounced in the apical one third of the cell.

References

Haynes, J. F., Burnett, A. L., and Davis, L. E. (1968). *J. Exp. Zool.* **167**, 283–294.
Mueller, J. F. (1950). *Trans. Amer. Microsc. Soc.* **96**, 133–147.
Slautterback, D. B. (1967). *Z. Zellforsch. Mikrosk. Anat.* **79**, 296–318.
Wood, R. L. (1959). *J. Biophys. Biochem. Cytol.* **6**, 343–352.

CHAPTER 9

Regeneration of a *Hydra* Containing No Interstitial Cells from an Isolated Basal Disc

ALLISON L. BURNETT AND PHILIP G. LAMBRUSCHI

I. Introduction

It has been generally agreed by investigators studying regeneration in *Hydra* that virtually any part of the animal when excised will regenerate. There have been two notable exceptions: the isolated tentacle and basal disc. There is one report in the literature by the Russian authors (Tokin and Gorbunowa, 1934) that *Hydra* can regenerate from a single basal disc if it is traumatized by pricking the excised base with a pin. These investigators claimed that the animal formed a new hypostome and tentacles and contained epidermal interstitial cells capable of forming cnidoblast cells, which in turn formed nematocysts.

This observation was of interest to us because the basal disc of *Hydra pseudoligactis* when examined histologically is found to contain no interstitial cells, cnidoblast cells, gastrodermal gland or zymogen cells, gastrodermal mucous cells, or cells in division. The base of *H. pseudoligactis,* for example, contains epidermal mucous cells which liberate an acid mucopolysaccharide (so-called gland cells of the basal disc), plus

239

nerve cells. Examination of hundreds of sections of the base has never revealed the presence of an interstitial cell. However, Davis (1964), has observed a few animals with some interstitial cells in this area. The gastrodermis of the disc contains digestive cells with large reserves of fat droplets plus protein reserve droplets. Thus, regeneration of this animal from an isolated base would entail a significant amount of dedifferentiation on the part of the three specialized cell types found in this region.

In an early experiment (Burnett, 1959), basal discs were isolated from 300 animals and all failed to regenerate. In fact, only in one or two cases was there any regeneration if the proximal third of the peduncle of the animal were attached to the bases. Thinking that perhaps there was not enough tissues in a single basal disc to permit regeneration, discs from several animals were chopped into a mince and placed in close contact until they fused into a single mass (Burnett, 1961). Out of twelve such sections which fused successfully, three miniature animals regenerated, but unfortunately they were lost while being prepared for histological study.

It appeared possible that, although interstitial cells cannot be detected histologically in the basal disc, perhaps they stained weakly in this area and were not recognized after toluidine blue staining. Squash preparations of basal discs revealed small cells that approximated the size of interstitial cells, and this seemed to bear out the foregoing possibility. However, in subsequent papers (Burnett and Diehl, 1964; Davis *et al.,* 1966) which employed vital staining, histological sectioning, and studies with the electron microscope, we found that these "small" cells were not interstitial cells but nerve cell bodies. These observations rekindled our interests in basal disc regeneration and the following studies were undertaken.

II. Materials and Methods

Hydra pseudoligactis was used as the experimental animal. This species was chosen because the basal disc is well demarcated from the adjacent peduncle and its rather elongated shape provides more tissue for ensuing regeneration. It is absolutely essential that no peduncle tissue be included when the bases are amputated. This is not a simple problem to overcome. The slightest contraction of the animal will invariably compress some peduncular tissue against the base and a cut exactly at the peduncle-base junction is difficult. It seemed preferable to cut through the base and actually leave some basal tissue behind to ensure that no peduncle was included (Fig. 1, p. 244).

The reason for this fine cutting is as follows. First, some nematocytes invariably pass down into the peduncle, but they are eliminated at the junction of the basal disc and peduncle. We wanted to be certain that this cell type was not included in our preparations. Also, mucous cells of the gastrodermis, although sparse in the peduncle, can occur at the level of the peduncle and basal disc, and occasionally they have been seen in the base itself.

Thus, we decided that we would perform excisions on a large number of animals, hoping that at least some bases would be devoid of peduncular tissue. For the following experiment 120 isolated bases and a similar number of controls were employed.

For 3 days following excision the experimental bases were pricked several times with a sharp pin once a day. Controls were left untouched. After 3 days the control and experimental bases were placed at a temperature of 12°C and observed daily.

III. Results

During the first 10 days of the experiment the most noticeable change in experimental animals was their elongation from the early "round ball" state to the tubular shape which was twice as long as it was wide. In many cases, it appeared certain that tentacles would arise from one end of the tube because the food materials from the digestive cells was well distributed within the tubes. Control animals remained in a rounded condition.

Between 12 and 14 days after excision 3 animals in the experimental group regenerated tentacles. All the control animals and the remaining experimental animals showed no regeneration and invariably perished after their food reserves were exhausted.

Although the regeneration percentage is small, histological examination of the animals revealed interesting information. In one animal which had regenerated a hypostome and two tentacles, the following was observed. There was not a single cnidoblast cell or interstitial cell in the entire epidermis. The tentacles, therefore, were completely devoid of nematocysts (Fig. 6, p. 246). The gastrodermis consisted of only digestive cells and was entirely lacking in zymogen and mucous cells. The small base of the regenerate contained epidermal basal mucous cells similar to those in the normal animal (Figs. 4 and 5, pp. 244, 245). However, the epidermal cells which formed the gastric column contained no mucous granules characteristic of the base; instead they had transformed into epitheliomuscular cells (Figs. 2 and 3, pp. 243, 244). Normally, when a cell reaches the basal disc it sloughs off the column and dies. In this case, the cells in the column were found in all stages of division. Nerve cells were still present in the epidermis, but their numbers had greatly reduced. This is probably because they had not divided and were now spread out over a much larger region than at the beginning of the experiment.

The gastrodermis of the animal, as we have stated previously, was composed of only digestive cells even in the region of the hypostome which normally contains hundreds of mucous cells (Fig. 6, p. 246).

The remaining two animals regenerated long, single, medial tentacles. In one of these animals the tentacle was completely devoid of nematocysts, but a few basophilic cells were found in the epidermis. Of these, none was forming nematocysts (Fig. 3, p. 245). The third animal contained a few isolated nematocysts in the tentacle, and perhaps a dozen basophilic cells which resembled interstitial cells. The gastrodermis of these two animals contained only digestive cells (Fig. 3, p. 245). This suggests that one or two interstitial cells were present in the base after excision.

IV. Discussion

From the three animals that regenerated, a few definitive conclusions can be drawn. 1. The general form of the *Hydra* is not dependent upon the presence of interstitial cells, zymogen cells, or mucous cells. Morphogenesis can be accomplished by the presence of epithelial cells alone. 2. Although we have never observed divisions in gland cells in the base of the epidermis of this species, these cells are capable of eliminating their mucous secretion and dividing.

The influence of pricking the cells with sharp needles is not known. We can think of two possibilities. Although in our studies with the electron microscope (Davis *et al.*, 1968) we have observed neurosecretory droplets in the cells of the base, we have not observed the elimination of these droplets as we have in the hypostomal area after the hypostome is excised. The fact that no control animals regenerated suggests that the initial excision may not be an adequate stimulus to evoke neurosecretion, but continued pricking of the base may cause some of the nerves to eliminate their enclosed neurosecretory droplets. This could presumably stimulate division of the basal cells (Burnett and Diehl, 1964; Burnett, 1966, 1968).

Another possibility is that control animals round up and remain in this condition. Presumably these pieces could regulate their internal ionic environment in much the same way the intact animal does. Animals subjected to pricking would during early days of regeneration be subjected to fluctuations in the internal and external ionic milieu and stimulated to grow. Burnett (1966), Macklin and Burnett (1966), and Schulz and Lesh (1970) have stressed the important role of ions in control of growth and differentiation. Davis (1970a,b) has demonstrated with the electron microscope that, under certain ionic conditions, cnidoblast cells containing nematocysts can divide. Presumably the outcome of such a division would be one cell with a nematocyst and another cell which would be identical to an interstitial cell. Therefore, the few cnidoblasts and interstitial cells observed in two animals could have resulted from contamination of basal pieces by a few nematocytes.

Acknowledgment

This work was supported by the National Science Foundation (Grant #GB 17917) and an Institutional Grant from the National Institutes of Health (#6060-301-9303).

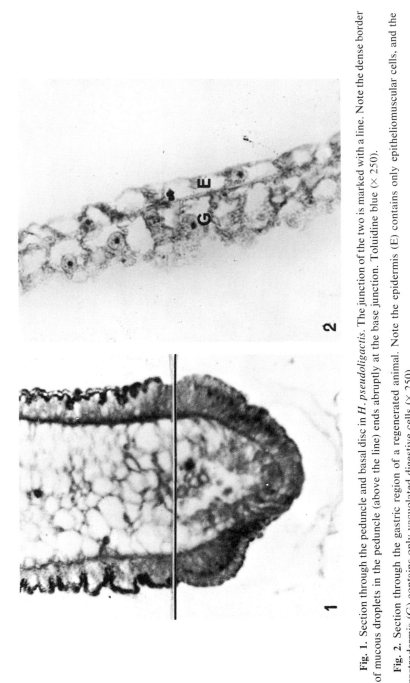

Fig. 1. Section through the peduncle and basal disc in *H. pseudoligactis*. The junction of the two is marked with a line. Note the dense border of mucous droplets in the peduncle (above the line) ends abruptly at the base junction. Toluidine blue (× 250).

Fig. 2. Section through the gastric region of a regenerated animal. Note the epidermis (E) contains only epitheliomuscular cells, and the gastrodermis (G) contains only vacuolated digestive cells (× 250).

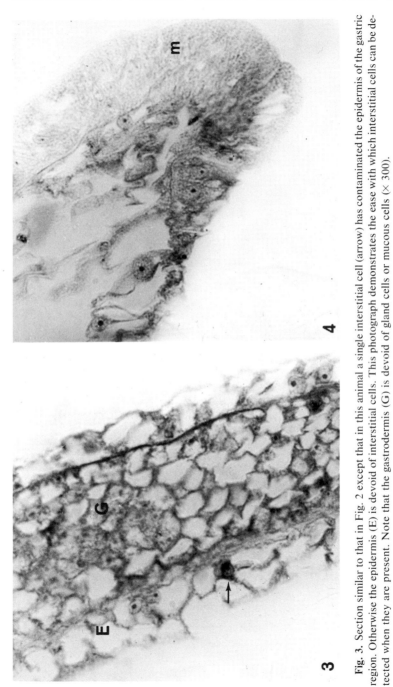

Fig. 3. Section similar to that in Fig. 2 except that in this animal a single interstitial cell (arrow) has contaminated the epidermis of the gastric region. Otherwise the epidermis (E) is devoid of interstitial cells. This photograph demonstrates the ease with which interstitial cells can be detected when they are present. Note that the gastrodermis (G) is devoid of gland cells or mucous cells (× 300).

Fig. 4. Basal disc of regenerated animal. Fine droplets within the epidermal mucous cells of the disc (m) can be recognized (× 300).

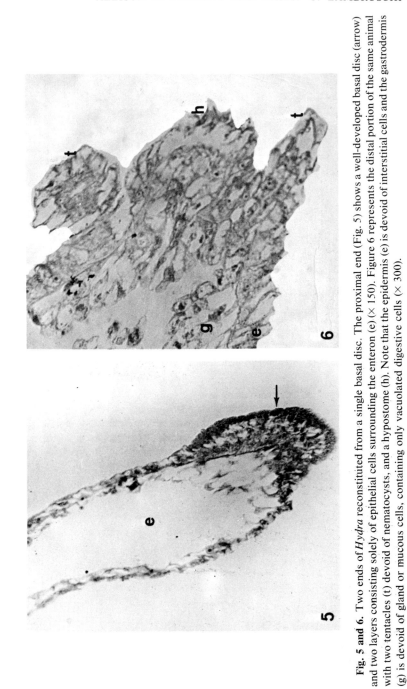

Fig. 5 and 6. Two ends of *Hydra* reconstituted from a single basal disc. The proximal end (Fig. 5) shows a well-developed basal disc (arrow) and two layers consisting solely of epithelial cells surrounding the enteron (e) (× 150). Figure 6 represents the distal portion of the same animal with two tentacles (t) devoid of nematocysts, and a hypostome (h). Note that the epidermis (e) is devoid of interstitial cells and the gastrodermis (g) is devoid of gland or mucous cells, containing only vacuolated digestive cells (× 300).

References

Burnett, A. L. (1959). Unpublished data.

Burnett, A. L. (1961). *J. Exp. Zool.* **146,** 21–84.

Burnett, A. L. (1966). *Amer. Natur.* **100,** 165–189.

Burnett, A. L. (1968). *In* "Results and Problems in Cell Differentiation" (H. Urpsrung, ed.), Vol. 1, pp. 109–127.

Burnett, A. l., and Diehl, N. (1964). *J. Exp. Zool.* **157,** 217–226.

Davis, L. (1964). Personal communication.

Davis, L. (1970a). *Exp. Cell Res.* **60,** 127–132.

Davis, L. (1970b). *Z. Zellforsch. Mikrosk. Anat.* **105,** 526–537.

Davis, L., Burnett, A. L., Haynes, J., and Mumaw, V. (1966). *Develop. Biol.* **14,** 307–329.

Davis, L., Burnett, A. L., and Haynes, J. (1968). *J. Exp. Zool.* **167,** 295–332.

Macklin, M., and Burnett, A. L. (1966). *Exp. Cell Res.* **44,** 665–668.

Schulz, J. K. R., and Lesh, G. (1970). *Growth* **34,** 31–55.

Tokin, B., and Gorbunowa, G. (1934). *Biol. Zh.* **3,** 294–306.

CHAPTER 10

Interspecific Grafting of Cell Layers

ALLISON L. BURNETT, RALPH LOWELL, AND LE MING HANG

I. Introduction

Although investigators have been grafting various body regions of the *Hydra* to one another for over two centuries, the grafts and the hosts invariably contained the two cell layers of the animal placed into contact. Another graft combination, one which has not been attempted before, is to graft the inner layer of one species to the outer layer of another species. This technique, involving the separation of the two cell layers and their subsequent recombination, was developed in our laboratory (Lowell and Burnett, 1969) and has been employed successfully between different species of brown *Hydra*.

The present paper involves the grafting of the gastrodermis of *Hydra viridis* to the epidermis of *Hydra pseudoligactis,* and the results of such a graft on two animals sectioned for histological study. The reason for the small number of animals employed is simple. Out of the dozens of combinations attempted only two were completely successful. In order for such a graft to be a success, the gastrodermis of the green must form the entire lining of the enteron. Although this has not been a special problem with brown *Hydra* of various species, we have been less successful with green and brown combinations for two reasons. First, the explants of green tissues have usually been too small to cover the entire enteron. Often they float free in the enteron and the epidermis of *H. pseudoligactis* merely forms a new gastrodermis from epidermal tissues (Lowell and Burnett, 1969). Second, although portions of green gastrodermis may become attached to the epidermis, there are usually large spaces of non-attachment. Epidermal cells from *H. pseudoligactis* migrate in and quickly form a new gastrodermis in these areas and the green cells are often forced to detach. In only two cases did the gastrodermis of green animals attach along the entire enteron; these animals were sectioned for study at 4 days and 6 days after grafting.

The reason that these experiments are especially rewarding hinges on the nature of the species in question. First, the mucous cells of *H. viridis* are concentrated only in the hypostome of the animal and are found nowhere else along the body column. The mucous cells of *H. pseudoligactis,* on the other hand, are abundant along the gastric column and even extend in large numbers into the peduncle. Second, the mucous cells of *H. viridis* are small (about 8–10 μ in width) and stain very dark red (almost violet at times) with toluidine blue at pH 7. The mucous cells of *H. pseudoligactis* are at least twice the size of *H. viridis* and often even larger (25 μ); they stain a light pink. Third, the digestive cells of *H. viridis* contain algal symbionts which serve as excellent markers to demonstrate that the gastrodermis is not contaminated by cells from the epidermis of *H. pseudoligactis.*

II.   Methods

The removal of the epidermis of *H. pseudoligactis* is described by Lowell and Burnett (1969) and that of removing the gastrodermis is described by Davis *et al.* (1968). The isolated gastrodermis is merely placed into contact with the epidermis and within 24 hours the epidermis will surround or overgrow the gastrodermis (Figs. 5 and 6).

Explants used in these experiments were taken from the mid-gastric region of both species. It must be remembered that the gastrodermis of the green animals never contains mucous cells in this area (Fig. 1).

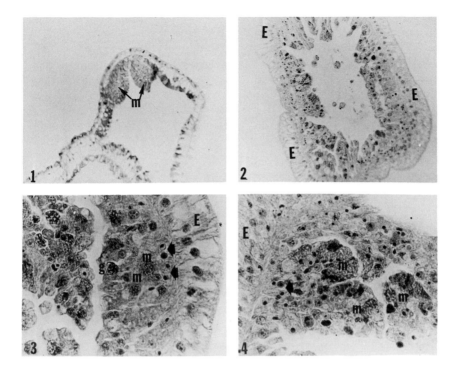

Fig. 1. Section through the hypostomal region of *H. viridis*. Note that the mucous cells (m) are confined to lobes beneath the apex of the hypostome. Toluidine blue (× 100).

Fig. 2. Section through gastric region of an animal containing a *H. pseudoligactis* epidermis and a *H. viridis* gastrodermis. Note that the epidermis consists solely of epitheliomuscular cells with their large basal nuclei. Interstitial cells are conspicuously absent (× 150).

Fig. 3. Higher power magnification of gastric region in animal described in Fig. 2. Note the mucous cells (m) and the gland cell (g). Similar cells are seen throughout the remainder of the gastrodermis. Arrows denote algal symbionts in the digestive cells. Note that the epidermis (E) is devoid of interstitial cells (× 375).

Fig. 4. Similar to Fig. 3 except that mucous cells (m) are present in large groups and line the enteron. Arrow denotes algal symbionts in digestive cells. Note that the epidermis (E) is devoid of interstitial cells (× 375).

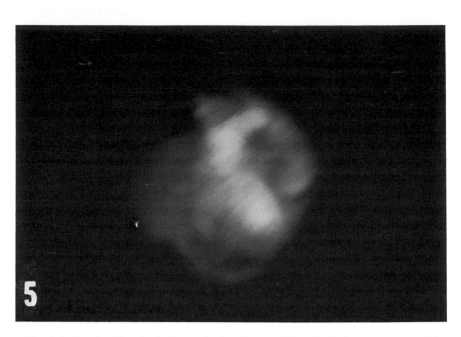

Fig. 5. Isolated epidermis of a brown hydra, *H. pseudoligactis,* beginning to surround the isolated gastrodermis of *H. viridis* after the two are placed into contact (× 200).

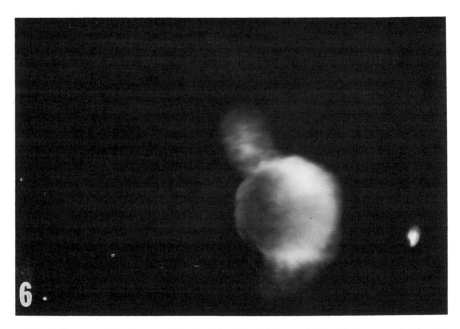

Fig. 6. Same as Fig. 5 except that epidermis of *H. pseudoligactis* has completely surrounded the gastrodermis of *H. viridis.* The animal is now capable of contracting (× 200).

III. Results and Discussion

The primary questions we asked were as follows. Which of the two cell layers will determine the cellular pattern in the recombinant? Will the gastrodermis resist the crossing-over of interstitial cells from the epidermis, as it apparently does in the normal green animal (except at the hypostome), or will the epidermis in some manner "sense" the lack of mucous cells in the gastrodermis and will interstitial cells invade the gastrodermis and form mucous cells? Second, will these mucous cells be those of *H. viridis* or of *H. pseudoligatis*?

The animal examined after 4 days revealed that hundreds of interstitial cells had invaded the gastrodermis of the green animal. Although some interstitial cells remained in the epidermis their numbers were severely diminished. At this stage some mucous cells had already formed. The algal bodies inside the digestive cells revealed that the green gastrodermis was intact and surrounded the enteron.

The animal examined on the sixth day showed a remarkable change. The epidermis of *H. pseudoligactis* was virtually devoid of interstitial cells, all of them having invaded the gastrodermis (Fig. 2). The gastrodermis, on the other hand, was totally lined by mucous cells in every section examined in the recombinant. Furthermore, all of the mucous cells were of the *H. pseudoligactis* type. Interstitial cells just behind the internal border of the gastrodermis were also beginning to form mucous as evidenced by their metachromasia (Figs. 3 and 4).

Previously we had thought that perhaps mucous cells did not form in the normal *H. viridis* column because of some inhibition released either through the enteron or adjacent digestive cells. If this is correct, then it certainly does not apply to interstitial cells of *H. pseudoligactis*. We also thought that perhaps a mesoglea had not formed between the two cell layers of the recombinant allowing for easy passage of the interstitial cells. This also is not the case because the mesoglea was intact on the fourth day, and all remaining interstitial cells in the epidermis crossed over the mesoglea during the next two days.

Rather, these results suggest to us that the distribution of secretory cells of the body column of the animal is determined by a different type of feedback mechanism from the gastrodermis to the epidermis. This mechanism operates in the hypostomal region of every species of *Hydra*, because in this region mucous cells invariably line the mouth. The continual sloughing off of mucous cells from the hypostome is presumably a stimulus for interstitial cells to migrate into the gastrodermis to repair the loss. However, this mechanism must operate in a gradient fashion extending apicobasally. Possibly, in some species, such as *H. viridis,* the gradient is weak and does not stimulate interstitial cells to invade the gastrodermis to form mucous cells below the mouth region. There must be a differential sensitivity to the gradient in the interstitial cells of various species. For example, in *H. fusca* mucous cells extend only to the junction of the budding region and peduncle. The same is true for *H. pirardi. Hydra pseudoligactis,* the species whose mucous cells extend in abundance even into the peduncle, may contain interstitial cells that are more sensitive to the feedback gradient than those of other species.

We are presently attempting to elucidate this problem by grafting a *H. viridis* epidermis to a *H. pseudoligactis* gastrodermis. Thus far, we have not had success because of the small amount of epidermis that can be removed intact from the green animal. Grafts between various species of brown *Hydra*, which are easier to perform, and which remain intact for months, may give more definitive conclusions.

Acknowledgment

This work was supported by the National Science Foundation (Grant # GB 17917) and an Institutional Grant from the National Institutes of Health (# 6060-301-9303).

References

Davis, L., Burnett, A. L., and Haynes, J. (1968). *J. Exp. Zool.* **167,** 283–294.
Lowell, R., and Burnett, A. L. (1969). *Biol. Bull.* **137,** 312–320.

CHAPTER 11

Regeneration of a Complete *Hydra* from a Single, Differentiated Somatic Cell Type

ALLISON L. BURNETT, RALPH LOWELL, AND

MARSHALL N. CYRLIN

I. Introduction

In this paper we shall discuss a single question in some detail using the common, freshwater *Hydra* as an experimental model. The question is: What is the role of the neoblast (in *Hydra,* interstitial or I-cell) in regeneration?

The term "neoblast" means many different things to many different investigators. To offer a concrete definition to be used as a backdrop for our discussion is to invite immediate controversy, because inherent in the definition is the conflict we wish to discuss. For example, if a neoblast is defined functionally as an embryonic reserve cell in adult tissue that differentiates into specialized adult cell types during wound healing, regeneration, gamete formation, asexual reproduction, etc., we shall be provided with an overwhelming body of evidence that during regeneration adult specialized cells contribute more significantly than reserve cells to regeneration. It will be further argued that cells identified as reserve cells are actually descendents of specialized cells that have morphologically dedifferentiated in response to wounding or excision of a body part.

On the other hand, a morphological definition is also subject to ready attack. If we say that a neoblast is a basophilic cell with no distinguishable organelles at the level of the light microscope, and ultrastructurally contains no significant endoplasmic reticulum (only scattered ribosomes), no Golgi complex, and a few scattered mitochondria, the following arguments appear. Differentiated cells during regeneration eliminate their cytoplasmic organelles (secretory droplets, muscle fibers, etc.), degrade their endoplasmic reticulum, and assume an "embryonic" character. It is often further argued that there is no such thing as embryonic reserve at all, and that until now we have been observing only differentiated cells in various stages of dedifferentiation during tissue repair. Obviously, even the unamputated adult requires continual tissue repair. An argument such as this places one in the impossible position of defining a cell type that does not exist.

We think it should be apparent by now that our original question concerning the neoblast needs rephrasing. Instead of asking what is the role of the neoblast, we should be asking: Is there a neoblast cell type existing as a discrete cell line? If so, what is its origin? How much does it contribute to regeneration? Is its contribution necessary? If the contribution to regeneration is made exclusively by specialized cell types, what are the conditions or mechanisms that control their dedifferentiation and subsequent redifferentiation? Then perhaps definitions can follow.

We shall review several seemingly paradoxical results of our experiments on *Hydra* regeneration. Although our investigations do not provide concrete answers to all the questions posed, we feel they at least provide the conceptual framework necessary to ask meaningful questions of a system that has been examined for over 200 years. In fact, it was the first regenerating system to be studied under controlled conditions (Trembley, 1744).

II. Normal Regeneration

If a *Hydra* is transected through the middle of the gastric column, according to the species used for the operation, regeneration of a new hypostome and tentacles occurs within 1 to 4 days. Histological examination of the five species used in our laboratory for such experiments reveals the following. Interstitial cells begin to multiply within a few hours after excision. Their accumulation at the wound surface appears to be due mainly to division near the amputation site and migration (as cnidoblasts) from more proximal regions. At the wound surface some interstitial cells differentiate into cnidoblast cells and form nematocysts. Others enter the gastrodermis and form mucous cells. However, another line of differentiation here is into nerve cells. Therefore, during the so-called differentiation phase much of the interstitial cell population near the wound disappears as the new hypostome is being formed (Burnett, 1968; Rose and Burnett, 1968a,b).

Examination of more proximal regions of regenerating animals reveals that some interstitial cells invariably "escape" the differentiation sequence and remain as dividing cell populations. It was observations such as these that influenced us and many former investigators to state that interstitial cells were indeed a discrete cell line, formed early during embryogeny and persisting throughout the life of the organism.

III. Dedifferentiation of Specialized Cell Types into I-Cells

A unique displacement of cells in one of our species of green *Hydra* led us to reexamine our conclusions. In the green form the gastric region contained only two cell types, digestive cells and gland cells. Mucous cells ordinarily present throughout the gut of other species of *Hydra* are limited solely to the hypostome (Rose and Burnett, 1968a). Therefore, if the gastrodermis could be separated from the epidermis, the gastrodermis from the gastric region would consist of only two cell types.

This separation was accomplished by placing the animal in an ionically balanced solution developed by Muscatine in 1963. By lowering the pH of the solution to pH 2.5 the epidermis contracts and the gastrodermis is revealed as an isolated core. The gastrodermis is then transferred immediately to another ionic solution developed by Haynes and Burnett in 1963; although the epidermis is destroyed by the treatment with Muscatine's solution, the gastrodermis survives (Davis *et al.,* 1966; Burnett *et al.,* 1966).

Examination of the isolated gastrodermal explant over the following days through light and electron microscopy (Davis *et al.,* 1966) revealed remarkable changes in the morphology of the two specialized cell types.

Only those cells at the exterior of the explant, that is, those in direct contact with the ionic medium, underwent change. Gland cells at the periphery shed their enclosed secretory granules and lost their well-developed endoplasmic reticulum. Without dividing, they reached a stage where they could not be distinguished ultrastructurally from interstitial cells. These cells then divided to form nests and thereafter differentiated into cnidoblast cells which formed functional nematocysts. The interstitial cells in the area of the animal destined to form the hypostomal region differentiated into nerve cells. Animals cloned from a two-cell-type regenerate were able to form normal sperm cells from their interstitial cells (Burnett *et al.,* 1966).

Digestive cells on the periphery of the explant broke down their enclosed algal bodies, elaborated longitudinal muscle fibers, and began secreting the mucoprotein border characteristic of epidermal cells. Gastrodermal digestive cells normally never form this mucous product at any level of the body column. The transformation from digestive cells to epidermal cells is a direct one and need not involve cell division.

From these observations it became obvious to us that interstitial cells need not arise from a stem population but could be formed under experimental conditions from specialized cells already existing in the animal. However, this observation did not demonstrate that in the intact animal dedifferentiation of specialized cells occurs. We shall return to this point later.

IV.   Epidermal Regeneration

Although many attempts had been made in the past no one had been able to obtain successful regeneration of whole *Hydra* from isolated epidermis. In our laboratory we had come to the conclusion that chemical techniques employed to separate the two cell layers invariably damaged the epidermis, and that physical techniques such as manual dissection produced pieces of epidermis too small for regeneration of whole animals.

Recently, we succeeded in isolating large pieces of viable epidermis by perfusing the enteron of the *Hydra* with Haynes' solution (Haynes and Burnett, 1963). The epidermal explants which survived were capable of forming an inner layer of gastrodermis containing digestive cells, gland cells, and mucous cells. Tentacles and a histologically normal hypostome were formed (Lowell and Burnett, 1969).

This experiment demonstrated for the first time that each cell layer of a single species of a hydroid was capable of forming the missing layer. Histological examination of isolated epidermis during regeneration revealed that during regeneration the inner layer of cells was formed by the internal migration of interstitial cells. These cells lining the interior of the original epidermis differentiated into digestive, gland, and mucous cells.

The foregoing observations present the seemingly paradoxical situation mentioned in Section I. Gastrodermal regeneration into whole animals can be accomplished by specialized cells which revert to the "neoblast" state to form certain epidermal cells. Epidermal regeneration into whole animals appears to depend almost completely on the capacity of the interstitial cells to form the three cell types characteristic of the gastrodermis. Thus, it appears that no regeneration can occur without interstitial cell participation.

V. Regeneration of Animals Lacking I-Cells

The paradox arises when one considers that in the earlier experiments of Brien and Reniers-Decoen (1955) and Diehl and Burnett (1964) animals whose interstitial cells had been eliminated by X irradiation or nitrogen mustard were able to bud and regenerate a new hypostome and tentacles after transection of the gastric column. Further complications arise when it is considered that animals lacking interstitial cells, although they are able to regenerate several times, invariably die. Histological observations after the fourth hypostomal regeneration reveal that the tentacles are devoid of nematocysts and that no new nerves are regenerating to replace those sloughed off in the hypostomal region (Diehl and Burnett, 1965).

Futhermore, in animals treated with nitrogen mustard, interstitial cells never reappear although the animal may live for several weeks. If, in the isolated gastrodermal explants, gland cells were capable of dedifferentiating into interstitial cells, why is not this same process occurring in animals treated with nitrogen mustard?

It can be argued that, in addition to selectively destroying interstitial cells, nitrogen mustard also inhibits dedifferentiation of specialized cell types. Although, as we shall see later, this possibility cannot be completely ruled out, we suggest an alternative. It is possible that when both cell layers are present there is a stable ionic environment both in the external culture medium and inside the gut. The internal environment depends upon the osmoregulatory systems operating in the epidermal and gastrodermal epithelial cells, that is, the digestive cells of the gut and the epidermal epithliomuscular cells. Elimination of the interstitial cells does not provide the stimulus for gland cells to differentiate because their environment remains unchanged. However, after separation of the gastrodermis, the gland cells at the exterior of the explant face a modified environment, and this induces gland cells at the periphery of the explant to void their secretory droplets and dedifferentiate into interstitial cells.

Another explanation is that proposed by Burnett and Lambruschi that when both cell layers are intact, interstitial cells invade the gut to replace zymogen cells or mycous cells which have sloughed off in the enteron.* This suggests a feedback mechanism is operating between the two cell types. However, there is no evidence that the feedback mechanism operates in both directions, that is, loss of interstitial cells in the

---

*See Chapter 9, this volume.

epidermis does not induce gland cells to migrate to epidermis and form I-cells.

From these observations one point is certain. *Hydra* does not require I-cells for the realization of its two major morphological entities, namely, the head (hypostome, mouth and tentacles) and the foot or basal disc. This point has been especially established by Burnett and Lambruschi who demonstrated that regeneration of a hypostome and two tentacles can occur from a single isolated basal disc.* One regenerated animal contained no I-cells whatsoever.

VI. Regeneration of Whole Hydras from Explants Consisting Solely of Epitheliomuscular Cells

This experiment was done as follows. Hydras (*H. pseudoligactis*) were treated with a 0.01% solution of nitrogen mustard for 10 minutes to destroy their interstitial cells (Diehl and Burnett, 1964). After 8 days (cnidoblasts are eliminated by this time) the epidermis was removed initially by the method of Lowell and Burnett (1969), but later by a much improved technique that allows the investigator to obtain large epidermal tubes completely free from gastrodermal contamination.

This latter technique is executed as follows. The animals are placed in a 10^{-5} solution of reduced glutathione which elicits mouth opening. Watchmaker's forceps are passed into the mouth opening and through the enteron until the basal disc is grasped. The animal is then everted by pulling the base through the mouth opening and placed in a 2% urethane solution. If the head region and base are amputated at this time, a cylinder consisting of an external gastrodermis and internal epidermis results. Cylinders are then shaken by hand in a small vial containing 2% urethane. Several rapid shakes succeed in peeling off the gastrodermis within 30 seconds. It is advisable to examine the vial every few seconds during shaking to ensure that the epidermal pieces remain intact. The tubes are quickly transferred to fresh culture medium and the epidermis reverted to its normal orientation by pulling one end of the cylinder through the other with the use of fine forceps.

By this method epidermal explants of large size are readily obtained; histological examination reveals that they consist solely of epidermal epitheliomuscular cells (Figs. 1–4). Animals are examined histologically each day for the next 10 days. Since the pace of regeneration varies in each animal, we have broken up the regeneration sequence into stages rather than by specific days. These stages are as follows:

1. The ends of the epidermal cylinders close and the animal rounds up into a ball (Figs. 1–4).

*See Chapter 9, this volume.

2. Some epidermal cells begin to round up and their basophilia increases greatly. These cells can in no way be likened to interstitial cells because their nucleus alone is much larger than an ordinary interstitial cell. Some of these cells contain vacuoles reminiscent of those found in normal epitheliomuscular cells (Figs. 5 and 6).

3. Other epidermal cells do not round up or become basophilic; instead their nuclei contain dense basophilic bodies resembling small nucleoli. Similar bodies are also observed in the cytoplasm surrounding the nucleus. This stage does not represent a transitional stage in the formation of the basophilic cells mentioned above, because they persist in this condition throughout the course of the experiment (Fig. 10).

4. After 3 or 4 days the basophilic cells migrate to the interior and stretch out against the overlying layer of epidermis (Fig. 7).

5. During the next 2 days epidermal cells on the interior differentiate into zymogen cells, mucous cells, and digestive cells. Differentiation into mucous cells is characterized by an appearance of metachromasia within the cell. During early stages of differentiation, the metachromatic area is densely concentrated within the basophilic cytoplasm, giving the cell a deep red appearance (Fig. 8). As the cell enlarges the typical form of the spumous cell (Rose and Burnett, 1968a) is assumed and large pink droplets fill all of the cytoplasm except for the small basophilic area which surrounds the nucleus (Fig. 9).

It is interesting to note that some of the basophilic cells in the epidermis also differentiate into mucous cells, but they never grow into the large spumous type. Rather they are identical to the early stage of differentiation when the metachromasia first appears (Fig. 11). In some of the epidermal cells which have not condensed, metachromasia identical to that of the mucous cells forms in a ring around the nucleus with its characteristic dense droplets. It is not known whether any of these mucous cells ever migrate into the interior as mucous cells or whether they perish in the epidermis. Normally, of course, this cell type never appears in the epidermis.

Zymogen cells are formed by the accumulation of secretory droplets throughout the cytoplasm of the epidermal cells which have migrated to the interior. None of them was observed in the epidermis. It should be noted that they were fewer in number in the reconstituted gastrodermis than in the normal animal (Fig. 9).

Digestive cells were formed by the inwandering epidermal cells by a lengthening of the cell toward the enteron with the concomitant formation of a large vacuole characteristic of this cell type (Figs. 7, 11).

At no time during this entire regeneration sequence did interstitial cells appear in the epidermis or the gastrodermis (Figs. 7–10, 12).

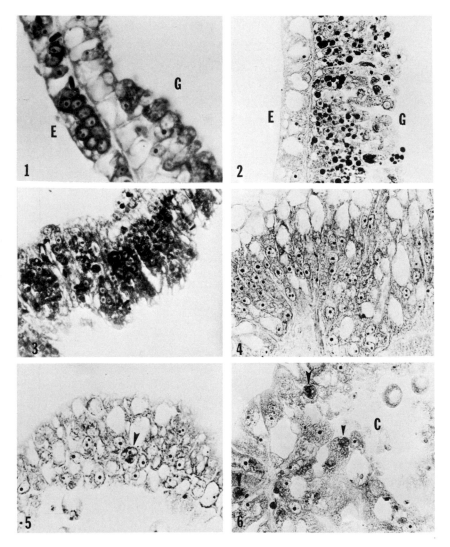

Fig. 1. Normal epidermis of *H. pseudoligactis*. Note the large nest of 9 interstitial cells adjacent to E (epidermis). Other interstitial cells are also visible on either side of the nest. The gastrodermal side (G) shows large vacuolated digestive cells and a peripheral border of darkly staining secretory cells (× 200).

Fig. 2. Same as above except that animal has been treated with nitrogen mustard. After 8 days it is observed that all interstitial cells are lacking from the epidermis (E) (× 150).

6. Differentiation of epidermal cells into nerve cells and cnidoblasts was difficult to observe histologically. It would seem most reasonable if cnidoblasts arose from epidermal cells that became basophilic and then formed the nematocyst droplet. This may be what is occurring in Fig. 5. However, nematocysts were observed forming in epidermal cells which had not condensed and which were not highly basophilic (Fig. 12). It will be observed in Fig. 12 that the nucleus of the cell has taken the condensed half-moon appearance of a typical cnidoblast cell, but the remainder of the cell is typical of a normal epitheliomuscular cell.

Nerve cells, although rare, were identified by their small size and multinucleolar bodies within the nucleus. A study at the ultrastructural level will have to be done before their derivation can be confirmed (Fig. 11).

7. Until this stage no cell divisions were observed. Most animals remain in this rounded-up condition; although they have formed both a circular and longitudinal muscle and are capable of contraction they do not form a hypostome, mouth, and tentacles. However, we believe that this is because of their small size. Larger epidermal isolates are capable of forming a hypostome, mouth opening, and at least two tentacles (Figs. 13 and 14). Such an animal is capable of capturing and ingesting a single *Artemia* nauplius. There were a few cell divisions observed in animals that underwent tentacle formation, but undoubtedly if the organisms had been sectioned at hourly intervals many more divisions would have been recorded.

We have been unable to raise a clone from regenerated animals; in fact, if not fixed for histological sectioning the regenerates perish. The reason for this appears to be that once a gastrodermal layer is established, there is no longer any condensation of epidermal cells into inwandering cell types.

Fig. 3. Epidermis isolated by shaking method (normal animal). Note the huge nests of densely basophilic interstitial cells. No gastrodermal cells are present (× 150).

Fig. 4. Isolated epidermis 8 days after the animal had been treated with nitrogen mustard. Note the homogenous population of epitheliomuscular cells with their characteristic vacuoles. Also note that nematocysts are lacking in this preparation. All interstitial cells have been destroyed (× 175).

Fig. 5. Condensation of an epidermal cell (arrow) with a rise in basophilia. Note the vacuoles or droplets within the cytoplasm (× 175).

Fig. 6. Further condensation of epitheliomuscular cells to basophilic condition (arrows). Some cells have sloughed off into the cavity (C) enclosed by the epidermis (× 175).

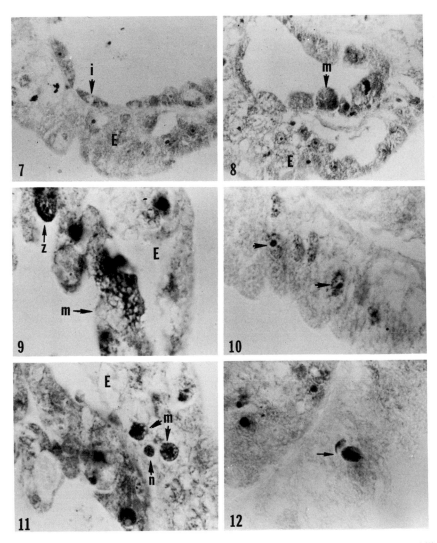

Fig. 7. Section through epidermis (E) which is devoid of interstitial cells. Basophilic inwandering epithelial cells (i) have begun to line the interior of the cavity. Note on far right of inner layer that one inwandering cell is forming a vacuole characteristic of digestive cells (× 225).

Fig. 8. Section at later stage than Fig. 7 showing an inwandering cell that is developing metachromasia characteristic of mucous cell (m). The cell to the left is undergoing similar differentiation. Note that the epidermis (E) is still devoid of interstitial cells (× 200).

The stimulus for this migration appears to be the lack of gastrodermis. Since there are no interstitial cells in the animal, the differentiated cell types such as cnidoblasts and nerve cells, which do not ordinarily divide are not replenished.

VII. Discussion

At the outset, it should be stated that our title is misleading because although whole *Hydra* were regenerated from explants consisting of a single specialized cell type, the animal never formed any interstitial cells. To investigators who would claim that interstitial cells are only dedifferentiated products of specialized cells this would present no problem because they are not recognized as a discrete cell line.

Nevertheless, this population of undifferentiated cells cannot go unrecognized for several reasons. First, and most important, although *Hydra* can live for weeks without any interstitial cells, the animals invariably perish. Second, during embryogeny interstitial cells arise before any of the differentiated cell types are formed. Third, X rays and nitrogen mustard will specifically eliminate this cell population. This indicates some kind of physiological or metabolic uniqueness which distinguishes these cells from all others in the animal. Fourth, an animal cannot form gametes without these cells present.

For the above reasons we strongly urge that the name neoblast or interstitial cell not be dropped. They are formed early in embryogenesis and are a self-replicating population. Thus, they certainly are not initially derived from specialized cell types. When they are formed from specialized

---

Fig. 9. Later stage showing gastrodermis with fully formed spumous, mucous cells (m) and a gland or zymogen cell (z). Epidermis (E) is devoid of interstitial cells (× 450).

Fig. 10. Epidermis of animal showing the large granulated nuclei of the epidermal epitheliomuscular cells (arrows). Note the complete absence of interstitial cells (× 450).

Fig. 11. Mucous cells (m) formed in the epidermis (E) from the differentiation of basophilic epitheliomuscular cells. A nerve cell nucleus with multinucleolar bodies (n) is seen between the mucous cells (× 450).

Fig. 12. Nematocyst (arrow) is forming within an epitheliomuscular cell. The nucleus of this cell has taken on the characteristic half-moon appearance of a cnidoblast cell (× 450).

cell types such as gland cells (Haynes and Burnett, 1963; Davis *et al.,* 1966) it is under very unusual conditions when the gland cells are placed in a specific ionic medium. There is no evidence that specialized cell types in the normal animal ever revert to a completely undifferentiated state, that is, to a cell type that contains no endoplasmic reticulum, Golgi apparatus, microtubules, etc.

This brings us to the point which we believe is crucial in discussion of neoblasts in general: First, what do these cells do in the normal animal; and second, are these cells the only ones that can perform a certain role under any condition? Here we can give some definitive answers to specific questions.

1. Do interstitial cells play a role in normal regeneration? Yes, they form cnidoblast cells, nerve cells, gland cells, mucous cells, as well as divide to maintain their reserve in the animal.

2. Are interstitial cells necessary for regeneration? No. Regeneration of basal disc and hypostome goes on perfectly well in their absence. The same is true for asexual budding.

We could continue this type of questioning for pages. In this paper we have shown that any type of cell normally formed by the interstitial cell (save the gametes) can be formed from epitheliomuscular cells. There is not a shred of evidence that this occurs in the normal animal, however.

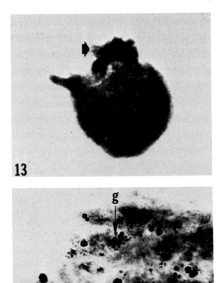

Fig. 13. Whole mount of *Hydra* reconstituted from explant of epidermal epitheliomuscular cells. This animal contains two tentacles and was able to ingest *Artemia* nauplii. Arrow points to section where animal was crushed during mounting and dozens of gland and mucous cells were forced through mouth opening ($\times$ 50).

Fig. 14. Enlargement of area designated by arrow in Fig. 13. Large numbers of highly metachromatic mucous cells (m) and zymogen of gland cells (g) were spewed through the mouth opening, indicating that the gastrodermis of the hypostome was normal ($\times$ 200).

At the present time we feel certain that we will be able to form an entire *Hydra* from a single differentiated epitheliomuscular cell once the proper medium for its attachment and division is obtained. Also, we are certain that we could induce this population of epitheliomuscular cells to dedifferentiate into interstitial cells. However, until someone can maintain indefinitely a culture of hydras which are devoid of I-cells, then we maintain that the I-cell is here to stay.

Acknowledgment

This work was supported by the National Science Foundation (Grant # GB 17917) and an Institutional Grant from the National Institutes of Health (# 6060-301−9303).

References

Brien, P., and Reniers-Decoen, M. (1955). *Bull. Biol. Fr. Belg.* **89,** 259–325.
Burnett, A. L. (1968). *In* "Results and Problems in Cell Differentiation" (H. Ursprung, ed.), Vol. 1, pp. 109–127.
Burnett, A. L., Davis, L., and Ruffing, F. (1966). *J. Morphol.* **120,** 1–8.
Davis, L., Burnett, A. L., Haynes, J., and Mumaw, V. (1966). *Develop. Biol.* **14,** 307–329.
Diehl, F., and Burnett, A. L. (1964). *J. Exp. Zool.* **155,** 253–260.
Diehl, F., and Burnett, A. L. (1965). *J. Exp. Zool.* **158,** 283–298.
Haynes, J., and Burnett, A. L. (1963). *Science* **142,** 1481–1485.
Lowell, R., and Burnett, A. L. (1969). *Biol. Bull.* **137,** 312–320.
Rose, P. G., and Burnett, A. L. (1968a). *Wilhelm Roux' Arch. Entwicklungsmech. Organismen* **161,** S281–S297.
Rose, P. G., and Burnett, A. L. (1968b). *Wilhelm Roux' Arch. Entwicklungsmech. Organismen* **161,** S298–S318.
Trembley, A. (1744). "Mémoires pour servir à l'histoire naturelle d'un genre de polypes d'eau douce, à bras en forme de cornes." Leyden.

PART VI

DIFFERENTIATION OF NERVOUS ELEMENTS IN *HYDRA*

In the past there have been excellent studies by Slautterback and Fawcett on the differentiation of interstitial cells into cnidoblasts. Also, as mentioned in the dedication of this book, the study of differentiation of interstitial cells into dividing cells, gland cells, and mucous cells has been thoroughly studied by Rose. The pioneer in investigations of differentiation of interstitial cells into nerves was Dr. Thomas Lentz at Yale University. However, we include this part as a most important contribution, because of the excellent treatment by Dr. Lowell Davis of three types of nerve differentiation from interstitial cells into sensory, ganglionic, and neurosecretory cells. Dr. Davis, after examining thousands of sections, not only demonstrates the "missing links" in the differentiation story, but also provides strong evidence as to the mechanism of neurosecretion in this primitive nervous system. Previous chapters have dealt with the importance of the nerves in controlling growth and differentiation, but we believe that the most compelling evidence is at the ultrastructural level, as exemplified in the following three chapters.

CHAPTER 12

Ultrastructure of Neurosensory Cell Development

LOWELL E. DAVIS

I. Introduction and Historical Review

Coelenterates represent the lowest multicellular organisms in which a nervous system exists. Little is known about the structure of the nervous system in *Hydra,* and even recently, the presence of a nervous system has been either disregarded or doubted (Hess *et al.,* 1957; Slautterback and Fawcett, 1959; Hess, 1961). As a result, when compared to the body of information on the nervous system of other organisms, specific data on the structure, function, origin, and development of the nervous system of *Hydra* are limited.

Since this is the first chapter devoted to the nervous system, it seems appropriate to review briefly some of the more pertinent structural data concerning the nervous system. The nervous system is considered mainly

as an epidermal plexus containing nerve cells distributed diffusely throughout the body column and a concentration of nerve cells in the tentacles,
hypostome, and basal disc (Hadzi, 1909; Marshall, 1923; Hyman, 1940).
Bullock and Horridge (1965), however, have expressed doubts as to the
hypostomal concentration of nerves. There are suggestions that a gastrodermal plexus also exists but this layer contains fewer and smaller cells
(Hyman, 1940).

The problem concerning "continuity throughout the nerve net" has
been the subject of several early investigations (Hadzi, 1909; Marshall,
1923; McConnell, 1932). Although their findings are not in complete
agreement, it is generally believed that while some processes apparently
end freely, many processes unite such that the nerve cell bodies lie in a
so-called network. In his work on the development of an epidermal nerve
net in the buds of *Hydra,* McConnell (1932) stated that, "The formation
of the nerve net takes place by the growing together of the processes from
the ganglion cells: These processes advance between the epitheliomuscular cells until they meet other processes from ganglion cells with
which they fuse. Other processes from the ganglion cells grow out in
various directions and end among the muscular cells." More recently,
Spangenberg and Ham (1960), using a modified version of the original
McConnell technique, have also confirmed the existence of an epidermal
nerve net. According to these authors ". . . it is easy to distinguish a well-
organized continuous nerve network both in the tentacles and in the
stalk and pedal disk regions — the observable network of the tentacles
extending for a short distance into the column region, and the nerves of
the pedal disk forming a circle around the aboral pore." It should be
pointed out that all the studies referred to above were performed at the
light microscopic level and utilized one of two basic methods: (1) specific
chemicals to dissociate cells without destroying them, and (2) selective
staining, usually with methylene blue. Some of the details of electron
microscopical studies on the nervous system will be presented later, but
it may be indicated at this point that the relatively few published ultrastructural data on this subject have not been able to confirm or reject the
existence of a continuous nerve net. This failure is due to the fact that the
nerve processes are long and extend in different directions and in
different planes. As a result, it is extremely difficult to obtain processes
in one plane for electron microscopy, and securing serial sections
throughout the entire lengths of such long processes further increases the
difficulty. It becomes apparent, not only from this particular detail, that
almost every aspect of the nervous system requires extensive study.
What has been observed at the ultrastructural level, however, is the
presence of intracellular bridges joining certain early developing nerve

cells (Davis, 1969). No more than two cells have been seen with this structural communication. Both cells are of the same type of nerve cell (neurosensory) and in the same stage of development. Since such "continuities" are temporary and involve cell bodies rather than processes, they cannot be regarded as elements of the continuous nerve net.

The types of cells composing the nervous system have also interested several investigators. Some of the earlier studies indicate that there are two types of nerve cells, ganglionic and neurosensory and transitions between them (Hadzi, 1909; Marshall, 1923; McConnell, 1932; Burnett and Diehl, 1964; Bullock and Horridge, 1965). The ganglionic cells, located at the base of epitheliomuscular cells, are bipolar or multipolar and the processes may divide and subdivide before they terminate or join other cell processes. Slight swellings are also observed along the processes. The processes extend in various directions, some terminating at the surface of the animal, others surrounding various parts of epitheliomuscular cells (Hadzi, 1909; Marshall, 1923; McConnell, 1932; Burnett and Diehl, 1964). In their study on the morphology of nerves, Spangenberg and Ham (1960) have indicated that nerve cells usually contain two to seven processes. They did not specify, however, the types of nerve cell involved. Neurosensory cells, also located among the epitheliomuscular cells, contain processes. According to McConnell, ". . . from their [neurosensory cells] proximal ends [they] send out typical processes which eventually find and coalesce with the processes of the ganglion cells." Thus the network referred to earlier is achieved. The distal processes extend to the surface of the animal where sensory hairs are formed. Whether the number of hairs varies from cell to cell is not clear, but from one to five hairs have been reported (Hadzi, 1909; Marshall, 1923; McConnell, 1932; Burnett and Diehl, 1964; Bullock and Horridge, 1965). Although electron microscopic studies of these sensory hairs will be presented later, it may be stated here that such studies have described the hairs as cilia or modified cilia (Lentz and Barrnett, 1965; Davis *et al.,* 1968; Davis, 1969).

The introduction of electron microscopical techniques in studying the nervous system of *Hydra* has not only confirmed the existence of ganglionic and neurosensory cells, but has led to the discovery of a third type of cell—the neurosecretory cell (Lentz and Barrnett, 1965; Davis *et al.,* 1968; see also Burnett *et al.,* 1964). These studies presented morphological descriptions of the three types of cells and suggested ultrastructural criteria for recognizing and identifying them. The results were highly significant, in that they demonstrated the presence of neurosecretory droplets in a group of organisms more primitive than flatworms, which were, until then, believed to be the most primitive animals containing neurosecretory droplets (Lender and Klein, 1961). Incidently, neuro-secretory droplets have been reported in sponges (Lentz, 1966), but this system has been approached only limitedly in this respect and therefore requires further investigation.

The origin of the various types of cells composing the nervous system has been studied by several investigators. There is much greater agreement in this area of study than in any other aspect of the nervous system. Generally, it is believed that all nerve cells arise from interstitial cells (Marshall, 1923; McConnell, 1932; Burnett and Diehl, 1964; Lentz, 1965a,b; Davis, 1969, 1972). Since nerve cells do not divide, unlike some specialized cells in *Hydra* (e.g., epitheliomuscular cells, mucous cells, digestive cells), their origin is considered to stem exclusively from the differentiation of interstitial cells. Some of the ultrastructural changes during the differentiation of neurosensory and ganglionic cells have been published recently and these studies confirmed the origins of nerve cells (Davis, 1969, 1972). Although similar studies involving neurosecretory cells are not available, as far as we are aware, it seems reasonable to assume that these cells also arise from interstitial cells.

II. Neurosensory Cell Development

A. INTERSTITIAL CELLS

Interstitial cells are the undifferentiated cells in *Hydra* from which several cell types originate. These include cnidoblasts, germ cells, ganglionic cells, digestive cells, and, in this particular reference, neurosensory cells (Slautterback and Fawcett, 1959; Slautterback, 1961; Lentz, 1965a,b; Burnett, 1966; Davis, 1968, 1969). Although the ultrastructure of interstitial cells has been described by several investigators (Slautterback and Fawcett, 1959; Slautterback, 1961; Hess, 1961; Lentz, 1965a; Davis, 1968), a brief description will be presented here in order that a meaningful comparison may be made between these cells and the early stages of nerve cell development.

Interstitial cells are round or oval, measuring approximately 5–6 μ in diameter (Fig. 1). They are located among epitheliomuscular cells, usually at the bases adjacent to the longitudinal myonemes, and may occur singly or in groups. The nucleus, containing a prominent nucleolus, is centrally located and occupies a considerable portion of the cell. The cytoplasm is unmistakably embryonic, in that it contains numerous ribosomes. A few mitochondria, an occasional inconspicuous Golgi complex, and small vesicles are also present. These cells undergo division and later differentiate into the various cell types indicated in Section I. An interstitial cell which appears to be preparing for division is seen in Fig. 2.

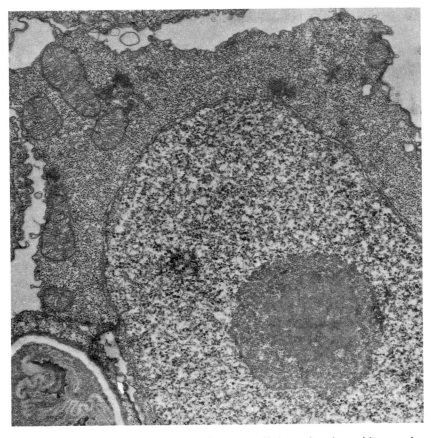

Fig. 1. Portion of an interstital cell showing a centrally located nucleus with a prominent nucleolus. The cytoplasm contains numerous ribosomes, a few mitochondria, and occasional small vesicles; sometimes an extremely small Golgi complex is also observed (× 16,500).

This cell is similar to that seen in Fig. 1, except that there are several mitochondria (about twice as many as are normally present), several vesicles, and elements of granular endoplasmic reticulum.

B. Early Stages of Development

It has already been indicated that interstitial cells are usually located near the longitudinal myonemes of the epitheliomuscular cells. Developing neurosensory cells (Fig. 3) are located in precisely the same area. As a result, they may be surrounded, partially or completely, by epitheliomuscular cells, or they may be adjacent to other nerve cells in various stages of development, interstitial cells and cnidoblasts.

At the onset of neurosensory cell differentiation, the interstitial cell

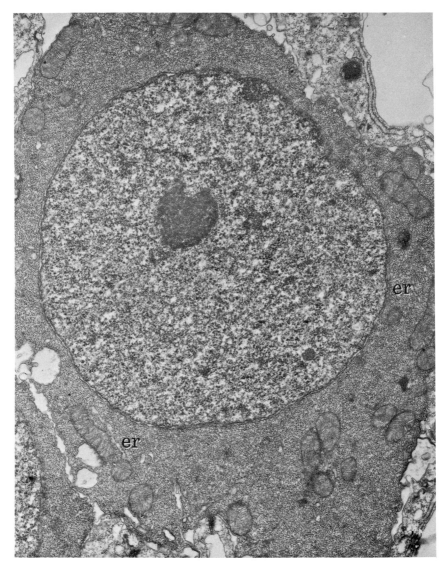

Fig. 2. Interstitial cell believed to be preparing for division. This cell is similar to that in Fig. 1 except that there are about twice as many mitochondria, several vesicles, and small elements of granular endoplasmic reticulum (er) (× 17,600).

assumes a spindle shape, and subsequently the cytoplasm elongates, forming what will later be designated as neurites. At this early stage of development, except for the cytoplasmic processes and a developing cilium, this cell appears identical to normal interstitial cells (Figs. 1 and 4). As a consequence of this similarity, together with certain structural

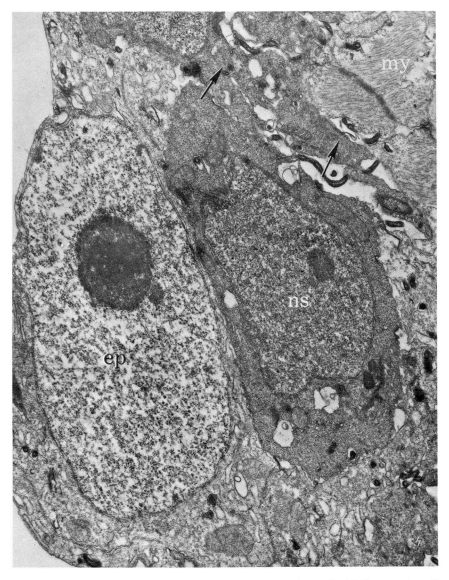

Fig. 3. Developing neurosensory cell (ns) located at the base of epitheliomuscular cells (ep) and almost completely surrounded by them. A neurosecretory cell neurite (arrows) lies between the developing cell and the myonemes (my) of the epitheliomuscular cells (× 9,900).

similarities among the three types of nerve cells that will be described later, it is absolutely imperative that extensive serial sections be examined in order to recognize and accurately identify the type of nerve cell involved. The differentiating neurosensory cell, however, is easily dis-

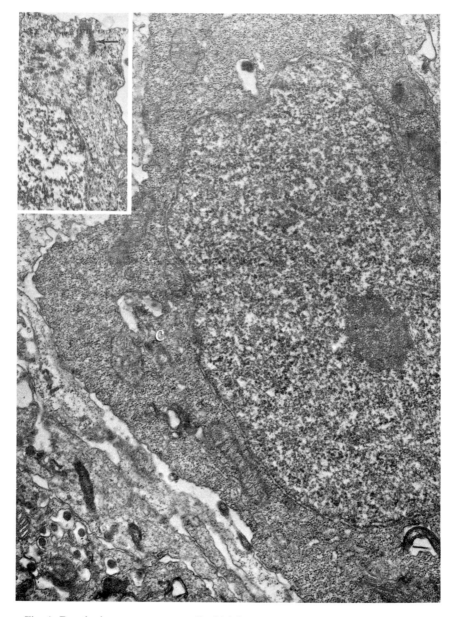

Fig. 4. Developing neurosensory cell which has assumed a slightly elongated shape. The cytoplasm extends in two directions (top and bottom) for the formation of neurites. Note the developing cilium (c). Neurosecretory cell neurites (bottom, left) containing neurosecretory droplets and microtubules are in close proximity to the developing cell (× 18,700). Inset: Centriole (arrow) aligned immediately below the plasma membrane and dense granules (400–1300 Å in diameter) at the base of the centriole (× 18,700).

tinguishable from other cell types originating from interstitial cells, e.g., cnidoblasts, by the presence of a developing cilium and the absence of active Golgi complexes and extensive segments of granular endoplasmic reticulum.

The presence of intercellular bridges is sometimes observed between two cells, and no more than two cells have been observed with this continuity. The presence of these bridges is not peculiar, however, to developing neurosensory cells, since they have been observed between interstitial cells, between developing cnidoblasts, and between differentiating spermatozoa (Slautterback and Fawcett, 1959; Slautterback, 1961; Hess, 1961; Burnett et al., 1966; Davis, 1970). According to Slautterback and Fawcett (1959), intercellular bridges between interstitial cells and between developing cnidoblasts are formed as a result of incomplete cytokinesis during division of interstitial cells. It is also suggested that since only one such bridge exists between two cells and these cells are of the same type and in exactly the same stage of development, the primary function of intercellular bridges is to synchronize differentiation. In the case of neurosensory cells containing intercellular bridges, their stages of development appear to be identical. These structures, however, are apparently transitory, since no mature neurosensory cells have been observed with intercellular bridges.

Finally, insofar as the intercellular bridges are concerned, their presence in neurosensory cells offers support to the belief that neurosensory cells arise from interstitial cells. Since the latter cell type also contains these structures, it seems reasonable to assume that cells originating from interstitial cells contain intercellular bridges, if only temporarily. In considering the intercellular bridges in relation to the "continuity throughout the nerve net," there is no doubt that the bridges do offer some type of cytoplasmic continuity. However, it is suggested that they cannot be responsible for the "continuity" described by several earlier investigators, because they are transient in nature and have not been observed in fully mature cells. Besides, they are most often found linking cell bodies rather than neurites, and cell types other than neurons also contain cytoplasmic bridges.

C. DEVELOPMENT OF CILIARY STRUCTURES

The processes involving the formation of centrioles and ciliogenesis have been investigated in a variety of cell types and organisms (Roth and Shigenaka, 1964; Dirksen and Crocker, 1966; Outka and Kluss, 1967; Sorokin, 1968; Steinman, 1968; Boquist, 1968). According to Davis (1969), some of these processes occur in a similar manner during the development of the ciliary apparatus. One of the first signs of the

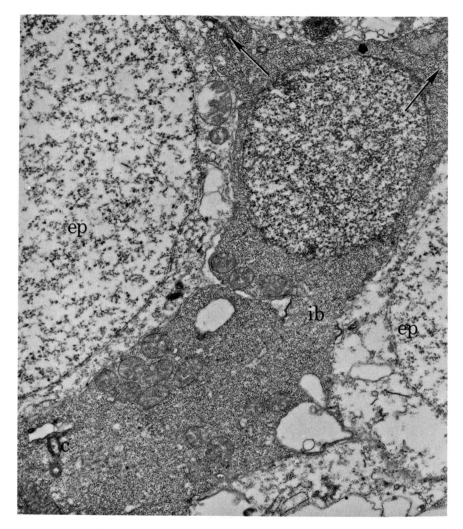

Fig. 5. Early differentiating neurosensory cells, one with a developing cilium (c), located between epitheliomuscular cells (ep). Note especially the intercellular bridge (with its characteristic thickened membrane) joining both cells (ib). Arrows indicate the direction of forming neurites (× 12,300).

development of this structure is the appearance of several osmiophilic dense granules, sometimes circularly arranged, and located in close proximity to the cell membrane. These granules average about 500 Å in diameter and appear to be similar to the procentriole precursor bodies (300–800 Å in diameter) described by Steinman (1968). Eventually, two centrioles are observed oriented at right angles to each other, one of which is in close contact with the plasma membrane (Figs. 4 and 5). It is

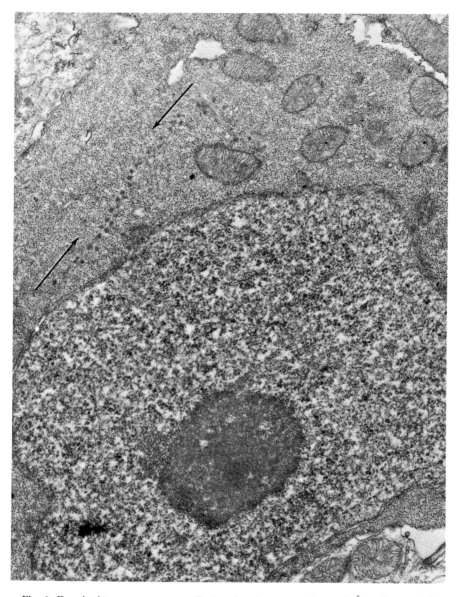

Fig. 6. Developing neurosensory cell, showing dense granules (700 Å in diameter) linearly arranged (arrows) and extending for up to 4.0 μ. Note that the nucleus, nucleolus, and cytoplasmic structures strongly resemble those of interstitial cells ($\times$ 18,700).

of interest to note that when interstitial cells divide for the final time prior to differentiation, one centriole remains near the plasma membrane (Slautterback, 1961). A second type of dense granule (650–850 Å in diameter) is sometimes seen at the base of the centriole which approaches the plasma membrane (Fig. 4). These granules actually appear fibrous and resemble the structures described by Sorokin (1968) as fibrogranular aggregates, which represent one type of precursor for basal body formation.

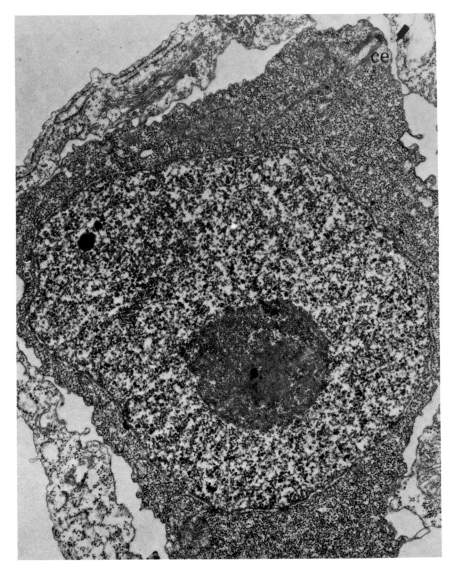

Fig. 7. Centriole (ce) located adjacent to the plasma membrane of a developing neurosensory cell. Dense fibers extend from the base of the centriole into the interior of the cell and small granules (similar to those in Fig. 6) aligned along the fibers (× 17,600).

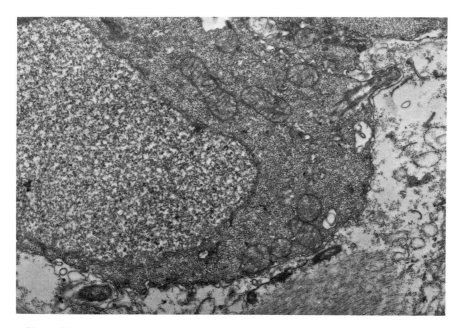

Fig. 8. Emerging ciliary bud (top, right) protruding into the extracellular space, and completely surrounded by plasma membrane (× 13,900).

A third type of electron-dense granule (700 Å in diameter) is observed in association with the developing cilium (Fig. 6). These granules are arranged linearly, extending from the base of the cilium to the interior of the cytoplasm for a distance of up to 4.0 μ (see also Doolin and Birge, 1966). Later, long, dense fibers which appear to emanate from the base of the developing cilium are observed among the linearly arranged granules, suggesting that these structures may be precursor materials for rootlet formation (Fig. 7). It should be pointed out that the distinction among the three types of granules described above is based solely on their dimensions, arrangement, and location within the cell.

As differentiation of the neurosensory cell progresses, the emerging ciliary bud extends into the extracellular space and is completely surrounded by the plasma membrane (Fig. 8). The young cilium contains microtubules, a few dense granules, and an amorphous material. A later stage of development is seen in Figs. 9 and 10. The ciliary shaft is completely elongated, and the internal microtubules extend its entire length. Dense fibers composing the rootlets have appeared with a corresponding decrease or disappearance of the electron-dense granules which originally extended linearly from the base of the centriole.

A single well-developed cilium complete with ciliary shaft, basal

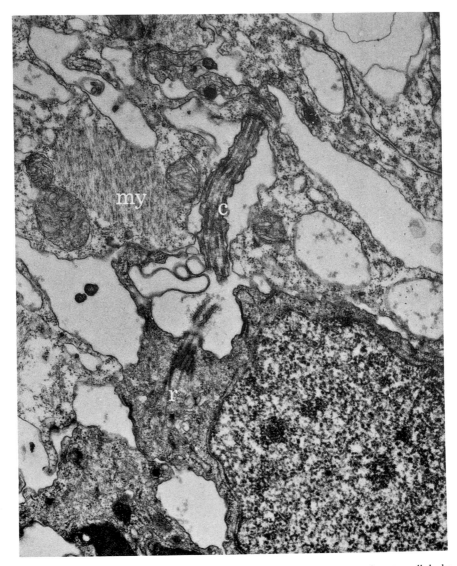

Fig. 9. Section passing through the developing cilium (c) which extends extracellularly and adjacent to a longitudinal myoneme (my). Internal microtubules are clearly visible. Rootlets (r) are observed at the base of the cilium but they are not striated. A portion of a neurosecretory cell (bottom, left) is also observed (× 19,800).

body and rootlets is seen in Fig. 11. The shaft contains microtubules throughout its length. At this stage of development the rootlets contain typical striations. Transverse sections of the cilium at various levels indicate that the internal tubules have a typical 9 + 2 arrangement, but

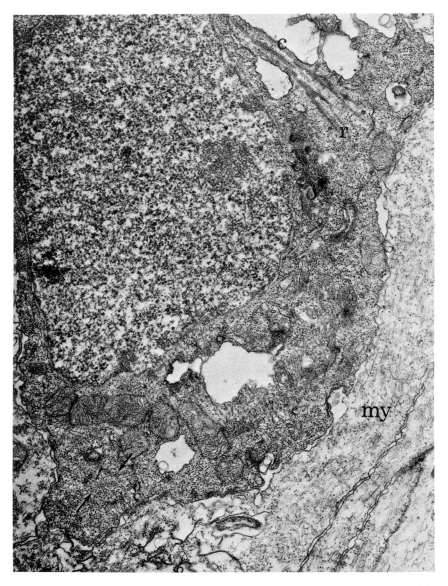

Fig. 10. Stage of development similar to that in Fig. 9. Note that the cilium (c), containing unstriated rootlets (r), extends away from the longitudinal myonemes (my). The base of a neurite (bottom, left) is observed, and the cross-sections of microtubules (arrows) indicate the orientation of the neurite (× 19,800).

the number and location of the tubules may vary from one level to another (Figs. 12 and 13; see also Roth and Shigenaka, 1964; Boquist, 1968).

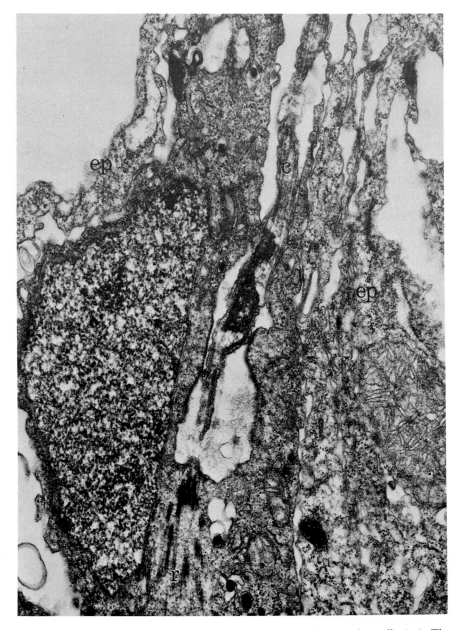

Fig. 11. Mature neurosensory cell located between epitheliomuscular cells (ep). The fully developed cilium (c) containing internal microtubules is surrounded by a cytoplasmic collar. The plane of section reveals a small part of the basal body and rootlets (r) which are seen to be striated for the first time. Note the small, dense, membrane-bound droplets (700–1000 Å in diameter) located mainly near the rootlets; the elongated and peripherally located nucleus with dense accumulations; and the drastic decrease in ribosomes (× 25,800).

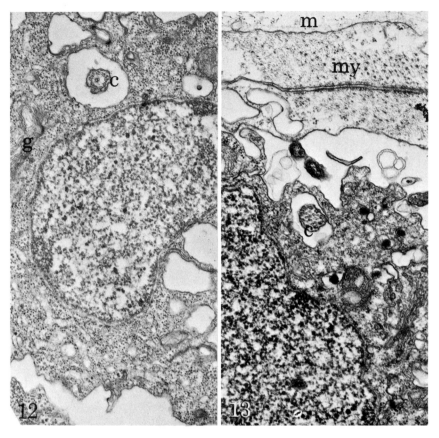

Figs. 12 and 13. Transverse sections of the cilium (c) at two different levels within its cytoplasmic collar. The internal tubules reveal a typical 9 + 2 arrangement (Fig. 12), but the number and location of the tubules vary from one level to another (Fig. 13). Golgi complex, g; epithelial myonemes, my; mesoglea, m (Fig. 12: × 24,400; Fig. 13: × 26,000).

Reference has been made earlier to the number of "hairs" (now called "cilia") in neurosensory cells, in that one to five may be present in each cell. Electron microscopical studies of mature neurosensory cells have shown the existence of only a single cilium (Lentz and Barrnett, 1965; Davis *et al.,* 1968; Davis, 1969). It has been argued that if neurosensory cells contained more than one cilium, serial sections would certainly indicate their presence (Davis, 1969). Furthermore, in bi- or multiciliated sensory or receptor cells of other organisms, cilia are located in the supranuclear cytoplasm so that a few adjacent serial sections reveal their presence (Bannister, 1965; Frisch and Reith, 1966; Wheatley, 1967; Thornhill, 1967). It seems reasonable to assume that if neurosensory cells contained two or more cilia, they would be located in one region and therefore be easily recognized in a few sections. It has been suggested that the apparent discrepancy may be explained on the basis that neurosensory cells differ in the number of cilia they contain, i.e., they may be uni-, bi-, or multiciliated (Davis, 1969).

D. GOLGI COMPLEX AND NEUROSECRETORY DROPLETS

The increase in Golgi complex activity and the formation of neurosecretory droplets are intimately associated and therefore will be de-

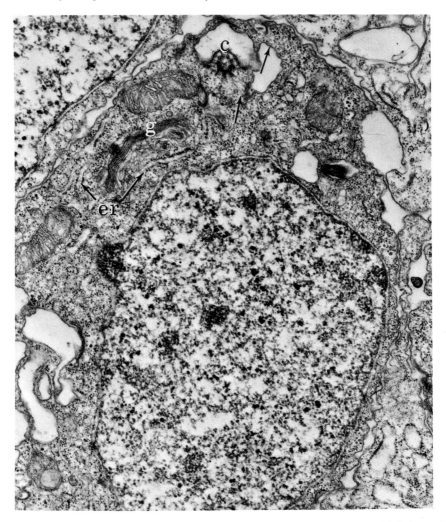

Fig. 14. During the development of the cilium (c), one Golgi complex (g) is located characteristically at its base. Short segments of granular endoplasmic reticulum (er) located near the Golgi complex, and microtubules (arrows) are also present (× 24,400).

scribed together. It will be recalled that the Golgi complex of interstitial cells is extremely small and inactive, and consequently not easily recognized. During early differentiation of the neurosensory cell, the lamellar system of the Golgi complex increases to the extent that by the time the cilium is formed and prior to the elaboration of droplets, there may be as many as three Golgi complexes. An interesting parallel is seen in the

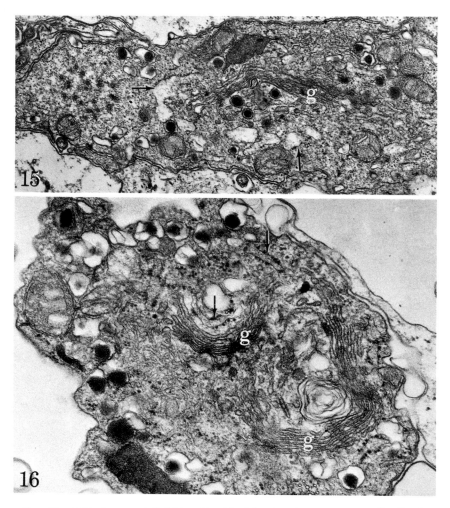

Figs. 15 and 16. Increased Golgi lamellae (g) of developed neurosensory cells. The droplets immediately adjacent to the Golgi membranes are homogeneously dense and average 1000 Å in diameter (Fig. 15). Those dispersed throughout the cell body vary in density, occupy only a portion of their vesicles, and range between 650 and 1300 Å in diameter. Short segments of granular endoplasmic reticulum (arrows) are observed near the Golgi vesicles (Fig. 15: × 26,000; Fig. 16: × 38,800).

developing vertebrate sensory neuroblasts, where there may be as many as four Golgi complexes (Tennyson, 1965). One of the Golgi complexes is observed near the base of the developing cilium (Fig. 14). Associated with this Golgi complex are short segments of granular endoplasmic reticulum. Although it is tempting to suggest that these two organelles participate in the formation of the ciliary apparatus, their exact functional relationship is unknown.

The Golgi complexes located in the cell body become extremely active during the production of droplets. On occasion, materials of high density are observed within the lamellae and also in the peripheral vesicles which ultimately become distended and finally separate from the Golgi membranes (Figs. 15 and 16). The isolated droplets, especially those which remain in the vicinity of the Golgi membranes, are uniformly dense, average about 1000 Å in diameter, and occupy the entire membranes which surround them (Fig. 15). Other droplets (650–1300 Å in diameter), which become scattered throughout the cell body, and eventually the neurites, occupy only a portion of the vesicles enclosing them and often reveal individual variations in densities (Fig. 16).

The droplets described above have been reported in previous publications and have been shown to be neurosecretory droplets (Burnett and Diehl, 1964; Davis et al., 1968). Whether located in the cell bodies where they are formed or in the neurites to which they are eventually transported, these droplets are strikingly similar to droplets in known neurosecretory cells (Bern et al., 1962; DeRobertis, 1962; Oosaki and Ishii, 1965; Scharrer, 1967, 1968). It has been suggested that the Golgi complexes and/or granular endoplasmic reticulum are involved in the development of neurosecretory droplets (Bern et al., 1962; Zambrano and DeRobertis, 1966; Zambrano and Mordoh, 1966; Oosaki and Ishii, 1965; Afzelius and Fridberg, 1963; Scharrer, 1968). From a structural point of view, it appears that as far as neurosensory cells are concerned, the Golgi complexes are the major sites of droplet formation. The actual mechanisms by which droplets are released have been suggested previously (Davis et al., 1968). These mechanisms will be described in detail later when the neurosecretory cells are considered.

E. OTHER CYTOPLASMIC STRUCTURES

1. Droplets

Another type of electron-dense droplet is observed in developing and mature neurosensory cells, and may be located both in the cell body and neurites (Fig. 17). They vary greatly in size (0.4–1.0 μ), shape, densities and internal structure. They appear early during development and apparently persist for an indefinite time. Their origin is uncertain, but

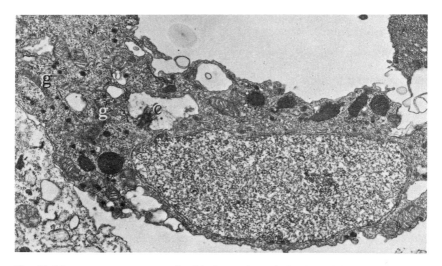

Fig. 17. Mature neurosensory cell with dense, irregularly shaped droplets ranging between 0.4 and 1.0 μ in diameter. They are observed in the cell body, but are also present in neurites. Golgi complex, g; cilium, c ($\times$ 11,250).

due to certain structural changes which mitochondria undergo during differentiation, it has been assumed that these dense bodies may arise from mitochondria (Davis, 1969).

2. Mitochondria

Mitochondria undergo certain morphological changes during differentiation from interstitial cells into neurosensory cells. Although their number increases slightly in each cell, the most conspicuous change is the increase in density of the matrix with a corresponding reduction in the number of cristae (compare Figs. 1, 2, 4, and 6 with Figs. 10, 15, 17, and 19). Some mitochondria also appear to decrease in size. The significance of these changes is not known. However, from certain structural evidences which are far from conclusive, it has been suggested that mitochondria may be responsible for the formation of the larger droplets described above (Davis, 1969).

3. Endoplasmic Reticulum

Only sparse segments of granular endoplasmic reticulum are observed either during differentiation or in the mature neurosensory cell. The few short fragments are usually observed in close proximity to the Golgi complex in the vicinity of the developing cilium (Fig. 14) and also in association with the Golgi complexes which form neurosecretory droplets (Figs. 15 and 16). The latter situation has been interpreted as indicating a limited role of the endoplasmic reticulum in the formation of neuro-secretory materials.

4. Ribosomes

As pointed out earlier, ribosomes are the most predominant organelles in interstitial cells (Figs. 1 and 2) and they persist throughout the early stages of neurosensory cell differentiation (Figs. 4 and 8). By the time the cilium is formed there is a noticeable decrease in number, and most ribosomes disappear when the fully differentiated stage is achieved (Figs. 11, 17, 18–21).

5. Microtubules

Microtubules are observed from the beginning of ciliary formation to the mature neurosensory cell. They find their greatest development, however, in the fully differentiated cell body and particularly in the neurites (Figs. 20 and 21). Davis (1969) has shown that microtubules, aligned along the long axis of the cell, extend for considerable distances from the vicinity of the rootlets to the neurite.

6. Changes in the Nucleus

Up to this point little has been said about the nucleus. This is because it is generally accepted that during cellular differentiation nuclear changes are much less striking than cytoplasmic modifications (Grobstein, 1959). The nuclei of neurosensory cells, however, reveal certain recognizable changes throughout their development. The small, oval-shaped nuclei of the interstitial cells from which they arise are finely granular and contain conspicuous nucleoli (Figs. 1 and 2). As differentiation proceeds, the structural changes become obvious until the mature neurosensory cell is formed (Figs. 11, 18, and 19). The nucleus may be oval or highly ir-regularly shaped, and is peripherally located. The original finely granular material disappears and is replaced with coarse granules and accumula-tions of these materials. The nucleolus becomes so reduced in size that only an occasional section may reveal its presence.

III. The Mature Neurosensory Cell

The ultrastructure of the mature neurosensory cell has been described previously by several investigators (Lentz and Barrnett, 1965; Davis et al., 1968; Davis, 1969). Several different profiles of them are seen in Figs. 11, 15–21. Generally, these cells are elongated, containing two or more neurites. They possess a cilium (maybe two or more) and active Golgi complexes which elaborate neurosecretory droplets. It should be borne in mind that it is extremely difficult to trace entire neurites in the

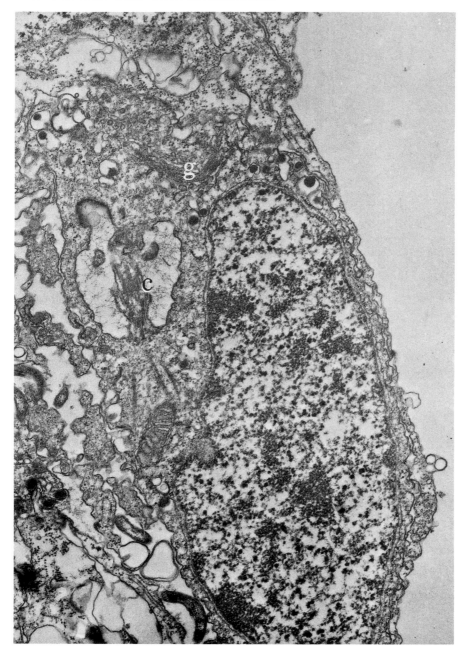

Fig. 18. Mature neurosensory cell showing a small portion of the ciliary apparatus (c). Note the Golgi complex (g), and the small dense droplets (900–1300 Å in diameter) occupying a portion of the vesicles. The elongated nucleus reveals dense accumulations of chromatin materials (× 22,000).

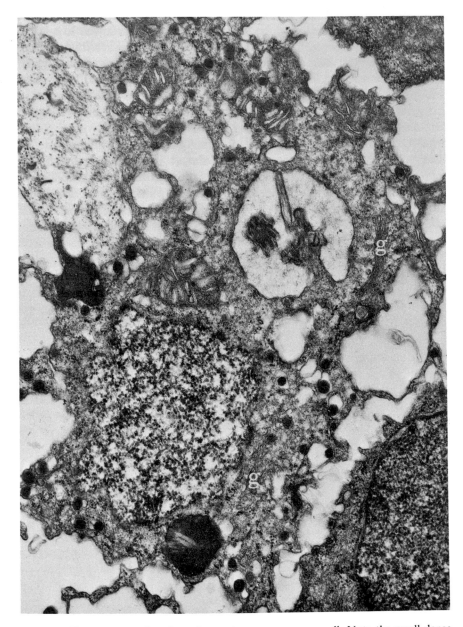

Fig. 19. Transverse section through a mature neurosensory cell. Note the small dense droplets (900–1200 Å in diameter) located mainly around the periphery of the cell and mitochondria with dense matrices; Golgi complex, g (× 27,500).

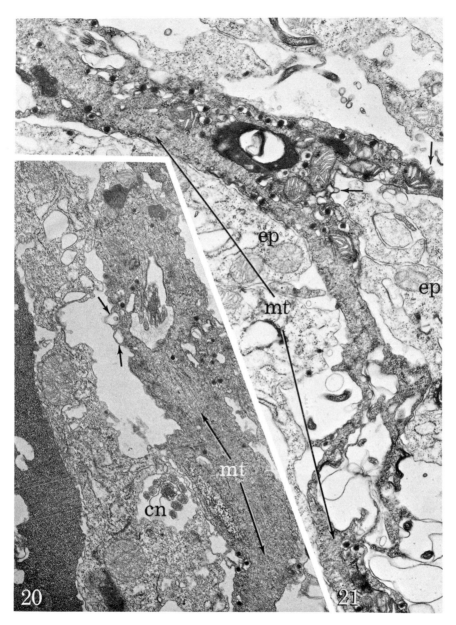

Fig. 20. Neurite of a mature neurosensory cell located immediately adjacent to a cnidoblast (cn). The neurite contains mostly microtubules (mt), with a few secretory droplets (700 Å in diameter), and ribosomes; arrows indicate possible areas of release of neurosecretion (× 11,900).

Fig. 21. Branching neurite of a mature neurosensory cell located between epitheliomuscular cells (ep). This neurite contains many microtubules (mt), dense secretory droplets (450–900 Å in diameter), small mitochondria with dense matrices, and a few of the larger type of dense droplets; arrows indicate possible area of release of neurosecretion (× 18,300).

electron microscope. As a result, branching neurites are seldom observed. Figures 20 and 21 show two neurites, one of which is unbranched, the other branched. In Fig. 20, except for a few neurosecretory droplets and ribosomes, the unbranched neurite is completely filled with microtubules. The branched neurite in Fig. 21 passes between epitheliomuscular cells. It contains many microtubules, several neurosecretory droplets (450–900 Å in diameter), small mitochondria with dense matrices, and a few of the large, dense droplets referred to earlier. It is emphasized that no specialized synaptic junctions similar to those of higher invertebrates and vertebrates have been observed in neurosensory cells or in other types of nerve cells.

IV. Fate of Neurosensory Cells

The fate of neurosensory cells or nerve cells in general has received little or no attention. This failure is probably due to the fact that investigators have focused their interest on the recognition and identification of the once dubious nervous system, its cell types, cellular origins, developmental stages, and possible functions of the cell types. It is known, however, that nerve cells are concentrated in the hypostome and basal regions. In the former region, cells are pushed distally and finally slough off the

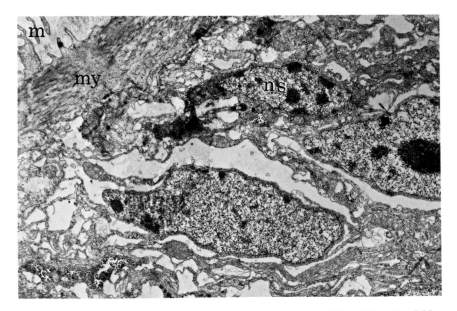

Fig. 22. Degenerating neurosensory cell (ns) located in the basal disc of the animal. Note the increased density of the nucleus. Mesoglea, m; epithelial myonemes, my (× 8,000).

mouth and the tips of the tentacles, while in the latter region, cells are pushed proximally and are discarded at the aboral pore. These processes, therefore, should account for the presence of dying or dead cells in the extremities indicated above. Figure 22 shows a degenerating neurosensory cell in the extreme base of the animal. Both the nucleus and the cytoplasm have assumed a greater degree of density than is normally present. The absence of neurites in this cell does not necessarily indicate that they have already degenerated, but may be due to the plane of section. In any event, it seems clear that nerve cells in the various extremities degenerate and are eventually discarded.

Acknowledgment

Some of the material presented in this section was obtained as a result of a National Science Foundation Grant (No. GB-8384). The author also acknowledges the technical assistance of Linda M. Bookman.

References

Afzelius, B., and Fridberg, G. (1963). *Z. Zellforsch. Mikrosk. Anat.* **59**, 289–308.
Bannister. L. H. (1965). *J. Microsc. Sci.* **106**, 333–342.
Bern, H. A., Nishioka, R. S., and Hagadorn, I. R. (1962). *In* "Neurosecretion" (H. Heller and R. B. Clark, eds.), pp. 21–34. Academic Press, New York.
Boquist, L. (1968). *Z. Zellforsch. Mikrosk. Anat.* **89**, 519–532.
Bullock, T. H., and Horridge, G. A., eds. (1965). "Structure and Function in the Nervous System of Invertebrates," Vol. I. Freeman, San Francisco, California.
Burnett, A. L. (1966). *Amer. Natur.* **100**, 165–189.
Burnett, A. L., and Diehl, N. A. (1964). *J. Exp. Zool.* **157**, 217–226.
Burnett, A. L., Diehl, N. A., and Diehl, F. A. (1964). *J. Exp. Zool.* **157**, 227–236.
Burnett, A. L., Davis, L. E., and Ruffing, F. (1966). *J. Morphol.* **120**, 1–8.
Davis, L. E. (1968). *Exp. Cell. Res.* **52**, 602–607.
Davis, L. E. (1969). *J. Cell. Sci.* **5**, 699–726.
Davis, L. E. (1970). *Z. Zellforsch. Mikrosk. Anat.* **105**, 526–537.
Davis, L. E. (1972). *J. Exp. Zool.* **176**, 107–128.
Davis, L. E., Burnett, A. L., and Haynes, J. F. (1968). *J. Exp. Zool.* **167**, 295–332.
DeRobertis, E. (1962). *In* "Neurosecretion" (H. Heller and R. B. Clark, eds.), pp. 3–20. Academic Press, New York.
Dirksen, R., and Crocker, T. (1966). *J. Microsc. (Paris)* **5**, 629–644.
Doolin, P., and Birge, W. (1966). *J. Cell Biol.* **29**, 333–346.
Frisch, D., and Reith, E. J. (1966). *J. Ultrastruct. Res.* **15**, 490–495.
Grobstein, C. (1959). *In* "The Cell" (J. Brachet and A. E. Mirsky, eds.), Vol. 1, pp. 437–496. Academic Press, New York.
Hadzi, J. (1909). *Arb. Zool. Inst. Univ. Wien.* **17**, 1–44.
Hess, A. (1961). *In* "The Biology of Hydra" (H. M. Lenhoff and W. F. Loomis, eds.), pp. 1–49. Univ. of Miami Press, Coral Gables, Florida.
Hess, A., Cohen, A. I., and Robson, E. A. (1957). *Quart. J. Microsc. Sci.* 315–326.
Hyman, L. (1940). "The Invertebrates," Vol. I. McGraw-Hill, New York.

Lender, T., and Klein, N. (1961). *C. R. Acad. Sci.* **253**, 331–334.

Lentz, T. L. (1965a). *J. Exp. Zool.* **159**, 181–194.

Lentz, T. L. (1965b). *Z. Zellforsch. Mikrosk. Anat.* **67**, 547–560.

Lentz, T. (1966). *J. Exp. Zool.* **162**, 171–180.

Lentz, T., and Barrnett, R. J. (1965). *Amer. Zool.* **5**, 341–356.

McConnell, C. (1932). *Quart. J. Microsc. Sci.* **75**, 495–510.

Marshall, S. (1923). *Quart. J. Microsc. Sci.* **67**, 593–616.

Oosaki, T., and Ishii, S. (1965). *Z. Zellforsch. Mikrosk. Anat.* **66**, 782–793.

Outka, D., and Kluss, B. (1967). *J. Cell Biol.* **35**, 323–346.

Roth, L., and Shigenaka, Y. (1964). *J. Cell Biol.* **20**, 249–270.

Scharrer, B. (1967). *Amer. Zool.* **7**, 161–169.

Scharrer, B. (1968). *Z. Zellforsch. Mikrosk. Anat.* **89**, 1–16.

Slautterback, D. B. (1961). *In* "The Biology of Hydra" (H. M. Lenhoff and W. F. Loomis, eds.), pp. 77–129. Univ. of Miami Press, Coral Gables, Florida.

Slautterback, D. B., and Fawcett, D. W. (1959). *J. Biophys. Biochem. Cytol.* **5**, 441–452.

Sorokin, S. (1968). *J. Cell Sci.* **3**, 207–230.

Spangenberg, D. B., and Ham, R. G. (1960). *J. Exp. Zool.* **143**, 195–201.

Steinman, R. M. (1968). *Amer. J. Anat.* **122**, 19–56.

Tennyson, V. (1965). *J. Comp. Neurol.* **124**, 267–318.

Thornhill, R. A. (1967). *J. Cell Sci.* **2**, 591–602.

Wheatley, D. N. (1967). *J. Anat.* **101**, 479–485.

Zambrano, D., and DeRobertis, E. (1966). *Z. Zellforsch. Mikrosk. Anat.* **73**, 414–431.

Zambrano, D., and Mordoh, J. (1966). *Z. Zellforsch. Mikrosk. Anat.* **73**, 405–413.

CHAPTER 13

Ultrastructure of Ganglionic Cell Development

LOWELL E. DAVIS

I. Introduction

It was indicated in Chapter 12 that there is general agreement among investigators concerning the origin of nerve cells, that is, that nerve cells originate from interstitial cells (Marshall, 1923; McConnell, 1932; Burnett and Diehl, 1964; Lentz, 1965; Davis, 1972). However, the presence of at least three types of nerve cells (i.e., neurosensory, ganglionic, and neurosecretory) raised several questions regarding their individual development. Since it is known also that there are certain structural similarities among the three types of cells (Davis *et al.,* 1968) it may be suspected that any two types, or even all three types, represent different developmental stages of essentially one type. In fact, it has been suggested that ganglionic and neurosecretory cells may represent the same type of nerve cell in different stages of development and function (Lentz and Barrnett, 1965). Recent ultrastructural evidences showed progressive structural changes during differentiation of neurosensory and ganglionic cells. The studies further indicated that the two types of nerve cells arise directly and independently from interstitial cells, and inferred a similar origin and independent development for neurosecretory cells (Davis, 1969, 1972).

II. Early Development

The initial stages of ganglionic cell differentiation are usually difficult to recognize and identify accurately because, except for slight cytoplasmic extensions, such cells are almost identical to certain interstitial cells that may be somewhat irregularly shaped. Consequently, in order to ascertain the identity of the cell type, particularly the early differentiative stages, it is necessary to study serial sections.

Following nuclear division of interstitial cells, one often sees the daughter cells connected by cytoplasmic bridges. It has been suggested that these bridges are formed as a result of incomplete cytokinesis (Slautterback and Fawcett, 1959). The plasma membrane of the bridge thickens, apparently becomes more supportive for a time, but eventually ruptures. In this conjoined condition the two cells have been shown to be capable of differentiating into such cell types as cnidoblasts, neurosensory cells, and germinal cells (Slautterback and Fawcett, 1959; Slautterback, 1961; Hess, 1961; Burnett et al., 1966; Davis, 1969). Two cells joined by an intercellular bridge are seen in Fig. 1. Both cells are structurally identical to interstitial cells as revealed by the presence of numerous ribosomes, few mitochondria and a paucity of other cell organelles. Examination of serial sections about 3–4 μ removed from the plane of section seen in Fig. 1 shows that these cells contain cytoplasmic processes extending in the direction as indicated by the arrows. It has been pointed out recently that the early developmental stages of ganglionic and neurosensory cells are similar, except that in the latter case, the early differentiating stages also involve the formation of the ciliary apparatus (Davis, 1972). Since such structures were not observed in serial sections of the cells shown in Fig. 1, they have been temporarily identified as early ganglionic cells. The same argument is applicable to Fig. 2, which shows, as in Fig. 1, a change in shape of the originally rounded or oval-shaped interstitial cells. The initiation of neurite formation is indicated by arrows seen in Fig. 2. The cytoplasm extends into the extracellular spaces (surrounded by epitheliomuscular cells), which are sometimes unusually wide and consequently offer little resistence to the growing neurite. Depending on the number of neurites, these cells are classified as bipolar. tripolar, or multipolar cells. Accordingly, since there are four cytoplasmic extensions (Fig. 2), this cell would be considered a multipolar cell. Since neurites extend in different directions, only an occasional section of a

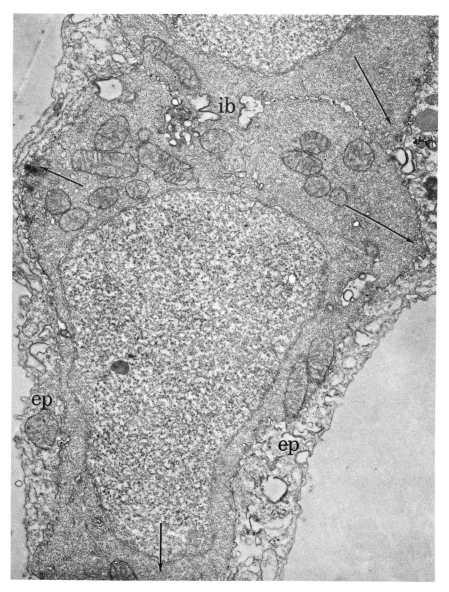

Fig. 1. Two cells believed to be very young ganglionic cells joined by an intercellular bridge (ib). Arrows indicate the directions in which long neurites have been observed in sections 3–4μ removed from the plane of section in this micrograph. The nucleus is elongated while the neurites are being formed. Note the numerous ribosomes and mitochondria, especially in the regions which give rise to neurites; epitheliomuscular cell, ep (× 13,100).

young ganglionic cell normally reveals such profiles. It is recognized that the cell seen in Fig. 2 possibly could be interpreted as a migrating inter-

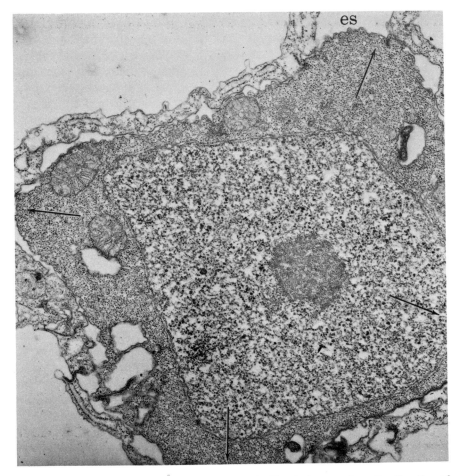

Fig. 2. Isolated cell, but similar to those seen in Fig. 1. Arrows show the direction of four forming neurites (two shown completely) which extend into wide extracellular spaces (es). The nucleus and cytoplasmic structures are similar to those of interstitial cells (× 16,500).

stitial cell. As such, it may contain similar cytoplasmic extensions, which in this case would be considered pseudopodia. When examined carefully, however, this possibility seems unlikely, for, unlike pseudopodia which normally contain no cell organelles, young neurites do contain certain organelles, as will be discussed later. Furthermore, as in the case of young neurosensory cells which are immediately recognized by the presence of a developing ciliary apparatus, short, blunt neurites are also present during early differentiation. It is clear, therefore, that although there are obvious difficulties in identifying early differention stages, the possibility referred to above seems unlikely.

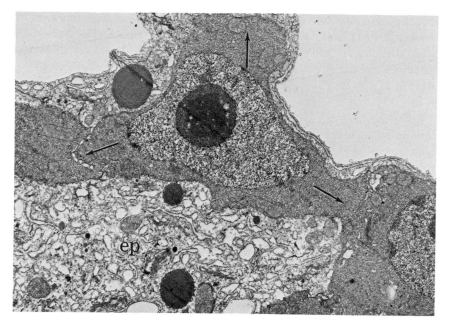

Fig. 3. Early stage of developing ganglionic cell showing three processes (arrows). Except for the change in cell shape and the restriction of mitochondria to the processes, the cell resembles an interstitial cell; epitheliomuscular cell ep (× 6600).

Another aspect of early developing ganglionic cells is seen in Fig. 3. This cell contains three cytoplasmic extensions, but unlike the cell in Fig. 2, two neurites of this cell are closely associated with other developing cells. Consequently, it is assumed that the growth of these neurites and the ultimate lengths achieved may be more limited than those in Fig. 2. An interesting structural feature observed in early differentiation is the grouping of mitochondria in certain regions of the cytoplasm (Figs. 3 and 4). We have noticed that, in most instances, the areas which contain mitochondrial accumulations are the same portions of the cell which elongate during the formation of neurites. As differentiation of the ganglionic cell proceeds, the cell becomes more elongated and the neurites thrust farther into the extracellular space (Fig. 4). These cells are located at the base of epitheliomuscular cells, and therefore may be surrounded by the latter cell type, cnidoblasts, or other nerve cells. Except for the long processes, the bases of which contain several mitochondria (Fig. 4), there are no striking structural changes up to this stage of development. The nucleus and cytoplasmic characteristics are still somewhat reminiscent of interstitial cells. A slightly later stage of development is seen in Fig. 5. Two or more Golgi complexes usually develop at the base of the neurite where mitochondria still continue to

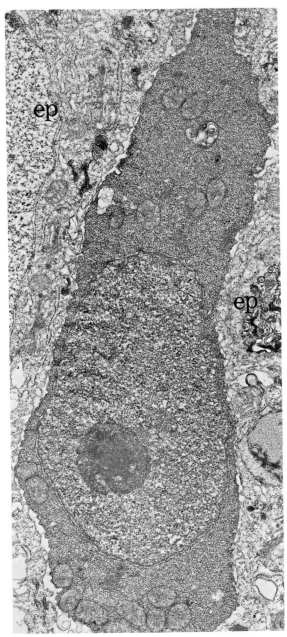

Fig. 4. Slightly more elongated developing ganglionic cell with two neurites (top and bottom) surrounded by epitheliomuscular cells (ep). Note that there are still numerous ribosomes, and that mitocondria accumulate at the base of the developing neurites (× 11,600).

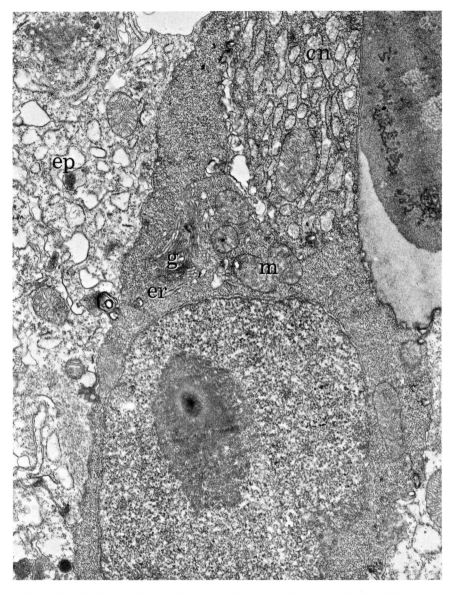

Fig. 5. Developing ganglionic cell showing Golgi complexes (g), mitochondria (m), and endoplasmic reticulum (er) located at the base of the neurite. The cell body and neurite contain numerous ribosomes. The cell is situated between epitheliomuscular cells (ep) and a cnidoblast (cn) (× 13,900).

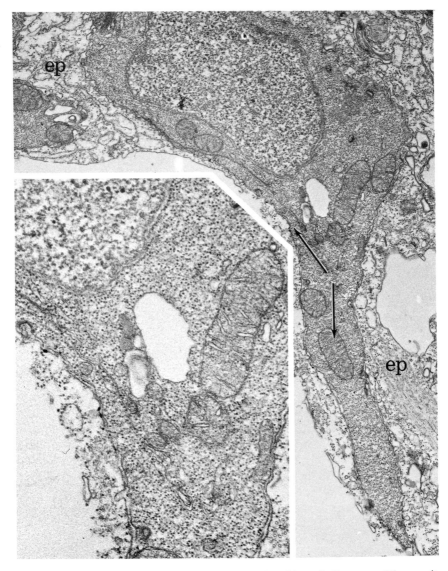

Fig. 6. Further elongated neurite containing mitochondria and ribosomes. The neurite is divided at the base, forming two neurites which extend in different directions (arrows) (× 15,400). Inset: Higher magnification of the dividing neurite seen in the accompanying micrograph; epitheliomuscular cell, ep (× 28,600).

accumulate. A few short segments of granular endoplasmic reticulum and small vesicles appear in close proximity to the Golgi complexes. The continuation of differentiation involves the movement of mitochondria from the bases of the neurites into the neurites themselves (Fig. 6),

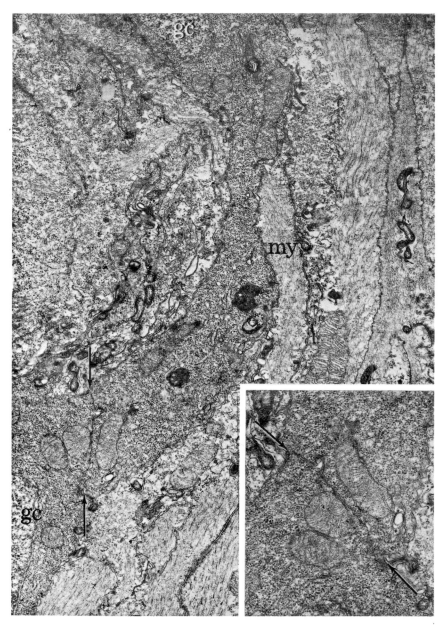

Fig. 7. Two young ganglionic cells (gc) located adjacent to the longitudinal myonemes (my) of epitheliomuscular cells. The neurite (containing ribosomes, short segments of endoplasmic reticulum, and mitochondria) of one cell (top) is closely associated with the cell body or a short neurite of the other cell (arrows) (× 15,400). Inset: Slightly higher magnification showing the point of contact between the two cells (arrows). There is no type of fusion or specialized junction (× 19,800).

where even in the fully differentiated cells some may still be found. A branching neurite seldom observed in electron microscopy is seen in Fig. 6. It appears that branching of neurites occurs when the neurites are still undeveloped, that is, containing mostly ribosomes and a few mitochondria.

The existence of a continuous nerve net was discussed in Chapter 12. Reference was made to McConnell's (1932) results in which the author suggested that the proximal processes of neurosensory cells eventually "coalesce" or "fuse" with processes of ganglionic cells. Associations of this type give rise to the continuous nerve net. Although ultrastructural studies have not confirmed or rejected the existence of such fusions, there are indications that neurites do approach each other forming what could be considered as a continuous system at the light microscope level. The type of relationship as seen electron microscopically is shown in Fig. 7. The neurites of two young ganglionic cells located adjacent to the epitheliolongitudinal myonemes are observed in close contact with each other. Higher magnification reveals that the plasma membranes of both neurites are intact, that is, there is no sign of fusion or specialized junctions.

III. Later Development

It was mentioned earlier that ganglionic cells may be bipolar, tripolar, or multipolar. As differentiation progresses, however, the neurites may become extremely long, extending in different planes and directions. In fact, even in young ganglionic cells, neurites are sometimes tortuous and branching. As a result, it is extremely difficult to obtain two neurites in one plane for electron microscopical study. The difficulty becomes even more acute in attempting to secure serial sections throughout the lengths of all or most neurites. Accordingly, the mature cells to be described below will contain only one neurite.

Further differentiation of the ganglionic cell is observed in Figs. 8–10. In addition to the increased elongation of the neurites, there is also a decrease in width. Figures 8 and 9 show the appearance of microtubules for the first time and a decrease in the number of ribosomes. The proximal region of the neurite contains numerous ribosomes, some microtubules, and few mitochondria. In contrast, the distal region is filled with microtubules and few ribosomes are present. A fully mature ganglionic cell is seen in Fig. 10. With the exception of a few mitochondria and ribosomes, the neurites contain only microtubules oriented along their long axis. In some micrographs glycogen deposits are seen in the cell body as well as in the neurites (Fig. 11). This neurite is oriented at right angles

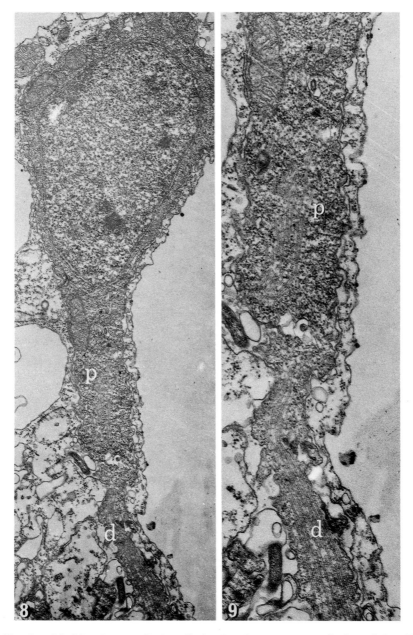

Figs. 8 and 9. Maturing ganglionic cell showing the appearance of microtubules. The proximal portion of the neurite (p) contains microtubules and many ribosomes, while the distal region (d) contains mostly microtubules. The oval-shaped nucleus with its dense clumps of materials, is surrounded by a small amount of cytoplasm (Fig. 8: × 13,900; Fig. 9: × 26,900).

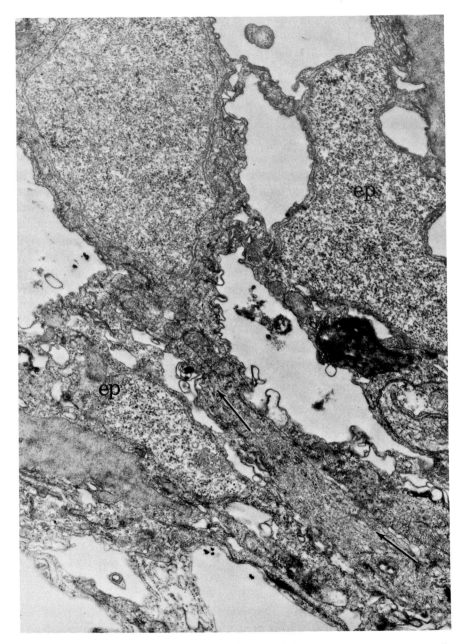

Fig. 10. Fully differentiated ganglionic cell located between epitheliomuscular cells (ep). The neurite contains mostly microtubules (arrows) that appear to extend throughout the length of the process (× 13,900).

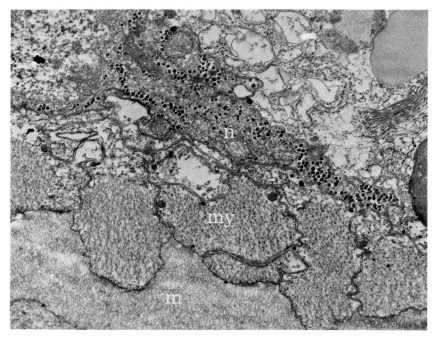

Fig. 11. Ganglionic cell neurite (n) oriented at right angles to the longitudinal myonemes (my) of epitheliomuscular cells. Glycogen granules are present in the cell body and neurite; mesoglea, m (× 17,600).

to longitudinal myonemes as evidenced by transverse sections of the muscles.

The nucleus also reveals certain changes during differentiation. These are obviously not as dramatic as cytoplasmic changes. The uniformly granular nucleoplasm and conspicuous nucleolus of the interstitial cells from which the ganglionic cells arise are replaced by dense clumps of materials throughout the nucleus and along the nuclear membrane.

IV. Mature Ganglionic Cell

Although all nerve cells in *Hydra* contain long neurites, the long and narrow type of ganglionic neurite seen in Figs. 8–10 can be distinguished from neurites of neurosecretory and neurosensory cells. A mature neurosecretory neurite is observed in Fig. 12. This neurite is structurally similar to neurosensory cell neurites and proper identification can only be made by examining serial sections which contain the respective cell bodies. In comparing Figs. 8–10 with Fig. 12 it is clear that the neuro-

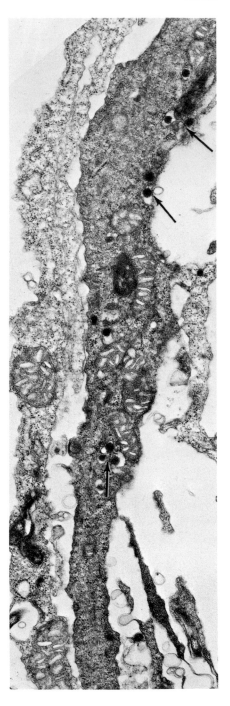

Fig. 12. Typical neurite of neurosensory and neurosecretory cell. Although it contains microtubules and ribosomes similar to ganglionic cell neurites, it may be distinguished from ganglionic cell neurites by the presence of neurosecretory droplets (arrows) in various stages of release (× 21,400).

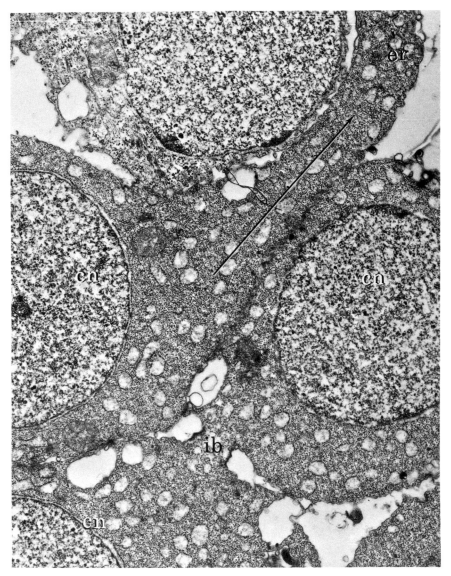

Fig. 13. Developing cnidoblasts (cn), one of which contains an unusually long process (arrow). This process differs from ganglionic cell processes by the presence of vesiculated endoplasmic reticulum (er). Microtubules have not been observed in processes of this type; intercellular bridge, ib (× 13,100).

secretory cell neurite contains several dense droplets which are in different stages of release. There have been suggestions that ganglionic and neurosecretory cells may be the same type of cell but in different

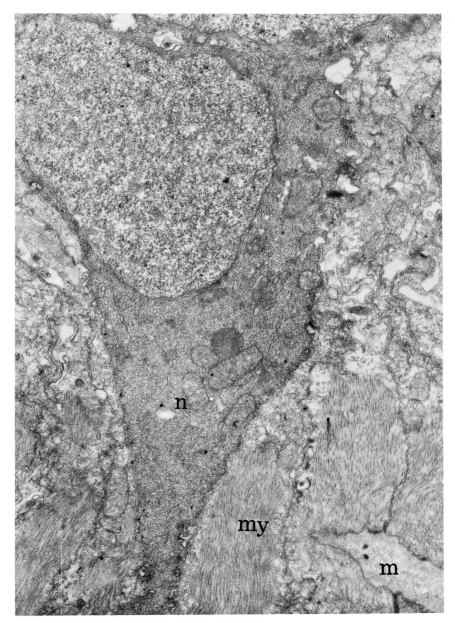

Fig. 14. Ganglionic cell showing a second type of neurite (n). The neurite has a broad base and tapers sharply between the myonemes (my) of epitheliomuscular cells. Few mito-chondria, a Golgi complex, and segments of endoplasmic reticulum are located at the base of the neurite. Numerous ribosomes are also present; mesoglea, m (× 13,900).

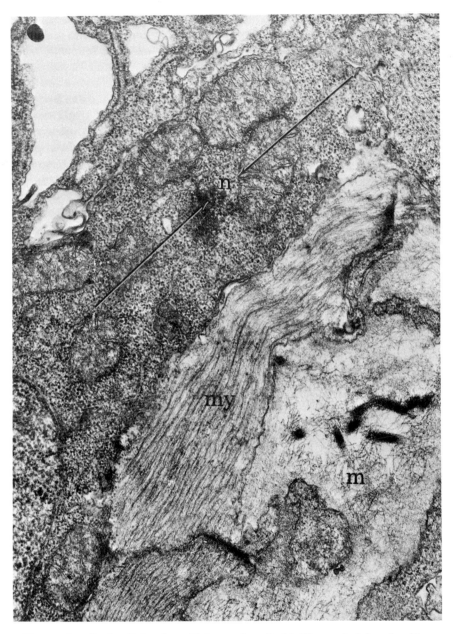

Fig. 15. Ganglionic cell showing a third type of neurite (n). The neurite is broad and tapers only slightly. Mitochondria, a few segments of endoplasmic reticulum, and ribosomes are present. Longitudinal myonemes, my; mesoglea, m (× 26,900).

stages of development and function (Lentz and Barrnett, 1965). Present evidence does not support this suggestion (Davis, 1972). Another structure which could possibly be misinterpreted as a neurite is seen in Fig. 13. Developing cnidoblasts normally do not contain long cytoplasmic extensions. However, in some instances these cells reveal long processes. Although they also contain numerous ribosomes, they are characterized by the presence of vesiculated endoplasmic reticulum. The latter organelles have not been observed in developing ganglionic cells.

Based on certain structural evidences, it was suggested that there may be three types of ganglionic cell neurites (Davis et al., 1968). The neurites up to this point represented the long and narrow type. A second type of neurite is seen in Fig. 14. This neurite contains a broad base, tapers sharply between epithelial myonemes, and runs along the long axis of the animal. As in the previously described neurite, this neurite also contains numerous ribosomes; there are several mitochondria, segments of granular endoplasmic reticulum and a Golgi complex at the base of the neurite. A third type of neurite is observed in Fig. 15. This neurite also runs parallel to the epithelial myonemes. Numerous ribosomes and mitochondria are located within the neurite. The three types of neurites described show obvious differences in their diameters. However, the most significant difference appears to be in their respective stages of development. The neurite seen in Fig. 10 represents a mature neurite; developmental stages of this same neurite are seen in the preceding micrographs (Figs. 8 and 9). The remaining two types of neurites (Figs. 14 and 15) contain mostly ribosomes and mitochondria and therefore resemble the early stages of the first type of neurite. If we assume that these two latter types of neurites undergo a type of development similar to that seen in Figs. 1–10, then it is reasonable to expect mature neurites of comparable dimensions to contain microtubules. Since such broad and tapering neurites have not been observed with numerous microtubules, it may be that the neurites differ only in their early developmental stages and ultimate sizes and are basically one type of neurite.

It is clear from these ultrastructural studies that ganglionic cells are derived directly and independently from interstitial cells. Since they do not divide, interstitial cells represent their sole origin.

Acknowledgement

A portion of the material presented in this section was obtained as a result of a National Science Foundation Grant (No. GB-8384). The author also acknowledges gratefully the technical assistance of Linda M. Bookman.

References

Burnett, A. L., and Diehl, N. A. (1964). *J. Exp. Zool.* **157,** 217–224.
Burnett, A. L., Davis, L. E., and Ruffing, F. (1966). *J. Morphol.* **20,** 1–8.
Davis, L. E. (1969). *J. Cell. Sci.* **5,** 699–726.
Davis, L. E. (1972). *J. Exp. Zool.* **176,** 107–128.
Davis, L. E., Burnett, A. L., and Haynes, J. F. (1968). *J. Exp. Zool.* **167,** 295–332.
Hess, A. (1961). *In* "The Biology of Hydra" (H. M. Lenhoff and W. F. Loomis, eds.), pp. 1–49. Univ. of Miami Press, Coral Gables, Florida.
Lentz, T. L. (1965). *J. Exp. Zool.* **159,** 181–194.
Lentz, T. L., and Barrnett, R. (1965). *Amer. Zool.* **5,** 341–356.
McConnell, C. H. (1932). *Quart. J. Microsc. Sci.* **75,** 495–509.
Marshall, S. (1923). *Quart. J. Miscosc. Sci.* **67,** 593–616.
Slautterback, D. B. (1961). *In* "The Biology of Hydra" (H. M. Lenhoff and W. F. Loomis, eds.), pp. 77–129. Univ. of Miami Press, Coral Gables, Florida.
Slautterback, D. B., and Fawcett, D. W. (1959). *J. Biophys. Biochem. Cytol.* **5,** 441–452.

CHAPTER 14

Structure of Neurosecretory Cells with Special Reference to the Nature of the Secretory Product

LOWELL E. DAVIS

I. Introduction

The two preceding chapters on the nervous system were concerned mainly with origin and differentiation of neurosensory and ganglionic cells. It was shown that both cell types originated solely and independently from interstitial cells, and several morphological aspects of their development were presented. Although ultrastructural studies on the origin and development of the third cell type—the neurosecretory cell—have not been completely determined, it seems reasonable to assume that this cell type also originates exclusively and independently from interstitial cells.

Ultrastructural studies on the mature neurosecretory cell are limited. Perhaps this is because it has only been recently that neurosecretion was discovered in *Hydra* (Lentz, 1963; Burnett *et al.,* 1964). Burnett *et al.* (1964), using several classic histochemical stains, showed positively stained droplets in certain types of neurites. These droplets represent the neurosecretory material. Although staining reactions alone are inadequate to indicate the presence of neurosecretory droplets, the information served as an excellent basis for later electron microscopical studies. Ultrastructural investigations showed that the neurites mentioned above contained membrane-bound secretory droplets ranging from 600 to 1800 Å in diameter (Lentz and Barrnett, 1965; Davis *et al.,* 1968). A few larger droplets (0.5–1.0 μ in diameter) were sometimes observed in these cells but they may be of a different chemical nature. Thus the discovery of neurosecretory droplets in *Hydra* and other coelenterates indicates that these organisms are the most primitive metazoans in which neurosecretion has been observed. Neurosecretorylike substances, however, have been reported in certain sponges but neither well-defined neurites or synaptic vesicles have been observed (Lentz, 1966b).

Although each of the three types of mature nerve cells (neurosensory, ganglionic, and neurosecretory) is morphologically distinct, there are certain similarities among them. For example, both neurosensory and neurosecretory cells produce secretory droplets and both have long neurites in which many droplets are located. This similarity makes it extremely difficult to identify accurately a neurite as belonging to a neurosecretory or neurosensory cell unless serial sections are made in which the cell bodies are also included. This chapter, therefore, will deal in part with the structure of the mature neurosecretory cell. It will also present certain observations concerning the nature of the secretory product, that is, its synthesis, transport, and release of these materials. Since, as has been indicated above, the neurites of the neurosensory and neurosecretory cells are indistinguishable, it may be assumed that the activities referred to earlier occur in a similar manner in both types of cells. Accordingly, the two types of neurites will be described together.

II. The Neurosecretory Cell

The neurosecretory cells, like other nerve cells, are located at the base of epitheliomuscular cells, adjacent to the longitudinal myonemes. Consequently, they are surrounded by epitheliomuscular cells or may lie immediately adjacent to cnidoblasts, interstitial cells, or other nerve cells. The most distinguishing feature of the cell body is the presence of active Golgi complexes and dense membrane-bound droplets ranging from 700 to 1200 Å in diameter (Figs. 1–3). The immature neurosecretory cell (Fig. 1) is identified by Golgi complexes which have begun to produce secretory droplets, the absence of many isolated droplets, and the persistence of numerous ribosomes. Mature cell bodies are seen in Figs.

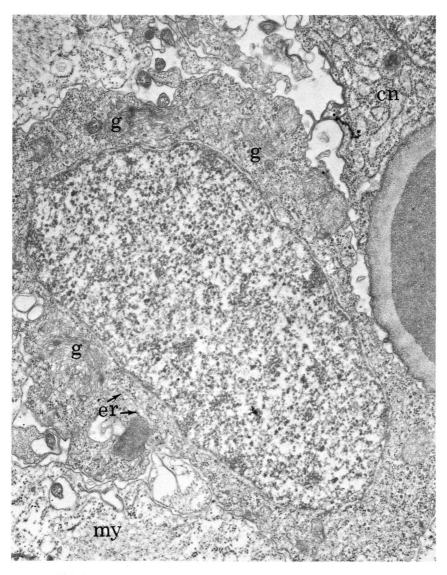

Fig. 1. Slightly immature neurosecretory cell located between epithelial myonemes (my) and a cnidoblast (cn). The elongated nucleus contains scattered clumps of chromatin material. Three Golgi complexes (g), one with dense droplets (700 Å in diameter), ribosomes, glycogen particles, and a few mitochondria are seen in the cytoplasm. Note the sparse segments of granular endoplasmic reticulum (er) and the lack of isolated droplets (as seen in Fig. 2) in the cytoplasm (× 24,500).

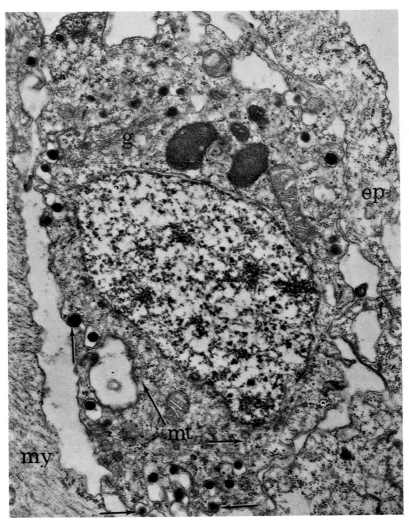

Fig. 2. Mature neurosecretory cell body showing the characteristic small, isolated secretory droplets (700–1200 Å in diameter), a Golgi complex (g) to which droplets are still attached, a few mitochondria with dense matrices, glycogen particles, a few ribosomes, large dense droplets (0.4 μ in diameter), and microtubules (mt). The cell is bordered by epithelial myonemes (my) and normal cytoplasm of epitheliomuscular cells (ep). Between the myonemes and the cell body are moderately dense droplets (340 Å in diameter). Note the fusion of the plasma membrane and the membrane surrounding some of the droplets (arrows) ($\times$ 25,700).

2 and 3 where the droplets (700–1400 Å in diameter) are scattered throughout the cytoplasm and the Golgi complexes are still active. In some instances, it appears that several of these membranes surrounding the droplets fuse, such that larger vacuoles are frequently observed. The

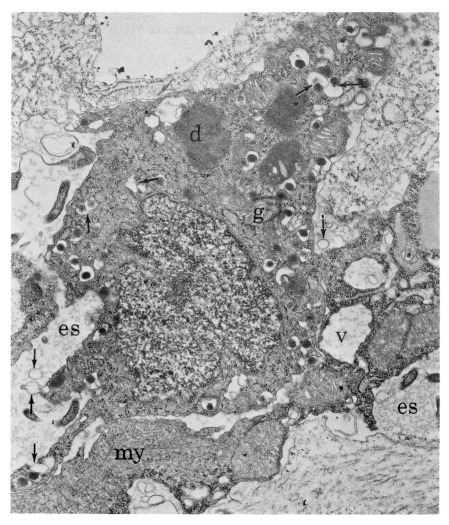

Fig. 3. Cell body of mature neurosecretory cell observed in a regenerating animal. Note especially small droplets in the cell body, some of which seem to have fused, and empty vesicles (arrows, top right); larger droplets (d) up to 0.8 μ in diameter, evaginated membranes suggesting release of droplets (arrows, bottom left) and moderately dense granules 350 Å in diameter) in the extracellular space (es) as well as in the vacuoles (v) of epitheliomuscular cells; epithelial myonemes, my ($\times$ 19,300).

densities of these droplets vary greatly, indicating partial release of some of them. The release of these droplets will be discussed later. Larger dense droplets (approximately 1.0 μ in diameter), a few mitochondria with dense matrices, microtubules, and occasional short segments of granular endoplasmic reticulum are present (Fig. 2). The mature cell also shows a drastic reduction in the number of free ribosomes (Figs. 1–3). Certain changes apparently occur in neurosecretory cells observed in regenerating animals (Fig. 3). The density of the entire cell increases and many empty vesicles are observed along the periphery of the cell. The density of the entire cell is greater than that observed in normal animals (compare Figs 2 and 3). Several of the characteristic neurosecretory droplets are found in the cell body, as well as in the neurites where many of them normally accumulate. In addition, in such animals, there are small, moderately dense droplets (350 Å in diameter) in the extracellular space surrounding these cells. The possible significance of these droplets will be discussed later.

The nature of the neurosecretory product, that is, its synthesis, transport, and release, is a problem with which several investigators are concerned. In neurosecretory cells of other organisms, the granular endoplasmic reticulum and Golgi complexes are implicated in the origin and formation of the secretory droplets (Bern et al., 1962; Zambrano and DeRobertis, 1966; Zambrano and Mordoh, 1966; Oosaki and Ishii, 1965; Afzelius and Fridberg, 1963; Scharrer, 1967, 1968). It is believed that the "raw protein material" is synthesized by the granular endoplasmic reticulum and is then transferred to the Golgi complexes, the ultimate source of elementary secretory droplets (Bern and Knowles, 1966). As far as *Hydra* is concerned, the ultrastructural evidence suggests that the Golgi complexes, which are usually very active organelles in these cells, are the major sites of droplet elaboration (Fig. 4; see also Davis et al., 1968). This suggestion, however, does not preclude the possibility that the granular endoplasmic reticulum may participate to some extent in the formation of the droplets. However, since only sparse segments of granular endoplasmic reticulum are ever observed in these cells, the suggestion seems valid insofar as their limited role is concerned. The formation of the droplets occurs in the cell body, sometimes near the base of the neurites. Once the membrane-bound droplets have been formed they are separated from the Golgi complexes and become scattered throughout the cell body. The orientation of the Golgi complexes, that is, their alignment along the long axis of the cell, together with many microtubules which extend from the limits of the nucleus into the neurites, apparently permit the movement and ultimate transport of the droplets into the neurites (Fig. 4). Since Golgi complexes from which the droplets originate have not been observed in these neurites as in some organisms (Knowles, 1958; von Euler, 1958), it seems reasonable to assume that their only source is from the Golgi complexes located in the cell body. As will be discussed later, not all the droplets are transported to the neurites. In many instances droplets remain in the cell body where they are later released.

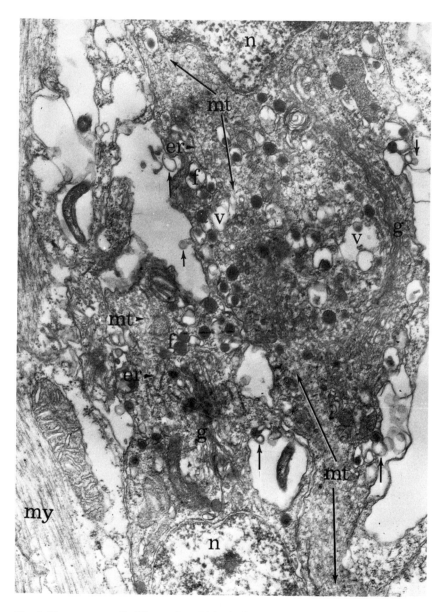

Fig. 4. Two mature cells. The nucleus (n) is similar to that seen in Fig. 2. The cell bodies contain Golgi complexes (g), membrane-bound droplets (800–1600 Å in diameter) of various densities, a few segments of endoplasmic reticulum (er) and microtubules (mt), and vacuoles (v) which may have been formed from fused vesicles; droplets which seem to be fusing (f) are also observed. One neurite (bottom, right) contains mostly microtubules. Note the empty or partially empty vesicles (arrows) along the plasma membrane; myonemes, my (× 25,300).

III. Mechanisms of Neurosecretory Release

The neurites which will now be discussed concern both neurosensory and neurosecretory cells. As indicated earlier, it is almost impossible to identify neurites of the respective nerve types unless cell bodies are included in the sections examined. There are apparently different types of neurites in neurosecretory and neurosensory cells. This difference is based on their ultimate lengths, diameters, and location (Figs. 5–7). Regardless of such differences, however, they contain small, dense neurosecretory droplets which range from 450 to 1100 Å in diameter (Figs. 5–7). High magnification of droplets that are already in the process of "diffusion," and consequently are only moderately dense, reveal a definite substructure. Such droplets are composed of minute particles averaging between 35 and 45 Å in diameter. Although these particulate materials cannot be observed in the droplets of higher density, it is believed that they too have a similar composition.

Some neurites contain numerous microtubules and a few dense droplets in different stages of release (Fig. 5). Other neurites, which apparently divide, also contain the secretory droplets but fewer microtubules. This neurite shows that the membranes surrounding the droplets fuse, forming larger vesicles in which may be two droplets of different densities (Fig. 6). Still other neurites contain many microtubules and secretory droplets. This type of neurite is considered more active in releasing neurosecretion as evidenced by the appearance of membranous elements along the plasma membrane (Fig. 7). Neurites extend in various directions and in different planes and consequently may be surrounded entirely by epitheliomuscular cells, or partially by cnidoblasts, interstitial cells, or other nerve cells (Figs. 8 and 9). There seems to be, however, a concentration of neurites immediately adjacent to epithelial myonemes and many run parallel to these myonemes, as evidenced by the transverse section of both neurites and myonemes.

Neurites occur not only singly; as many as four have been observed running adjacent to each other (Fig. 10). Whether individually or together, they are sometimes in close contact with cnidoblasts and, in some instances, neurites appear to terminate on the nematocysts themselves (Fig. 11). Neurites are also closely associated with interstitial cells, which relationship could exert a strong local effect and therefore be important for the differentiation of these cells (Fig. 12).

There are several mechanisms by which neurosecretion is released from neurosecretory cells. According to DeRobertis (1962, 1964), neurosecretory droplets pass from the vesicles, leaving dense droplets or empty membranes. It has also been indicated that the presence of

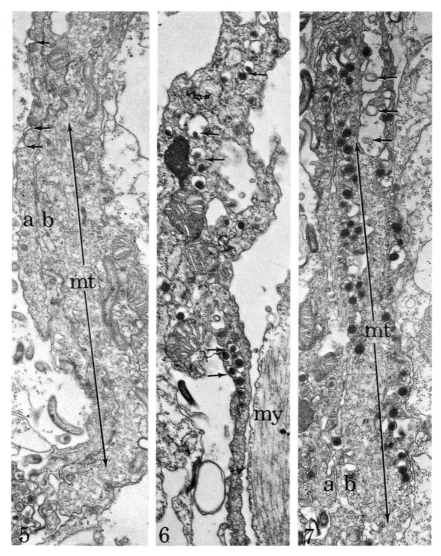

Figs. 5, 6, and 7. Mature neurites of different shapes and sizes. Two neurites (Fig. 5) adjacent to each other (a and b). They contain mostly microtubules (mt), droplets (approximately 900 Å in diameter) of moderate density, and mitochondria. Arrows indicate areas where vesicles fused to plasma membrane may have ruptured (× 18,700). Neurite (Fig. 6) with dense droplets (450–1100 Å in diameter). The neurite tapers sharply and lies immediately adjacent to epithelial myonemes (my). Note that in some cases there appears to be a fusion of plasma membrane and membranes surrounding some droplets (bottom, arrows) (× 18,700). Two neurites (a and b) (Fig. 7) containing dense droplets (700–1100 Å in diameter) and microtubules (mt). Note the empty vesicles (arrows) which appear to be the remnants of discarded droplets (× 18,700).

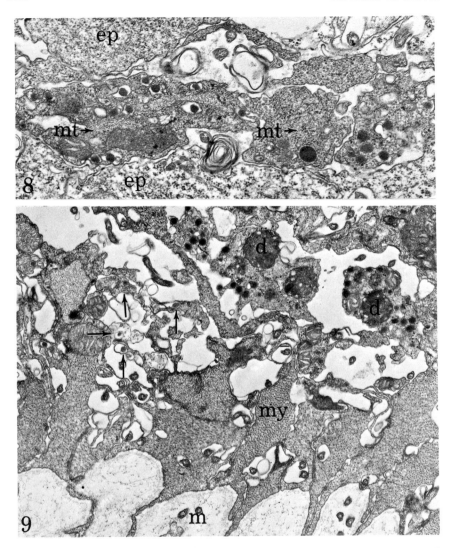

Figs. 8 and 9. Transverse sections of neurites surrounded by epitheliomuscular cells (ep) (Fig. 8), and adjacent to the longitudinal myonemes (my) (Fig. 9). In Fig. 8, note the cross-sections of microtubules (mt) and droplets ranging from 800 to 1000 Å in diameter (× 25,300). In Fig. 9, in addition to the small dense droplets (950–1300 Å in diameter) there are larger dense droplets (d; 0.7 μ in diameter). Note the very small neurites (arrows) which contain droplets of various densities and membranous elements surrounding them; mesoglea, m (× 13,100).

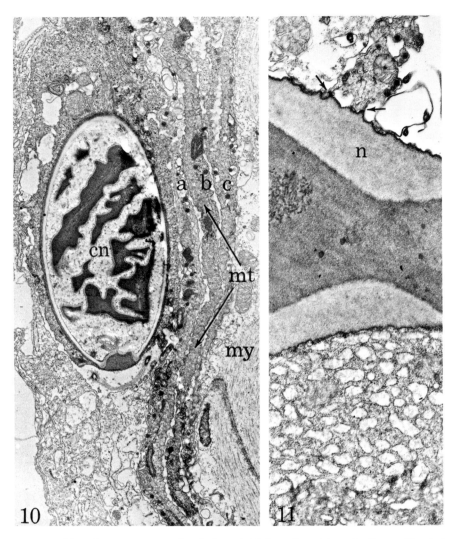

Fig. 10. Three long, narrow neurites (a, b, and c) lying adjacent to each other and located between a cnidoblast (cn) and longitudinal myonemes (my). They contain dense droplets (approximately 900 Å in diameter), microtubules (mt), and a few mitochondria (× 10,400).

Fig. 11. Neurite containing droplets (approximately 1200 Å in diameter) which appear to terminate directly on the nematocyst (n) of a cnidoblast (see arrows) (× 13,100).

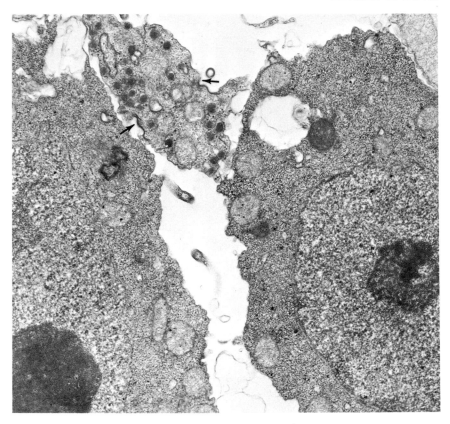

Fig. 12. Neurite with dense droplets (approximately 900 Å in diameter) closely associated with two interstitial cells. Arrows indicate possible areas of ruptured vesicles (× 18,700).

numerous synaptic vesicles in axon terminals may be due to the fragmentation of the membranes surrounding neurosecretory droplets (Bern and Knowles, 1966). Lentz (1966a) and Davis *et al.* (1968) suggested one possible mechanism for the release of neurosecretion in *Hydra*. These investigators showed that the membranes surrounding the droplets fuse with the plasma membrane, thereby providing a route of release for the enclosed droplet. This method of release is observed in Figs. 2, 6, 13, and 19. After the droplets are isolated from the Golgi lamellae, some remain in the cell body, while others are transported into the neurites. In either location, the membranes of the vesicles fuse with the plasma membrane to accomplish the release of the droplets. The release of droplets does not occur spontaneously. Instead, there is a gradual depletion of vesicular contents by mere diffusion as evidenced by the appearance of several droplets of different densities (Figs. 6, 13, and 16). It is at this stage of partial diffusion that the particulate materials (35–45 Å in diameter) may be observed. Whether the droplets occur along the periphery of the cell body and neurite or are located more interiorly, a certain degree of fusion of individual droplets results. Figures 3, 4, 6, and 13 show fusion of the surrounding membranes of some droplets. This fusion results in the formation of much larger vesicles. In some cases, droplets

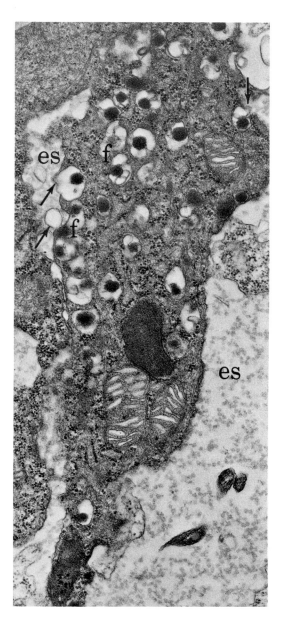

Fig. 13. Neurite, observed in regnerating animal, containing droplets of various densities (850–1700 Å in diameter). Some of these droplets seem to have fused or were in the process of fusion (f). Unlike the newly formed droplets which occupy the entire vesicle, these droplets fill only a portion of these enlarged vesicles. Note the empty vesicles and fused membranes (arrows) along the plasma membrane, overall density of the neurite, and droplets (350 Å in diameter) in the extracellular space (es) (× 28,700).

of different densities are observed in the process of fusion (Fig. 3) within the larger vacuole. It is interesting to note that fusion of similar droplets also occurs in more advanced organisms (Weiss, 1965; Bunt and Ashby, 1968). The mechanism described above represents one method for release of neurosecretion in *Hydra*.

The second possible mechanism also involves the fusion of the vesicle membranes with the plasma membrane. The fused membrane ruptures, forming an aperture which is in direct continuity with the extracellular space. The droplets in this case are not extruded wholly but also diffuse gradually into the extracellular space (Figs. 5, 12, and 19). This type of release has been described as exocytosis and occurs in a variety of higher organisms. In some instances the droplets released in this manner may be intact or may assume a granular appearance (Weiss, 1965; Bunt, 1969; Rodriguez, 1969; Weitzman, 1969; Normann, 1969). It appears that although this method of release may be present in *Hydra*, it does not represent the primary method of release.

The third suggested mechanism is somewhat similar to the first and second in that there is a fusion or partial fusion of the vesicle membranes with the plasma membrane of the cell body or neurite. Shortly after fusion occurs, the combined membranes evaginate into the extracellular space (Figs. 3, 4, 7, 9, and 14). The droplets diffuse gradually, such that droplets of various densities may be observed within the evaginated membranes. This method of release, therefore, eventually produces many empty evaginated vesicles along the plasma membrane. In some sections, membranes of this nature are observed detached from the cell. Whether they are completely separated or represent merely sections of extremely evaginated membranes is not clear. The constriction at the base of certain of these evaginated vesicles, however, suggests that, at least in some cases, vesicles may be entirely isolated from the cell. Occasionally, dense droplets with their surrounding membranes are observed intact in the extracellular space (Fig. 15). Since this latter condition occurs seldom, it is believed that such profiles represent a slight modification of the third mechanism.

The fourth means of release appears to involve the separation of small parts of the neurite and their eventual degeneration, as shown in Figs. 16–18. It is possible that the ends of the neurites with their secretory droplets may break off from the remainder of the cells and gradually degenerate until only a mass of isolated vesicles remains. An alternative explanation could be the degeneration of the entire cell, such that in appropriate sections the same sequence of neurite degeneration would be apparent (Figs. 16–18). It will be shown later that nerve cells perish at

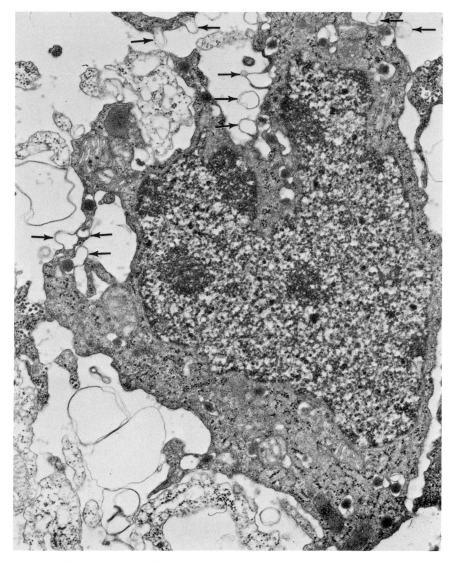

Fig. 14. Neurosecretory cell observed in a regenerating animal. The overall density of the cell is greater than that in normal animals. The droplets in the cell body are approximately 1100 Å in diameter. Note the empty or partially empty vesicles and evaginated membranes (arrows) along the plasma membrane (× 24,300).

the extremities of the animal, and therefore this mechanism may be of doubtful existence. The suggested methods of release are presented diagrammatically in Fig. 19.

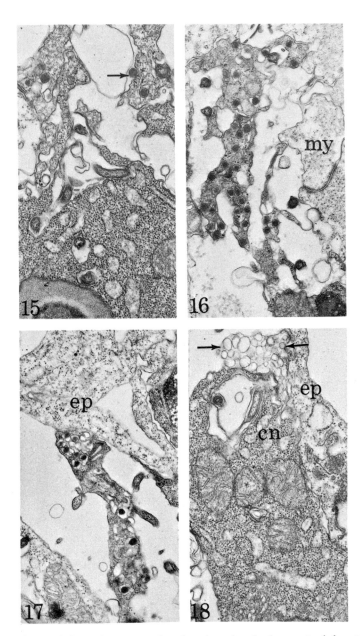

Regardless of the release mechanism involved, the material enters the extracellular space and apparently undergoes further diffusion. It is noted that, in some other systems, released materials are not observed in the

Fig. 15. Neurites with droplets approximately 1100 Å in diameter. Note the droplet (arrow) which is membrane-bound and appears to be entirely separated from the neurite (× 18,700).

Figs. 16, 17, and 18. Sequential stages of degenerating neurites which may have separated from cell bodies or of neurites from intact degenerating cells. Neurites (Fig. 16) with droplets (900–1400 Å in diameter) located close to epithelial myonemes (my). Note the variations in density (× 21,400). Neurite (Fig. 17) with droplets (470–1100 Å in diameter) in contact with an epitheliomuscular cell (ep). The droplets at the point of contact are smaller and less dense than those in the proximal region and their membranes appear to coalesce (× 18,300). Group of vesicles (arrows; 700–1600 Å in diameter) located near a cnidoblast (cn) and an epitheliomuscular cell (ep). These vesicles are believed to represent the vestiges of neurite degeneration (× 18,700).

surrounding external lamina or perivascular space. It is therefore assumed that the droplets may be in a molecularly dispersed state (Afzelius and Fridberg, 1963; Shivers, 1969). Scharrer (1968), on the other hand, showed that the released material was clearly observable in the interneuronal gap. Furthermore, the released and unreleased materials were similar in appearance, that is, moderately dense and granulated. In attempting to ascertain the presence of released material in *Hydra,* the extracellular spaces were examined closely for evidences of peculiar droplets, especially in the vicinity of neurosecretory neurites. Since it is believed that the production of neurosecretion increases during the first several hours of regeneration and, presumably, a concomitant increase in release results, regenerating animals could provide a clue as to the state of the released material. Figures 2, 3, and 13 reveal small, moderately dense granules (340–350 Å in diameter) in the extracellular space immediately adjacent to the neurosecretory cell. These granules are seldom observed in normal animals (Fig. 2), but many appear commonly in regenerating animals (Figs. 3 and 13). It is noted, however, that the appearance of these granules, even in regenerating animals, is not consistent, as evidenced by the presence of very few of them around some nerve cells in regenerating systems (Fig. 14). Whether or not these granules represent the resynthesized release material is not known.

The conditions that regulate the actual release of neurosecretory material are varied (Ishii and Kobayashi, 1963). According to Bern and Knowles (1966), chemical changes, especially ionic factors in the extracellular fluid, electrotonic transmission of impulses from adjacent activated neurosecretory neurons, hormones, and other chemical factors could result in the release of the materials. The conditions that trigger the

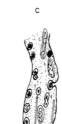

Fig. 19.

release mechanism in *Hydra* are unknown. It is known, however, that during the initial stages of regeneration, the amount of neurosecretion increases to a point well above the normal limits and apparently, a corresponding increase in the rate of release occurs. Also, immediately prior to the formation of germ cells, the amount of neurosecretion decreases, such that by the time the animal has become sexual there are no secretory droplets. Since in both these processes cell differentiation occurs, it may be that the release mechanism is intimately associated with cell differentiation.

IV. Nature of Neurosecretory Material

Studies by Lesh and Burnett (1964, 1966) have shed some light on the nature of the neurosecretory material in *Hydra*. The investigators extracted an inducer that is concentrated in the hypostomal region and apparently in a gradient fashion from head to base. They suggested that the inducer controls cell division and head formation along the body column. The fact that the activity of the inducer was diminished when nerve cells were destroyed suggested that the inducer was probably produced by neurosecretory cells (Burnett and Diehl, 1964; Lentz and Barrnett, 1965). In addition, electron microscopical examination of the extract showed the presence of particulate materials averaging 950 Å in diameter (Lesh and Burnett, 1964). This observation is in excellent agreement with more recent studies which showed that most of the

---

Fig. 19. Diagrammatic interpretation of four mechanisms of neurosecretory release in neurosecretory and neurosensory cell neurites. Although only neurites are shown in the diagram, the processes indicated in 1–3 also occur in the cell bodies. (1a–1e): Dense membrane-bound droplets in the cell body and neurites eventually fuse with the plasma membrane. The droplets diffuse gradually from the vesicles, leaving empty or partially empty vesicles. This method of release occurs commonly in *Hydra*. (2a–2e): Fusion of the droplets with the plasma membrane. Eventually the fused membrane ruptures and the droplets are diffused in the extracellular space (exocytosis). This mechanism is not considered one of the primary methods of release. (3a–3e): Following fusion or partial fusion of the vesicle membrane and plasma membrane, the membranes evaginate into the extracellular space. During this process the droplets diffuse gradually, leaving many empty vesicles along the plasma membrane. It is believed that some of the evaginated vesicles eventually separate from the cell body or neurite. This method, together with that shown in 1a–1e, represents the primary mechanisms of release. (4a–4e): Rupture of the distal portion of neurites. The isolated portion eventually degenerates until only groups of vesicles are observed. At the same time the droplets are released. This sequence of diagrams could also be interpreted as different planes through entire degenerating cells. It is doubtful that this method of release occurs in *Hydra*.

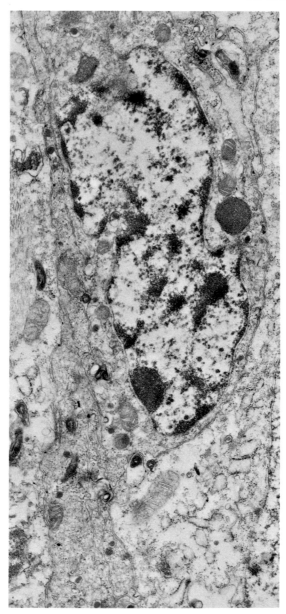

Fig. 20. Neurosecretory cell believed to be in the early stages of degeneration. Note the increased density of the nucleus and accumulation of nuclear material ($\times$ 15,400).

neurosecretory droplets are approximately 1000 Å in diameter (Lentz, 1966a; Davis *et al.,* 1968; Davis, 1969). It was therefore proposed that neurosecretory cells in the hypostome produced the inducer material (Lesh and Burnett, 1966).

Biochemical characterization of the inducer revealed that the material was "relatively heat stable, not extractable with lipid solvents, digested by proteolytic enzymes and slowly dialysable" (Lesh and Burnett, 1964, 1966). It is interesting to note that several compounds including glycoprotein, carbohydrate, phospholipid, sulfur-rich protein, and basic polypeptides have been reported in neurosecretion of other organisms (Bern and Hagadorn, 1965; Adams, 1965; McCann and Dhariwal, 1966; Hagadorn, 1967). Although the chemical nature of the inducer is presently being investigated, biochemical analyses suggest that it may be a low-molecular-weight polypeptide (Lesh and Burnett, 1964).

Most studies involving the nervous system have neglected to offer even a brief suggestion as to the fate of nerve cells. Reference has been made as to the fate of neurosensory cells in Chapter 12. It is well established that nerve cells are concentrated in the hypostome and basal regions of the animal. Since there is movement of cells, distally and proximally, one would expect to find a variety of dead or dying cells (Fig. 20), especially near the mouth, tips of the tentacles, and basal disc. Figure 21 shows a degenerating neurosecretory cell located at the tip of the tentacle. Although a few mitochondria, remnants of microtubules, and the characteristic secretory droplets (approximately 900 Å in diameter) are present, the most conspicuous structures are membranous debris. A transverse section of a neurite is also seen in the basal disc (Fig. 22); it contains microtubules, secretory droplets (approximately 1000 Å in diameter), larger, irregularly shaped droplets, and glycogen particles.

Returning to the last mechanism of release which was mentioned earlier, that is, the suggestion that tips of neurites may be broken off and ultimately degenerate, it may be that this type of mechanism does not exist at all. The appearance of such neurites could be interpreted as different planes through degenerating cells. An important question arises here as to whether the nerve cells release all secretory droplets and finally die or do they continue to produce droplets until they are finally discarded at the extremities. Figures 21 and 22 reveal that secretory droplets are present in dying or dead cells. It is therefore assumed that the cells continue the synthesis of neurosecretion throughout their existence.

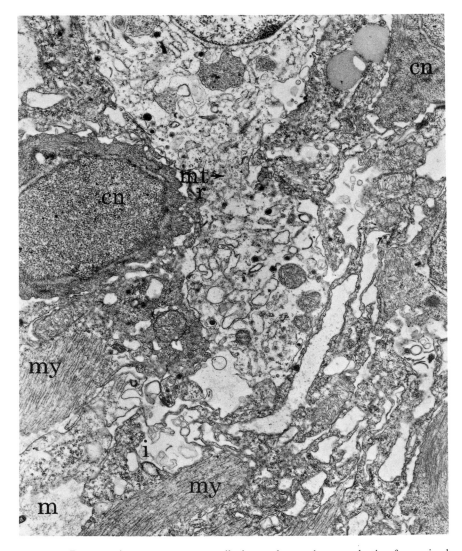

Fig. 21. Degenerating neurosecretory cell observed near the tentacle tip of an animal. Note the large, moderately dense bodies (near nucleus, top), microtubules (mt), dense droplets (900 Å in diameter), small mitochondria, and vesicles of various sizes. Epithelial myonemes, my; cnidoblasts, cn; mesoglea, m (× 14,400).

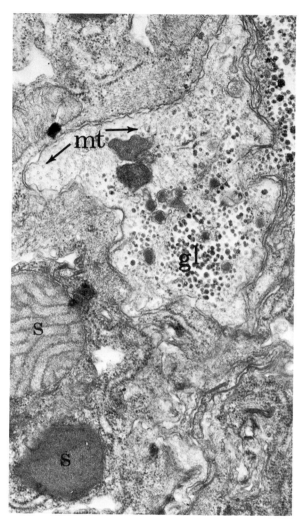

Fig. 22. Transverse section of a degenerating neurite observed in the basal disc of the animal. Note the microtubules (mt) in cross-section, small, dense droplets (1000 Å in diameter), glycogen deposits (gl) and the larger, irregularly shaped dense droplets. Secretory droplets (s) of the epitheliomuscular cells, one of which (top) is characteristic of the basal disc, are also observed (× 30,600).

Acknowledgment

A portion of the material presented in this section was obtained as a result of a National Science Foundation Grant (No. GB-8384). The author also acknowledges gratefully the technical assistance of Linda M. Bookman.

References

Adams, C. W. M. (1965). "Neurohistochemistry." Amer. Elsevier, New York.
Afzelius, B., and Fridberg, G. (1963). *Z. Zellforsch. Mikrosk. Anat.* **59**, 289–308.
Bern, H. A., and Hagadorn, I. R. (1965). *In* "Structure and Function in the Nervous Systems of Invertebrates" (T. H. Bullock and G. H. Horridge, eds.), pp. 353–429. Freeman, San Francisco, California.
Bern, H. A., and Knowles, G. W. (1966). *In* "Neuroendocrinology" (L. Martini and W. F. Ganong, eds.), Vol. 1, pp. 139–186. Academic Press, New York.
Bern, H. A., Nishioka, R. S., and Hagadorn, I. R. (1962). *In* "Neurosecretion" (H. Heller and R. B. Clark, eds.), pp. 21–34. Academic Press, New York.
Bunt, A. H. (1969). *J. Ultrastruct. Res.* **28**, 411–421.
Bunt, A. H., and Ashby, E. A. (1968). *Gen. Comp. Endocrinol.* **10**, 376–382.
Burnett, A. L., Diehl, N. A., and Diehl, F. A. (1964). *J. Exp. Zool.* **157**, 227–236.
Burnett, A. L., and Diehl, N. A. (1964). *J. Exp. Zool.* **157**, 217–226.
Davis, L. E. (1969). *J. Cell Sci.* **5**, 699–726.
Davis, L. E., Burnett, A. L., and Haynes, J. F. (1968). *J. Exp. Zool.* **167**, 295–332.
DeRobertis, E. (1962). *In* "Neurosecretion" (H. Heller and R. B. Clark, eds.), pp. 3–20. Academic Press, New York.
DeRobertis, E. (1964). "Histophysiology of Synapses and Neurosecretion." Macmillan, New York.
Hagadorn, I. R. (1967). *In* "Neuroendocrinology" (L. Martini and W. F. Ganong, eds.), Vol. 2, pp. 439–484. Academic Press, New York.
Ishii, S., and Kobayashi, H. (1963). *Japan J. Exptl. Morphol.* **17**, 56–67.
Knowles, F. G. W. (1958). *Proc. Int. Symp. Neurosecretion. 2nd, 1957,* 105–109.
Lentz, T. L. (1963). *Anat. Rec.* **145**, 344.
Lentz, T. L. (1966a). "The Cell Biology of Hydra." Wiley, New York.
Lentz, T. L. (1966b). *J. Exp. Zool.* **162**, 171–180.
Lentz, T. L., and Barrnett, R. J. (1965). *Amer. Zool.* **5**, 341–356.
Lesh, G. E., and Burnett, A. L. (1964). *Nature (London)* **204**, 492–493.
Lesh, G. E., and Burnett, A. L. (1966). *J. Exp. Zool.* **163**, 55–78.
McCann, S. M., and Dhariwal, A. P. S. (1966). *In* "Neuroendocrinology" (L. Martini and W. F. Ganong, eds.), Vol. 1, pp. 261–296.
Normann, T. (1969). *Exp. Cell Res.* **55**, 285–287.
Oosaki, T., and Ishii, S. (1965). *Z. Zellforsch. Mikrosk. Anat.* **66**, 782–793.
Rodriguez, E. M. (1969). *Z. Zellforsch. Mikrosk. Anat.* **93**, 182–212.
Scharrer, B. (1967). *Amer. Zool.* **7**, 161–169.
Scharrer, B. (1968). *Z. Zellforsch. Mikrosk. Anat.* **89**, 1–16.
Shivers, R. R. (1969). *Z. Zellforsch. Mikrosk. Anat.* **97**, 38–44.
von Euler, U. S. (1958). *Recent Progr. Horm. Res.* **14**, 483–512.
Weiss, M. (1965). *Z. Zellforsch. Mikrosk. Anat.* **68**, 783–794.
Weitzman, M. (1969). *Z. Zellforsch. Mikrosk. Anat.* **94**, 147–154.
Zambrano, D., and DeRobertis, E. (1966). *Z. Zellforsch. Mikrosk. Anat.* **73**, 414–431.
Zambrano, D., and Mordah, J. (1966). *Z. Zellforsch. Mikrosk. Anat.* **73**, 405–413.

PART VII

CELL PROLIFERATION AND MORPHOGENESIS IN *HYDRA*

Probably nothing has done more to confuse the story of growth in *Hydra* than the conflict over where divisions actually occur along the body column of the animal. First, Brien reported a subhypostomal growth region in *Hydra* which through his own papers, and also through the papers of the present editor, was reinterpreted by some investigators to mean that the *only* cell divisions in this organism were subhypostomal. This claim is, of course, ridiculous, and anyone who reads Brien's excellent monographs will be soon convinced that cell divisions occur in the gastric and budding regions of the animal. For some unknown reason the idea of uniformity of cell divisions along the body column began to grow. This is a false notion and one that must be corrected. Dr. Corff, in the following chapter, has not only counted mitoses in every cell of several hydras, but has also recorded the stages of division, orientation of spindle fibers, and precise location of the dividing cells. It is hoped that this paper will settle once and for all the spurious notions of "steady-state" *Hydra* and uniformity of cell division along the column of the animal.

CHAPTER 15

Organismal Growth and the Contribution of Cell Proliferation to Net Growth and Maintenance of Form

SONDRA CORFF

Part I. ORGANISMAL GROWTH

I. Introduction

A. ORGANISMAL GROWTH

Hydras can be maintained for years without any changes in morphology or signs of aging, although they continuously produce buds. Continual growth of the body column is easily demonstrated, however, by marking a region of the body column and observing the movement and subsequent disappearance of the marker at the bud region or at the extremities. As the marker moves distally or proximally along the body column, the intact *Hydra* itself does not appear to undergo any change in size or morphology. These observations raise two important questions which will, in fact, constitute the basis for most of the subsequent discussion in this chapter. How is the marker displaced along the body column? What is the underlying mechanism that permits simultaneous growth and maintenance of the body column morphology and size as the marker is displaced?

Another major problem which must be considered in a discussion of organismal growth is concerned with the correlation of data from studies at both the organismal and cellular levels of organization. At the organismal level, growth can be analyzed quantitatively in terms of the production of buds and by the rate of movement of markers on the body column. Organismal growth can also be studied at the cellular level of organization by histological analysis of the displacement of marked cells along the body column or by the pattern of mitosis along the body column. Direct correlation of data from organismal and cellular levels requires consideration of certain qualitative aspects of *Hydra* growth. Some of these aspects will be discussed in the section on organismal growth and others will be discussed more fully in the section on cell proliferation.

B. CELL PROLIFERATION

Morphological and physiological characteristics observed at the cellular level of organization can be directly related to the total morphology of *Hydra* at the organismal level. An excellent system is thus provided for investigating the relationships between mitosis, cell division, cell differentiation, and growth and morphogenesis. *Hydra* size and morphology appear to remain constant under certain conditions, but continual tissue renewal is evident from the distal or proximal movement of marked regions relative to the body column from a region under the hypostome. The movement of the marker thus reflects net growth in the body column which results from the continual addition of cells to the column by cell division and the removal of cells from the column by cell death, budding, and sloughing at the extremities or into the gastric cavity. The movement of the markers away from the subhypostome region suggested the concept of a growth zone in this region, even though mitosis had been observed in most regions of the body column by McConnell (1930, 1933a,b, 1936). Since no meristematic region of growth exists in the subhypostome, recent studies have tried to analyze mitotic patterns at the cellular level in an attempt to elucidate the components contributing to the net growth pattern as reflected by marker movements and also to explain the nature of the growth zone which is apparent at the organismal level. The results of these studies have led to conflicting interpretations regarding the contribution of cell division to growth patterns and morphogenesis (Burnett, 1966; Campbell, 1967a–d; Clarkson and Wolpert, 1967; Corff, 1969). An analysis of mitotic distribution in *Hydra littoralis* presented by Campbell (1967a) indicated a uniform distribution of cell division along the gastric column of budding *Hydra*. Since no sharp localization of cell division occurred, Campbell concluded that *Hydra* lacked a subhypostomal growth region, and that morphogenesis and maintenance of form was unrelated to the pattern of cell division along the body column. However, the results of other studies (Burnett, 1966; Campbell, 1967d; Corff, 1969) indicate a pattern of nonuniform distribution of cell division along the body column. This pattern has suggested a possible relationship between mitosis and form in *Hydra* and the presence of a subhypostomal growth region (Burnett, 1966; Corff, 1969).

Determination of a representative pattern of mitotic activity along the body column is difficult mainly because of the dynamic nature of growth, the flexibility of *Hydra* form, and the variance of growth patterns expressed by individual hydras in a culture population. Unless certain aspects inherent in the system are carefully considered, a nonrepresentative and possibly misleading pattern of mitotic activity will emerge, resulting in erroneous interpretation of the relationship or contribution of cell division to growth patterns, morphogenesis, and the maintenance of form in *Hydra*. Several aspects of mitotic analysis which could directly or indirectly influence determination of the actual mitotic pattern will therefore be discussed in some detail along with the results obtained from mitotic analysis of budding and nonbudding hydras.

II. Analyzing Growth at the Organismal Level

A. The Basic Pattern of Growth

The general pattern of *Hydra* growth at the organismal level has been frequently studied by workers observing the movement of a variety of markers along the body column (see Burnett, 1961, for early studies; Campbell, 1967b; Corff, 1969). Our present concept of *Hydra* growth, however, is mainly based on observations and theories advanced by two workers. Tripp (1928) grafted a peduncle excised from one *Hydra* to the subhypostome region of another and observed that the peduncle moved down the body column to its original position. This experiment plus the observation of Issajew (1926) that a fork in a tentacle gradually moved distally until it disappeared led Tripp to postulate the existence of a growth region under the hypostome that forced cells distally and proximally. He further postulated that *Hydra* did not grow longer indefinitely because the cells at the base of the peduncle and at the tips of the tentacles would continually slough off.

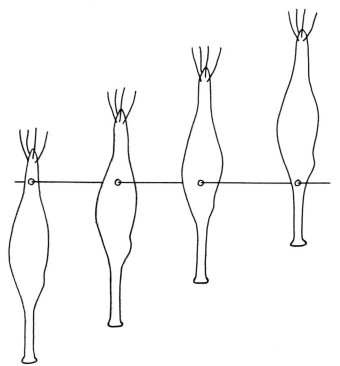

Fig. 1. Diagrammatic representation of the relationship between marker displacement and growth of body column. The marked region is stationary and only appears to move proximally as the body column moves distally.

Brien (1953) observed the movement of vitally stained distal regions grafted to nonstained proximal regions. After 3 to 5 weeks, all the stained tissue had moved proximally to the basal disc. He postulated that *Hydra* grew continually, replacing its tissue from a single, active subhypostome region, the growth region. Brien further concluded that the movement of the marker proximally was due to the formation of new body column in the region between the marker and the hypostome and that this growth was balanced by cell loss at the bud and at the extremities. According to Brien's theory, if the *Hydra* were suspended in space, it would be displaced distally while maintaining its size and morphology. The marked region only appears to move proximally relative to the entire body column when it is actually our frame of reference, i.e., the body column, which is moving distally (Fig. 1). The word "movement" then, is only used to describe the changing position of the marker relative to the body column and does not constitute an explanation of the underlying mechanism of marker displacement.

B. TYPES OF MARKERS

The use of markers for analyzing growth assumes that no migration of the epitheliomuscular cells in the epidermis or digestive cells in the gastrodermis occurs. These cell types constitute most of the *Hydra* structure and since they do not migrate as individual cells relative to each other, tissue marker movement away from the subhypostome must represent the rate of tissue formation above the marker. The rate of marker movement should therefore provide some indication of the underlying pattern of growth (cell division). A brief description of the most common types of markers and some difficulties encountered by their use will provide a foundation for our discussion of recent growth studies involving these markers.

1. Gastrodermal Markers

In order to graft tissue from one *Hydra* to another, the gastrodermis of both must be in contact. Consequently, when tentacle or peduncle segments are grafted to the body column, they are assumed to measure the growth of gastrodermal tissue above and through the marker. There are several potential drawbacks to this marking method, particularly in the case of tentacle markers. Since a large number of nerves are located at the base of the tentacles, the graft sometimes stimulates the growth of a new hydranth from the host. Since cells are continually lost from the tips of the tentacles, mitosis at the base of the tentacle graft may produce cells which do not contribute to growth of the body column but which migrate up the tentacle. Even if growth is not stimulated at the region of the graft, abnormal growth may be stimulated as the tentacle graft moves away from the inhibitory effects of the hypostome. Both tentacle and peduncle markers are frequently lost at the bud region with the initiation of a new bud.

Hydra can be stained with methylene blue and the stained region excised and grafted onto a nonstained body column (Brien and Reniers-Decoen, 1949; Brien, 1953; Burnett, 1959, 1961; Campbell, 1967b). Most of the stain accumulates in the gastrodermis. Several difficulties may arise when tracing this type of marker for several weeks. The stain tends to fade with time. Stained gastrodermal cells can detach from the mesoglea and distribute stained material throughout the distal body regions (Burnett, 1959). Methylene blue is toxic and if the animal is stained too intensely, it will die. Even when lightly stained, the tissue may not be completely normal. The stain frequently accumulates in the nucleus of the cell and when this occurs, the cell dies (Burnett, 1961). Methylene blue can contribute to abnormal growth patterns. Yao (1945) found that methylene blue can induce tentacles. As with tentacle and peduncle markers, methylene blue markers are frequently lost in the bud region as the stained tissue is incorporated into the growing bud.

Green *Hydra* can be bleached and grafts made between green and white animals. The marker is extremely stable and easy to follow over a long period of time. This marker too, however, is usually lost at the bud region by incorporation of the tissue into the growing bud.

2. Epidermal Markers

If the region of the body column of a sexual *Hydra* that contains the testes is excised and grafted onto a nonsexual *Hydra,* its movement along the epidermis can be measured for a short time. Unfortunately, when a testis moves onto the body column of the nonsexual *Hydra,* it is usually absorbed (Shostak *et al.,* 1965). Measurements of marker movement on sexual animals are unreliable for information regarding asexual *Hydra* since growth and budding in most sexual animals ceases (Burnett, 1961).

3. Epidermal and Gastrodermal Markers

Both the epidermis and gastrodermis can be simultaneously marked by labeling the *Hydra* with H^3-thymidine. A segment of the labeled animal is grafted onto a nonlabeled animal and the subsequent movement of the two layers analyzed at the cellular level by autoradiography techniques. Movement of the marked layers with time must of course be followed in different animals; consequently, this method requires precise grafting technique. The general growth state of the animal may also play a role in the subsequent movement of the marked tissue. Shostak *et al.* (1965) reported that the epidermis moved faster than the gastrodermis in studies on *Hydra viridis*. In rapidly budding *H. littoralis,* however, the gastrodermis moved faster than the epidermis (Campbell, 1967c). The epidermis and gastrodermis not only move as coherent sheets of tissue (Burnett and Garofalo, 1960) but they also move at different rates over the mesoglea.

Movement of both layers of the *Hydra* have also been studied by combining a testis (epidermal marker) segment of a bleached sexual *Hydra* with a green *Hydra* body column (Shostak *et al.,* 1965). In these studies, the testis was observed to move faster than the corresponding gastrodermal tissue, eventually crossing the border of the graft between the green and bleached segments.

4. Epidermal, Gastrodermal, and Mesogleal Marker

A marker which appears to measure the production of both cellular and acellular elements above the marker and not just the rate of tissue formation in either the epidermis or the gastrodermis has been described (Corff, 1969). The marker is established by partially bisecting the *Hydra* along the distoproximal axis from either the distal or proximal ends. The V-shaped junction between the regenerated halves of the longitudinally split animal is used as the marker. This method maintains the original gradient of the *Hydra* and eliminates problems imposed by the staining technique. In addition, the marker is not lost in the bud region, but moves completely through the entire animal to the basal disc.

C. QUALITATIVE ASPECTS

In some instances, workers have referred to cultures of *Hydra* maintained under identical conditions for several weeks as animals maintained in a steady-state condition. It must be recognized, however, that each *Hydra* maintains its own steady state which may or may not be identical with other hydras in the population. Reference to a steady-state popula- is not valid.

Even though the rate at which cells are added and lost from the body column may differ between animals, it is important that each group of animals be maintained under identical conditions.

D. GENERAL COMMENTS

All the methods previously described are useful for certain experiments. Both tissue markers (epidermal and gastrodermal) and split markers reflect the same general pattern of growth discussed earlier, i.e., the markers move distally or proximally from a region directly under the hypostome. If the movement of the epidermal or gastrodermal markers is viewed without reference to split-marker movement or vice versa, the impression obtained is that each marker measures the rate of body column formation above the marker. Since split and single tissue markers do move at different rates relative to the body column, some differences must exist between the phenomena being measured. These differences in rates of marker movement lead us to question more closely the processes actually being measured and the relationship between these measurements and growth measured at the cellular level in terms of mitosis. An understanding of these differences should further enhance our knowledge of the processes underlying marker movement along the body column.

III. General Patterns of Marker Movements

A. DISTAL MOVEMENT OF MARKERS

Methylene blue markers, tentacle grafts, and split markers situated in a small region directly under the hypostome move distally. This displacement of the marked tissue from the tip of the hypostome takes approximately 20 to 30 days (Fig. 2). The rate of movement distally is much slower than the rate of movement through more proximal regions of the body column.

When a split marker is established from the distal end into the subhypostome region, two hypostomes are situated on one body column. There is no influence on budding rate and approximately the same number of buds are produced as recorded for a single hypostome. The two hypostomes gradually become one as the marker moves distally. Maintenance of the hypostome, therefore, does not appear to depend on the existing hypostome, but rather on the number of subhypostome regions.

B. PROXIMAL MOVEMENT OF MARKERS

The movement of a split marker through the body column occurs more slowly than the movement of single tissue markers (tentacle grafts or methylene blue markers). Campbell (1967b) showed that in *H. littoralis,* methylene blue markers and tentacle grafts moved from the subhypostome region to the proximal bud in approximately 8 days, and down the peduncle and basal disc in approximately 20 days. In *Hydra oligactis,* split-marker movement was much slower through most of the morphologically distinct regions (Fig. 2).

When the movement of both a split marker and a peduncle graft on one *Hydra* was recorded (Corff, 1969), the two markers were observed to move through the mid-gastric and upper bud regions at approximately the same rate. In the bud region, however, the single tissue marker moved faster than the split marker as the portion of the body column between the two markers was removed as bud. In the peduncle, the two markers again move at approximately the same rate.

The difference in rates of movement of split markers and tissue markers observed in *H. oligactis* suggests, at this point, that two different phenomena are being measured. There are several reasons for suggesting that the split marker measures the rate of production and maintenance of both cellular and acellular elements above the marker, whereas the gastrodermal marker (tentacle marker) measures only the rate of production of the gastrodermal tissue. (1) As the split marker moves proximally, an actual measurable body column consisting of epidermis, gastrodermis, and mesoglea is formed above the marker. (2) Campbell (1967c) has pre-

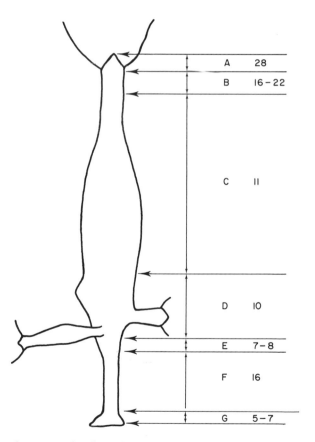

Fig. 2. General pattern of split-marker movement along the body column of *Hydra*. Numbers represent time in days required for marker to move through various regions of the body column. A, hypostome; B, subhypostome; C, upper and mid-gastric regions; D, bud region; E, bud–peduncle; F, peduncle; G, basal disc.

sented autoradiographic evidence for the more rapid movement of gastro-dermis in budding *Hydra* compared with the epidermis. This suggests that more gastrodermal cells may be formed than directly contribute to the production of a new body column. They may simply increase the number of villi in the gastrodermal cavity. (3) The split marker always moves completely through the body column, whereas the other markers are frequently incorporated into bud tissue. This observation suggests that the split marker does not just follow the movement of the cellular elements but also measures the production of another element contained within the total structure of the body column. This element must be the mesoglea. (4) The rate of split-marker movement is much slower than that of the tentacle-marker movement in regions which show a high number of mitosis relative to the rest of the body column. This indicates that all mitoses do not contribute directly to the displacement of the marker away from the hypostome. (5) Split markers take approximately 28 days to move through the gastric column and into the peduncle while tentacle markers are incorporated into the bud in approximately 8 days. (6) Approximately the same amount of time is required for production of body column above the bud region as is required for its subsequent removal in the bud region.

C. CORRELATION OF MARKER MOVEMENT WITH MORPHOLOGY

Markers situated 15% or more of the total body column from the hypostome invariably move proximally. The proportional distance of the marker from the hypostome can be calculated using two different frames of reference as the total length. In one method, the total length of the body column from hypostome tip to basal disc is used; in the other method the distance between the hypostome tip and the bud–peduncle junction is used. As seen in Fig. 3, the rate of marker movement is expressed differently, depending upon the method of calculation: The rate of marker movement is faster when the marker position is based on the distance between hypostome and bud–peduncle than when the marker position is based on the total body column.

The duration each marker remains in a morphologically distinct region of the body column can be determined by visual observation at the time of measurement. The morphological position of the split marker sometimes appears to fluctuate, especially as the marker moves from the bud region into the bud-peduncle region and the peduncle (Table I). Fluctuation however, also can occur between the subhypostome and the upper gastric regions. Although the rate of marker movement through the low gastric and bud regions may appear faster than the rate of movement of more distally positioned markers, the marker actually remains in the

TABLE I

DURATION OF SPLIT MARKER IN MORPHOLOGICAL REGIONS OF THE BODY COLUMN[a]

Cut from distal or proximal end	Duration in morphological region (days)								No. of buds	No. of days
	Subhypostome region	Upper gastric region	Mid-gastric region	Upper bud region	Bud region	Bud-peduncle region	Peduncle region	Basal disc region		
Distal (D)	4-Hypo(16)	—	—	—	—	—	—	—	13	20
"	—	3	7	2	13	7	—	—	37	32
"	4-Hypo(28)	—	—	—	—	—	—	—	22	32
"	6-Hypo(26)	—	—	—	—	—	—	—	22	32
"	5-Hypo(25)	4	8	—	—	10	—	—	17	30
"	16	—	13	3	4	13	—	—	22	28
"	1	—	3	—	7	13	8	—	26	31
"	—	4	6	2	12	6	2	—	45	31
"	—	10	5	2	11	—	—	—	33	30
"	—	—	—	—	—	—	—	—	14	28
Proximal (P)	—	4	7	4	15	2	—	—	21	32
"	—	—	4	1	5	8	—	—	17	18
"	—	—	8	—	10	13	—	—	27	31
"	—	—	9	5	16	—	5	—	19	30
"	—	—	—	2	3	4	8	—	12	14
"	—	—	—	2	10	7	—	—	35	27
"	—	—	—	2	3	22	—	—	19	27
(D) and (P)	6	5	4	1	5 2[b]	6 6[b]	— 13[b]	—	24	27
"	15	3	8	—	— 2[b]	— 13[b]	— 11[b]	—	21	27
"	7	4	7	5 2[b]	3 5[b]	1 12[b]	— 7[b]	—	16	27
"	—	—	—	—	15 —	2 —	4 14[b]	6 3[b]	31	27
"	—	2	7	—	6 3[b]	6 5[b]	6 7[b]	— 1[b]	23	27
"	—	8	3	2	8 2[b]	4 10[b]	— —	—	32	27
"	—	—	—	—	10 —	3 —	12 8[b]	— 5[b]	28	25
"	—	—	4	—	7 —	3 —	9 10[b]	1 —	24	24
"	—	—	4	6	9 7[b]	4 6[b]	2 11[b]	—	25	25

[a] Recorded from individual *Hydra*.   [b] Duration of proximal marker.

morphologically distinct bud region longer than in the mid-gastric region. This occurs even though the actual length of the upper and mid-gastric regions is much greater than the actual length of a budding region.

Although a new bud region is continually formed distally along the body column, the movement of the bud–peduncle junction away from the hypostome occurs very slowly. This is probably due to the removal of most gastric tissue in the bud region. Only a few cells slip past to the peduncle region. Split markers positioned at both the subhypostome and the bud–peduncle remain at a constant distance from each other although the gastric tissue is constantly being replaced.

Some interesting observations result from analyzing the movement of two split markers on one *Hydra*. The hydras are bisected from the distal and the proximal ends. In one *Hydra*, for example, the distal marker was situated in the subhypostome region and the proximal marker in the bud–peduncle region. Both markers moved at the same rate and the distance between the two markers remained the same. If longitudinal growth in the body column was occurring faster in the bud region than above the subhypostome, as suggested by the large number of mitotic figures observed in the bud region, the proximal marker would move away from the gastric region more rapidly than the distal marker moves away from the sub-

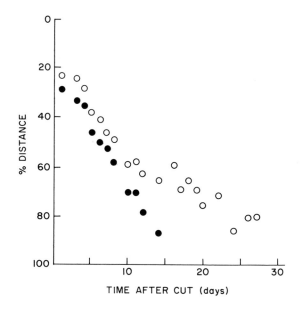

Fig. 3. Movement of split marker along the body column. Open circles, proportional distance (% distance) from hypostome to marker based on total body column length; closed circles, proportional distance (% distance) from hypostome to marker based on length of gastric column (hypostome to bud–peduncle junction).

hypostome. Divisions in the parent body column directly above the peduncle are numerous but evidently do not contribute to longitudinal growth of the column to any great extent.

In Fig. 4, the individual patterns of split-marker movement observed in over 20 hydras were visually superimposed to produce a combined plot of marker movement. The general pattern indicates that in two regions of the body column (subhypostome and bud–peduncle junction), body column formation above the marker occurs very slowly. These regions demarcate areas of high cell division from areas of low cell division. The slow movement of the split marker at the bud–peduncle junction does not correlate with the high mitotic activity observed in the bud region and suggests that most of the mitoses observed must contribute to the bud and not to growth of the body column in this region.

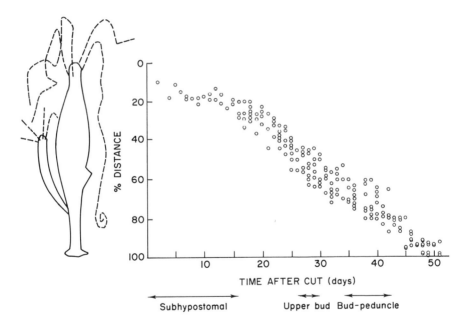

Fig. 4. Combined data on split-marker movements.

IV. Relationship between Organismal Growth and Mitosis

A. RELATIONSHIP BETWEEN MARKER MOVEMENT AND MITOSIS

Most of the actual movement of the split marker away from the hypostome occurs in the distal half of the animal. In the bud region, although mitoses are numerous, marker movement away from the hypostome appears to slow down and the marker remains in the region for a longer period of time than in the more distal region. The slow movement of the marker through the bud region suggests that the large number of mitoses there do not contribute to growth of the body column in a longitudinal direction, but mostly to the budding process and growth in circumference of the body column. Campbell (1967a,b) suggested that the broad distribution of mitosis in the gastric column correlated well with the movement of both methylene blue markers and tentacle graft markers down the gastric column. Since an increase in cell number through mitosis contributes not only to the longitudinal growth, but also to circumferential growth, as well as to the formation of buds, direct comparison of marker movement with mitotic frequency and distribution without consideration of these aspects may lead to misleading conclusions. In general, the rate of body column formation exhibited by split-marker movement compares favorably with the small number of cells whose mitotic spindle is oriented along the longitudinal axis of the animal. The rate of bud–peduncle junction movement distally is extremely slow compared with the rate of bud initiation distally; consequently form in starving hydras is maintained even though few mitotic figures can be observed.

B. Correlation between Body Column Formation and Mitosis

The approximate length of time required for a split marker to move through each segment of the body column and the approximate percentage distance from the hypostome tip to the marker has been diagrammatically represented to show the rate of body column formation as a marker moves proximally (Fig. 5). Since the marker is considered stationary with regard to the body column, its movement proximally is due to the addition of new body column above the marker. If we take a marker positioned 15% of the body column away from the hypostome tip and plot the rate of body column proximally by morphological segments (upper gastric, mid-gastric, bud, and bud–peduncle), we see that the marker is displaced by 15% of the body column through the upper gastric region in 5 days, by 25% of the body column through the mid-gastric region in 6 days, by 15% of the body column through the bud region in 10 days, and by 5% of the body column through the bud–peduncle junction in 7 days. Body column formation therefore occurs in the upper gastric region at approximately 3% per day, in the mid-gastric region at approximately 4% per day, in the bud region at 1.5% per day, and in the bud–peduncle region at approximately 0.7% per day. In the bud and bud–peduncle regions, very little longitudinal growth is needed to account for the displacement of the marker.

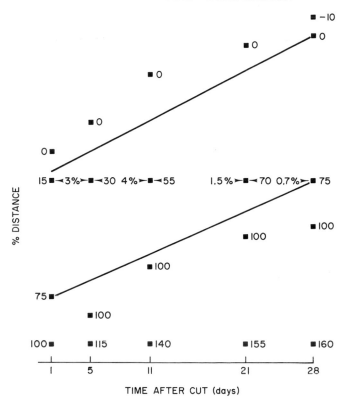

Fig. 5. Diagram representing rate of body column formation above split marker. Hypostome, 0; bud–peduncle, 75; basal disc, 100. Numbers represent proportional distance from hypostome. Arrows point to marker position relative to body column over a 28-day period. From days 1 to 5, marker is in the upper gastric region; from days 5 to 11, marker is in the mid-gastric region; from days 11 to 21, marker is in the bud region; from days 21 to 28, marker is in the bud–peduncle region (see text for further explanation).

If *Hydra* forms 70% of its body column in 28 days, approximately 2.5% of the column must be formed each day. Histological studies have shown that there are approximately 700 histological (5 μ) sections in a large, budding *H. oligactis,* which was the species used in these studies. Each histological cross-section of the gastric region contained approximately 100–175 digestive cells although the peduncle and hypostome possessed fewer. The total body column would therefore contain approximately 70,000 digestive cells. If the rate of body column formation is 3% per day, *Hydra* would require about 2100 new cells each day. Histological studies on the number and distribution of mitoses in *Hydra* have also shown approximately 500 cells in mitosis at one time in the body column. These studies indicate that cycles of synchronous mitotic activity may occur in *Hydra*. If the duration of mitosis for each cycle is approximately 2 hours (12 divisions in 24 hours), 500 cells dividing during each cycle would produce 6000 cells in 24 hours. Since our studies have also shown that approximately 30% of the dividing cells have spindles oriented parallel to the longitudinal axis of the body column which probably contribute to growth in this direction, 2000 cells would be added to the column per day. This is close to the estimated 2100 cells needed per day to increase body length by 3%.

V. Underlying Mechanism of Marker Movement

A. Possible Influences on Rate of Marker Movement

Differences in rates of tissue and split-marker movements and differences in rates of epidermal and gastrodermal movements have raised questions concerning the value and accuracy of correlating growth at the organismal level and mitotic distribution at the cellular level without greater knowledge of other possible forces or mechanisms that could influence these growth processes. For example, is the rate of marker movement influenced by other processes such as the rate of cell migration over the mesoglea (as sheets of tissue), the rate of mesoglea formation, the stability of the mesogleal structure, the permanance of cell attachment to the mesoglea, or the process of fold or villi formation? Does the addition of new cells to the body column exert a pushing force, especially in the bud region, or does bud formation itself initiate a pulling force on cells in the body column? Does mitosis contribute simultaneously and equally to all growth phenomena observed at the organismal level?

Campbell (1967b) has offered an explanation for the rate of marker movement that is based on a concept of localized growth versus uniform growth. According to this concept, if growth were localized in the sub-hypostome region, the movement of a marker with time would be linear; if growth were uniform, the marker would move exponentially. Campbell's data showed that the rate of marker movement was compatible with both uniform and localized growth. Since mitosis is observed throughout the body column, Campbell favors the concept of uniform growth along the body column. He does not, however, take into consideration growth in circumference of the body column or any other possible influence on the rate of marker movement.

B. Body Column Components and Rate of Marker Movement

Hydra structure is most simply described as two layers of cells separated by a noncellular mesoglea. With this concept, it is difficult to visualize addition of cells to the gastrodermis and epidermis above the marker contributing to displacement of the marker, but not contributing to the formation of the body column structure actually observed above the split marker. However, this appears to be the situation described by the relative movements of tissue and split markers. Brien's concept of growth implies the displacement of a tissue marker proximally due to the addition of cells above the marker and the simultaneous advancement of the basal disc distally. The tissue marker was assumed to measure formation of the body column above the marker, as shown in Fig. 6A. Recent observations of differences in rates of epidermal and gastrodermal movement, however, indicate that migration of cells over a mesogleal structure may occur, and together with the differences in split- and tissue-marker movements indicate that the two markers measure different phenomena: tissue replacement and body column formation. This concept is diagramed in Fig. 6B.

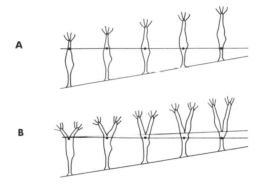

Fig. 6. A. Diagrammatic representation of Brien's concept of body column formation. Tissue marker moves proximally due to the addition of cells above the marker and the continual advancement of the basal disc in a distal direction. B. Diagrammatic representation of observations on both split- and tissue-marker movements. Tissue formation and body column formation appear as two separate phenomena (see text for explanation).

Since epidermis and gastrodermis move independently over the mesoglea, the only remaining layer that could account for the rate of formation of the body column above the split marker would be the mesoglea, although at present the nature of mesogleal production is unknown, Haynes et al. (1968) showed that some digestive cells send deep cytoplasmic attachments into the mesoglea while others show a smooth attachment. If the deep attachments are permanent in any particular segment of the mesoglea, the independent movement of the gastrodermis and epidermis would be difficult. If independent movement does reflect the cell's ability to migrate as sheets of tissue, the differences in rates of tissue- and split-marker movements could be explained by the slower production of the mesoglea structure relative to the rate of cell migration. The association of cells with the mesoglea, however, is not uniform throughout the animal. In the gastric region, not all cells are closely associated with the mesoglea. The cells are thrown up into folds or villi, so that a large number of cells are associated with a small area of mesoglea. In the peduncle, the base of each cell is in close association with the mesoglea regardless of the nature of its attachment. It is possible, therefore, for cells added by mitosis in the gastric region to contribute to folds or villi without significantly contributing to the observed gross structure of the body column that is seen above the split marker.

Mitosis as a positive force in the movement of cells may be reflected by the difference between split- and tissue-marker movements. The split marker measures the formation of body column above the marker on the apposing sides of the V-shaped split. The peduncle marker was attached to the nonapposing sides of the V-shaped split. Cells migrating on the inside length of the mesogleal structure must eventually drop off into the gastric cavity so that the only force exerted distally would be that of cell addition to the body column. The peduncle marker on the outside of the body column, however, is also under the influence of any proximal forces such as, perhaps, pulling forces resulting from the removal of tissue in the bud region. This pulling force may contribute to faster movement of the tissue marker.

These suggestions indicate a number of possible activities at the cellular level that could affect the movement of a marker at the organismal level. It is apparent that some caution must be exercised in accepting conclusions drawn from data correlating growth at the cellular and organismal levels.

Part II.   THE CONTRIBUTION OF CELL PROLIFERATION
TO NET GROWTH AND MAINTENANCE OF FORM

VI.   Methods of Analyzing Mitosis in *Hydra*

A.   SELECTION OF EXPERIMENTAL HYDRAS

1. Budding Hydras

In order to determine a general pattern of mitotic frequency and distribution for *Hydra,* individual patterns of mitosis must be determined in a number of animals. Under the same culture conditions, each *Hydra* reaches its own steady-state level where cells produced by mitosis are equal to the number of cells lost from the body column by budding or by sloughing into the gastric cavity or at the extremities. Hydras maintained in low density cultures appear larger and more uniform in size than hydras maintained in high density or mass cultures and continually possess several buds on the body column. They nevertheless maintain their own steady-state growth independent of the other animals in the culture dish.

The results of one study indicate that no precise temporal correlation between feeding and frequency of mitosis exists that can be utilized in selecting experimental hydras for mitotic analysis (Corff, 1969). Hydras (*H. oligactis*) were exposed to colchicine for 4 hours prior to fixation at different times over a 24-hour period following feeding and the mitotic index in the distal half of the body column was determined. The difference in mitotic index between two animals fixed at the same time after feeding was frequently greater than the difference between two animals fixed at different times after feeding (Table II). Campbell (1967a), however, counted mitoses in *H. littoralis* fixed at intervals over a 24-hour period and concluded that a temporal relationship exists between feeding and mitosis in epithelial and nonepithelial cells. Since mitotic patterns vary as much between individuals fixed at the same time as between animals fixed at different times, it would seem that the more important factor in obtaining a representative pattern of mitosis involves obtaining animals with a large number of mitotic figures for analysis. For example, frequently very few mitoses are found in epithelial cells of some hydras fixed at any particular time after feeding, while others fixed at the same time exhibit numerous mitotic figures. If patterns from both types are averaged, the potential for mitosis in some regions of the body column are drastically affected (Corff, 1969). This aspect will be examined more closely in a later section.

TABLE II

AVERAGE MITOTIC INDEX IN DISTAL HALF OF COLCHICINE-TREATED HYDRAS AT VARIOUS TIMES AFTER FEEDING

Colchicine incubation (hours after feeding)	Hydra	Average mitotic index (M. I.)	Difference in M. I. between hydras fixed at same time	Difference in M. I. between hydras fixed at different times
0– 4	(1)	0.578	—	(1) and (4), 0.052
4– 8	(2)	—	—	(1) and (5), 0.065
8–12	(3)	—	—	(1) and (6), 0.155
12–16	(4)	0.630	(4) and (5), 0.177	(1) and (7), 0.021
12–16	(5)	0.513	—	(1) and (8), 0.267
16–20	(6)	0.423	—	(6) and (4), 0.217
20–24	(7)	0.599	(7) and (8), 0.246	(6) and (5), 0.090
20–24	(8)	0.845	—	(6) and (7), 0.176
				(6) and (8), 0.422

2. Nonbudding Hydras

Since different mitotic patterns of frequency and distribution exist in budding hydras, is it possible to determine meaningful differences between budding and nonbudding hydras? Some nonbudding hydras can be starved for several days and still produce buds. This suggests that all hydras lacking buds should not be considered as representing a truly nonbudding state, since change from a nonbudding to a budding state implies that factors which initiate budding are still active. Consequently, mitotic frequency and distribution observed in a *Hydra* without buds may not actually represent the mitotic pattern of a truly nonbudding animal. In an attempt to obtain a morphologically and physiologically nonbudding *Hydra,* the following method has been employed (Corff, 1969). Buds which had detached from hydras maintained in low density cultures during a 24-hour period following feeding were placed in a separate bowl. After 24 hours, these buds possessed buds of their own which detached during the next 48 hours. These young buds were transferred to a separate bowl for an additional 48 hours. The hydras, which had been starved for 5 days, were then fed and considered 24 hours later as representative of a nonbudding state.

B. DETERMINATION OF MITOTIC FREQUENCY AND DISTRIBUTION

In order to evaluate the relationship of mitosis to morphogenesis and the maintenance of form, an accurate and representative mitotic pattern (frequency and distribution) must be determined. Factors directly or indirectly contributing to the mitotic pattern will therefore be examined in this section specifically to determine their effect on the mitotic pattern of a single animal and also on a general pattern formed by combining patterns from several individual hydras.

There are three major difficulties associated with mitotic analysis of *Hydra*. First, fixation necessarily imposes a static condition on an extremely dynamic system. Second, very few mitotic figures are observed in any one histological section. An estimation of mitotic frequency in a larger segment of the body column from a count of one histological section does not accurately represent the mitotic frequency in that segment and consequently may distort the picture of mitotic frequency and distribution along the body column. Third, integration of data from several hydras into a general pattern that will accurately correlate mitosis with *Hydra* morphology is difficult due to variation in length of fixed animals and variation in proportional length of the three major body regions (hypostome and tentacles, gastric, peduncle and basal disc).

The number of mitotic figures in every histological section of four hydras have been counted and recorded (Corff, 1969). With these data, several methods of counting mitotic figures and analyzing mitotic distribution can be compared and the method permitting the most accurate and and representative picture of mitotic frequency and distribution determined. Mitotic figures were counted in the epitheliomuscular cells of the epidermis and the digestive cells of the gastrodermis only. These cells (the largest cell types in *Hydra*) maintain contact with the mesoglea (von Gelei, 1924; Hess, 1961; Wood, 1961; Haynes *et al.*, 1968) and con-

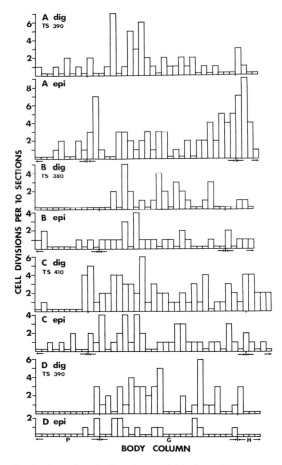

Fig. 7. Mitotic distribution along body column of 4 hydras. Mitoses counted by Method I and mitotic counts plotted by Procedure I. 1 bar = 10 histological sections; apposed arrows = bud–peduncle junction or hypostome–gastric junction. Epi, epitheliomuscular cells of epidermis; dig, digestive cells; H, hypostome region; G, gastric region; P, peduncle and basal disc region; TS, total number of histological sections. A, *Hydra* 1; B, *Hydra* 2; C, *Hydra* 3, D, *Hydra* 4.

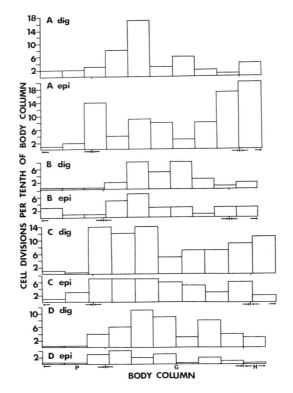

Fig. 8. Mitotic distribution along body column of 4 hydras. Mitoses counted by Method I and mitotic counts plotted by Procedure II. 1 bar = tenth of body column. Abbreviations and symbols, the same as in Fig. 7.

tribute most to the actual mass of the animal. Cnidoblasts and interstitial cells do not attach to the mesoglea and migrate within the epidermis (Lenhoff, 1959; Burnett, 1960; Diehl and Burnett, 1966). In the gastro-dermis, the majority of gland cells do not appear to be attached to the mesoglea, although a few cells may do so by a thin filament (Campbell, 1967c).

In all the counting methods to be described, the histological sections obtained from each *Hydra* were numbered consecutively from the proximal to the distal end of the animal so that cell divisions in each section could be accurately recorded and the mitotic count plotted in the proper position along the body column. The position of the bud–peduncle junction and the hypostome–gastric junction was recorded for each *Hydra*. The junction between the peduncle and the gastric region will be referred to as the bud–peduncle junction even when the hydras examined do not possess buds.

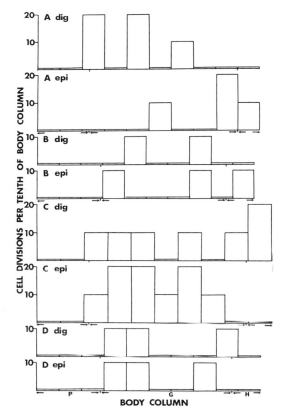

Fig. 9. Mitotic distribution along body column of 4 hydras. Mitoses counted by Method II and mitotic counts plotted by Procedure II. 1 bar = tenth of body column. Abbreviations and symbols, the same as in Fig. 7.

With Counting Method I, every histological section of four large, nonbudding hydras (fixed 24 hours after feeding) was analyzed and the mitotic figures plotted (Fig. 7). The hydras were then divided into 10 segments of equal length and the total number of mitotic figures for each body-column tenth plotted (Fig. 8). This method is time-consuming and inefficient, but provides a basis for comparison of other methods.

Another method of counting and estimating mitotic figures from a small segment of the body column (Campbell, 1967a) was used (Counting Method II) and the mitotic pattern shown in Fig. 9 obtained. With this method, mitotic frequency in each tenth of the body column is estimated from the number of mitotic figures counted in one histological section every tenth section, multiplied by 10. As seen in Fig. 9, however, this method enhances or diminishes the number of mitotic figures in each tenth

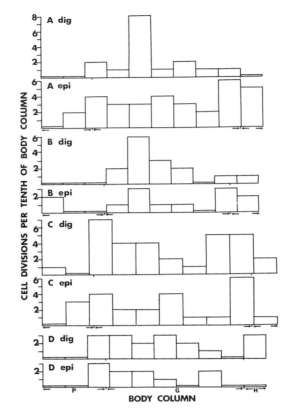

Fig. 10. Mitotic distribution along body column of 4 hydras. Mitoses counted by Method III and mitotic counts plotted by Procedure II. 1 bar = tenth of body column. Abbreviations and symbols, the same as in Fig. 7.

of body column. In addition, the relative distribution of mitoses along the column differs from the actual distribution established by direct count of all sections (Fig. 8).

Since the small number of mitotic figures in one histological section prevents an accurate estimation of mitotic frequency in a larger adjacent segment of the body column, another method of estimating mitotic frequency was used (Counting Method III). Ten consecutive sections every twenty-fifth section were counted so that ten sections at the peduncle and hypostome junctions were included in the count (Fig. 10). Comparison of the mitotic pattern obtained by this method (Fig. 10) with those obtained by a direct count (Fig. 8) and by a count of one histological section every ten sections (Fig. 9) indicates that this method (Fig. 10) provides a more representative pattern of mitotic frequency and distribution. Regions of relatively higher numbers of mitosis observed in individual mitotic patterns (Fig. 7) are retained. The total number of mitotic figures was obviously reduced, but the general distribution as seen in Fig. 8 is retained. The individual patterns obtained for the four hydras with each method were added (Fig. 11, A, B, and C). The mitotic frequency and distribution obtained with Method III compared favorably with that obtained with Method I where each section was counted (Fig. 11, A and C). The pattern obtained with Method II, however, greatly enhances or diminishes the number of mitosis in some segments. In addition, extreme regional differences in mitotic frequency such as the bud–peduncle junction are masked and the pattern seems to indicate a high number of mitoses in the peduncle.

In each 25 section segment of the body column, 40% of the sections have actually been counted. In order to estimate the total number of mitotic figures, those directly counted are multiplied by 2.5. Comparison

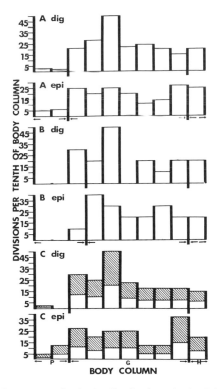

Fig. 11. A. Integrated pattern of mitotic distribution obtained by adding the mitotic counts of hydras 1–4 as shown in Fig. 8. B. Integrated pattern of mitotic distribution obtained by adding the mitotic counts of hydras 1–4 as shown in Fig. 9. C. Integrated pattern of mitotic distribution obtained by adding the mitotic counts of hydras 1–4 as shown in Fig. 10. 1 bar = tenth of body column. Abbreviations and symbols, the same as in Fig. 7.

of the number of estimated mitoses with those directly counted for each segment indicated that approximately 40% of the total possible mitoses were actually counted (Table III). The largest deviation from the expected mitotic estimate occurred where relatively few mitotic figures were directly counted.

These methods of estimating mitotic frequency have been discussed in detail in order to demonstrate how a quantitative analysis of mitosis may actually convey a misleading and nonrepresentative pattern of mitotic frequency and distribution if (1) mitotic frequency is estimated from a direct count of too small a sample of histological sections for each segment, and (2) if the total number of mitotic figures in the body column is not sufficient to establish a definite pattern.

TABLE III

COMPARISON OF THE NUMBER OF MITOSES COUNTED BY METHOD III WITH THE TOTAL NUMBER OF MITOSES DIRECTLY COUNTED IN EACH *Hydra* BY METHOD I

Hydra	Total number of mitoses (Method I)		Total number of mitoses (Method III)		Percent mitoses counted by Method III	
	Epithel.	Digestive	Epithel.	Digestive	Epithel.	Digestive
1	86	48	32	16	37	33
2	30	29	13	15	43	52
3	47	80	24	31	51	38
4	15	48	10	17	67	35

C. CORRELATION OF MITOTIC FREQUENCY AND DISTRIBUTION WITH HYDRA MORPHOLOGY

There are two possible methods for determining the potential for mitosis in a particular segment of the body column. Mitotic figures can be counted in a large number of hydras and only patterns from animals exhibiting sufficiently large numbers of mitotic figures selected. A second method employs the use of mitotic inhibitors such as colchicine to accumulate mitoses over a short period of time without detrimental effects. The response of batches of *Hydra* and individuals within a batch to colchicine (0.015–0.040%) is not always consistent. Normal intact hydras injected with colchicine (into the gastric cavity) respond more favorably and exhibit fewer effects of colchicine on the tissue than observed in regenerating hydras incubated in colchicine. The effects of colchicine on regenerating hydras are discussed in Section VIII. These effects are not usually observed in intact hydras, but if an animal responds unfavorably, it can be eliminated from the mitotic analysis after viewing a few histo-logical sections. Colchicine metaphase figures can be easily observed in the epithelial cells; no mitotic spindles are visible. In noncolchicine-treated hydras, epithelial cells undergoing mitosis appear to round up and, in the case of digestive cells, appear to lie close to the mesoglea. After colchicine treatment, some of these cells may detach from the mesoglea and, after long incubation in colchicine, the cells may be expelled com-pletely from the body column. Detachment from the mesoglea after colchicine treatment is similar to the response of fibroblasts in hanging drop cultures, where colchicine initiates withdrawal of cell processes from the substratum (Miszurski, 1949).

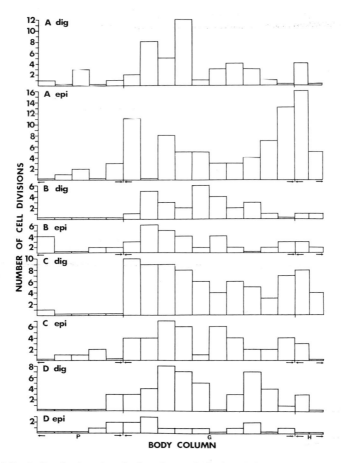

Fig. 12. Mitotic distribution along body column of 4 hydras. Mitoses counted by Method I and mitotic counts plotted by Procedure III. 1 bar = fifth in peduncle region; tenth in gastric region; half in hypostome region. Abbreviations and symbols, the same as in Fig. 7.

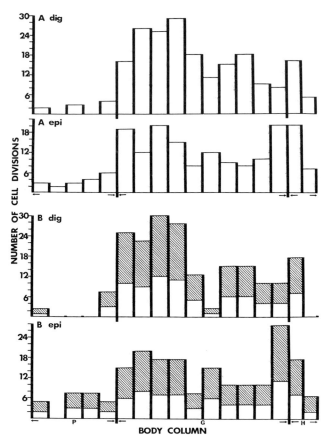

Fig. 13. A. Integrated pattern of mitotic distribution obtained by adding the mitotic counts of hydras 1–4 as shown in Fig. 12. B. Integrated pattern of mitotic distribution obtained by adding the mitotic counts of hydras 1–4 as shown in Fig. 14. 1 bar = fifth in peduncle region; tenth in gastric region; half in hypostome region. Abbreviations and symbols, the same as in Fig. 7.

Before describing the mitotic patterns obtained from both colchicine- and noncolchicine-treated hydras, a discussion of some aspects concerning the correlation of mitotic figures with *Hydra* morphology is necessary. In determining a general pattern of mitosis for budding and nonbudding hydras, patterns exhibited by individual animals must be combined. Comparison of Figs. 7, 8, and 11A indicate that combining mitotic distribution by axial tenths of the body column shifts the bud–peduncle junction proximally and obscures the sharp drop in mitosis observed in the individual *Hydra* at the peduncle and hypostome junctions. It is apparent that the larger the number of patterns integrated into one by this means, the

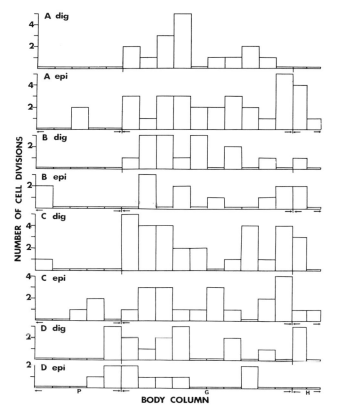

Fig. 14. Mitotic distribution along body column of 4 hydras. Mitoses counted by Method III and mitotic counts plotted by Procedure III. 1 bar = fifth in peduncle region; tenth in gastric region; half in hypostome region. In order to obtain estimated total number of mitoses for each segment, multiply the number of mitoses plotted by 2.5. Abbreviations and symbols, the same as in Fig. 7.

greater the chance of obscuring the distinct mitotic pattern in these regions and possibly the more subtle mitotic patterns within the gastric column. The following procedure was found to be practical and most representative of several alternative procedures for correlating mitotic distribution with the morphology of the intact animal.

Each *Hydra* was divided into three major body regions (hypostome, gastric, and peduncle and basal disc) by determining histologically the junction between consecutive regions of animals that had been sectioned transversely from the distal to the proximal ends of the body column. The total number of histological sections counted for each region was then divided equally: the peduncle into 5 segments; the gastric region into 10 segments; and the hypostome region into 2 segments. Thus approximately equal numbers of sections are allocated to each segment. Comparison of mitotic distribution achieved by this method (Fig. 12) with the direct count method (Fig. 7) and the tenth of body column method (Fig. 8) indicates a more representative mitotic distribution is obtained by the method employed for Fig. 12. Changes in mitotic frequency associated with morphological demarcations are not masked or obscured as frequently occurs when other procedures are used for plotting mitotic distribution. Mitotic patterns of individual animals can now be combined by averaging the same segments for each animal (Fig. 13A).

The number of mitotic figures obtained by Method III (10 consecutive sections every twenty-fifth section) were replotted for each *Hydra* using the three body region procedure (Fig. 14) and the individual patterns combined into one distribution pattern (Fig. 13B).

The results obtained by Method III indicate that if the number of mitotic figures obtained are plotted by body regions, an accurate pattern of relative distribution is achieved without counting mitotic figures in every section. This method of counting also permits an estimation of the total number of mitotic figures for each body region. The total number of mitotic figures for each segment can be estimated by multiplying the number counted for each segment by 2.5 (Table IV). This estimate was superimposed on Fig. 13A (direct count of all sections) as shown in Fig. 15. The positive and negative differences between the actual and estimated number of mitotic figures for each segment plotted, varies from bar to bar. If the differences for two adjacent segments are added, however, the total number of mitotic figures estimated for the doubled segment closely approximates the number of mitotic figures directly counted (Fig. 13A) for that same segment (Table IV).

General Comments

The total body length of each *Hydra* varies after fixation. This slight difference in length can alter the generalized pattern obtained from integrating individual patterns, since the three main regions of *Hydra* — peduncle, gastric, and hypostome — comprise different proportions of the total length in each animal. The difference in proportion of distinct regions is disregarded when each animal is divided into ten segments. Morphologically distinct regions overlap and obscure the normally sharp histological and mitotic demarcations exhibited by individual mitotic patterns. Only four hydras were used in this procedure; the combination of 18 or 20 patterns would obscure even more the mitotic pattern in morphologically distinct regions. These effects on combined patterns are eliminated by plotting mitotic distribution according to the three major body regions.

TABLE IV

COMPARISON OF NUMBER OF MITOSES COUNTED BY METHOD I AND METHOD III IN EACH SEGMENT OF BODY COLUMN

Segment No. and body region	(1) Actual number of mitoses counted by Method III		(2) Total number of mitoses estimated from Method III		(3) Total number of mitoses directly counted (Method I)		Difference between columns (2) and (3)[a]	
	Epithel.	Digestive	Epithel.	Digestive	Epithel.	Digestive	Epithel.	Digestive
Peduncle and basal disc								
1	2	1	5	3	3	2	+2	+1
2	0	0	0	0	2	0	−2	0
3	3	0	8	0	3	3	+5	−3
4	3	0	8	0	4	0	+4	0
5	2	3	5	8	6	4	−1	+4
Gastric								
1	6	10	15	25	19	16	−4	+9
2	8	9	20	23	12	26	+8	−3
3	7	12	18	30	20	25	−2	+5
4	7	11	18	28	15	29	+3	−1
5	3	5	8	13	8	18	0	−5
6	6	1	15	3	12	11	+3	−8
7	4	6	10	15	9	15	+1	0
8	4	6	10	15	8	18	+2	−3
9	4	4	10	10	10	9	0	+1
10	11	4	28	10	20	8	+8	+2
Hypostome								
1	7	7	18	18	20	16	−2	+2
2	2	0	5	0	7	5	−2	−5

[a] + = number of mitoses overestimated by use of Method III; − = number of mitoses underestimated by use of Method III.

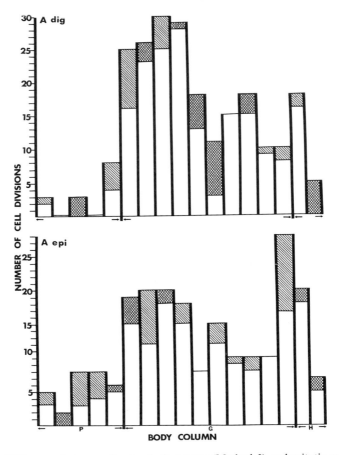

Fig. 15. Difference between direct mitotic counts (Method I) and mitotic counts estimated from Method III for 4 hydras as shown in Fig. 13. Lined segments represent number of mitotic figures overestimated by use of Method III. Cross-hatched segments represent number of mitotic figures underestimated by use of Method III.

If mitotic patterns from animals with a small number of mitoses are added or averaged with mitotic patterns from animals with a large number of mitotic figures, the actual potential for cell division at a given segment for a particular time after feeding is either enhanced or diminished. It would seem, therefore, that in formulating a generalized pattern of mitotic activity only hydras exhibiting enough cell divisions to establish a pattern of mitosis should be included in the integrated data. For example, if the mitotic distribution in epitheliomuscular cells shown in Fig. 8A and D are averaged, the frequency of mitosis in the most distal tenth segment is reduced 50%. The number of mitosis in the adjacent segment is also reduced 50%. Since, in one *Hydra*, these two segments actually contain twice the average number of mitotic figures, it would be misleading to assume that the potential for mitosis in this region is represented by the averaged data.

VII. Analysis of Growth at the Cellular Level

A. DISTRIBUTION OF MITOTIC FIGURES IN BUDDING AND NON-BUDDING HYDRAS

In general, the results obtained from a mitotic analysis of budding and nonbudding hydras support those reported in most histological studies. Fewer mitoses occur in the peduncle region than in the gastric region. No mitosis occurs in the tentacles and mitotic activity is virtually absent in the basal disc. Mitosis is rarely observed in the hypostome, especially in the distal tip. Differences in mitotic frequency and distribution within the gastric region become apparent, however, by counting and plotting mitoses according to the three body regions. When the pattern of mitotic frequency and distribution in the gastric region of budding and non-budding hydras is compared, several distinct patterns are observed in both colchicine- and noncolchicine-treated animals (Corff, 1969).

1. Nonbudding Hydras

Although mitoses occur in all segments of the gastric column, the number of mitotic figures is highest in the subhypostome region and the number decreases in a proximal direction toward the peduncle. Few mitoses are found at the peduncle junction relative to the more distal regions. Digestive cells in 3 colchicine-treated hydras were analyzed for mitotic figures (Fig. 16) and the above pattern is evident. In noncolchi-cine-treated hydras, mitotic figures were analyzed for stage of mitosis and

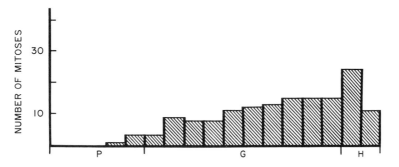

Fig. 16. Estimated mitotic distribution in three colchicine-treated, nonbudding hydras. P, peduncle and basal disc region; G, gastric region; H, hypostome region.

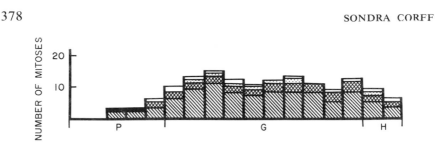

Fig. 17. Average mitotic distribution in noncolchicine-treated, nonbudding hydras. P, peduncle and basal disc; G, gastric region; H, hypostome region. Diagonal lines, spindles oriented perpendicular to longitudinal axis; cross-hatch, spindles oriented parallel to longitudinal axis; stipple, spindles oriented perpendicular to circumference; white segments, prophase.

spindle orientation. The general pattern obtained from 4 animals is shown in Fig. 17 together with spindle orientation. Because of the small number of mitotic figures, the general distribution appears somewhat uniform, but the number of mitotic figures in the subhypostome and upper gastric regions are higher relative to the proximal segments of the body column compared with budding hydras. Approximately 70% of the mitotic figures were oriented perpendicular to the longitudinal axis and 28% parallel to the longitudinal axis of the body column. The mitotic pattern obtained when colchicine- and noncolchicine-treated hydras were averaged is shown in Fig. 18. Mitoses decrease in the mid-gastric region and increase slightly in the lower gastric region, just distal to the peduncle.

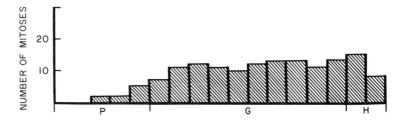

Fig. 18. General pattern of mitosis for nonbudding hydras, colchicine- and noncolchicine-treated. P, peduncle and basal disc; G, gastric region; H, hypostome region.

2. Budding Hydras

Budding hydras were divided into (1) animals that were maintained so that they always possessed several buds, and (2) animals that possessed just a Stage 0 bud (thickening of bud region and accumulation of lipid) or Stage 1 bud (bud without tentacles protruding from parent body column). Mitoses were counted in the parent body column only and not in the buds themselves. The mitotic pattern for digestive cells in 5 colchicine-

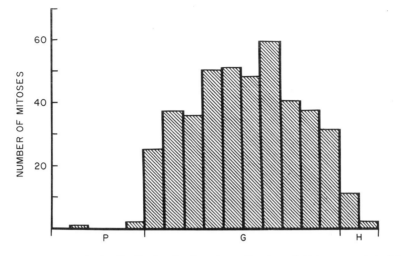

Fig. 19. Average mitotic distribution in digestive cells of 5 colchicine-treated, budding hydras. P, peduncle and basal disc region; G, gastric region; H, hypostome region.

treated hydras is shown in Fig. 19 and for digestive cells in 3 noncolchi-cine-treated hydras in Fig. 20. Fewer mitotic figures are found in the subhypostome segments relative to the rest of the gastric and budding regions in hydras possessing several buds. In hydras just initiating a new bud (Stage 0), mitoses are higher in the subhypostome than in the mid-

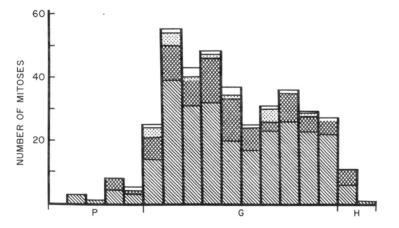

Fig. 20. Average mitotic distribution in digestive cells of noncolchicine-treated, budding hydras. P, peduncle and basal disc; G, gastric region; H, hypostome region. Diagonal lines, spindles oriented perpendicular to longitudinal axis; cross-hatch, spindles oriented parallel to longitudinal axis; stipple, spindles oriented perpendicular to circumference; white segments, prophase.

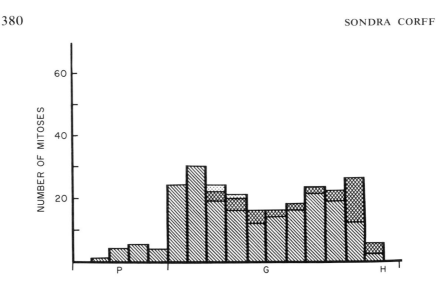

Fig. 21. General pattern of mitosis in colchicine- and noncolchicine-treated hydras (Stage 0 bud). P, peduncle and basal disc; G, gastric region; H, hypostome region. Diagonal lines, spindles oriented perpendicular to longitudinal axis; cross-hatch, spindles oriented parallel to longitudinal axis; stipple, spindles oriented perpendicular to circumference; white segments, prophase.

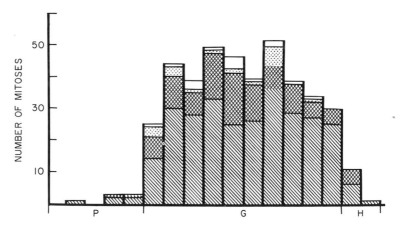

Fig. 22. General pattern of mitosis for budding hydras, colchicine- and noncolchicine-treated. P, peduncle and basal disc; G, gastric region; H, hypostome region. Diagonal lines, spindles oriented perpendicular to longitudinal axis; cross-hatch, spindles oriented parallel to longitudinal axis; stipple, spindles oriented perpendicular to circumference. white segments, prophase.

gastric region (Fig. 21) and somewhat higher than in the bud region. In hydras possessing a Stage 1 bud, mitoses are slightly higher in the bud region, relative to more distal regions of the gastric column. A general pattern for budding hydras was obtained by averaging the total number of mitoses for each segment of 5 colchicine-treated and 3 noncolchicine-treated hydras (Fig. 22). In each segment, a higher percentage of cells appear to be contributing to growth in the circumferential direction than in the longitudinal direction. The percentage of cells dividing longitudinally is higher in the region of the subhypostome and in the peduncle, although fewer mitoses were observed in these segments compared with those in the gastric column.

3. Buds

Buds, just detached from the parent body column, frequently lack a sharp demarcation between the peduncle and gastric regions when viewed

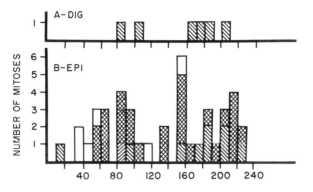

Fig. 23. Mitotic distribution in digestive and epitheliomuscular cells of a bud, just detached from parent body column. Plotted as 10 histological sections/segment. Diagonal lines, spindles oriented perpendicular to longitudinal axis; cross-hatch, spindles oriented parallel to longitudinal axis; stipple, spindles oriented perpendicular to circumference; white segments, prophase.

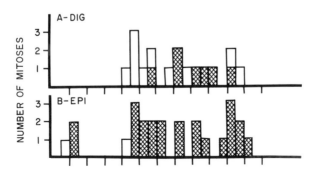

Fig. 24. Mitotic distribution in digestive and epitheliomuscular cells of a 24-hour detached bud. Plotted as 10 histological sections/segment. P, peduncle and basal disc; G, gastric region; H, hypostome region. Diagonal lines, spindles oriented perpendicular to longitudinal axis; cross-hatch, spindles oriented parallel to longitudinal axis; stipple, spindles oriented perpendicular to circumference; white segments, prophase.

under a dissecting scope. This morphology is reflected in the mitotic frequency and distribution (Fig. 23). Mitotic figures are found throughout the body column. Buds, detached for 24 hours, show the normal demarcation at both the organismal and cellular levels (Fig. 24). Mitosis in the peduncle is much lower than in the gastric region.

B. ADDITIONAL ASPECTS INFLUENCING PATTERNS OF NET GROWTH

1. Spindle Orientation

The gastric column of *Hydra* is essentially a tapered tube, which increases in circumference proximally. Mitosis must therefore contribute to growth and maintenance of form in this direction as well as to growth in length of the body column. As previously indicated, mitotic figures in noncolchicine-treated hydras were analyzed according to mitotic spindle orientation, and these data were incorporated into the mitotic patterns exhibited by each animal. The results indicate that spindle orientation is not random. Most of the spindles are oriented either parallel to the distoproximal axis of the animal or perpendicular to the axis (tangential to the circumference). Spindles oriented parallel to the longitudinal axis can be visualized by tracing the dividing cell over three to five histological sections; it would appear that they contribute to growth in length of the body column. Mitotic figures oriented tangential to the circumference of the section and perpendicular to the longitudinal axis are usually observed in one or two histological sections and appear to contribute to growth in the circumference of the body column. Almost all divisions are located close to the mesoglea between the gastrodermal folds. Daughter cells of a cell in late anaphase or telophase visually appear to be contributing to adjacent folds. In digestive cells of budding hydras, approximately 70% of the spindles were oriented perpendicular to the distoproximal axis. In nonbudding hydras, 60% of the spindles were oriented in this direction. This difference may possibly relate to the observed increase in folds and villi in the gastrodermis of budding hydras. Approximately 20–30% of the digestive cells possessed spindles oriented parallel to the distoproximal axis of the body column in both budding and nonbudding animals. A very small number of cells contained spindles oriented perpendicular to the circumference of the section (facing toward the gastric cavity). These cells may contribute to formation of villi in the gastrodermal folds.

In the epidermis, the epitheliomuscular cells exhibit a larger number of spindles oriented parallel to the longitudinal axis than to the perpendicular. Since the epidermis is not oriented in folds, spindle orientation may reflect this difference between epidermis and gastrodermis.

2. Possible Synchronous Mitotic Activity

Although no temporal correlation between feeding and mitotic frequency is apparent that could aid in selecting hydras for analysis, another aspect of mitosis in *Hydra* may influence the mitotic frequency observed in fixed animals. In addition to spindle orientation, each mitotic figure counted was recorded according to its stage in the mitotic cycle (prophase, metaphase, anaphase, or telophase). Prophase is usually the longest phase of a mitotic cycle. In 3 budding hydras, however, only 2–4% of the mitotic figures were in prophase. In other hydras, all mitotic figures in both digestive and epitheliomuscular cells were in prophase. Hydras are frequently sectioned in which no mitosis is apparent in these cell types. It seems possible that these animals were fixed during a period of mitotic inactivity which may occur between periods of synchronous mitotic activity.

It is possible to accumulate c-metaphase figures in the body column of *Hydra* by exposure to colchicine. Unless histological observations are made, it is difficult to assume that all animals in a batch are responding in a similar manner. This aspect may complicate results obtained from biochemical analysis of hydras treated with mitotic inhibitors or inhibitors of protein and nucleic acid synthesis. However, if synchronous waves of mitosis occur as suggested, they could determine the extent of effectiveness and the response of hydras to short periods of incubation in colchicine.

3. General Comments

The difference in mitotic patterns observed in budding and nonbudding hydras indicates that mitosis does not occur randomly or uniformly in the gastric column, but fluctuates in response to some controlling mechanism or process that influences the general state of growth of the entire animal. According to Burnett (1966), mitosis is controlled by the level of inducer, normally produced in the hypostome region. This suggests that in nonbudding hydras, mitosis should be higher in the subhypostome region and lower in the more proximal regions. In budding hydras, however, inducer is also produced by the buds and diffuses proximally and distally along the parent column. Mitosis would therefore be expected to occur with approximately the same frequency in the bud region and in the subhypostome. This general pattern is observed in hydras possessing Stage 0 or Stage 1 buds. In hydras that are continually budding and possess several buds at one time over a long duration, inducer levels in the low gastric and bud regions would be expected to be very high. The relatively high frequency of mitosis in these regions in animals possessing several buds supports this possibility.

VIII. Effects of Mitotic Inhibitors on Regeneration and Morphogenesis

A. COLCEMID, COLCHICINE, AND LOW TEMPERATURE

The effects of colcemid on various excised regions of the body column and their ability to subsequently induce hypostome formation has been investigated by Webster (1967) as part of a larger study on pattern regulation (Webster and Wolpert, 1966; Webster, 1966a,b, 1967). Hydras regenerating in colcemid for 24 to 48 hours formed normal monopolar forms (with delay) while some formed multiple distal structures or tentacles arranged in a random fashion. If the hypostome and tentacles were not removed, hydras exposed to colcemid for 48 hours subsequently regenerated only monopolar forms. When hypostomes from colcemid-treated hydras were grafted onto the gastric region of a host animal, their ability to induce a secondary axis was not affected by colcemid treatment. The ability of subhypostome regions to induce a secondary axis was suppressed by colcemid treatment. Webster and Wolpert explain these effects in terms of colcemid action on a postulated system for polarized regulation which includes axial gradients in time for hypostome determination, inhibition of hypostome formation, and a threshold for inhibition.

The effects of colchicine and low temperature on regeneration and morphogenesis have been examined (Corff and Burnett, 1969, 1970). Colchicine and low temperature frequently prevent completely normal regeneration of distal structures, but an unexpected result is sometimes obtained: formation of a peduncle and basal disc at the distal cut surface. Hicklin *et al.* (1969) independently reported the same phenomenon following exposure of hydras to dithiothreitol, an SH inhibitor.

How does colchicine elicit this unusual response and how does this response contribute to our understanding of the mechanisms controlling growth, morphogenesis, and the maintenance of form in *Hydra?* The first question can be answered in part by a discussion of the action of colchicine on cells. Colchicine alters or prevents normal regeneration by interfering with the processes of cell division and neurosecretion, and this interference subsequently affects morphogenesis and the maintenance of form. Part of the answer to the second question lies in the fact that hydras do not respond to colchicine in an "all or none" manner suggested by Ham and Eakin (1958) from their results and those of Sturtevant *et al.* (1951), who reported that tentacle formation was inhibited or reduced in low concentrations of colchicine. After 1–4 hours incubation in concentrations that inhibit mitosis (0.015–0.025%), hydras subsequently regenerate normally, exhibit a reduced number of tentacles or abnormally positioned tentacles, or produce a single medially placed tentacle where the hypostome normally forms. Some do not regenerate any structure at the distal end, some disintegrate, and some animals form a peduncle and basal disc at the distal end of the body column (Corff and Burnett, 1969). The frequency of each response is related to three parameters: (1) concentration of colchicine, (2) the length of exposure to colchicine, and (3) the duration of regeneration in normal culture water prior to transfer to colchicine. Colchicine action is not localized since mitoses are blocked throughout the body column, but maximum effectiveness is localized at the distal end. If a small piece of the distal end is excised following colchicine treatment, normal regeneration occurs, while the small piece of excised tissue sometimes forms a peduncle and basal disc. Normal peduncle regeneration at the proximal end of the body column is not affected by colchicine, so that its effect appears to be directed toward inhibition of distal structures. Since colchicine appears to inhibit or repress those factors responsible for normal hypostome and tentacle formation (Lentz and Barrnett, 1963; Burnett *et al.,* 1964; Lesh and Burnett, 1964, 1966; Lentz, 1965a,b), the varied morphological forms produced at the distal end after treatment with colchicine suggest that different degrees of response to colchicine occur in individual animals. At high levels of colchicine repression (related to high concentration and long exposure), distal tissue produces proximal tissue (peduncle and basal disc). If the morphological forms observed after colchicine treatment are assumed to

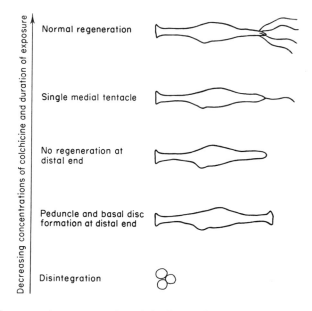

Fig. 25. Diagrammatic representation of the four main categories of response to colchicine arranged according to a morphogenetic hierarchy.

reflect lesser degrees of colchicine effectiveness, and consequently, a smaller tendency for production of proximal tissue, the observed forms can be arranged according to a morphogenetic hierarchy that indicates not only the different degrees of effectiveness of colchicine action on individual *Hydra* (repression of normal distal structures), but also the actual distoproximal distribution of tissue and form in normal animals (Fig. 25).

Both colchicine and low temperatures cause disintegration of microtubules in *Actinosphaerium* (Tilney, 1965). Hydras exposed to low temperatures sometimes form peduncle and basal disc at the distal end of the body column. This only occurs, however, when the animals are exposed to cold and then permitted to regenerate at room temperature. The other regeneration responses observed with colchicine treatment are also induced by cold treatment. Hydras maintained in the cold after excision of the hypostome and tentacles eventually regenerate normally but with some delay. The delay depends on temperature and on the length of regeneration permitted at room temperature prior to transfer to the cold. These observations are discussed more fully elsewhere in terms of morphogenesis and maintenance of form (Corff and Burnett, 1970). It is suggested that in the cold-adapted or starving *Hydra,* the factors responsible for normal polarity and morphology are in balance with the amount of growth permitted. When *Hydra* are returned to room temperature, this balance is disrupted and the potential for growth due to the higher temperature no longer corresponds with these factors.

B. OTHER INHIBITORS

1. SH Inhibitors

Hicklin *et al.* (1969) have shown that regenerating hydras incubated in dithiothreitol (DTT) can form basal discs at the distal end of the body column. They conclude from their results that basal disc formation is an autonomous process lacking any dependence on a dominant region and that distal and proximal structures are specified separately.

2. Nucleic Acid and Protein Synthesis Inhibitors

Quantitative measurements of DNA, RNA, and protein synthesis along the body column of intact and regenerating hydras have been reported (Clarkson and Wolpert, 1967; Clarkson, 1969a,b). The results indicate an essentially uniform pattern of DNA synthesis along the body column and support some studies of mitotic patterns in *Hydra* (Campbell, 1967a; Clarkson and Wolpert, 1967), which suggest that mitosis is uniform along the body column and not related to morphogenesis. There are several difficulties associated with biochemical analyses that should be noted here: (1) Excision of identical regions from hydras possessing identical states of growth would of necessity be extremely difficult due to flexibility of the body column and to growth differences indicated by mitotic pattern data. (2) ^{3}H-thymidine incorporation studies must indiscriminately measure incorporation into not only the epitheliomuscular and digestive cells, but also into interstitial cells which divide rapidly, as well as other nonepithelial types. This point seems relevant since budding and regeneration can continue in the absence of interstitial cells. Gradients of DNA, RNA, and protein synthesis along the body column may not be representative of those patterns exhibited by the epitheliomuscular and digestive cells, or to those processes involved in morphogenesis and maintenance of form. (3) Another possible difficulty stems from long periods of incubation in radioactive precursors. If mitotic frequency in different regions of the body column continually fluctuate as suggested by Corff (1969), pooling of similar regions from different animals may essentially mask differences in synthesis in different regions.

The effects of inhibitors of nucleic acid and protein synthesis have been analyzed using biochemical assays and the time required for hypostome formation from the subhypostome region or the production of a secondary axis from a host *Hydra*. Hydroxylurea delays hypostome formation but the delay is small compared to the decrease in ^{3}H-thymidine incorporation (Clarkson, 1969b), so that DNA synthesis did not appear to play a major role in hypostome initiation. Hypostome determination was delayed threefold by 5-fluorouracil; this delay was accompanied by large inhibition of label into DNA and RNA. Actinomycin D inhibited RNA synthesis and hypostome regeneration was partially inhibited. Treated hypostomes did not induce secondary axes as well as controls. Chloramphenicol inhibited protein synthesis and delayed hypostome determination in similar grafting experiments. Although all the inhibitors delayed tentacle regeneration, none was observed to cause alteration in polarity. Puromycin does not completely inhibit hypostome formation, but hypostomes from treated animals do not completely induce secondary axes in grafts.

C. Peduncle Formation, a Theory

The initiation of peduncle formation at a certain level of the body column is probably controlled by a chemical gradient. The results of histological studies, however, suggest some possible mechanisms for the actual achievement of the characteristic peduncle form and histology (Corff and Burnett, 1969). (1) The characteristic peduncle form is due to the physical detachment of cells and large clumps of villi from the mesoglea at the peduncle junction. This detachment of villi was first observed by McConnell (1929, 1931), who suggested a process of "endogenous fragmentation" to facilitate distribution of food particles to other regions of the body column. (2) The increased number of nerve cells in the peduncle and basal disc probably arise from the numerous interstitial cells present in the epidermis of the gastric region and thus account for their depletion in the peduncle. Interstitial cells are known to differentiate into nerve (Lentz, 1965b). (3) Migration and phagocytosis are two processes that may contribute to normal peduncle formation and tissue characteristics. In colchicine-treated hydras, cnidoblasts and possibly interstitial cells appear to have migrated into the gastrodermis where they are phagocytosed by the digestive cells. Colchicine treatment may therefore permit observation of an enlarged and extended step in the normal process of peduncle formation, that of cell detachment and phagocytosis. Even though villi appear to detach at the bud–peduncle region in normal hydras, one layer of digestive cells always remains. Although detachment of cells occurs in colchicine-treated animals, at least one layer of digestive cells always remains attached in all regions.

References

Brien, P. (1953). *Biol. Rev. Cambridge Phil. Soc.* **28**, 308–349.
Brien, P., and Reniers-Decoen, M. (1949). *Bull. Biol. Fr. Belg.* **82**, 293–386.
Burnett, A. L. (1959). *J. Exp. Zool.* **140**, 281–342.
Burnett, A. L. (1960). *Ann. Soc. Zool. Belg.* **90**, 269–280.
Burnett, A. L. (1961). *J. Exp. Zool.* **146**, 21–84.
Burnett, A. L. (1966). *Amer. Natur.* **100**, 165–189.
Burnett, A. L., and Garofalo, M. (1960). *Science* **131**, 160–161.
Burnett, A. L., Diehl, N. A., and Diehl, F. (1964). *J. Exp. Zool.* **157**, 227–236.
Campbell, R. D. (1967a). *Develop. Biol.* **15**, 487–502.
Campbell, R. D. (1967b). *J. Morphol.* **121**, 19–28.
Campbell, R. D. (1967c). *J. Exp. Zool.* **164**, 379–391.
Campbell, R. D. (1967d). *Trans. Amer. Microsc. Soc.* **86**, 169–173.
Clarkson, S. G. (1969a). *J. Embryol. Exp. Morphol.* **21**, 33–54.
Clarkson, S. G. (1969b). *J. Embryol. Exp. Morphol.* **21**, 55–70.
Clarkson, S. G., and Wolpert, L. (1967). *Nature (London)* **214**, 780–783.
Corff, S. C. (1969). Ph.D. Dissertation, Case Western Reserve University, Cleveland, Ohio.
Corff, S. C., and Burnett, A. L. (1969). *J. Embryol. Exp. Morphol.* **21**, 417–443.
Corff, S. C., and Burnett, A. L. (1970). *J. Embryol. Exp. Morphol.* **24**, 21–32.
Diehl, F. A., and Burnett, A. L. (1966). *J. Exp. Zool.* **163**, 125–140.
Ham, R. G., and Eakin, R. E. (1958). *J. Exp. Zool.* **139**, 35–54.
Haynes, J. F., Burnett, A. L., and Davis, L. E. (1968). *J. Exp. Zool.* **167**, 283–294.
Hess, A. A. (1961). *In* "The Biology of Hydra" (H. M. Lenhoff and W. F. Loomis, eds.), pp. 1–9. Univ. of Miami Press, Coral Gables, Florida.
Hicklin, J., Hornbruch, A., and Wolpert, L. (1969). *Nature (London)* **221**, 1268–1271.
Issajew, W. (1926). *Wilhelm Roux' Arch. Entwicklungsmech. Organismen* **108**, 1–67.
Lenhoff, H. M. (1959). *Exp. Cell Res.* **17**, 570–573.
Lentz, T. L. (1965a). *Science* **150**, 633–635.

Lentz, T. L. (1965b). *J. Exp. Zool.* **159**, 181–194.

Lentz, T. L., and Barrnett, R. J. (1963). *J. Exp. Zool.* **154**, 305–328.

Lesh, G. E., and Burnett, A. L. (1964). *Nature (London)* **204**, 492–493.

Lesh, G. E., and Burnett, A. L. (1966). *J. Exp. Zool.* **163**, 55–78.

McConnell, C. H. (1929). *Biol. Bull.* **56**, 341–346.

McConnell, C. H. (1930). *Science* **72**, 170.

McConnell, C. H. (1931). *J. Morphol.* **52**, 249–263.

McConnell, C. H. (1933a). *Biol. Bull.* **64**, 86–95.

McConnell, C. H. (1933b). *Biol. Bull.* **64**, 96–102.

McConnell, C. H. (1936). *Wilhelm Roux' Arch. Entwicklungmech. Organismen* **135**, 202–210.

Miszurski, B. (1949). *Exp. Cell Res., Suppl.* **1**, 450–451.

Shostak, S., Patel, N. G., and Burnett, A. L. (1965). *Develop. Biol.* **12**, 434–450.

Sturtevant, F. M., Sturtevant, R. P., and Turner, R. C. (1951). *Science* **114**, 241–242.

Tilney, L. G. (1965). *Anat. Rec.* **151**, 426.

Tripp, K. (1928). *Z. Wiss. Zool.* **132**, 476–525.

von Gelei, J. (1924). *Z. Zellforsch. Mikrosk. Anat.* **1**, 471–498.

Webster, G. (1966a). *J. Embryol. Exp. Morphol.* **16**, 105–122.

Webster, G. (1966b). *J. Embryol. Exp. Morphol.* **16**, 123–141.

Webster, G. (1967). *J. Embryol. Exp. Morphol.* **18**, 181–197.

Webster, G., and Wolpert, L. (1966). *J. Embryol. Exp. Morphol.* **16**, 91–104.

Wood, R. L. (1961). *In* "The Biology of Hydra" (H. M. Lenhoff and W. F. Loomis, eds.), pp. 51–67. Univ. of Miami Press, Coral Gables, Florida.

Yao, T. (1945). *J. Exp. Biol.* **21**, 150–155.

PART VIII

THE MESOGLEA OF *HYDRA*

Any histological description of *Hydra* written within the past five years will describe the mesoglea or mesolamella of *Hydra* as being that little strip of "stickum" that holds the two cell layers together. The reading of the following section will show that Dr. Hausman has not only discovered that the mesoglea has a ladderlike, collagenous structure heretofore undiscovered, but that this structure may be basic in cell movement, budding, reproduction, regeneration, and cell sloughing at the extremeties. His studies on the basic structure of the mesoglea, in the editor's view, will never allow a developmental biologist to view *Hydra* or many other organisms again without considering the role of that *"ground mat"* to which all cells bind or which they employ as a pathway of locomotion.

CHAPTER 16

The Mesoglea

ROBERT E. HAUSMAN

I. Mesoglea as Connective Tissue

A. DEFINITION

Mesoglea is the connective tissue of the three most primitive surviving metazoan phyla: the sponges, the coelenterates, and the ctenophores. A specific descriptive definition is difficult to formulate because the size, structure, and organization of mesogleas are so variable. Thickness alone, may vary from 1 μ in some hydras to 30 cm in some anemones. This diversity is expressed in the number of alternate terms for mesoglea: mesolamella, mesenchyme, and collenchyme: These terms attempt to differentiate among the mesogleas of various species on the basis of the three variables recognized by light microscopists: the presence or absence of cells, the presence or absence of fibers, and the thickness of the mesoglea itself. Hyman (1940) considered a mesolamella to be a thin, non-fibrous, noncellular layer, a mesenchyme as a thick gel with a fiber matrix and wandering cells, and a collenchyme as a thick gel with organized sublayers of fibers and organized cells.

While these terms are more descriptive of the tissue cytology than the general term "mesoglea," they are unsatisfactory in the light of electron microscopy studies which emphasize the common structural organization of all connective tissues. In fact, there is very little to differentiate mesoglea structurally from the connective tissue of higher forms, and the limitation of the term to these three acoelomate phyla seems arbitrary. It might better be applied to all organisms with a single unspecialized type of connective tissue. However, since the nomenclature for connective tissues is presently in a state of flux, the term is best retained with the understanding that it refers to a structurally heterogeneous group of tissues in these three phyla, which, along with all other animal connective tissues, share a few general functions.

B. FUNCTION

Though mesoglea may contain wandering cells, it is basically an extra-cellular material. It lies between two more-organized layers of cells (epithelia), either in the walls of sponges or between the epidermis and gastrodermis of coelenterates and ctenophores. As an intercell-layer material, mesoglea has obvious skeletal-supportive potential, and probably its most widely recognized and agreed-on function is that of a skeleton (Hyman, 1940; Chapman, 1953a,b). In this role it may be augmented by inorganic material, as in the spicules of sponges, or by configuration specializations, such as the septa of anemones.

The sessile, filter-feeding sponges show little, if any, muscular movement, but in the two more active phyla the mesoglea performs a second function related to its supportive role; it is a place of insertion for the longitudinal and circular muscles (Hyman, 1940; Batham and Pantin, 1951; Holmes, 1950; Chapman, 1953a,b; Robson, 1957; Hess *et al.,* 1957; Shostak *et al.,* 1965). In this capacity it plays a rather important role in the muscular movement of the organism. Especially in the sea anemones, the thick mesoglea has definite elastic properties (Bouillon and Vandermeersche, 1956) and acts as a combination tendon–ligament antagonist in its relation to muscle. Chapman (1953b) was able to demonstrate, using *Calliactis* mesoglea, that the viscous–elastic properties of the anemone's body wall were all clearly shown by the mesoglea alone, without the muscle cells. Robson (1957), working with *Metridium,* considered the mesoglea–muscle as a unit system for contraction and relaxation. In many anemones this close degree of interaction might be a necessity since at some points in the body wall the circular muscles are either absent or too sparse to effectively stretch the longitudinals. Instead, the elastic mesoglea serves as the antagonist. Chapman (1970) suggested mesoglea as the force involved in reextending scyphistoma tentacles. He raised the question in *Hydra,* specifically, whether the muscle insertion actually transmits force to the mesoglea as a skeleton, or, as he maintains, acts as a complicated hydraulic system reponding to a continuous sheath of contractile myonemes. Presumably, in this latter scheme, the complicated cell insertions might only serve to attach the two epithelia to the mesoglea.

The question cannot be answered on morphological evidence alone, and more work on the physiology of mesoglea–muscle, especially in *Hydra,* needs to be done.

These two functions, support and muscle insertion-antagonist, are universal for mesoglea and probably constitute its evolutionary raison d'etre. However, there are numerous other roles that have been proposed for mesoglea and a few that have been impressively demonstrated in particular organisms. Whether they are properties of all mesogleas remains to be demonstrated.

The mesoglea has frequently been implicated in food storage or transfer. De Beer and Huxley, in 1924, demonstrated that the mesoglea of the scyphozoan *Aurelia* decreases greatly in size when the animal is starved. They claimed that the mesoglea served as a reserve food source which the animal digested as needed. Hatai (1917) claimed changes occurred in the mesoglea of *Cassiopeia xanachana* with starvation. The question that must be asked of these observations is whether it is mesogleal material being broken down or a reserve material, stored in the mesoglea temporarily, being withdrawn. Burnett (1959) demonstrated that *Hydra* has glycogen present in its mesoglea 6 hours after feeding, but noted its subsequent disappearance and suggested it was being transferred from the gastrodermis to the epidermis and was not stored in the mesoglea. Gauthier (1963) described particles on the ultrastructural level which she considered to be glycogen and which disappeared after starvation. This observation, however, has not been subsequently confirmed (see Section II,A).

It is clear, then, that the mesoglea plays some role in food transfer, but this may be a purely passive one; a fact made necessary by its location between the energy-ingesting cells and the energy consumers. The question of storage requires further investigation. However, I suspect that this is a function which will vary greatly from one species to another.

Since mesoglea is the prime extracellular material of coelenterates, it most likely serves the filter and ionic "sink" roles proposed for other extracellular materials (Bennett, 1963). Macklin (1967) has presented evidence for large ionic potentials across the mesoglea of *Hydra*. This is an area that requires further work and which might go far in explaining the enigma of osmoregulation in the freshwater *Hydra*.

Mesoglea plays a role in cell movement. Shostak *et al.* (1965), also working with *Hydra,* demonstrated that the two cell layers move in sheets independently of each other over the mesoglea, and concluded that the mesoglea served as a substratum for cell movement. Subsequently, I have suggested that the mesoglea may play a more active role and actually exert a control over the movement of cells (Hausman and Burnett, 1969, 1970, 1972; Burnett and Hausman, 1969).

Shostak *et al.* (1965) also observed that the isolated mesoglea of *Hydra* was sticky and suggested it was an intercellular adhesive material. This suggestion has been confirmed by the observation that besides forceps and glass needles, the mesoglea will adhere to isolated cells (Hausman and Burnett, 1969).

A material having the properties of a cell substratum and an inter-cellular adhesive material is not as improbable as it might sound because of the various cell specializations and variety of cell–mesoglea inter-actions. These will be described below and hopefully reconcile the apparent contradiction.

In summary, then, all mesogleas play a structural role and serve as the basis for muscle attachment–antagonist and potential movement. Some mesogleas may store food reserves or passively function as a food dis-persion system. *Hydra* mesoglea plays a complex role in cell adhesion and movement.

While few of these properties of mesoglea are surprising, and some might even seem like a belaboring of the point, the localization of all these functions by a single, often very thin, tissue inspires a certain amount of admiration. An analogy might be if your liver, subcutaneous fat, tendons, and skeleton were all one organ, a few millimeters in thickness underlying your skin.

C. *Hydra* SPECIFICALLY

The mesoglea underlying the epidermis of *Hydra* is a thin, 0.5–3.0 μ acellular material that extends throughout most of the animal. It is thicker in the peduncle (Hess *et al.,* 1957; Noda, 1968; Hausman and Burnett, 1969) and thinner in the tentacles (Davis and Haynes, 1968; Burnett and Hausman, 1969). While the relative proportions remain constant in a relaxed *Hydra,* the thickness of the entire mesoglea or local areas may be greatly changed by muscle contraction (Hyman, 1940).

In the body column of *Hydra* the mesoglea is always present between the two cell layers (except for short times during developmental events, as will be discussed later), but at the proximal and distal ends of the body column there are certain areas where it is conspicuously absent. Proximally, the mesoglea is absent from the aboral pore at the center of the basal disc. Distally, the mesoglea is absent, of course, from the mouth, and, surprisingly, from the tips of the tentacles (Burnett and Hausman, 1969). When it can be isolated with tentacles intact, the mesoglea retains the form of a perfect *Hydra.*

The elasticity of *Hydra* mesoglea can be dramatically demonstrated by stretching the isolated mesoglea with microforceps or glass needles. It will stretch six to seven times it normal length and twice it width before pulling free or tearing, and return to approximately its normal length. Presumably, this does not damage the mesoglea because an intact *Hydra* can frequently be observed to extend to this length. No quantitative work has been done on the elasticity of *Hydra* mesoglea, but Chapman (1953b), using *Calliactis* mesoglea, found the immediate elastic expansion to be nearly directly proportional to load except for very small loads.

Hydra mesoglea is apparently unaffected by short exposures to strong base (pH 12), but exposure to acid below pH 4 causes a shrinkage of both *Hydra* (Hausman, 1968) and *Calliactis* (Chapman, 1953b) mesoglea by about one third. After dehydration in air and subsequent rehydration, *Hydra* mesoglea is destroyed.

D. PLACE IN THE CONNECTIVE TISSUE HIERARCHY

According to most presently accepted evolutionary hierarchies, *Hydra* is among the most primitive coelenterates and consequently among the most primitive metazoans in the mainline of animal evolution (Hyman, 1940). Only in this class, the Hydrozoa, is the mesoglea devoid of cellular elements (mesolamella).

In the anthozoans the mesoglea consists of a gelatinous mesenchyme with fibers and wandering ameboid cells (mesenchyme). In the scyphozoans, the true jellyfish, the cells are often confined to the outer and inner edges of the mesoglea and spaced at orderly distances; layers of fibers are also present. Hyman (1940) terms this a collenchyme. The mesoglea of ctenophores is also of collenchyme complexity.

Though not properly a mesoglea, the mesenchyme of flatworms is often cytologically indistinguishable from the mesoglea of anemones. With the annelids, connective tissue begins to split up into the various classes that we recognize in the vertebrates: cartilage, tendons, blood vessel binding, bone matrix, and basement membrane (basal lamina).

The relation of mesoglea to higher metazoan connective tissue has been speculated on for at least the past century. Krukenberg, in 1880, claimed that the mesoglea of *Aequorea* and *Rhizostoma* yielded neither gelatin nor mucin and so was chemically unrelated to other connective tissues. His results notwithstanding, by the early 1950's it was recognized that mesoglea was structurally and chemically very similar to vertebrate connective tissue (Chapman, 1953a; Grimstone *et al.*, 1958; Burnett and Hausman, 1969). As we have previously mentioned, much of this evidence comes from a common ultrastructural pattern. Recently, chemical similarities have been demonstrated between invertebrate and vertebrate connective tissue (Hunt, 1970).

Once this relationship was established, the speculation that mesoglea might be the primeval connective tissue was inevitable. Chapman (1953a) speculated that the study of coelenterate mesoglea "might shed some light on the origin and composition of connective tissue in general."

The particular connective tissue that mesoglea is most like in structure is basement membrane (basal lamina). Weiss (1957) noted similarities between mesoglea and the basement membrane of amphibian larvae. Fawcett (1961) commented that the mesoglea of *Hydra* might be a useful place to obtain information that could be carried over to the study of basement membranes. Recent papers on basement membranes in other organisms demonstrate an ultrastructure that is virtually identical to *Hydra* mesoglea (Dilly, 1969).

II. Physicochemical Structure of Mesoglea

A. Ultrastructure

Hydra mesoglea contains no apparent structures when viewed in paraffin sections under the light microscope, except for the numerous cell insertions. Hadzi (1909) interpreted these as cytoplasmic processes traversing the mesoglea. Only with the use of the electron microscope was *Hydra* mesoglea seen to have structure.

1. Cell Insertions

Hess *et al.* (1957) and Hess (1961) demonstrated that Hadzi's cytoplasmic processes were not regions of cytoplasmic continuity between the two cell layers, but always contained two apposing cell membranes. What Hadzi saw were deeply inserted processes of epitheliomuscular or digestive cells which may terminate in the mesoglea (Fig. 1), or on another process (Fig. 2), or on the cell membrane of the other layer.

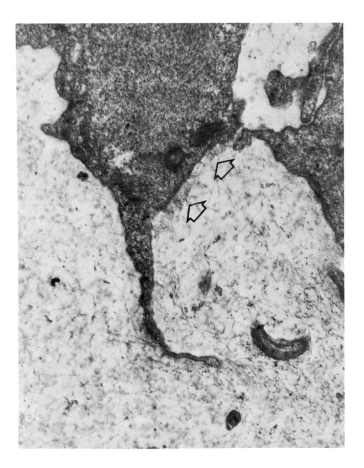

Fig. 1. Electron micrograph of *Hydra pseudoligactis* showing the process of an epitheliomuscular cell inserted into the mesoglea. The mesogleal fibrils at the cell membrane (arrows) are suggestive of mesoglea synthesis ($\times$ 39,000). (From Hausman and Burnett, 1972.)

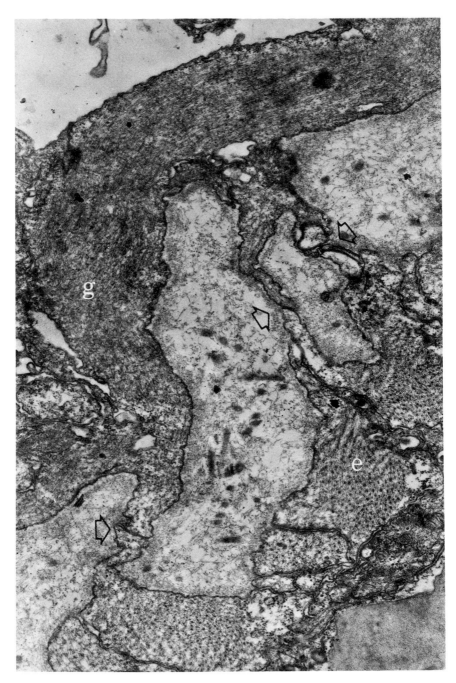

Fig. 2. Cytoplasmic elongations of the epidermis (e) and gastrodermis (g) extend into the mesoglea sometimes forming contacts (arrows). The dense bodies within the mesoglea are the electron-dense structures characteristic of *Hydra pirardi* ($\times$ 22,000). (From Davis and Haynes, 1968.)

Haynes *et al.* (1968) demonstrated that the myonemes of the epitheliomuscular cells do not run into the processes inserted into the mesoglea,
and, when cut in cross-section, the insertions appear highly branched.
Haynes *et al.* describe these as a series of arching loops which link the
base of the cell to the mesoglea (Fig. 3). A single cell may have as many
as five or six insertions into the mesoglea. This extreme specialization of
both cell layers, but especially the epidermis, in their contacts with the

Fig. 3. Longitudinal section through the bases of several epitheliomuscular cells. Cell
processes extend into the mesoglea but the myonemes (my) do not extend into the processes.
Note that most of the mesogleal fibrils are cut in cross-section (× 12,000). (From Haynes
et al., 1968.)

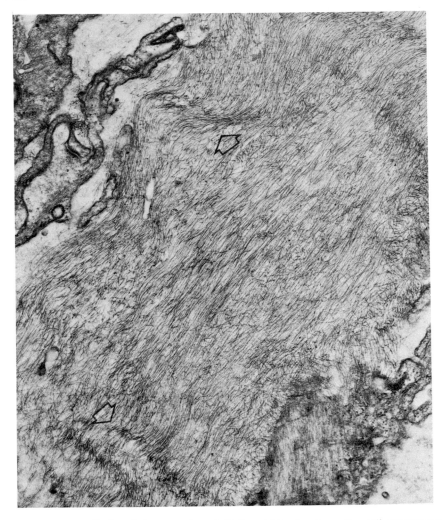

Fig. 4. Dense fibrils of the mesoglea of *Hydra viridis* showing a "wavy" appearance (arrows). In this section of the fibrils are closely associated with the epidermis (e) and absent immediately adjacent to the gastrodermis (g) (× 23,000). (From Davis and Haynes, 1968.)

mesoglea demonstrates quite impressively the importance of the mesoglea as a base for cell attachment.

2. Fibrils

The most conspicuous elements of mesogleal ultrastructure are small fibrils (Davis and Haynes, 1968). The distribution of the fibrils throughout the mesoglea is variable, as is their orientation. They may be compacted in bundles and oriented along one plane (Figs. 4 and 5), or sparsely

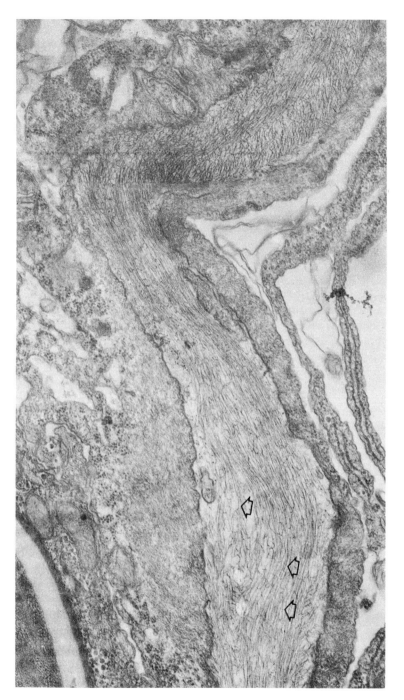

Fig. 5. Slightly oblique section through the mesoglea of a relaxed animal (*H. viridis*). The fibrils are arranged more orderly than those in Fig. 6. Many of the fibrils appear "beaded" (arrows). (× 30,600). (From Davis and Haynes, 1968.)

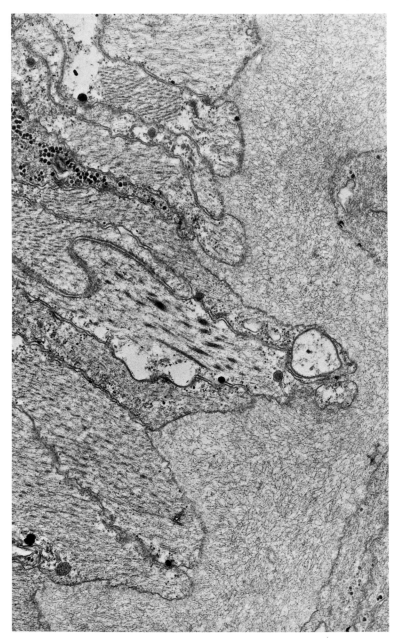

Fig. 6. Low magnification electron micrograph showing fibrils randomly dispersed in the amorphous ground substance (× 19,800). (From Davis and Haynes, 1968.)

distributed and randomly oriented (Figs. 6 and 7). These fibrils had been observed earlier and described as a distinct fibrous background (Hess *et al.*, 1957; Hess, 1961), as fine oriented filaments (Slautterback and Fawcett, 1959), as a meshwork of randomly arranged filaments (Gauthier, 1963; Wood, 1961; Noda, 1968), and as 60–80 Å fibers by Haynes *et al.* (1968).

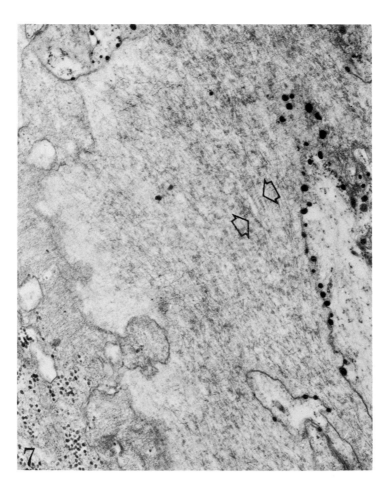

Fig. 7. Randomly arranged fibrils, a few of which appear "banded" (arrows) as distinct from the "beading" seen in Fig. 5. The banded fibrils are approximately 400 Å thick and the periodicity of the banding is approximately 300 Å ($\times$ 22,000). (From Davis and Haynes, 1968.)

There is no doubt that all these authors are describing the same structures. Better resolution has come with improvements in electron micrography technique, particularly fixation. As Davis and Haynes (1968) point out, glutaraldehyde fixation followed by osmium postfixing preserves the fibrils better than fixation osmium alone.

I have been referring to these structures as fibrils; previously, they have been called filaments and Davis and Haynes (the definitive work to date) have called them fibers. The rationale for each of these names can be easily understood in the context of the state of knowledge at that time. For the same reason I suggest fibrils as the name for these structures. We now know there is at least one higher level of organization (to be discussed below) which would logically be called fibers (Hausman and Burnett, 1969). There is a precedent for this in *Metridium* (Grimstone *et al.,* 1958).

Because of the variable orientation of the fibrils, they may appear in section as side view or end-on view. In most sections, the majority of fibrils run parallel to the oral–aboral axis of *Hydra* (Davis and Haynes, 1968), and would therefore appear in side view in a longitudinal section of *Hydra*. However, contraction results in a disorientation of the fibrils, and sections through contracted animals demonstrate a disordered pattern (Davis and Haynes, 1968).

Davis and Haynes describe two types of fibrils, a small threadlike fibril with a diameter of 70–90 Å and of indeterminate length with frequent swellings, resulting in a beaded appearance, and a thicker (360–450 Å in diameter) fibril which exhibits a periodicity of 300 Å (Fig. 7). The 70–90 Å fibril is much more common. They also describe short, thin fibrils extending from the plasma membrane of epitheliomuscular cells into the mesoglea (Fig. 8). In some sections they note that these fibrils are replaced by a moderately dense amorphous material. We have suggested that both these areas are a localization of mesoglea synthesis (Hausman and Burnett, 1972) and they will be dealt with under that heading.

3. Particles

All investigators have reported the mesoglea as granular or identified large particles in it. Gauthier (1963) described these as 300–400 Å in diameter and suggested they were glycogen because they disappeared when the animal was starved. With glutaraldehyde and osmium, Davis and Haynes (1968) described these same particles as 450 Å in diameter and of low density (Fig. 9). They do not appear in all sections.

The question of whether they are glycogen or not remains unanswered. They are too large to be glycogen β-granules, whose size ranges up to

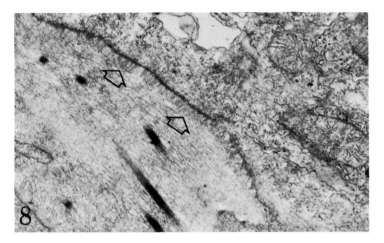

Fig. 8. Bundles of short fibrils (arrows) extending into the mesoglea from the base of an epitheliomuscular cell. These fibrils are perpendicular to the oral–aboral axis and may be indicative of fibril synthesis. Note also the electron-dense bodies characteristic of *H. pirardi* (× 22,000). (From Davis and Haynes, 1968.)

300 Å, but could be α-granules. However, in most uranyl acetate–lead citrate preparations they do not appear electron-dense enough to be glycogen.

4. Other Materials

Bacteria are an occasional feature of mesoglea (Fig. 10) and are sometimes present in large numbers (Davis and Haynes, 1968). Their relationship with *Hydra* is unknown but can be presumed to be analogous to that of the intracellular bacteria.

Davis and Haynes examined the mesoglea of four species of *Hydra* in section: *H. viridus, H. oligactis, H. pseudoligactis,* and *H. pirardi.* The mesogleal ultrastructure of the first three was virtually identical, but *H. pirardi* mesoglea contained an additional moiety not found in the others. These are extremely electron-dense structures (Figs. 2, 11–13) approximately 790 Å in diameter and are sometimes found attached to the bases of epitheliomuscular cells (Figs. 12 and 13). Hausman and Oschman (1971) have observed electron-dense structures of similar size in the isolated mesoglea of *H. pseudoligactis.* Davis and Haynes noted a fibrous material associated with the outer limits of these dense structures; in isolated mesoglea they appear to be made up of small fibrils tightly compacted together. Noda (1968) observed these same structures

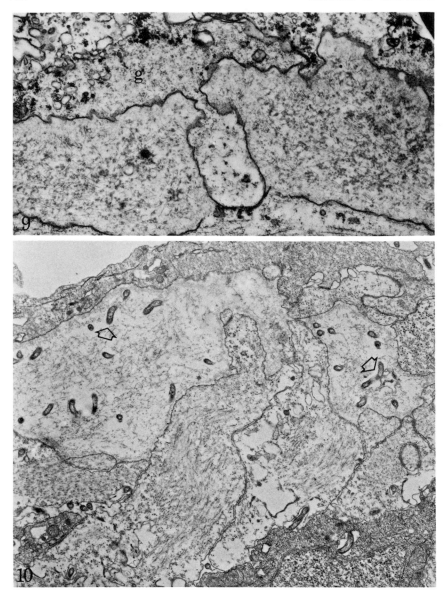

Fig. 9. Small low-density droplets approximately 450 Å in diameter are scattered throughout the mesoglea of *H. viridis*. The fibrils appear disorganized. A large cell extension crossed the mesoglea from the gastrodermis (g) (× 16,500). (From Davis and Haynes, 1968.)

Fig. 10. Low magnification electron micrograph of *H. pseudoligactis* showing bacteria (arrows) in the mesoglea. These have been observed in all species of *Hydra* (× 11,550). (From Davis and Haynes, 1968.)

in *Hydra magnipapillata*. He called them tubular bodies and described them as 600 Å in diameter and at least 1.3 μ long. Often, they were enclosed within a fibrous covering.

The mesoglea sometimes contains a material that appears lipidlike. It is contained in droplets which may be as large as 0.6 μ in diameter and are frequently associated with membranes (Fig. 14). The function of either of these moieties, the lipid material or the tubular bodies, is totally unknown.

Finally, there is the electron-lucent background material in which all these structures are embedded. On the basis of light microscopy histochemistry, this material has been theorized to be a mucopolysaccharide; this subject will be dealt with below.

B. ULTRASTRUCTURE VS. MICROSTRUCTURE (PROLOGUE)

As we begin to talk about the structure of *Hydra* mesoglea as seen under the light microscope, it will become apparent that there is a large, presently difficult-to-bridge gap between the structures seen at the two levels, light vs. electron microscope. With this in mind, it is, perhaps, pertinent to consider the interpretation and limitations of both electron and light microscopy as applied to *Hydra* mesoglea.

All ultrastructural studies, with the exception of some preliminary work (Hausman and Oschman, 1971), have been on the thin 0.5–3.0 μ in diameter cross-sections of mesoglea cut at less than a few hundred angstroms. Identical "thick" sections stained with methylene blue and observed under the light microscope demonstrate no mesoglea structure. The structures described below in isolated *Hydra* mesoglea virtually never appear in sections cut at 4 μ for light microscopy, although one recent chance section out of 1500 of the author's does show the structures seen in isolated mesoglea.

As an extracellular connective tissue, mesoglea is of a class of tissues that have been particularly refractile to traditional electron stains. Uranyl and lead acetate, lead citrate, and potassium permananate have been used in the past on *Hydra* and other tissues with very little success in staining polysaccharides. Perhaps new electron-staining techniques for polysaccharides (Rambourg and Leblond, 1967; Rothman, 1969) will result in greater agreement with light microscopy.

C. MICROSTRUCTURE (LIGHT MICROSCOPY)

The fibrous nature of coelenterate mesoglea was recognized as early as 1879 by the Hertwigs. Since then, numerous authors have described light

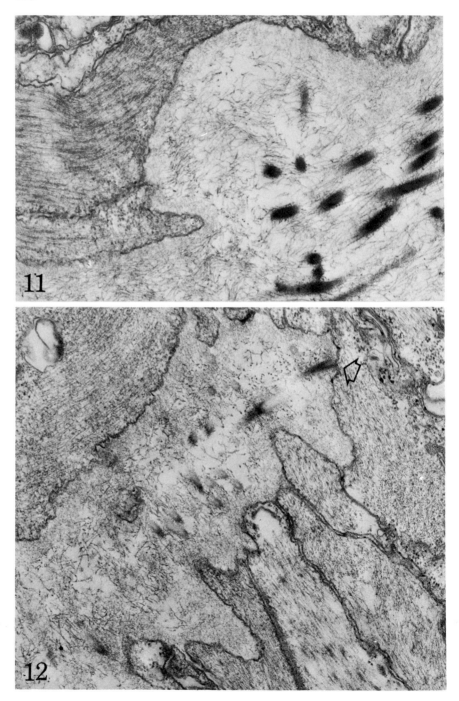

microscopal fibers in various scyphozoans and anthozoans (Chapman, 1953a; Batham, 1960; Mackie and Mackie, 1967; Torelli, 1953, 1969; Robson, 1957; Grimstone *et al.,* 1958). Chapman noted that mesogleas like "connective tissues generally, consist of a ground substance in which are present more or less independent cells and more or less independent and clearly defined fibers."

Hydrozoan polyps (of which *Hydra* is one) were thought to be anomalous in two of three ways. We have already noted that their mesoglea is acellular, and until recently it was thought to be nonfibrous. Hyman (1940) considered *Hydra* mesoglea a thin, noncellular cement, and proposed it be called a mesolamella, to differentiate it from true mesogleas.

Holmes (1950), in an intriguing paper, suggested that the mesoglea of the green *Hydra* (*H. viridis*) contained muscle fibers embedded in it. He noted:

> The mechanics of the behaviour of hydra, with its extremely thin mesoglea and enormous powers of elongation, are likely to show differences from the conditions in such higher forms as the anemones of which we now have a good deal of information. It is possible that the possession of a mesoglea with a fiber structure of varying stability, elastic, or even contractile, is a part of the basis of these differences.

Holmes was mistaken — it is the higher forms that have epidermal muscle fibers totally embedded in their mesoglea — and his suggestion of buried muscle fibers was not supported by subsequent investigation. Hess *et al.* (1957) specifically noted that all muscle fibers in *Hydra* were located within the cells, separated by a cell membrane from the mesoglea, and no subsequent electron microscopy has demonstrated isolated muscle fibers embedded in the mesoglea of *H. viridis* (Davis and Haynes, 1968). Nevertheless, Holmes' intuition was on the right track and much of his last statement may still be true.

The microstructure described below is seen in *Hydra* mesoglea isolated by a nonchemical procedure and stained with a variety of general protein and polysaccharide stains (Hausman and Burnett, 1969). As mentioned previously, none of this structure is apparent in fixed, sectioned paraffin material.

Fig. 11. Longitudinal section through the mesoglea of *H. pirardi* showing the electron-dense structures in longitudinal section. They have a fibrous material associated with them and frequently appear to be cut tangentially as they pass through the plane of section ($\times$ 30,600). (From Davis and Haynes, 1968.)

Fig. 12. Longitudinal section through *H. pirardi* mesoglea shows electron-dense material attached to the base of an epitheliomuscular cell (arrow). This electron-dense material is approximately 750 Å thick ($\times$ 30,000). (From Davis and Haynes, 1968.)

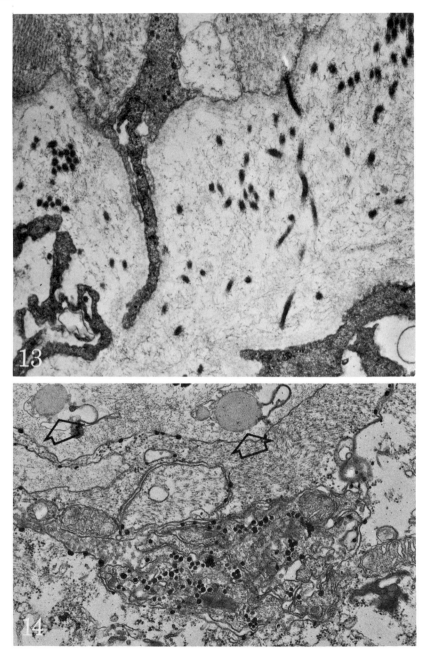

1. Gel

The bulk of the mesoglea consists of a structureless gel which is refractile to staining with most histological stains. This is probably because of its high water content and consequent low concentration of potentially stainable material (Hausman and Burnett, 1969).

2. Fibers

Embedded in the gel is an extensive rectolinear* fiber system which extends throughout the mesoglea (Figs. 15–17), though its state of organization may be affected by development changes, as we shall see below. Since the structure of the fiber system is not rigid, its dimensions are variable. The larger fibers vary in thickness, from 0.3 to 1.0 μ, depending on the stretch of the mesoglea and location in the body column. The fibers in the peduncle are generally thicker. The edges of the largest (peduncle or stretched) fibers are not sharply delineated, giving the impression that they are not qualitatively distinct from the gel. The interfiber distance between the oral–aboral fibers is 2 μ in the stained preparations. The spacing of the circular (around the body column) fibers is more variable, and in some areas on some mesogleas they are absent. The length of the fibers is also variable, but individual fibers may be traced more than three quarters of the way along the body column.

In regions of the body column (see next section) these thick, very long fibers do not appear; instead, short 0.3 μ diameter fibers, randomly oriented, fill the mesoglea as a matrix (Fig. 18). These fibers are particularly evident under Nomarsky interference–contrast illumination. Where the larger fiber system is present, the smaller fibers are aligned parallel to, and are usually part of the larger fibers (Figs. 19 and 20). With Nomarsky illumination, the large fibers are not evident. This suggests that they are of nearly equal index of refraction to the gel.

The interfiber distance of the short fibers seen with Nomarksy illumination is 1.5 μ instead of the 2.0 μ seen in stained material. The difference, however, is due to the difference in the state of the tissue. Nomarsky material is examined unfixed in water, while stained material is fixed, dehydrated, and mounted before being examined.

---

*The adjective "rectolinear" was suggested to the author by Dr. S. A. Wainwright and seems particularly useful for describing a primarily linear fiber system with cross-fibers at right angles.

Fig. 13. Cross-section through *H. pirardi* mesoglea showing an electron-dense structure attached to the base of an epitheliomuscular cell. It is approximately 790 Å thick (× 22,000). (From Davis and Haynes, 1968.)

Fig. 14. Lipidlike droplets in *H. oligactis* mesoglea ranging up to 0.6 μ in diameter (arrows), often associated with membranes (× 22,000). (From Davis and Haynes, 1968.)

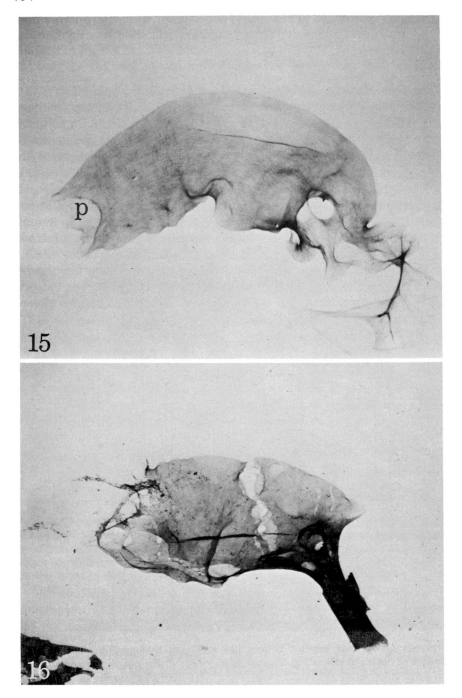

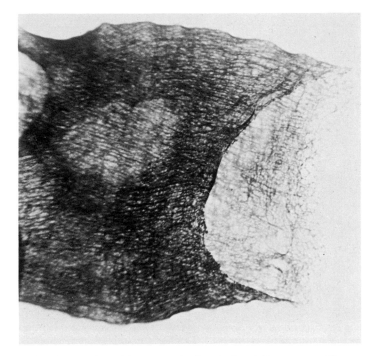

Fig. 17. Isolated mesoglea with an organized oral–aboral fiber system. The cut perpendicular to the oral–aboral axis is the result of a preisolation excision of the base (PAS technique; × 160) (From Hausman and Burnett, 1969.)

3. Rings

Spaced along the fibers of the larger fiber system in stained material are 0.7 μ diameter particles. They are irregularly spaced along the fibers (Fig. 21), but never appear alone in the gel without a fiber. With Nomarsky illumination, in fresh tissue, these appear as rings of 1.0 μ outside diameter and 0.3 μ inside diameter (Fig. 20). Only when the smaller fibers are disorganized do the rings appear alone in the gel. When the larger fiber system appears broken down in stained mesoglea, an occasional particle will appear as a ring, demonstrating that the particles are rings condensed by fixation (Fig. 22). These may be points of cell attachment.

Fig. 15. Low-power light micrograph of the isolated mesoglea of *H. pseudoligactis*. The basal disc has torn off at the peduncle (p) (PAS technique; × 54).

Fig. 16. Low-power micrograph of isolated mesoglea demonstrating an extremely dark-staining peduncle. The tentacles have been lost in the process of isolation (PAS technique; × 40).

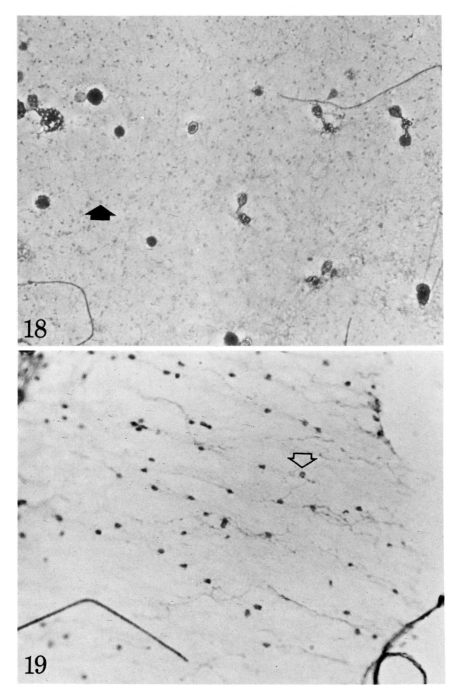

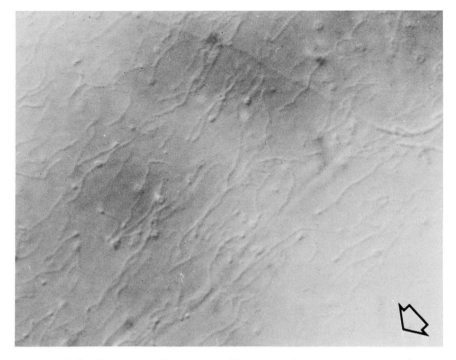

Fig. 20. Isolated mesoglea with Nomarsky illumination showing the short 0.3 μ diameter fibers aligned in the direction of the arrow, parallel to the oral–aboral axis of the animal. The 0.7 μ diameter rings are also present. The large, thick line is a discharged nematocyst thread ($\times$ 2100).

I had previously suggested that the spaces between the larger fibers (Fig. 23) were holes left by cell processes inserted in the mesoglea. Recent improvements in mesoglea isolation technique (Hausman and Burnett, 1972) and work on unfixed mesoglea with Nomarsky interference–contrast optics have changed the size estimate to 0.6 μ–2.0 μ in diameter and have cast some doubt on the original interpretation. There is no

Fig. 18. Isolated mesoglea from the gastric region of a *Hydra* fed 5 times weekly (so budding is continuous) under phase-contrast optics. The 0.7 μ particles (rings) and short fibers can be seen (arrow). An organized fiber pattern is absent (compare with Fig. 17). The goblet shaped objects are desmoneme nematocysts. (PAS–toluidine blue stained; $\times$ 350). (From Hausman and Burnett, 1970.)

Fig. 19. Isolated mesoglea with an organized oral–aboral fiber system showing the alignment of the small fibers in one direction and the identity of particles and rings (arrow) (toluidine blue stained; $\times$ 720).

Fig. 21. Isolated mesoglea showing the large (0.3–1.0 μ diameter) fibers and the 0.7 μ diameter particles spaced along the fibers (PAS–toluidine blue stained; $\times$ 2100). (From Hausman and Burnett, 1969.)

doubt that cell processes extend into the mesoglea, but 2000 Å-thick, methylene blue-stained sections, when viewed with the light microscope, demonstrate that the cell processes are not as regular in spacing as the spacing of the clear areas. Unfixed, unstained mesoglea exhibits no holes left by cell processes, suggesting that they close up when the cells are stripped away. Presumably, the clear areas between fibers are simply areas of lower affinity for polysaccharide stains (see Section II,E).

4. Distal and Proximal Specializations

We have already seen that mesoglea is absent from the aboral pore, the mouth, and the ends of *Hydra*'s tentacles. However, around the mouth and aboral pore the mesoglea is highly organized. As the fibers of the large fiber system converge on the mouth and aboral pore, they gradually occlude the intervening gel and form a fibrous mat (Figs. 24–26). Often, closely spaced circular fibers forms a dense band of fibrous matter around both these openings.

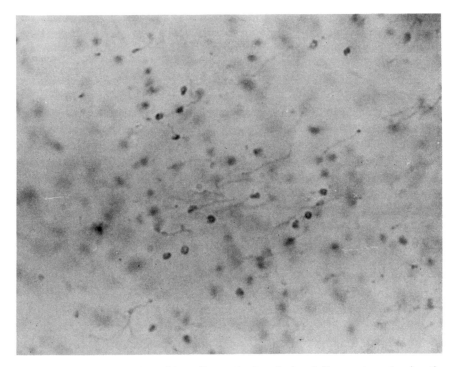

Fig. 22. Isolated mesoglea with a disorganized oral–aboral fiber system showing the random orientation of the small (0.3 μ diameter) fibers and the rings (toluidine blue stained; × 720).

D. ULTRASTRUCTURE VS. MICROSTRUCTURE (EPILOGUE)

Since I feel that work with electron stains for polysaccharides will provide much needed information in the near future, I hesitate to speculate too much on the possible relationships between the fibrils and other ultrastructural moieties and the microstructural fibers and rings. However, on the basis of electron micrographs (Figs. 27 and 28), I have already suggested (Hausman and Burnett, 1969) that bundles of fibrils form the fibers visible in the light microscope. Presumably, these are the small, 0.3 μ diameter fibers which appear under Nomarsky interference–contrast illumination. Grimstone *et al.* (1958) have already suggested such a relationship between fibrils and fibers in the sea anemone, *Metridium*.

E. CHEMISTRY OF MESOGLEA

There is current interest in the connective tissue chemistry of invertebrates. The impetus for this work stems from a number of sources:

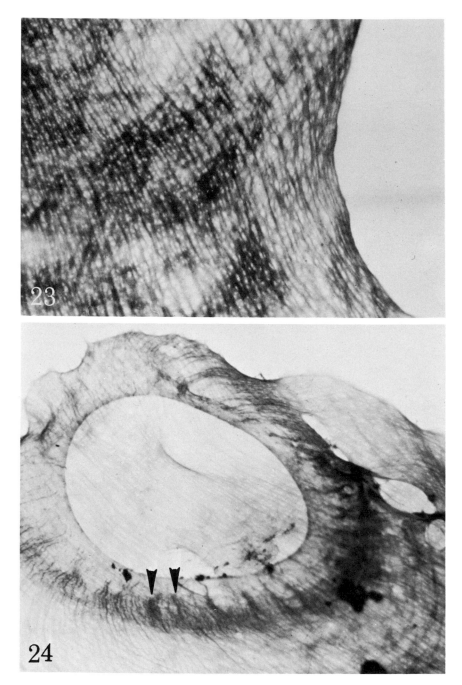

Fig. 23. Isolated mesoglea from the gastric region of a nonbudding *Hydra* showing highly organized oral–aboral fiber system and the spaces between the fibers (compare with Fig. 18) (PAS stained; × 216).

Fig. 24. Isolated mesoglea showing the oral pore (mouth). Note the thick, dense fibers around the opening (arrows) (× 160). (From Burnett and Hausman, 1969.)

a general "coming of age" of heteropolysaccharide chemistry, a continuing interest in structural proteins, correlations between connective tissue changes and aging, and a desire to find "simpler systems" on which to study connective tissues. Consequently there have been a number of recent papers on the chemistry of coelenterate mesoglea (see Katzman and Jeanloz, 1970, for references). Unfortunately, none of these have concerned *Hydra*. *Hydra* mesoglea, because of its small size, has not lured chemists. Therefore, much of the physical chemistry information we have will not be from *Hydra* specifically, but from other coelenterates. If we avoid the minor details which vary from species to species (Gross and Piez, 1960), I feel we are justified in applying findings on the physical chemistry of the other coelenterates to *Hydra*.

1. Coelenterate Mesoglea

Histochemistry, the periodic acid-Schiff reaction, and various protein stains had demonstrated by the middle of the last century that coelenterate mesogleas contained a polysaccharide and a protein component. Where distinct fibers were present in the light microscope, the protein could be localized in them by differential staining. In the absence of distinct fibers, as in *Hydra,* it was assumed that significant protein was absent and only a sticky gel was present (mesolamella).

On the basis of many histochemical techniques and the work of many investigators, it was generally agreed by the 1940's that the coelenterate mesogleas contained mucopolysaccharides (Goreau, 1956) and a protein that strongly resembled vertebrate collagen in its staining (Hyman, 1940; Chapman, 1953a; Bouillon and Vandermeersche, 1956). *Hydra* mesoglea, however, remained an enigma.

Marks *et al.* (1949), using X-ray diffraction, established that alcyonarian mesogleas contained a protein that could be called collagen. With the perfection of fixation techniques and electron microscopy, more evidence on the nature of mesoglea came from comparative ultrastructure. On the basis of the fibril structure, Grimstone *et al.* (1958) stated that the fibrils observed in *Metridium senile* were a collagen derivative. The discovery of similar fibrils in the mesoglea of *Hydra* (Hess *et al.,* 1957; Hess, 1961; Wood, 1961) led these workers to suggest that they too might be collagen.

Concurrently, Piez and Gross (1959; also Gross and Piez, 1960) had established, in a series of comprehensive experiments that included X-ray diffraction patterns, amino acid analysis, histochemistry, and electron microscopy, that a group of invertebrate mesogleas, including those of the coelenterates *Metridium* and *Physalia,* contained proteins that could be called collagens. They concluded that invertebrate collagens, while falling within the limits of collagen, contained less of the two imido acids,

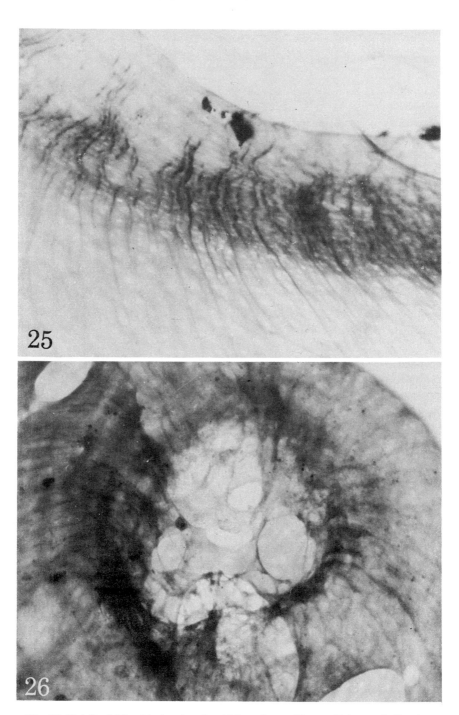

Fig. 25. Detail of Fig. 24 showing the thicker, denser fibers which practically obscure interfiber space (× 420). (From Burnett and Hausman, 1969.)

Fig. 26. Isolated mesoglea at the aboral pore (PAS–toluidine blue stained; × 160).

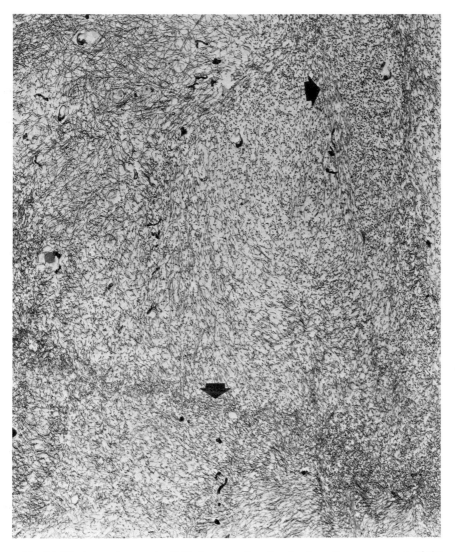

Fig. 27. Electron micrograph of *Hydra* mesoglea showing how the arrangement of the 70–90 Å fibrils might be seen as 0.3 μ diameter fibers (arrows) both parallel and perpendicular to the oral–aboral axis ($\times$ 16,000). (Courtesy of Dr. L. E. Davis from Hausman and Burnett, 1969.)

proline and hydroxyproline, more hydroxylysine, and fewer of the nonpolar amino acids. The coelenterate collagens contained the least proline and hydroxyproline.

Gross and Piez (1960) also looked at bound carbohydrates and concluded that there was no polysaccharide yet isolated with purified colla-

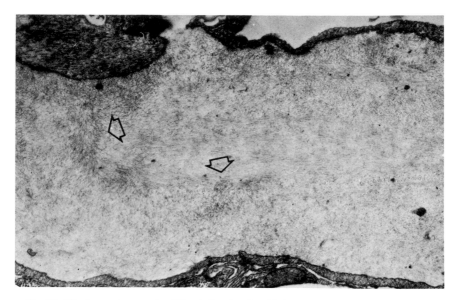

Fig. 28. Electron micrograph of *H. viridis* showing fibril orientation. Bundles of fibrils are cut obliquely (arrows) with longitudinal and cross-sections of fibrils scattered throughout the mesoglea. Note the concentration of fibrils at the epidermal border (e) (× 22,000). (From Davis and Haynes, 1968.)

gen, although the purified invertebrate collagens contained large amounts of bound sugars. This, of course, says nothing about the rest of the mesoglea, such as an unattached, not covalently bound polysaccharide gel. It does suggest, however, that invertebrate collagens, and especially coelenterate collagens with their low imido acid content, may have different chemical properties than vertebrate collagens.

Gross *et al.* (1958) suggested that there might be more than one molecular species of polysaccharide present. Rudal (1968) suggested that there might even be more than one type of carbohydrate–collagen association in a given invertebrate tissue, a situation unlike that in vertebrates.

Katzman and Jeanloz (1970) were recently able to purify *Metridium* collagen with an attached heteropolysaccharide. The large polysaccharide, 30% of the peptide isolated, contained fucose, xylose, mannose, and galactosamine. This suggests that the relationship between the collagen fibrils in coelenterate mesoglea and the polysaccharide amorphous gel may be more complex than simple physical proximity, one embedded in the other.

2. Hydra Mesoglea

Lenhoff *et al.* (1957) had identified an anomalous collagenlike protein (it has a low glycine content and lacks the characteristic wide-angle X-ray diffraction pattern) from the nematocysts of *Hydra,* but the first bio-chemical work on the mesoglea of *Hydra* was that of Shostak *et al.* (1965).

Using extracted and gelatinized *Hydra* mesoglea and rattail collagen, they found their behaviors in acrylamide gel electrophoresis to be similar, the only major difference being the absence of the slowest moving, or trimer, ring of collagen from the mesoglea extract. To further determine that this was a collagen, they subjected the gelatin to two-dimensional paper chromatography. They were able to identify lysine, hydroxylysine, hydroxyproline, proline, and glycine. Furthermore, they noted that the amount of imido acid was small and only detectable if large numbers of hydras were extracted.

This analysis coincides with that of Gross and Piez (1960). Even in the absence of X-ray diffraction data there is little doubt that there is a protein in *Hydra* mesoglea which is in the collagen family, and hence, a collagen.

Shostak *et al.* (1965), noting the descriptions of fibrils in the electron micrographs of *Hydra* mesoglea, took the obvious step and suggested that the collagen was located in these fibrils and the polysaccharide in the amorphous gel. This would have settled the question of *Hydra* mesoglea structure were it not for a number of unsettling observations. Shostak *et al.* (1965) noted some of them:

> It would be surprising if the collagenlike protein in the mesoglea was either stretchable or elastic, since collagen is generally nowhere near as elastic as were the mesogleas (Harkness, 1961). Rather than the elasticity of the mesogleas being an intrinsic property of the macromolecules (Bouillon and Vandermeersche, 1956) it is probably a function of the fabric into which the protein is woven.

As Shostak *et al.* (1965) noted, Bouillon and Vandermeersche (1956) and Bouillon (1959) have claimed there is an elastic prótein in *Hydra* mesoglea and, on the basis of orcein staining and other histochemical behavior, have identified it as an elastin. Recently, we have been able to demonstrate that *Hydra* mesoglea stains with the aldehyde–fuchsin technique, a characteristic of elastin. We have already noted the elasticity of *Hydra* mesoglea and also that exposure to acids decreases this elasticity. Elder and Owen (1967), using a potassium permangante–spirit blue technique which parallels the aldehyde–fuchsin technique in its specificity for elastin, made the generalization that actinians contained collagen fibers and scyphozoans an "elastin." They noted that any given coelenterate may contain either or both structural proteins. Consequently, in the Hydrozoan *Hydra,* we might expect either elastin, collagen, or both. Furthermore, the elastins they describe are anomalous in their staining and structural characteristics, and most resemble mammalian oxytalan fibers.

Biochemically, the discovery of collagen–polysaccharide bonds and the elastin question open many complex alternatives that were not considered earlier. But, by far, the greatest subsequent confusion introduced has been on the structural level.

As we have seen, Davis and Haynes (1968) described two types of fibrils and large electron-dense structures in the mesoglea of at least one *Hydra* species. Furthermore, they have observed that there is an apparent orientation to the fibrils that vanishes upon muscular contractions. On the light microscope level, the discovery of large protein–polysaccharide fibers, protein fibers, and proteinaceous rings (Hausman and Burnett, 1969, 1972) which can be distinguished histochemically (Table I) may account for the elastic properties, but also opens possibilities that were formerly not considered.

Using histochemistry (Table I) and enzyme digestion (Table II), I have further investigated the isolated mesoglea of *Hydra*. On the basis of these tests and previous results, I have tried to identify the chemical composition of each of the components of *Hydra* mesoglea.

The larger (0.5–1.0 μ in diameter) fibers, which may extend the length of the animal, are mostly polysaccharide, since they stain strongly with

TABLE I

STAINING PROPERTIES OF ISOLATED MESOGLEA[a]

Technique	Large fibers	Nomarsky fibers	Particles (rings)	Gel
PAS	+	−	−	−
Bauer	+	−	−	−
Schiff (no oxidation)	−	−	−	−
Toluidine blue, pH 7	−[b]	−[b]	+[c] (metachromatic)	−
Toluidine blue, pH 9.5	+[d] (orthochromatic)	+[d]	+ (metachromatic)	−
Light green	+	+	−	−
Sudan black B	−	−	−	−
Alcian blue–neutral red	−	−	+[e]	+
PAS–toluidine blue	+	+	+	−
PAS–light green	+	+	−	−
PAS–alcian blue	+	−	+	−
Gram reaction	−	−	+	−

[a] Modified from Hausman and Burnett (1969).

[b] At pH 7 some sections of fiber do stain lightly but the whole network does stain; general staining begins at pH 8.

[c] Particles stain metachromatically compared to those sections of fiber that stain.

[d] At pH 9.5 the stain is strongest; at higher pH the stain fades out.

[e] Staining is inconsistent; some stain + with alcian blue, others do not.

TABLE II

ENZYME SENSITIVITY OF ISOLATED MESOGLEA[a]

Enzyme	Large fibers	Small fibers	Particles (rings)	Gel
Collagenase	+[b]	+	+	+[c]
Elastase	+[b]	+	+	−
Amylase	+	−	−	+
Hyaluronidase	−	−	−	−[d]
Trypsin	−	+	−	+[c]
Proteinase	−	+	−	+[c]

[a]Modified from Hausman and Burnett (1969).

[b]May be due to its effect on the small fibers.

[c]Results in an initial greater transparency and may be an effect on a precursor tropocollagen.

[d]Though there is no visible change, mesoglea loses adhesiveness.

the periodic acid-Schiff reaction. The polysaccharide is not strongly acidic, since it does not stain with alcian blue, and is not sensitive to hyaluronidase.

The small shorter fibers (0.3 μ in diameter; Fig. 20) are primarily, and perhaps exclusively, protein. They are insensitive to the polysaccharide-digesting enzymes and sensitive to all the protein-digesting enzymes. They are the most likely loci for the collagen; however, their sensitivity to elastase makes it doubtful that the fibers are exclusively collagen. The question of the nature of the protein will be discussed below.

The toluidine blue-staining particles (0.7 μ in diameter) and the rings apparent under interference–contrast optics (0.3 μ inside diameter, 1.0 μ outside diameter), which I believe are identical, seem to be a muco-polysaccharide. They have a definite protein component, but occasionally give a positive reaction for acid mucopolysaccharide. Unless it is a function of the associated polysaccharide, the protein is different from that of the small fibers as judged by its lower pH toluidine blue staining. The remaining gel is primarily water, but contains enough polysaccharide to be extremely sensitive to amylase and to occasionally show a very light alcian blue staining indicating an acid mucopolysaccharide. However, this small amount of polysaccharide may be significant. Because of their polyionic nature, polysaccharides can contribute structurally and chemically to tissues when present only in amounts of 0.3% (Schubert, 1965). Judging from its initial collagenase sensitivity (it becomes more transparent) and the ubiquitousness of the presumably protein fibrils in electron micrographs (Fig. 27), the gel presumably contains protein elements. These may be a precursor of the protein found in the small fibers (Hausman and Burnett, 1972). This is discussed further in Section IV,B,2.

3. Collagen or Elastin?

I must first of all point out, to those who may be expecting an answer, that I cannot provide a solution. I can only give a perspective of the various possibilities based on a number of equivocal experiments. None of the histochemical techniques show any differentiation between the elastase-sensitive and collagenase-sensitive portions of the mesoglea. With the exception of a dilute collagenase-sensitive material in the gel, the action of both enzymes is on the small fibers.

This may be explained in two ways. Either the fibers are made up of two proteins, a collagen and an elastin, or they are made up of a single protein which, though a collagen/elastin, is extremely anomalous. The presence of two types of fibrils on the ultrastructural level could be evidence for the former, but the rarity of the thicker, banded fibrils and the extreme sensitivity of the mesoglea to elastase (it literally falls apart to the touch) make a separation of proteins on this level highly unlikely. We already know that as a collagen it is anomalous in a number of ways: its low imido acid and high hydroxylysine content and its unusual banding. The unusual, 300-Å banding is not significant in classifying the protein as a collagen or not, because of the large amount of polysaccharide present. Both Rudall (1968) and Hunt (1970) note that collagens with a high amount of carbohydrate tend to have no or abnormal banding. Furthermore, if we are dealing with a single protein, it is elastase sensitive and extremely elastic.

The suggestion of Shostak et al. (1965) that the elasticity resides in the polysaccharide of the gel is one I find very unsatisfactory unless there is an elastic protein present. Largely polysaccharide substances can be strong (chitin is an example) but they are not known to be capable of the elasticity that Hydra mesoglea exhibits. Besides, as we have seen, there is good histochemical evidence for the existence of an elastin.

The second possibility, that of a single protein, becomes more attractive when we realize that all of the evidence we have for the collagenous nature of the protein concerns primary structure. Properties such as enzyme sensitivity, stain affinity, and elasticity depend on secondary or higher orders of organization, all of which are influenced by the method of synthesis and the microenvironment, such as the presence of linked heteropolysaccharides. While secondary and higher orders of structure ultimately depend on primary structure, we have already mentioned collagens which, while falling within the primary structure limitations, differ in such higher order characteristics as banding and enzyme sensitivity (Gross and Piez, 1960).

If there is a single protein moiety, it is interesting in a number of ways. Since Hydra is from a stock that evolved very early in metazoan evolution, it may have some significance as an ancestral structural protein exhibiting both the strength of collagen and the elasticity of elastin. If it is an ancestral or "stem" protein, why was it lost in the normally conservative process of evolution?

III. Mesoglea as a Dynamic Structure

I have mentioned previously that the structure of *Hydra* mesoglea is affected by developmental changes. In this section I shall detail these changes as they appear on the light microscope level, and discuss a hypothesis relating the changes in mesoglea structure to morphogenesis (Hausman and Burnett, 1970).

A. MICROSTRUCTURE

Hydra maintained in culture, in the laboratory, under relatively constant conditions and fed so that most individuals do not either bud or degenerate (twice weekly) maintain a constant fiber system. This consists of the large (0.5–1.0 μ diameter) fibers extending in a rectolinear pattern from the aboral pore up to the mouth (see Section II). We have not observed these larger fibers to extend into the tentacles though the smaller short fibers are present there. The large fibers, along with the rest of the mesoglea, are thicker in the peduncle, and more cross-fibers (around the body column fibers) occur in this body region. Most of the individuals in a culture population fed twice (2 ×) weekly maintain this complete fiber system (Table III).

An individual *Hydra*, when fed, will exhibit one of three different mesoglea fiber system responses. Either (1) the rectolinear fiber system will disappear completely and only the short fibers and particles (rings) will remain; or (2) the rectolinear fiber system will disappear from the peduncle–gastric region junction distally while remaining intact in the peduncle (Figs. 29 and 30); or (3) the fiber system will disorganize only immediately below the hypostome in the growth region. All of these responses to feeding last for a little more than a day; by 28 hours the distribution of fiber system organization in the population is as it was before feeding.

If hydras are fed to satiation daily, they will bud continuously — a second bud forming before the first one has detached, and then a third or more before initial detachment occurs. These animals never rebuild the oral–aboral rectolinear pattern above the peduncle–gastric region (now bud–peduncle) junction. *Hydra* can apparently maintain this condition for long periods (Hausman and Burnett, 1970) making it highly unlikely that the large rectolinear organization is necessary for the structural

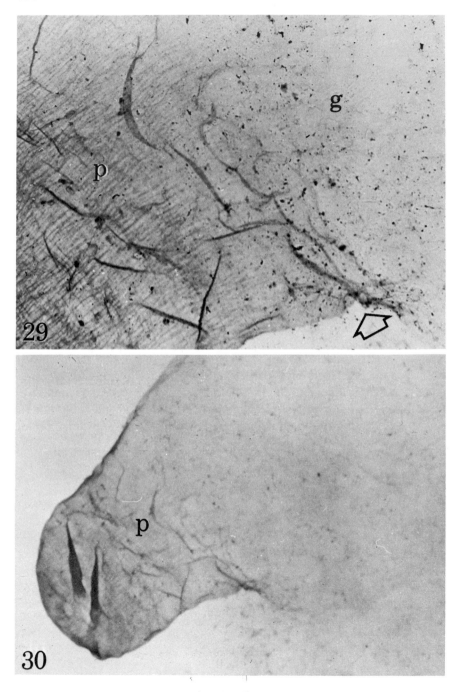

TABLE III

CULTURES FED TWICE OR 5 TIMES WEEKLY FOR AT LEAST
2 WEEKS PREVIOUS TO SAMPLING[a]

	Half-fiber system (%)	Complete fiber system (%)	No fiber system (%)
2 × [b]	3.2–13.3	50.0–71.4	25.4–39.0
5 × [c]	66.7–70.4	2.9–7.4	25.9–26.7

[a]Modified from Hausman and Burnett (1970).
[b]Data taken from an average of 9 cultures of 1500 animals/culture with about 500 animals sampled.
[c]Data taken from an average of 6 cultures of 300 animals/culture with about 500 animals sampled.

properties of the mesoglea. The distribution of fiber system organization in a population fed five times weekly (5 ×) is given in Table III.

In *Hydra* about to bud, the mesoglea fiber system breaks down in the budding region, and in some cases we have observed the fibers shifting temporarily so that the oral–aboral large fibers are aligned into the bud (Fig. 31). At this stage, the mesoglea at the point of budding has broken down totally and the epidermis and gastrodermis are apparently in direct contact. Subsequently, the large oral–aboral fiber system is broken down from the bud–peduncle junction distally and only the disoriented small fibers and rings remain (Fig. 32).

If a second bud does not initiate before the first bud detaches, the rectolinear fiber system will be organized again in the parent body column. By the time the bud has developed its own peduncle, both the bud and the parent will have a well-organized oral–aboral fiber system (Fig. 33).

The amount of information we have about the structure of the mesoglea does not allow much speculation on the mechanism of the change in fiber system organization. However, on the basis of a low rate of mesoglea synthesis (see Section III,B) and the speed at which the mesoglea breakdown response occurs there seems to be minimal loss of material. We

Fig. 29. Isolated mesoglea of the bud–peduncle junction. Arrow denotes the junction. Note that the oral–aboral fiber system is well developed in the peduncle (p) but lacking in gastric region (g) (PAS–toluidine blue stained; × 160). (From Burnett and Hausman, 1969.)

Fig. 30. Isolated mesoglea of an early-stage budding *Hydra* demonstrating the intense PAS staining of the peduncle mesoglea (p) compared with the bud or gastric region (PAS technique; × 40). (From Burnett and Hausman, 1969.)

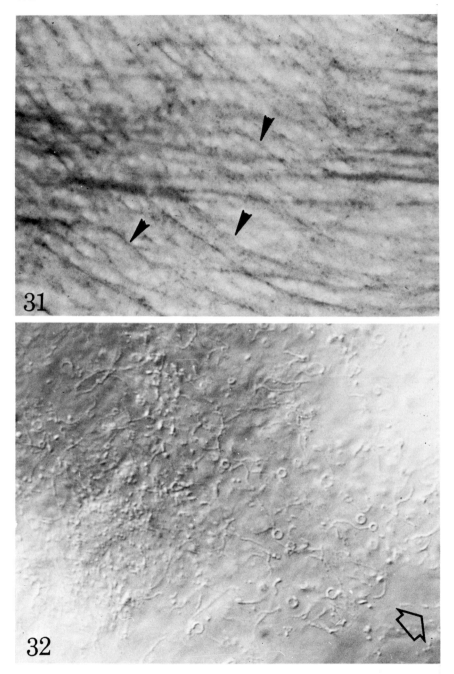

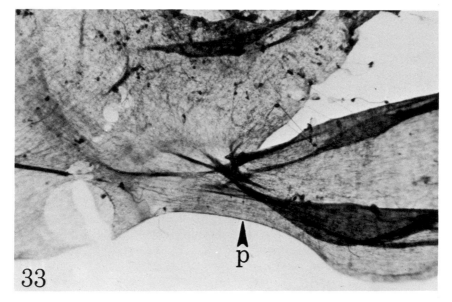

Fig. 33. Isolated mesoglea from the budding region of *Hydra* with an almost fully developed bud still attached. The well-developed peduncle of the bud (p) is apparent, as is the reestablished oral–aboral fiber system in the parent body column (PAS–toluidine blue stained; × 250). (From Hausman and Burnett, 1970.)

suggested that an enzyme "fiberase" might disorganize the large fiber components without destroying them. They could then be subsequently reorganized. The short (0.3 μ diameter) fibers may be these "building block" components. Whatever the mechanism of fiber disorganization is, it must take into account the inordinately long time, about 9 days, that it takes *Hydra* to reestablish the organized oral–aboral fiber system after it has been absent for a number of weeks because of continuous feeding. At present, there is no satisfactory explanation.

B. ULTRASTRUCTURE

There is no information, at present, on the ultrastructural changes that would correspond to the observed reorganization on the light micros-

---

Fig. 31. Longitudinal (arrows) and circular mesoglea fibers from the budding region of an early-stage budding *Hydra*. The oral–aboral fibers have shifted to align into the region of the developing bud (PAS–toluidine blue stained; × 420). (From Burnett and Hausman, 1969.)

Fig. 32. Isolated mesoglea of *Hydra* under Nomarsky illumination demonstrating the random orientation of the short, 0.3 μ diameter, fibers and particles when the fiber system has broken down. The oral–aboral axis is shown by the arrow (× 2100).

copy level. All recent work on the ultrastructure of *Hydra* mesoglea has been done on 24-hour starved animals previously fed five times, or less, weekly. Sections were taken from the gastric region. As we have seen, the fiber organization of the mesoglea in this area at this time after feeding is variable, and does not give any information on reorganization.

C. Summary

Observation of the mesoglea fiber system organization of *Hydra* population in the laboratory tells us (1) that the large rectolinear fiber system is apparently not necessary for the structural role of the mesoglea, since hydras function normally without the larger fibers, when fed five times or more weekly (these hydras bud continually); (2) that a *Hydra* with an organized fiber system disorganizes it temporarily when fed; (3) that before budding, the organized fiber system disorganizes first in the budding region and then distally. In the latter case the fiber system is not reorganized until late in budding.

D. A Working Hypothesis

To explain these observations, I suggested that the role of the large, oral–aboral, rectolinear fiber system was not a structural one, but rather a guide to cell movement (Burnett and Hausman, 1969; Hausman and Burnett, 1969, 1970). It has been known since 1928 that cells move down the body column of *Hydra,* away from the subhypostomal growth region, and up the hypostome into the mouth or tentacles (Tripp, 1928; Brien, 1953; Burnett, 1961; Shostak *et al.,* 1965). Shostak *et al.* (1965) demonstrated that the migration of cells in each cell layer is independent of the other layer and of the underlying mesoglea.

If the oral-aboral fiber system were a fiber cage which, though elastic, strictly limited cell movement to a direction parallel to the larger oral–aboral fibers and did not permit changes in the body column length, the fiber system would have to break down for growth or budding to occur. Without reorganizing the oral–aboral fiber system at least temporarily, *Hydra* would only be able to replace its lost cells and maintain its entity. Hydras fed twice weekly do just that: They maintain the organized fiber system and do not bud or grow in length.

There is as yet no direct evidence demonstrating that cells moving up or down the body column of *Hydra* are guided by the mesoglea fibers. There are a number of observations, however, which support the hypothesis. Diehl and Burnett (1966) have observed that cells moving down the body column often move in trains, which would be expected if they were following the tracks of the mesoglea. By following the movement of testes in sexual hydras, cells can be seen to move down the body column

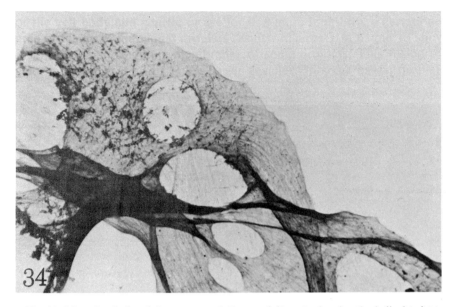

Fig. 34. Mesoglea isolated from a sexual *H. pseudoligactis* showing the helical twist to the oral–aboral fiber and the whole mesoglea (PAS–toluidine blue stained; × 160).

in a slow helix. The mesoglea fiber system exhibits this same helical pattern (Fig. 34). There are numerous data from tissue culture systems, dating back to the work of Harrison on axon growth, on the propensity of cells and cell processes to follow grooves or fibers in a substratum (Weiss, 1945).

1. Regeneration

If the mesoglea fiber system must reorganize for *Hydra* to undergo any growth or morphogenesis, then an animal should be unable to regenerate without first breaking down the oral–aboral fiber system. Hydras undergoing regeneration should exhibit a differently organized fiber system, and a change in fiber system organization should be observed before regeneration occurs. This can easily be tested in *Hydra* since the animal will regenerate any missing part. When the hypostome is excised, thereby forcing the animal to regenerate a new hypostome and tentacles, the oral–aboral fiber system breaks down throughout the animal (Table IV). Only the short (0.3 μ diameter) fibers and particles remain as a disorganized matrix, just as the gastric region appears during budding. Most hydras reorganize their mesoglea fiber system within 4 hours after excision. At this time, the wound has not yet closed off and visible morphogenesis will not begin for another few hours.

TABLE IV

Hypostome Excision[a]

Hours after excision	Half-fiber system	Complete fiber system	No fiber system[b]
0 + 4	11.4	58.0	30.5
8 + 10	24.0	21.2	54.9

[a] Modified from Hausman and Burnett (1970).
[b] Percentages rounded to nearest tenth.

2. Maintenance (Nonbudding)

As a basis for the hypothesis, we suggested that, in a nonbudding *Hydra*, cells from the subhypostomal growth region moving up into the hypostome adhere to the mesoglea by a combination of cell processes inserted into the mesoglea and chemical adhesion to the mucopoly-saccharide gel. At the rim of the mouth, the densely packed fibers in the

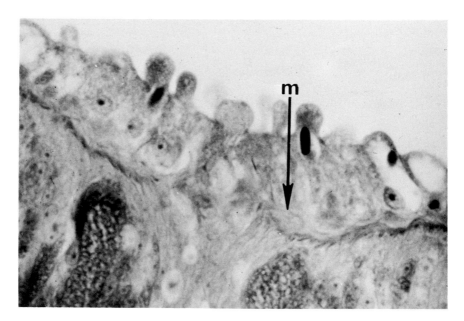

Fig. 35. Longitudinal section through the mouth region. One can observe the thickening in the mesoglea (m) and its "frayed" appearance where it becomes discontinuous (compare with Fig. 24). Several epidermal cells at the top are presumably in the process of sloughing off the body column and can be seen projecting from the border (toluidine blue stained; × 825).

mesoglea reduce the amount of adhesive material and make it difficult for the cells to insert processes. Consequently, perfectly viable cells are sloughed off the organism at the mouth to make room for the constant cell proliferation (Fig. 35). Sloughing also occurs at the tentacle tips where the mesoglea is absent and the two cell layers directly oppose each other. This sloughing allows a continual stream of cells to move into the tentacles at their bases.

Cells moving down the body column from the subhypostomal growth region move along the mesoglea fibers until they reach the gastric region–peduncle junction. There they meet resistance. Cell movement is slower in the peduncle (Corff and Burnett, 1969) and the cells attach much more strongly (Fig. 36) (Lowell and Burnett, 1969) to the thicker fiber system. The cells moving down through the gastric region meet the resistance posed by the strongly attached, slower moving peduncle cells and are forced to seek a path of less resistance in order to make room for those behind them. For most of these cells the path of least resistance is to

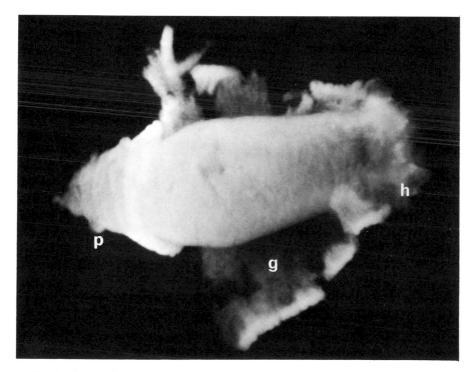

Fig. 36. Hayne–Muscatine's preparation of a whole *Hydra* showing the epidermis in the gastric region lifted off (g) while that in the peduncle (p) and hypostome (h) still adheres to the mesoglea (× 100). (Courtesy of Dr. Ralph Lowell.)

cross over the mesoglea (the case of epidermal cells) into the gastrodermis and slough off into the enteron through gastrodermal villi (Corff
and Burnett, 1969). Some, however, do cross over into the peduncle,
making up for the cells lost from that region, and make their way down
the thick fibers to the basal disc where they encounter thick, gel-occluding
fibers at the mouth, and slough off the animal.

3. Budding

   In well-fed hydras, the mechanism of bud initiation (as yet unknown)
causes a local weakening and breakdown of the mesoglea in a small area
of the budding region (Fig. 37). This is followed (or preceded) by a
temporary shifting of the oral–aboral fibers into the bud (Fig. 31). The
opening up of a new area of least resistance, the developing bud, and the
shifting of the tracks of cell migration into its shunts the cells moving
down the column into the bud instead of forcing them to cross over the
mesoglea and slough into the enteron.

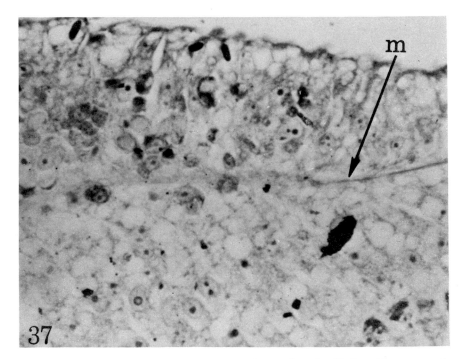

Fig. 37. Longitudinal section through the budding region of a *Hydra* with a very early
Stage I bud. The mesoglea (m) is "frayed" and appears to be discontinuous in places
(toluidine blue stained; × 350). (From Burnett and Hausman, 1969.)

There is also a shift in the direction of the mitotic spindles of epithelio-muscular cells in the budding region. They shift from predominately oral–aboral to a direction across the oral–aboral axis pointing into the bud (Corff, 1969). Thus may also be a result of the breakdown of the oral–aboral fiber system and could aid in shunting cells into the newly developing bud. As we have mentioned, the fiber system is subsequently broken down distally from the bud–peduncle junction up to the hypostome. Cells do not slough off the animal in this region because they are attached by the chemical adhesion of the mesoglea (since there are no organized oral–aboral fibers to loop around). However, the cells in the peduncle, which are attached by the same chemical adhesion and the cell processes looping around an organized fiber system, are easily able to resist invasion by the gastric region cells attached only by an adhesive gel. Consequently, few cells cross over into the peduncle. The result of this is a net loss of cells in the peduncle and a subsequent shortening of that region so that the old bud–peduncle junction and the nearly detached bud move down the body column. The bud finally detaches from a region below the budding zone, where the new bud is now forming.

Two or three days after initiation, when a bud has developed its own tentacles and subhypostomal growth region, it forms its own oral–aboral fiber system, with its own thick-fibered peduncle (Fig. 33). The parent body column, if it is not going to bud again immediately, reforms its oral–aboral fiber system (for further discussion see section on budding).

4. Column Growth

Newly detached buds must grow to a certain size before they will begin to bud. In order to lengthen and increase the circumference of the body column, the animal temporarily breaks down its oral–aboral fiber system to allow for expansion. Breakdown presumably allows a greater density of cells in an area, followed by an increase in the area of the mesoglea, and a spreading out of the cells and re-forming of the oral–aboral fiber system with the original normal density of cells maintained. If fed to satiation again within a 28-hour period the animal, of course, does not rebuild the large fiber system, and if feeding is continued the excess cells will be shunted into a bud. If not provided with sufficient nutrition to bud, *Hydra* will maintain the rebuilt oral–aboral fiber system until its next meal or until it degenerates from lack of nutrition 3 weeks later.

In regenerating *Hydra,* as we have seen, the organized oral–aboral fiber system breaks down throughout the entire organism, even into the peduncle. The reason why this normally resistant (in budding) region disorganizes is not yet clear. There is a parallel enigma in the question of mesoglea synthesis in the peduncle (see next section). To be consistent, fiber system breakdown in the peduncle should be able to be tied to cell movement. Little is known about cell movement in the peduncle during hypostome regeneration, but there is apparently no massive movement of cells from the more proximal areas into the regenerating hypostome (Burnett, 1965; Burnett and Yen, 1969). One possibility is that the peduncle breakdown is overreaction induced by the trauma of hypostome excision (Hausman and Burnett, 1972). Since it does not contribute to structure, the sudden loss of the oral–aboral fiber system in the peduncle would have no adverse effect on regeneration unless it was needed to guide cell movement.

5. Mechanism of Cell Movement

The method by which *Hydra* cells move up and down the body column is unknown. We know from cell marker studies (Shostak *et al.,* 1965) that cells move, and we know from micrographs that cells insert processes into the mesoglea. Whether it is the same cell that does both is not known. I have previously suggested that since the same cell types, epitheliomuscular and digestive cells, are involved in both movement and process insertion, the processes, instead of being antithetical to cell movement, are involved in the mechanism. The 1.0 μ diameter ring structures may also be involved in cell attachment and movement since their size and density roughly correspond to the size and number of processes underneath a single cell. Preliminary work suggests that *Hydra* cells are capable of extending long pseudopods on a glass substratum, and perhaps this is the mechanism of cell movement *in vivo*. Guided by the fibers, a long pseudopod may move over the mesoglea, take root, and pull the cell along after it. Cells would move up and down the body column as if crawling along a ladder.

IV. Mesoglea Origin

A. HISTORY

The cellular origin of mesoglea has long been speculated on but seldom experimented on. It has been a speculation very short of facts. Hyman (1940) confessed that there was nothing even known about the tissue layer origin (whether it came from the epidermis or gastrodermis) of mesoglea. Previous workers had speculated on mesoglea origin on the basis of the germ-layer theory. Since the mesoderm (read mesoglea) came from the ectoderm (read epidermis), the mesoglea, they concluded, must be of epidermal origin. Hyman pointed out the fallacy of this type of reasoning as applied to coelenterate embryology, but could only guess that both cell layers contributed to the mesoglea. Chapman (1953a) ventured the opinion that the cells embedded in the cellular mesogleas could hardly be responsible for mesoglea synthesis since this would leave those coelenterates with a cellular mesoglea, such as *Hydra,* in rather a bind. He also suggested that both the epidermis and the gastrodermis contributed to mesoglea origin. Shostak *et al.* (1965) recognized that knowledge of the origin of mesoglea was very critical to a consideration of its role in morphogenesis but, on the basis of no experimental facts, did not care to speculate on its origin. Consequently, until very recently there was no experimental work on the cell-layer origins of coelenterate mesoglea and few speculations on the cell types which might be involved. Mackie and Mackie (1967) suggested that the mesoglea of the siphonophore *Hippopodius* may be synthesized by a particular type of endodermal cell. These authors, however, provide no experimental evidence.

In sponges there have been numerous investigations of mesoglea origin, and a number of different cells have been demonstrated to contribute to its synthesis. Recently, Smith and Lauritis (1969) have identified the cell type responsible for mesoglea synthesis in the marine sponge *Cyamon neon de Laubenfels.* They point out, however, that the cell type involved may vary within the phylum. This may well be due to the persistent difficulty in identifying cell types in sponges.

B. *Hydra*

In *Hydra,* the cell types are well known and the system is open to the investigation of synthesis with radioautographic methods. I have recently investigated mesoglea synthesis in *Hydra,* using tritiated proline (Hausman and Burnett, 1972) and tritiated glucose.

Radioproline has long been used to study connective tissue synthesis on the basis of its concentration in collagen, both as proline and the unique-to-collagen amino acid, hydroxyproline. Most of the work has been done on vertebrate systems (Stetten, 1949; Peterkovsky and Udenfriend, 1963; Udenfriend, 1966), where the use of labeled proline is based on a number of well-accepted facts. First, it is known that hydroxyproline is not incorporated into growing peptide chains but that proline is incorporated, and some is later hydroxylated to hydroxyproline. Second, that once hydroxylated, the proline (now hydroxyproline) remains in a collagen polypeptide and is never used for anything else. Third, proline itself is not a common amino acid. Finally, hydroxyproline was virtually unknown in noncollagenous proteins. These last two facts led to the common assumption that any proline label being followed into connective tissue was collagen. However, the usefulness of labeled proline as a tool for studying collagen synthesis has been questioned recently (Nadol and

Gibbins, 1970) on the basis of this last assumption. With all this in mind, the question must be asked: Is the method applicable to *Hydra?*

Hydra can reasonably be assumed to synthesize its polypeptides in the same manner as vertebrates—incorporation and subsequent hydroxylation of proline. The third and fourth assumptions, however, cannot be made so confidently. We do not know whether proline and/or hydroxyproline are reused, and we do know that both these amino acids are characteristic also of elastin (Barnes *et al.,* 1970) and of at least one other protein. As we have noted previously, *Hydra* (and other coelenterate) nematocysts contain a hydroxyproline-containing, noncollagenous protein (Lenhoff *et al.,* 1957; Gross and Piez, 1960).

Fortunately, both these difficulties can be easily eliminated. The cellular source of nematocysts is well known and these cells (nested interstitial cells) are cytologically and topologically distinct from the mesoglea. The subsequent appearance of the label in mature nematocysts occurs long after the mesoglea exhibits label and confirms the non-mesogleal fate of this proline. By using short periods of exposure to label

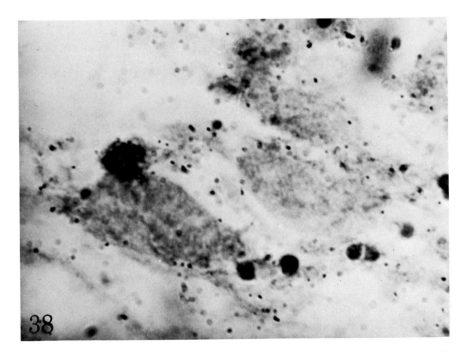

Fig. 38. Radioautograph showing tritiated proline label localized in the digestive cells (light region) and not over the three darker mucous cells. The large round spheres are protein-reserve droplets in the digestive cells (toluidine blue stained; × 2100). (From Hausman and Burnett, 1972).

and isolating mesoglea without cells, the complications of reused label can be eliminated and we can be sure we are following synthesis of mesoglea.

1. Cell Types Responsible

On the basis of electron micrographs (P. G. Rose, unpublished electron micrographs) (Figs. 1 and 8) I had suspected that both epidermal epitheliomuscular cells and gastrodermal digestive cells might be involved in mesoglea synthesis. Tritiated proline labeling established that only these two cell types (Fig. 38) and nested interstitial cells (discussed above) incorporated enough proline to be responsible for mesoglea synthesis. Furthermore, epitheliomuscular and digestive cells are distributed evenly over the body column of *Hydra* and are intimately connected to the mesoglea. The label in epitheliomuscular cells, in fact, was concentrated in that portion of the cell adjacent to the mesoglea (Fig. 39). Tritiated glucose, while not confined to these two cell types, was found in them and in the isolated mesoglea. On the basis of this evidence, I have suggested that both these cell types participate in mesoglea synthesis.

2. In the Mesoglea

After a pulse label, radioproline is initially distributed equally over the mesoglea fibers and the gel (Fig. 40). However, after 2 weeks in an organized oral–aboral fiber system, label is concentrated in the fibers (Fig. 41). There are two possible explanations for this observation: Either the labeled material in the gel is lost to the animal while that in the fibers remain; or the labeled material, previously in the gel, moves into the fibers and is replaced by new, unlabeled material. In the absence of quantitative data, neither possibility can be eliminated, but on the basis of what we know about collagen synthesis, we favor the latter (label moving into the fibers).

Collagen is released from cells as a precursor molecule, tropocollagen, which then organizes itself *in situ*. Tropocollagen is particularly sensitive to digestion with the enzyme collagenase, and we have already noted that the initial effect of collagenase on *Hydra* mesoglea is on the gel. If the tropocollagen organized itself into mature collagen within the short 0.3 μ diameter fibers, the label would concentrate there and newly synthesized (subsequent to the pulse label) "cold" tropocollagen would make up the gel.

We know we are following mesoglea synthesis, but have been assuming that the radioproline label is a collagen precursor. The other important connective tissue protein, elastin, also contains significant proline, however, (approximately 12 residues/100) and the label could just as

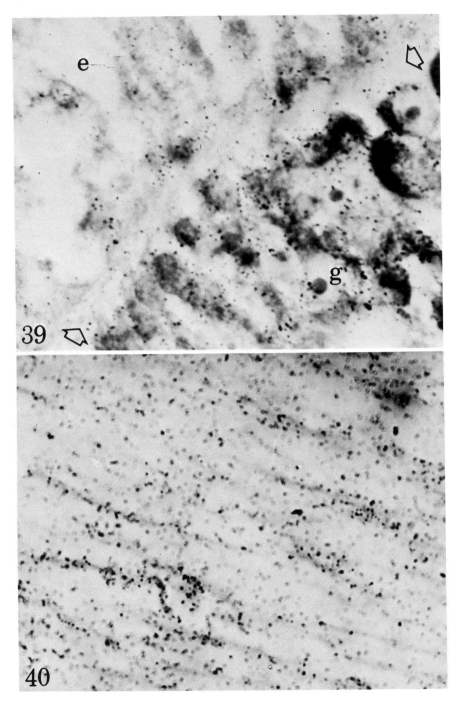

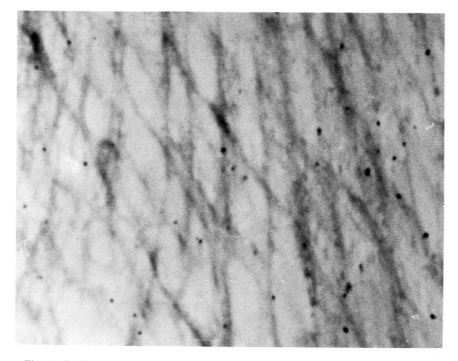

Fig. 41. Radioautograph of *Hydra* isolated mesoglea showing tritiated proline label only over the fibers after 2 weeks' maintenance feeding (PAS technique; × 2100).

well be localized there. This may be unnerving on the biochemical level, but it does not change the results for mesoglea synthesis.

3. Localization in the Animal

In the same study (Hausman and Burnett, 1972) it was demonstrated that mesoglea synthesis is not confined to any particular region of *Hydra,* such as a growth zone, but is distributed throughout the entire organism. This is in accord with the distribution of the cells responsible for synthesizing mesoglea, epitheliomuscular and digestive cells. There are, however, regional variations in the rate of mesoglea synthesis (as measured

---

Fig. 39. Radioautograph showing tritiated proline label both over the gastrodermis of *Hydra* (g) and over the epidermis (e). The arrows indicate the mesoglea and muscle fibers. Note that the epidermal label is concentrated along the mesoglea (toluidine blue stained; × 2100). (From Hausman and Burnett, 1972.)

Fig. 40. Radioautograph of isolated *Hydra* mesoglea showing tritiated proline label in its initial distribution over both the fibers and the gel (PAS technique; × 2100).

by the tissue label over the two cell types) and in the amount of label in the mesoglea of particular regions. These qualitative results are summarized in Figs. 42 and 43. I have suggested that this can be explained on the basis of the rate of cell movement over the various body regions.

a. Nonbudding (Maintenance). In a nonbudding animal, cells move relatively quickly distally from the subhypostomal growth region and are sloughed off at the mouth or tentacle tips. If the epitheliomuscular and digestive cells synthesize mesoglea at a constant rate, as they move, they will leave behind them a mesoglea whose amount of label is a function of this rate. With constant synthesis there must also be a constant loss of mesoglea; otherwise it would build up to unmanageable proportions. The low rate of incorporation, however, makes it likely that the necessary amount of mesoglea material is lost simply by wear and tear. An alternative drain on the amount of mesoglea material is suggested in Section V.

Cells moving proximally through the gastric region from the subhypostomal growth region move slower than those in the hypostome. Without any change in rate of synthesis they would leave behind a more heavily labeled and thicker mesoglea. This is exactly what occurs (Fig. 42) in the gastric region. As we have noted, cells in the peduncle move

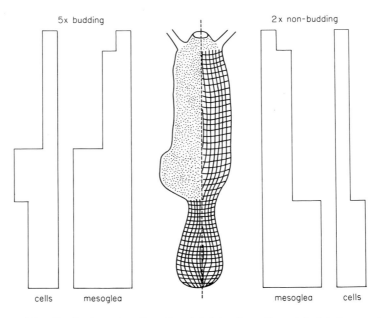

Fig. 42. The distribution of radioproline label in the cells and isolated mesoglea of *Hydra*. The amount of label is expressed by the width of the bar in the individual body region: basal disc–peduncle, budding region (if present), gastric region, hypostome. (From Hausman and Burnett, 1972.)

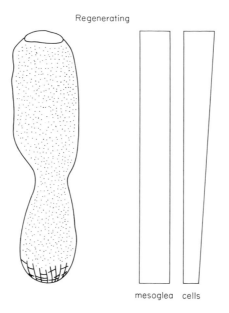

Regenerating

mesoglea cells

Fig. 43. The distribution of radioproline label in the cells and isolated mesoglea of regenerating *Hydra* where the hypostome has been excised. The amount of label in each body region is expressed by the width of the bar. Label decreases from the regenerating area proximally in the cells. (From Hausman and Burnett, 1972.)

slowest of all and would, therefore, be expected to leave behind them the most heavily labeled and thickest mesoglea, that with the greatest density of newly synthesized subunits. Figure 42 shows this increase in incorporated label in the peduncle, but this alone does not seem to be enough to account for the increase in incorporation.

b. Budding. The fiber structure in the peduncle of *Hydra* does not change when the animal is about to bud. Presumably, neither the speed nor the direction of cell movement changes in response to budding in the peduncle. Therefore, if the hypothesis is correct, we would not expect the rate of synthesis or incorporation of labeled mesoglea to change. Figure 42 shows that neither rate changes (as determined by autoradiography).

The rate of synthesis or incorporation does not change in the upper gastric region either, even though the oral–aboral fiber system breaks down. This correlates with the lack of evidence for any change in the rate of cell movement in this area during budding. In the lower gastric region, now the budding region, both the rate of synthesis and the rate of incorporation into the mesoglea are elevated. I think this increase in the rate of synthesis is a direct result of the budding process and allows for the production of new mesoglea for the developing bud, which grows and detaches as a complete small *Hydra* within 3 days.

   c. Regenerating.   In an analogous way, both mesoglea synthesis and the incorporation of newly synthesized material are elevated in an animal regenerating its hypostome (Fig. 43). Here, however, the cells nearest the excision seem to be carrying a larger portion of the burden of synthesis while sharing in none of its rewards. They exhibit a heavier label than do the more proximal cells, but the label in the mesoglea is evenly distributed throughout the animal. There is presently no satisfactory explanation for this, but it may be linked with the also-difficult-to-explain breakdown of the large, oral–aboral fiber system in the peduncle during the hypostome regeneration.

4. Orientation, Turnover, and Polysaccharides

   There are three major unsolved questions concerning the origin and turnover of *Hydra* mesoglea and coelenterate mesogleas in general. How permanent is the mesoglea? What is the origin of the fiber orientation? What is the origin of the polysaccharide?

   We know that a 3-hour pulse label will leave labeled material in the mesoglea fibers up to 2 weeks later, so *Hydra* mesoglea lasts this long and probably longer without being completely turned over. This will be discussed further in Section V.

   The question of fiber orientation in coelenterate mesogleas has concerned other workers. Chapman (1953b) noted that the fibers of anemone mesoglea lined up along the lines of greatest stress in the stretched mesogleas. He suggested that this was not only a passive effect on the mature fibers, but that stress played a role in the lining up of the smaller fibrils into the ordered, larger fiber during synthesis. The smaller fibrils organized, he suggested, along the lines of greatest stress. Grimstone *et al.* (1958), noting that the small fibrils are not unique to the fibers, but pass freely from one bundle of fibrils (a fiber) to the next, agreed with Chapman. This kind of direction is known to occur, of course, in development of bone, where the calcium is laid down preferentially along the lines of greatest stress. In view of the current work on mesoglea ultrastructure (see Section III,B), this seems to be the best available explanation for the orientation of the protein component of *Hydra* mesoglea. It may or may not be a good explanation for the orientation of the polysaccharides.

   There is little information on the synthesis of polysaccharides in *Hydra*. From the findings of Katzman and Jeanloz (1970) on *Metridium*, where they found the heteropolysaccharide chemically attached to the collagen peptide, it would seem that the same cells responsible for the synthesis of the mesoglea proteins would have to also synthesize the polysaccharide. Our preliminary results with glucose incorporation, while not specific, suggest that, in *Hydra,* both epitheliomuscular and digestive cells may synthesize all mesoglea precursors, both protein and polysaccharide.

V. Morphogenic Role

In the previous sections we have seen how the mesoglea of *Hydra* provides a structural support and place of cell insertion for the animal. It may play a role in food transport, and is both an adhesive material to which *Hydra* cells adhere chemically and physically and a substratum over which they migrate. Finally, I have provided evidence for cell movement, and suggested that the mesoglea directs cell movement and controls cell sloughing.

In the latter two roles, the mesoglea maintains the form of *Hydra;* it enforces a morphogenesis and morphology on a constantly proliferating system of cells. The morphological contribution of the mesoglea is particularly apparent when a whole mesoglea is isolated, intact, from the animal. What results is a perfect *Hydra* shape with tentacles, mouth, and basal disc, completely devoid of cells and an amorphous pile of cells. The mesoglea, unquestionably, contributes to the pattern or form of *Hydra.* For example, we have seen how it may maintain the form of the peduncle. A much more difficult question is how it contributed to the formation of that pattern or form.

A. PATTERN FORMATION

Baird and Burnett (1967) demonstrated pattern formation in both budding and in tentacle formation by new buds in *Hydra.* Pattern formation in development is, of course, the predetermination (prepatterning) of the locus and morphology of a structure or structures before their actual appearance. It often involves (and apparently does in *Hydra* budding) a process where the first morphological realization determines the position of later formations.

Preexisting chemical or physiological gradients have often been invoked to account for prepatterning and its resultant morphogenesis. The existence of gradients in *Hydra* can no longer be argued, and their role in the formation of both the head and the bud is well established (Burnett, 1968).

Once these morphological entities are established though they are not yet developed (the primary prepattern), the mechanism of further morphogenesis is not known. Here, in the determination of the position and order of tentacle formation on new hypostomes and in the positioning of the second, third, and subsequent buds (the secondary prepatterns), are where the mesoglea is of great importance.

In this capacity the mesoglea may direct cell interactions. Like the genome of each cell, the mesoglea is a locus of information — the genome for an individual cell, the mesoglea for populations of cells in particular regions of the animal. It "tells" groups of cells which direction (though, perhaps not backward or forward) to move in, how to attach, and when to slough off. Because of its size, its distribution throughout the body column, and its location underneath every attached epithelial cell, the mesoglea is also the means of communication between cells. Thus, a change in the mesoglea organization that begins in the budding region is quickly extended to the hypostome and the patterns of cell movement shift. In a broader sense, the pattern that the cells organize into the mesoglea is one of the important factors which make *Hydra* an organism and not a growth of cells.

Is this the morphogenic role of mesoglea? If so, it is an impressive list of functions for a thin, acellular, "nonliving," gel sandwiched between two epithelia. It seems presumptuous then, to ask: Is this all it does? I am only going to ask; but answer, I think not.

B. CELL COMMUNICATION

There are other mechanisms of cell-to-cell communication, other factors of cell population control in *Hydra*. These have been dealt with in other chapters of this book, but it is worthwhile to restate them here. First, there are the cellular conducting systems, both nerve-mediated, and epitheliomuscular cell conduction. Second, there are the two chemical means of communication proposed by Burnett (1961): the stimulator, presumably released by neurosecretory cells, which promotes cell division in neighboring cells, and the inhibitor, presumably released by dividing cells, which inhibits neighboring cells from dividing. Finally, there is the intercellular adhesive material, which plays an important role in cell-to-cell contacts and mediates the passage of materials from one cell to another.

Since the mesoglea itself is acellular, let us ignore the two cellular means of communication and consider only the relation of the three chemical, developmental controls on cell populations to the mesoglea. Counting the mesoglea, *Hydra* has four chemical controls over the complex processes of cell differentiation and movement. If we look more carefully at these four chemical controls we note some interesting similarities.

The extracellular adhesive material, which presumably fills the 200-Å spaces between cells, is obviously adhesive. We have already seen that the mesoglea is also adhesive. Since the cells are already manufacturing one sticky polysaccharide or mucopolysaccharide for the mesoglea, it would save energy if they could also use this for intercellular adhesion, and not have to manufacture another. Lowell Davis (in Chapter 6 of this volume) has noted that in regenerating *Hydra* gastrodermis, the origin of extracellular material and mesoglea is similar and that, for a time before fibrils appear, both materials appear identical in the electron microscope. If the mesoglea gel also serves as the intercellular adhesive material, we would expect that, in the presence of this gel, cells might be expected to adhere to each other more tightly. Since it is difficult to stimulate *Hydra* cell reaggregation at all this has not been directly tested, but in the presence of *Hydra* mesoglea extract sponge cells reaggregate more quickly and adhere more tightly (Sindelar, 1969). If the intercellular material is mesoglea gel without the protein fiber, it might be lost in the process of isolating the mesoglea. Virtually any physical or chemical method for isolating the mesoglea of *Hydra* will also cause each cell layer to fall apart.

An individual cell would need less genetic information and less internal synthetic structure if the intercellular and nonprotein-bound mesogleal polysaccharide were the same. Instead of secreting both mesoglea protein and mesoglea polysaccharide at the basal (proximal to the mesoglea) surface and a different, intercellular polysaccharide to every other surface (presumably it leaks off the free apical surface), it only has to direct the protein to its basal surface and can secrete the polysaccharide indiscriminately. So, there is an argument for and a possibility that the unbound mesoglea polysaccharide (or mucopolysaccharide) and the intercellular adhesive material may be the same.

None of this evidence proves that these materials are identical and many of the ideas are highly speculative; but, if correct, they may bring to light the full morphogenic role of the mesoglea in *Hydra* and connective tissue in higher organisms. At least, they will guide the direction of research in the near future on the developmental role of *Hydra* mesoglea.

> It is totally misleading to represent cells as isolated entities without regard to their environment. Both cells and what surrounds them are integral parts of a continuum and must be studied in that interrelation (Weiss, 1965).

References

Baird, R. V., and Burnett, A. L. (1967). *J. Embryol. Exp. Morphol.* **17**, 35–81.
Barnes, M. J., Constable, B. J., Morton, L. F., and Kodicek, E. (1970). *Biochem. J.* **119**, 575–585.
Batham. E. J. (1960). *Quart. J. Microsc. Sci.* **101**, 481–485.

452   ROBERT E. HAUSMAN

Batham. E. J., and Pantin, C. F. A. (1951). *Quart. J. Microsc. Sci.* **92**, 27–54.
Bennett, H. S. (1963). *J. Histochem. Cytochem.* **11**, 14–23.
Bouillon, J. (1959). *Bull. Biol. Fr. Belg.* **18**, 64–72.
Bouillon, J., and Vandermeersche, G. (1956). *Ann. Soc. Zool. Belg.* **87**, 9.
Brien, P. (1953). *Biol. Rev. Cambridge Phil. Soc.* **28**, 308–349.
Burnett, A. L. (1959). *J. Exp. Zool.* **140**, 281–342.
Burnett, A. L. (1961). *J. Exp. Zool.* **146**, 21–84.
Burnett, A. L. (1968). *In* "The Stability of the Differentiated State" (H. Ursprung, ed.),
      pp. 109–127. Springer-Verlag, Berlin and New York.
Burnett, A. L. (1965). Unpublished observations.
Burnett, A. L., and Hausman, R. E. (1969). *J. Exp. Zool.* **177**, 15–24.
Burnett, A. L., and Yen, C. (1969). Unpublished observations.
Chapman, D. M. (1970). *Can. J. Zool.* **48**, 931–943.
Chapman, G. (1953a). *Quart. J. Microsc. Sci.* **94**, 155–176.
Chapman, G. (1953b). *J. Exp. Biol.* **30**, 440–451.
Corff, S. C. (1969). Ph.D. Dissertation, Case Western Reserve University, Cleveland,
      Ohio.
Corff, S. C., and Burnett, A. L. (1969). *J. Embryol. Exp. Morphol.* **21**, 417–443.
Davis, L. E., and Haynes, J. F. (1968). *Zellforsch. Mikrosk. Anat.* **92**, 149–158.
de Beer, G. R., and Huxley, J. S. (1924). *Quart. J. Microsc. Sci.* **68**, 471–479.
Diehl, F. A., and Burnett, A. L. (1966). *J. Exp. Zool.* **163**, 125–140.
Dilly, P. N. (1969). *Z. Zellforsch. Mikrosk. Anat.* **97**, 69–83.
Elder, H. Y., and Owen, G. (1967). *J. Zool.* **152**, 1–8.
Fawcett, D. W. (1961). *Symp. Biol. Hydra, 1961* p. 65.
Gauthier, G. F. (1963). *J. Exp. Zool.* **152**, 13–40.
Goreau, T. (1956). *Nature (London)* **177**, 1029–1030.
Grimstone, A. V., Horne, R. B., Pantin, C. F. A., and Robson, E. A. (1958). *Quart J.
      Microsc. Sci.* **99**, 523.
Gross, J., and Piez, K. A. (1960). *In* "Calcification in Biological Systems," Amer. Ass.
      Advance. Sci., Washington, D.C.
Gross, J., Dumsha, B., and Glazer, N. (1958). *Biochem. Biophys. Acta* **30**, 293.
Hadzi, J. (1909). *Arb. Zool. Inst. Univ. Wien.* **17**, 225–268.
Harkness, R. D. (1961). *Biol. Rev. Cambridge Phil. Soc.* **36**, 399–463.
Hatai, S. (1917). *Carnegie Inst. Wash. Publ.* **251**.
Hausman, R. E. (1968). Unpublished observations.
Hausman, R. E., and Burnett, A. L. (1969). Unpublished observations
Hausman, R. E., and Burnett, A. L. (1969). *J. Exp. Zool.* **171**, 7–14.
Hausman, R. E., and Burnett, A. L. (1970). *J. Exp. Zool.* **173**, 175–186.
Hausman, R. E., and Burnett, A. L. (1972). *J. Exp. Zool.* **177**, 435–446.
Hausman, R. E., and Oschman, J. L. (1971). Unpublished observations.
Haynes, J. F., Burnett, A. L., and Davis, L. E. (1968). *J. Exp. Zool.* **167**, 283–294.
Hertwig, O., and Hertwig, R. (1879). *Jena. Z. Naturwiss.* **13**, 457.
Hess, A. (1961). *In* "The Biology of Hydra" (H. M. Lenhof and W. F. Loomis, eds.), pp.
      1–50. Univ. of Miami Press, Coral Gables, Florida.
Hess, A., Cohen, A. I., and Robson, E. A. (1957). *Quart. J. Microsc. Sci.* **98**, 315–326.
Holmes, W. (1950). *Quart. J. Microsc. Sci.* **91**, 419–428.
Hunt, S. (1970). "Polysaccharide-Protein Complexes in Invertebrates." Academic Press,
      New York.
Hyman, L. (1940). "The Invertebrates," Vol. I. McGraw-Hill, New York.
Katzman, R. L., and Jeanloz, R. W. (1970). *Biochem. Biophys. Res. Commun.* **40**, 628–635.

Krukenberg, C. F. W. (1880). *Zool. Anz.* **3**, 306.
Lenhoff, H. M., Kline, E. S., and Hurley, R. (1957). *Biochim. Biophys. Acta* **26**, 204–205.
Lowell, R. D., and Burnett, A. L. (1969). *Biol. Bull.* **137**, 312–320.
Mackie, G. O., and Mackie, G. V. (1967). *Vie Milieu, Ser. A* **16**, 47–71.
Macklin, M. (1967). *J. Cell Physiol.* **70**, 191–196.
Marks, M. H., Bear, R. S., and Blake, C. H. (1949). *J. Exp. Zool.* **121**, 55–78.
Nadol, J. B., and Gibbins, J. R. (1970). *Z. Zellforsch. Mikrosk. Anat.* **106**, 398–411.
Noda, K. (1968). *Zool. Mag.* **77**, 322–325.
Peterkofsky, B., and Udenfriend, S. (1963). *J. Biol. Chem.* **238**, 3966.
Piez, K. A., and Gross, J. (1959). *Biochim. Biophys. Acta* **34**, 24.
Rambourg, A., and Leblond, C. P. (1967). *J. Cell Biol.* **32**, 27.
Robson, E. A. (1957). *Quart. J. Microsc. Sci.* **98**, 256–278.
Rothman, A. H. (1969). *Exp. Cell Res.* **58**, 177–178.
Rudall, K. (1968). *In* "Treatise on Collagen" (B. S. Gould, ed.), Vol. 2, p. 83. Academic Press, New York.
Schubert, M. (1965). *Struct. Funct. Connect. Skeletal Tissue, Proc. Advan. Study Inst., 1964* p. 124–131.
Shostak, S., Patel, N. G., and Burnett, A. L. (1965). *Develop. Biol.* **12**, 434–450.
Sindelar, W. (1969). Personal communication.
Slautterback, D. B., and Fawcett, D. W. (1959). *J. Biophys. Biochem. Cytol.* **5**, 441–452.
Smith, V., and Lauritis, J. A. (1969). *J. Microsc. (Paris)* **8**, 179–188.
Stetten, M. R. (1949). *J. Biol. Chem.* **181**, 31.
Torelli, B. (1953). *Arch. Zool. Ital.* **38**, 333–341.
Torelli, B. (1969). *Pubbl. Sta. Zool. Napoli* **37**, 218–226.
Tripp, K. (1928). *Z. Wiss. Zool.* **132**, 476–525.
Udenfriend, S. (1966). *Science* **152**, 1335.
Weiss, P. (1945). *J. Exp. Zool.* **100**, 353.
Weiss, P. (1957). *J. Cell Comp. Physiol.* **49**, Suppl. 1, 105.
Weiss, P. (1965). *Struct. Funct. Connect. Skeletal Tissues, Proc. Advan. Study Inst., 1964* p. 256–263.
Wood, R. L. (1961). *In* "The Biology of Hydra" (H. M. Lenhoff and W. F. Loomis, eds.), p. 51–64. Univ. of Miami Press, Coral Gables, Florida.

Author Index

Numbers in italics refer to the pages on which the complete references are listed.

Subject Index

QL
377
H9
B96

Burnett, Allison L
    Biology of hydra. Contributors: Allison L. Burnett [and others] Edited by Allison L. Burnett. New York, Academic Press, 1973.

    xv, 466 p. illus. 24 cm.

    Includes bibliographies.

    1. Hydra.   I. Title.

270776 QL377.H9B87   593′.71   72–77331
        ISBN 0–12–145950–0   MARC
        Library of Congress   73 [4]